Main

YEAR ZERO

Taming the Gods: Religion and Democracy on Three Continents

The China Lover: A Novel

*Murder in Amsterdam: Liberal Europe, Islam,
and the Limits of Tolerance*

Conversations with John Schlesinger

Occidentalism: The West in the Eyes of Its Enemies

Inventing Japan: 1853–1964

*Bad Elements: Chinese Rebels from
Los Angeles to Beijing*

Anglomania: A European Love Affair

*The Missionary and the Libertine:
Love and War in East and West*

Playing the Game

God's Dust: A Modern Asian Journey

*Behind the Mask: On Sexual Demons, Sacred Mothers, Transvestites,
Gangsters, Drifters and Other Japanese Cultural Heroes*

The Japanese Tattoo
(text by Donald Richie, photographs by Ian Buruma)

YEAR ZERO

A HISTORY OF 1945

IAN BURUMA

THE PENGUIN PRESS

New York

2013

THE PENGUIN PRESS
Published by the Penguin Group
Penguin Group (USA) LLC
375 Hudson Street
New York, New York 10014

USA · Canada · UK · Ireland · Australia
New Zealand · India · South Africa · China

penguin.com
A Penguin Random House Company

First published by The Penguin Press, a member of Penguin Group (USA) LLC, 2013

Excerpt from a poem by A. P. Herbert. Used by permission of A P Watt at United Agents on behalf
of the Executors of the Estate of Jocelyn Herbert, MT Perkins and Polly MVR Perkins.

Excerpt from "Don't Let's Be Beastly to the Germans" by Noel Coward. Published by Warner
Chappell Music Ltd.

Excerpt from "My Little Sister" from *My Little Sister and Selected Poems 1965–1985* by Abba
Kovner, translated by Shirley Kaufman, Oberlin College Press.

LIBRARY OF CONGRESS CATALOGING-IN-PUBLICATION DATA

Buruma, Ian.
Year zero : A history of 1945 / Ian Buruma.
p. cm.
Includes bibliographical references and index.
ISBN 978-1-59420-436-4
1. History, Modern—1945–1989. 2. World War, 1939–1945—Peace. 3. World War,
1939–1945—Influence. I. Title.
D840.B88 2013
940.53'14—dc23   2013007702

Printed in the United States of America
1 3 5 7 9 10 8 6 4 2

Designed by Gretchen Achilles

To my father, S. L. Buruma,
and to Brian Urquhart

A Klee drawing named "Angelus Novus" shows an angel looking as though he is about to move away from something he is fixedly contemplating. His eyes are staring, his mouth is open, his wings are spread. This is how one pictures the angel of history. His face is turned toward the past. Where we perceive a chain of events, he sees one single catastrophe that keeps piling ruin upon ruin and hurls it in front of his feet. The angel would like to stay, awaken the dead, and make whole what has been smashed. But a storm is blowing from Paradise; it has got caught in his wings with such violence that the angel can no longer close them. The storm irresistibly propels him into the future to which his back is turned, while the pile of debris before him grows skyward. This storm is what we call progress.

—WALTER BENJAMIN
Ninth Thesis on the Philosophy of History

CONTENTS

PART THREE

NEVER AGAIN

YEAR ZERO

PROLOGUE

There was something about my father's story which baffled me for a long time. His experience of the Second World War was not a particularly unusual one for a man of his age and background. There are many worse stories, yet his was bad enough.

I was quite young when I first heard about my father's war. Unlike some people, he was not reticent about it, even though some memories must have been painful to recall. And I enjoyed hearing them. There was also an illustration of sorts provided by tiny black-and-white photographs, stuck in an album which I retrieved from a drawer in his study for my private pleasure. They were not dramatic images, but sufficiently strange for me to wonder at: pictures of a primitive workers' camp in eastern Berlin, of my father grimacing grotesquely to sabotage an official photograph, of officious-looking Germans in suits adorned with Nazi insignia, of Sunday outings to a lake in the suburbs, of blond Ukrainian girls smiling at the photographer.

These were the relatively good times. Fraternizing with Ukrainians was probably forbidden, but memories of those women still produce a wistful look in my father's eyes. There are no photographs of him almost dying from hunger and exhaustion, of being tormented by vermin, of using a waterlogged bomb crater as a common toilet as well as the only available bath. But these hardships were not what baffled me. It was something that happened later, after he had come home.

Home was the largely Catholic town of Nijmegen in the east of Holland, where the Battle of Arnhem took place in 1944. Nijmegen was taken by the Allies after heavy fighting, and Arnhem was the bridge too far. My grandfather had been posted there in the 1920s as a Protestant minister to take care of a relatively small community of Mennonites.* Nijmegen is a border town. You could walk to Germany from my father's home. Since Germany was relatively cheap, most family holidays were spent across the border, until the Nazi presence became insufferable even for tourists round about 1937. Passing by a Hitler Youth camp one day, my family witnessed young boys being severely beaten by uniformed youths. On a boat trip along the Rhine, my grandfather caused (perhaps deliberate) embarrassment among German passengers by reciting Heinrich Heine's poetic ode to the Rhine maiden, *The Lorelei*. (Heine was Jewish.) My grandmother decided that enough was enough. Three years later, German troops came pouring across the border.

Life went on, even under German occupation. It was, for most Dutch people, as long as they were not Jewish, still oddly normal, at least in the first year or two. My father entered Utrecht University in 1941, where he studied law. To have a future as a lawyer, it was (and to some extent still is) imperative to become a member of the fraternity, the so-called student corps, which was exclusive and rather expensive. Although socially respectable, being a Protestant minister did not earn enough to pay all my father's bills. So a maternal uncle from the more affluent side of the family decided to subsidize my father's social obligations.

However, by the time my father joined, student fraternities had already been banned by the German authorities as potential hives of resistance. This was soon after Jewish professors had been expelled from the

---

* To avoid confusion, I should mention that Dutch Mennonites are very different from their American brethren. Dutch Mennonites tend to be rather progressive, open to other faiths, and not at all reclusive. The opposite tends to be true of American and German Mennonites, which caused a certain degree of awkwardness when bearded figures in old-fashioned black suits turned up on formal visits to my grandfather in Nijmegen.

universities. At Leyden, the dean of the law faculty, Rudolph Cleveringa, protested against this measure in a famous speech, his bag packed with toothbrush and a change of clothes in case of arrest, which duly came. Students, many of them from the corps, went on strike. Leyden shut down. The fraternity in Amsterdam had already been dissolved by its own members after a German ban on Jewish students.

But Utrecht remained open, and the fraternity continued to function, albeit underground. This meant that the rather brutal hazing rituals for new members had to take place in secret. First-year students, known in the corps as "fetuses," were no longer forced to shave their heads, for this would have given them away to the Germans, but it was still customary to make the fetuses hop around like frogs, deprive them of sleep, treat them like slaves, and generally humiliate them in a variety of sadistic games that happened to catch the senior boys' fancy. My father, like others of his class and education, submitted to this ordeal without protest. It is the way things were (and still are) done. It was, as they rather pedantically put it in Latin, *mos* (the custom).

In early 1943, young men were put to another, more serious test. The German occupiers ordered all students to sign a loyalty oath, swearing to refrain from any action against the Third Reich. Those who refused would be deported to Germany, where they would be forced to work for the Nazi war industry. Like 85 percent of his fellow students, my father refused, and went into hiding.

Later that year, he received a summons from the student resistance in Utrecht to return to his hometown. The reason for this remains obscure. A stupid mistake, perhaps, made in a moment of panic, or it may just have been a case of incompetence; these were students, after all, not hardened guerrilla fighters. My father arrived at the station with his father. Unfortunately, the Nazis had chosen just that moment to round up young men for labor in Germany. The platform was blocked on both sides by the German police. Threats were made that parents would be held responsible for any escapes. Worried about getting his parents in trouble, my father signed up. It was a thoughtful, but not a particularly heroic act, which still bothers him on occasion. He was transported, with other men, to a nasty little concentration camp, where Dutch thugs were trained by the SS in the savage techniques of their trade. After a brief time there, my father spent the rest of the war working in a factory in Berlin manufacturing brakes for railway trains.

This was a mixed experience, at least at first. As long as they did not actively resist the Germans, Dutch student workers were not put in concentration camps. The tedium of factory work, the shame of laboring for the enemy, and the physical discomforts of sleeping in freezing and verminous barracks even had their compensations. My father recalls attending concerts of the Berlin Philharmonic conducted by Wilhelm Furtwängler.

Things at the Knorr Brakes factory may also not have been all that they seemed. A taciturn, dark-haired man called Herr Elisohn tended to slink away when approached by the Dutch student workers, and there were others who shunned too much contact, men with names such as Rosenthal. Much later, my father surmised that the factory might have been hiding Jews.

Things got much worse in November 1943, when the Royal Air Force started its long bombing campaign on the German capital. In 1944, the RAF Lancasters were joined by American B-17s. But the wholesale destruction of Berlin, and its people, really began in the first months of 1945, when bombs and firestorms were more or less constant. The Americans attacked by day, the British by night, and in April, the Soviet "Stalin Organs" started shelling the city from the east.

Sometimes the students managed to squeeze themselves into air-raid shelters and subway stations, not a privilege allowed to prisoners in concentration camps. Sometimes a hastily dug ditch was their only protection against the bombing raids, which, in my father's memory, the students both welcomed and feared. One of the worst torments was lack of sleep, for the bombing and shelling never really stopped. There was a constant din of air-raid sirens, explosions, human screams and falling masonry and glass. Yet the students cheered on the Anglo-American bombers that could so easily have killed them and in some cases did.

In April 1945, the workers' camp had become uninhabitable: roofs and walls were blown away by wind and fire. Through a contact, possibly made through one of the less Nazified Protestant churches, my father found refuge in a suburban villa. His landlady, Frau Lehnhard, had already taken in several other refugees from the wreckage of central Berlin. Among them was a German couple, Dr. Rümmelin, a lawyer, and his Jewish wife. Ever fearful of her arrest, the husband kept a revolver in the house, so they could die together if this should come to pass. Frau Lehnhard liked to sing German *Lieder*. My father accompanied her on the piano. It was, in his words, "a rare reminder of civilization" in the mayhem of Berlin's final battle.

On his way to work in eastern Berlin, my father passed through the ruined streets where Soviet and German troops were fighting from house to house. On the Potsdamer Platz, he stood behind the Stalin Organs as they bombarded Hitler's chancellery with their sinister screaming noise. It gave him a lifelong horror of big bangs and fireworks.

Sometime in late April, or possibly in early May, 1945, Soviet soldiers arrived at Frau Lehnhard's house. Such visits usually implied gang rapes of the women, no matter how old, or young, they were. This didn't happen. But my father almost lost his life when Dr. Rümmelin's revolver was discovered. None of the soldiers spoke a word of English or German, so explanations for the presence of the gun were useless. The two men in the house, Dr. Rümmelin and my father, were put up against the wall to be executed. My father remembers feeling fatalistic about this. He had seen so much death by then that his own imminent end did not come as much of a surprise. But then, through one of those freakish bits of luck which meant the difference between life and death, there appeared a Russian officer who spoke English. He decided to believe Dr. Rümmelin's story. The execution was called off.

A certain rapport was struck up between my father and another Soviet officer, a high school teacher from Leningrad. Without any language in common, they communicated by humming snatches of Beethoven and Schubert. This officer, named Valentin, took him to a pickup point somewhere in the rubble that had once been a working class suburb of western Berlin. From there my father had to find his way to a DP (displaced persons) camp in the east of the city. He was joined on his trek through the ruins by another Dutchman, possibly a Nazi collaborator, or a former SS man. Since it had been several weeks since my father had had any proper food or sleep, he could barely walk.

Before they got much farther, my father collapsed. His dubious companion dragged him into a broken building where the man's girlfriend, a German prostitute, lived in a room up several flights of stairs. My father cannot recall what happened next; he was probably unconscious for much of the time. But the prostitute saved his life by nursing him back to a state sufficient to make it to the DP camp, where more than a thousand people of all nationalities, including concentration camp survivors, had to make do with a single water tap.

A photograph of my father taken in Holland more than six months later shows him still looking puffy from hunger edema. He is wearing a rather ill-fitting suit. It might have been the one he received from a Mennonite charity organization in the United States, which had urine stains on the trousers. Or perhaps it was a hand-me-down from his father. But, although pudgy and a little pale, in the photograph my father looks cheerful enough, surrounded by other men of his age, raising their beer mugs, mouths opened wide, cheering, or singing some student song.

He was back in his fraternity at Utrecht. This would have been in September 1945. My father was twenty-two. Because wartime initiations to the corps had occurred in secret, it had been decided by senior figures in the fraternity that the hazing rituals had to be conducted all over again. My father does not recall having to hop like a frog, or being too badly knocked about himself. This kind of treatment was reserved for younger boys who had just arrived at university, some of them perhaps fresh from camps far worse than my father's. There may have been Jewish students among them who had been hiding for years under the floorboards of houses belonging to brave Gentiles prepared to risk their necks. But my father does not remember anyone being especially bothered about such things; no one was interested in personal stories, Jewish or otherwise; they all had personal stories, often unpleasant. As part of their initiation to the corps, the new "fetuses" were screamed at, humiliated, and even squashed into tiny cellars (a game later known in fraternity circles as "playing Dachau").

And this is what baffled me. How could my father have put up with such grotesque behavior after all he had gone through? Did no one find this peculiar, to say the least?

No, my father said repeatedly. No, it seemed normal. That is the way things were done. It was *mos*. No one questioned it. He later qualified this by saying that he would have found it unseemly to have abused a Jewish survivor, but couldn't speak for others.

It baffled me, but gradually I think I came to understand. The idea that this was *normal* seems to me to provide a clue. People were so desperate to return to the world they had known before the Nazi occupation, before the bombs, the camps, and the murders, that hazing "fetuses" seemed normal. It was a way back to the way things once were, a way, as it were, of coming home.

There are other possibilities. Perhaps to men who had seen serious violence, student games seemed relatively inoffensive, the healthy hijinks of youth. But it is more likely that the men who took to hazing with the greatest enthusiasm were those who had not experienced very much at all. Here was a chance to act tough, a pleasure that was all the more keenly felt if the victims were people who had been through a great deal more.

· · ·

THIS STORY OF MY FATHER—as I said, not as bad as many others, but bad enough—was what made me curious about what happened just after the most devastating war in human history. How did the world emerge from the wreckage? What happens when millions are starving, or bent on bloody revenge? How are societies, or "civilization" (a popular word at the time), put together again? The desire to retrieve a sense of normality is one very human response to catastrophe; human and fanciful. For the idea that the world as it was before the war could simply be restored, as though a murderous decade, which began well before 1939, could be cast aside like a bad memory, was surely an illusion.

It was, however, an illusion held by governments as much as by individual people. The French and Dutch governments thought that their colonies could be repossessed and life would resume, just as it had been before the Japanese invaded Southeast Asia. But it was only that, an illusion. For the world could not possibly be the same. Too much had happened, too much had changed, too many people, even entire societies, had been uprooted. Nor did many people, including some governments, want the world to go back to what it had been. British workers, who had risked their lives for King and country, were no longer content to live under the old class system, and voted Winston Churchill out of office just two months after Hitler's defeat. Joseph Stalin had no intention of letting Poland, Hungary, or Czechoslovakia restore any kind of liberal democracy. Even in western Europe many intellectuals saw communism, wrapped in the morally cozy gown of "antifascism," as a more viable alternative to the old order.

In Asia, the incipient change was, if anything, even more dramatic. Once Indonesians, Vietnamese, Malays, Chinese, Burmese, Indians, and others too had seen how a fellow Asian nation could humiliate Western colonial masters, the notion of Western omnipotence was smashed forever, and relations could never be the same again. At the same time, the Japanese, like the Germans, having seen the vainglorious dreams of their leaders turn to ashes, were receptive to changes that were partly encouraged and partly imposed by the victorious Allied occupiers.

British and American women, whom wartime circumstances had propelled into the workforce, were no longer so content to swap their economic independence for domestic subservience. Many still did, of course, just as it took time for colonies to gain full independence. The conservative desire to return to "normal" would always vie with the wish for change, to start again from scratch, to build a better world, where devastating wars would never happen again. Such hopes were inspired by genuine idealism. That the League of Nations had failed to prevent a (second) world war did not hamper the idealism of those who hoped, in 1945, that the United Nations would keep peace forever. That such ideals, in time, turned out to be as illusory as the notion of turning back the clock does not diminish their power, or necessarily devalue their purpose.

The story of postwar 1945 is in some ways a very old one. The ancient Greeks knew well the destructive force of the human thirst for revenge, and their tragedians dramatized ways in which blood feuds might be overcome by the rule of law; trials instead of vendetta. And history, in the East no less than the West, is littered with dreams of starting afresh, of treating the ruins of war as an open building site for societies based on new ideals, which were often not as new as people thought.

My own interest in the immediate postwar period was sparked partly by current affairs. We have seen enough examples in recent years of high hopes invested in revolutionary wars to topple dictators and create new democracies. But mainly I wanted to look back in time to understand the world of my father, and his generation. This is partly, perhaps, because of a child's natural curiosity about the experience of a parent, a curiosity that grows stronger as the child becomes older than the parent was at that time. Such curiosity is especially acute when the father was tested by hardships that the child can only imagine.

But it is more than that. For the world my father helped to create from the ruins of the war that so nearly killed him is the world that we grew up in. My generation was nurtured by the dreams of our fathers: the European welfare state, the United Nations, American democracy, Japanese pacifism, the European Union. Then there is the dark side of the world made in 1945: communist dictatorship in Russia and eastern Europe, Mao's rise in the Chinese civil war, the Cold War.

Much of this world of our fathers has already been dismantled, or is fast coming apart at the seams. To be sure, in almost every place that was affected by the last world war, life today is far better than it was in 1945, certainly in material terms. Some of things people feared most have not come to pass. The Soviet empire has fallen. The last battlegrounds of the

Cold War are on the Korean peninsula, or possibly the narrow Taiwan straits. Yet, as I write, people everywhere are talking about the decline of the West, of the United States as well as Europe. If some of the fears of the immediate postwar period have faded, so have many of the dreams. Few still believe that eternal peace will come from a kind of world government, or even that the world can be shielded from conflict by the United Nations. Hopes for social democracy and the welfare state—the very reason for Churchill's defeat in 1945—have been severely bruised, if not dashed, by ideology and economic constraints.

I am skeptical about the idea that we can learn much from history, at least in the sense that knowledge of past follies will prevent us from making similar blunders in the future. History is all a matter of interpretation. Often the wrong interpretations of the past are more dangerous than ignorance. Memories of old hurts and hatreds kindle new conflagrations. And yet it is important to know what happened before, and to try and make sense of it. For if we don't, we cannot understand our own times. I wanted to know what my father went through, for it helps me to make sense of myself, and indeed all our lives, in the long dark shadow of what came before.

PART 1

LIBERATION
COMPLEX

CHAPTER 1

EXULTATION

W hen Allied troops in Germany liberated millions of prisoners of Hitler's fallen Reich—in concentration camps, slave labor camps, prisoner of war camps—they expected to find them docile, suitably grateful, and happy to cooperate in any way they could with their liberators. Sometimes, no doubt, that is what happened. Often, however, they encountered what became known as the "Liberation complex." In the slightly bureaucratic words of one eyewitness: "This involved revenge, hunger and exultation, which three qualities combined to make displaced persons, when newly liberated, a problem as to behavior and conduct, as well as for care, feeding, disinfection and repatriation."[1]

The Liberation complex was not confined to inmates of DP (displaced person) camps; it could have been used to describe entire countries newly liberated, and even in some respects the defeated nations.

I was born too late, in too prosperous a country, to notice any effects of hunger. But there were faint echoes still of revenge and exultation. Vengeance, against people who had collaborated with the enemy or, worse, slept with him, continued to be exacted in a quiet, almost surreptitious way, mostly at a very low level. One did not buy groceries from a certain store, or cigarettes from another, for "everyone" knew that the owners had been "wrong" during the war.

Exultation, on the other hand, was institutionalized in Holland by turning it into a yearly ritual: May 5, Liberation Day.

As I remember it from my childhood, the sun always shone on May 5, with church bells ringing, and red, white, and blue flags snapping in the light spring breeze. December 5, the feast of St. Nicholas, may be a bigger family occasion, but Liberation Day is the great show of patriotic joy, or at least it was when I grew up in the 1950s and '60s. Since the Dutch did not liberate themselves on May 5, 1945, but were freed from German occupation by Canadians, British, American, and Polish troops, the annual outburst of patriotic pride is slightly odd. But still, since the Dutch, like the Americans and the British, like to believe that freedom defines the national identity, it makes sense that the German defeat became blurred in national consciousness with the collective memory of defeating the Spanish crown in the Eighty Years' War straddling the sixteenth and seventeenth centuries.

Sentimental tears come easily to someone of my generation, born just six years after the war, confronted with images of Scottish bagpipers walking through machine-gun fire on a Normandy beach, or French citizens singing the "Marseillaise," not, of course, through any memories of our own, but through Hollywood movies. But I saw a little bit of the old exultation, precisely fifty years after May 5, 1945, when the entry of Canadian Army soldiers in Amsterdam was reenacted to celebrate the anniversary. The fact that Allied troops didn't actually arrive in Amsterdam until May 8 is now beside the point. The original occasion must have been extraordinary. In the account of a British war correspondent on the spot: "We have been kissed, cried on, hugged, thumped, screamed at and shouted at until we are bruised and exhausted. The Dutch have ransacked their gardens so that the rain of flowers which falls on the Allied vehicles is endless."[2]

Fifty years later, elderly Canadian men, medals pinned to tight and faded battle dress, rode into the city once more on the old jeeps and armored cars, saluting the crowds with tears in their eyes, remembering the days when they were kings, days their grandchildren have long tired of hearing about, days of exultation before the war heroes settled down in Calgary or Winnipeg to become dentists or accountants.

What struck me more than the old men reliving their finest days was the behavior of elderly Dutch women, dressed like the respectable matrons they undoubtedly were. These women were in a state of frenzy, a kind of teenage ecstasy, screaming like girls at a rock concert, stretching their arms to the men in their jeeps, reaching for their uniforms: "Thank you! Thank you! Thank you!" They couldn't help themselves. They, too, were reliving their hours of exultation. It was one of the most weirdly erotic scenes I had ever witnessed.

. . .

IN FACT, AS ALREADY NOTED, the Canadians did not come to Amsterdam on May 5, nor was the war officially over on that date. True, on May 4, Grand Admiral Hans-Georg von Friedeburg and General Eberhard Hans Kinzel had come to the tent of Field Marshal Bernard Montgomery ("Monty") on the Lüneburg Heath to surrender all German forces in northwest Germany, Holland, and Denmark. A young British army officer named Brian Urquhart saw the German's rush along a country road to Monty's HQ in their Mercedes-Benzes. Not long before that he had been one of the first Allied officers to enter the nearby concentration camp of Bergen-Belsen, where most of the liberated prisoners "seemed beyond articulate speech, even supposing we had found a common language." What he thought were logs from a distance were piles of corpses "as far as the eye could see."[3] When Admiral von Friedeburg, still dressed in a splendid leather greatcoat, was confronted a few days later with an American news report of German atrocities, he took this as an insult to his country and flew into a rage.

On May 6, another ceremony took place in a half-destroyed farmhouse near Wageningen where General Johannes Blaskowitz surrendered his troops to Canadian lieutenant-general Charles Foulkes. There was little left of Arnhem itself, after having been pounded to rubble in September 1944, when British, American, and Polish troops had tried to force their way through Holland in the military catastrophe known as Operation Market-Garden. One of the people who had seen this disaster coming was Brian Urquhart, then an intelligence officer working for one of the operation's chief planners, General F. A. M. "Boy" Browning, a dashing figure with a great deal of blood on his hands. When Urquhart showed his commanding officer photographic evidence of German tank brigades waiting around Arnhem to blow the Allies away, he was told to take sick leave. No one, certainly not a lowly intelligence officer, was allowed to spoil Monty's party.*

But still the war was not over, even in Holland. On May 7 crowds had gathered on Dam Square in the center of Amsterdam in front of the Royal Palace, cheering, dancing, singing, waving the orange flag of the Dutch royal family, in anticipation of the triumphant British and Canadian troops whose arrival was imminent. Watching the happy throng from the windows of a gentlemen's club on the square, German naval officers decided in a last-minute fit of pique to fire into the crowd with a machine gun mounted on the roof. Twenty-two people died, and more than a hundred were badly injured.

Even that was not the very last violent act of the war. On May 13, more than a week after Liberation Day, two men were executed. They were German anti-Nazis, who had deserted from the German army and hidden among the Dutch. One had a Jewish mother. They emerged from their hiding places on May 5, and turned themselves in to members of the Dutch resistance, who handed them over to the Canadians. They then fell victim to a typical wartime muddle. When Montgomery accepted the German surrender on May 4, there were not enough Allied troops in

---

* In fact, the operation in its planning stages was commonly referred to as "the party." One of the most famous officers in the Battle of Arnhem, Colonel John Frost, had even planned to bring his golf clubs to Holland.

Holland to disarm the Germans or feed the POWs. For the time being
German officers were allowed to remain in command of their men. The
two unfortunate German deserters were placed among other German soldiers in a disused Ford assembly plant outside Amsterdam. A German
military court was hastily improvised by officers keen to assert their authority for the very last time, and the men were sentenced to death. The
Germans asked the Canadians for guns to execute the "traitors." The
Canadians, unsure of the rules and unwilling to disrupt the temporary
arrangement, complied. And the men were swiftly executed. Others apparently met a similar fate, until the Canadians, rather too late, put a stop
to such practices.[4]

The official date for the end of the war in Europe, V-E Day, was in fact
May 8. Even though the unconditional surrender of all German troops
was signed in a schoolhouse in Rheims on the evening of May 6, the celebrations could not yet begin. Stalin was furious that General Eisenhower
had presumed to accept the German surrender for the eastern as well as
western fronts. Only the Soviets should have that privilege, in Berlin.
Stalin wanted to postpone V-E Day till May 9. This, in turn, annoyed
Churchill.

People all over Britain were already busy baking bread for celebratory
sandwiches; flags and banners had been prepared; church bells were waiting to be tolled. In the general confusion, it was the Germans who first
announced the end of the war in a radio broadcast from Flensburg, where
Admiral Doenitz was still nominally in charge of what remained of the
tattered German Reich. This was picked up by the BBC. Special editions
of the French, British, and U.S. newspapers soon hit the streets. In London, large crowds gathered around Piccadilly Circus and Trafalgar Square,
expecting Churchill to announce victory so the biggest party in history
could finally begin. Ticker tape started raining in the streets of New York.
But still there was no official announcement from the Allied leaders that
the war with Germany was over.

Just before midnight on May 8, at the Soviet HQ in Karlshorst, near
my father's old labor camp, Marshal Georgy Zhukov, the brutal military

genius, at last accepted the German surrender. Once more, Admiral von Friedeberg put his signature to the German defeat. Field Marshal Wilhelm Keitel, expressionless, rigid, every inch the Prussian soldier, told the Russians that he was horrified by the extent of destruction wrought on the German capital. Whereupon a Russian officer asked Keitel whether he had been equally horrified when on his orders, thousands of Soviet villages and towns were obliterated, and millions of people, including many children, were buried under the ruins. Keitel shrugged his shoulders and said nothing.[5]

Zhukov then asked the Germans to leave, and the Russians, together with their American, British, and French allies, celebrated in style with teary-eyed speeches and huge amounts of wine, cognac, and vodka. A banquet was held in that same room the following day when Zhukov toasted Eisenhower as one of the greatest generals of all time. The toasts went on and on and on, and the Russian generals, including Zhukov, danced, until few men were left standing.

On May 8, crowds were already going crazy in New York. They were also pouring into the streets in London, but a peculiar hush still fell over the British crowds, as though they were waiting for Churchill's voice to set off the celebrations. Churchill, who had decided to ignore Stalin's wish to postpone V-E Day till the ninth, would speak at 3 P.M. President Truman had already spoken earlier. General Charles de Gaulle, refusing to be upstaged by Churchill, insisted on making his announcement to the French at exactly the same time.

Churchill's speech on the BBC was heard on radios around the world. There was no more room to move on Parliament Square outside Westminster, where loudspeakers had been installed. People were pressed against the gates of Buckingham Palace. Cars could no longer get through the crowds in the West End. Big Ben sounded three times. The crowd went quiet, and at last Churchill's voice boomed through the loudspeakers: "The German war is therefore at an end . . . almost the whole world was combined against the evil-doers, who are now prostrate before us . . . We must now devote all our strength and resources to the completion of our task, both at home and abroad . . ." And here his voice broke: "Advance Britannia! Long live the cause of freedom! God save the King." A little later, he made the V for Victory sign on the balcony of the Ministry of Health. "God bless you all. This is your victory!" And the crowd yelled back: "No it is yours!"

The *Daily Herald* reported: "There were fantastic 'mafficking' scenes in the heart of the city as cheering, dancing, laughing, uncontrollable crowds mobbed buses, jumped on the roofs of cars, tore down a hoarding for causeway bonfires, kissed policemen and dragged them into the dancing . . . Motorists gave the V-sign on their electric horns. Out on the river tugs and ships made the night echo and re-echo with V-sirens."

Somewhere in that crowd were my eighteen-year-old mother, who had been given time off from her boarding school, and her younger brother. My grandmother, Winifred Schlesinger, daughter of German-Jewish immigrants, had every reason to be happy, and her worship of Churchill knew no bounds. But she was nervous that her children might get lost in the "excited, drunken crowd—especially Yanks."

In New York, five hundred thousand people celebrated in the streets. Curfew was lifted. The clubs—the Copacabana, the Versailles, the Latin Quarter, the Diamond Horseshoe, El Morocco—were packed and open half the night. Lionel Hampton was playing at the Zanzibar, Eddie Stone at the Hotel Roosevelt Grill, and "jumbo portions" of food were on offer at Jack Dempsey's.

In Paris, on the Place de la République, a reporter for the *Libération* newspaper watched "a moving mass of people, bristling with allied flags. An American soldier was wobbling on his long legs, in a strange state of disequilibrium, trying to take photographs, two bottles of cognac, one empty, one still full, sticking from his khaki pockets." A U.S. bomber pilot thrilled the crowd by flying his Mitchell B-25 through the gap under the Eiffel Tower. On the Boulevard des Italiens "an enormous American sailor and a splendid negro" decided to engage in a competition. They pressed every woman to their "huge chests" and counted the number of lipstick marks left on their cheeks. Bets were laid on the two rivals. At the Arc de Triomphe, a bigger crowd than had ever been seen offered thanks to General de Gaulle, who flashed a rare smile. People belted out the "Marseillaise," and the Great War favorite, "Madelon":

> *There is a tavern way down in Brittany*
> *Where weary soldiers take their liberty*
> *The keeper's daughter whose name is Madelon*
> *Pours out the wine while they laugh and "carry on"* . . .
> *O Madelon, you are the only one*
> *O Madelon, for you we'll carry on*
> *It's so long since we have seen a miss*
> *Won't you give us just a kiss* . . .

And yet V-E Day in Paris was regarded by some as a bit of an anticlimax. France, after all, had already been liberated in 1944. Simone de Beauvoir wrote that her memory of that night was "much more confused than my memories of our other, earlier festivities, perhaps because my feelings were so confused. The victory had been won a long way off; we had not awaited it, as we had the Liberation, in a fever of anxiety; it had been foreseen for a long time, and offered no new hopes. In a way, this end was like a sort of death . . ."[6]

Muscovites, on the other hand, swept into the streets as soon as V-E Day was announced in the early morning of the ninth. Masses of people, many of them still in their nightgowns and pajamas, danced and cheered through the night, crying "Victory! Victory!" In a letter to the British historian Martin Gilbert, one of Stalin's interpreters, named Valentin Berezhkov, recalled: "The pride that victory was finally won over a treacherous and foul enemy, the grief for the fallen (and we did not know then that nearly thirty million were killed on the battlefields), hopes for a lasting peace and continued cooperation with our wartime allies—all this created a special feeling of relief and hope."[7]

Libération of May 8 was probably right: this was above all a party for the young. "It was only the young who felt exuberant. Only the young jumped onto the jeeps, which resembled a grandstand at the Longchamp races, running through the Champs-Élysées, flags around their heads and songs on their lips. And that is the way it should be. For the young the danger is over."

My grandmother in England, pining for her husband still serving in the British Army in India, could not share her children's exuberance. Her feelings were no doubt shared by many people who worried about faraway husbands or sons, or had lost far too much to rejoice. The reaction of this daughter of immigrants was also peculiarly English. "I missed you too much to celebrate," she wrote to my grandfather, "so I improved the shining hour by doing a bit of extra work in the garden."

My father cannot even remember the day the war officially ended. He vaguely recalls the sound of Russian guns fired in celebration. Marshall Zhukov mentions this in his memoir: "We left the banquet hall [on May 9] to the accompaniment of a cannonade from all types of weapons . . . the shooting went on in all parts of Berlin and its suburbs."[8] But my father was used to the sound of guns, and made no special note of it.

Brian Urquhart, the young British intelligence officer, stuck in northern Germany, fresh from the shock of witnessing Belsen, could not feel total joy either: "It is difficult to reconstruct what I actually felt at the time on such an overwhelming occasion. Nearly six years from despair to victory, many friends gone, fantastic waste and destruction . . . I wondered about all those nameless faces in war photographs, refugees, prisoners, civilians under bombing, Russians in the snow and wreckage of their country, crewmen on sinking freighters—how many of them would their families see again?"[9]

But such thoughts did not dampen the spirits of revelers in New York, Paris, and London. It was a festival of youth, but also of light. Quite literally. "The City Lights Up!" was the May 9 headline of the *New York Herald Tribune*. "The Night Sky of London was Aglow Again" said the London *Daily Herald* on May 8. In Paris the lights of the Opéra were lit for the first time since September 1939, in red, white, and blue. One after the other, the lights went back on illuminating the Arc de Triomphe, the Madeleine, and the Place de la Concorde. And the *Herald Tribune* proudly reported "large floodlighted Stars and Stripes, Union Jack and Tricolor" waving in front of their building on the Rue de Berri.

New York City had been going steadily darker since the "dimout" on April 1942, and then the "brownout" since October 1943. Only the torch on the Statue of Liberty remained dimly lit. But by 8 P.M., May 8, according to the *New York Daily News*, "all the jewels in Broadway's crown were full aglow, and the great chunky masses of humanity seemed to swim in the light and their spirits were warmed by it."

Nelson's Column on London's Trafalgar Square was picked out by a searchlight. St. Paul's, standing almost alone in the midst of the bombed City financial district, was bathed in floodlights. Cinemas lit up Leicester Square in lurid colors. And then there was the soft red glow of tens of thousands of bonfires lit all over London and beyond, all the way up to Scotland.

It wasn't just the relief that lights could be switched on again now that bombs and "doodlebugs" (German flying bombs) were no longer to be feared. There was something symbolically moving about the return of light. Reading these accounts I was reminded of a story I was told once by a Russian academic in Moscow. French literature was her subject and her passion. She had dreamed all her life of seeing France and other parts of western Europe, places she knew only from books. At last, in 1990, after the fall of the Berlin Wall, her dream came true; she was allowed to travel to Paris by train. I asked her what had impressed her most. She said it was the moment her train passed from East to West Berlin in the night, and suddenly there were lights.

. . .

FESTIVALS OF LIGHT, universal and as old as the first torch lit by man, often have a mystical origin, relating to the seasons and the beginning of new life. Some recollections of the early days of liberation have a distinct air of religious exultation. This is especially true of the rapturous reception of Allied soldiers by the female population. Maria Haayen, a young woman from The Hague, remembers seeing the first Canadian tank rumbling towards her, with the head of a soldier peering from the gun turret: "All the blood drained from my body, and I thought: *there comes our liberation*. And as the tank came nearer, I lost my breath and the soldier stood up—he was like a saint."[10]

This feeling was perhaps more common among young women, but it was shared by men. One Dutchman recalled that it "was a privilege even to touch the sleeve of a Canadian uniform. Each Canadian private was a Christ, a saviour . . ."[11]

In one important sense, the experience of the Allied soldiers in liberated countries in the summer of 1945 might be compared to what happened about twenty years later, when the Beatles arrived. Then, too, liberation was expressed as a form of mania, which was above all erotic. In 1945, men in countries such as Holland, Belgium, and France, and even more so in defeated Germany and Japan, were either absent, or in captivity, or poor, underfed, and demoralized. Foreign occupation and defeat had more or less destroyed male authority, at least temporarily. A Dutch historian at the time put it like this: "Dutch men were beaten militarily in 1940; sexually in 1945."[12] The same could be said for France, or Belgium, or any number of countries which had known occupation. One of the consequences of war was that many women had lost much of their female subservience. They had taken jobs, worked for the resistance, or been left to take care of their families. They were, in the deeply disapproving French phrase of the time, *hominisée*; they had begun to behave like men.

Compared to the skinny Dutchmen, or Frenchmen, or Germans, unwashed, shabbily dressed, the spruce Canadians and tall Americans, well-fed, well-paid, sharp-looking in the sexy uniforms of conquerors, must indeed have looked like gods. In the words of one of many Dutch women who ended up marrying a Canadian: "Let's face it, after what we had been through the Canadians looked delicious."

Nothing expressed the eroticism of liberation better than the music accompanying the Allied troops, music that had been banned by the Nazis: swing music, jazz, Glenn Miller's "In the Mood," Tommy Dorsey, Stan Kenton, Benny Goodman, Lionel Hampton, "Hey! Ba-Ba-Re-Bop."

In Paris, young people danced to "Victory discs," jazz records distributed to American troops. And the Franco-American spirit entered French chansons too. The hit song of 1945, sung by Jacques Pills, went:

Oh! Là là!
Bonjour mademoiselle
Oh! Là là!
Hello, qu'elle fait comme ça
Oh! Là là!
Je pense you are très belle
Oh! Là là!
You very beau soldat . . .

Fraternizing with the Germans was still officially forbidden to the Western Allies in 1945. In Holland and France it was actively encouraged. There was even something named Operation Fraternization. In July, the Entertainment Committee of the Netherlands was founded under the auspices of Princess Juliana and Prince Bernhard, specifically to offer English-speaking female company to the more than one hundred thousand Canadians. The idea was that these young women would accompany the soldiers to art shows, museums, movies, and properly supervised dances.

The hopeful and piously expressed expectation was that the women would "uphold the honor of our nation." My Dutch grandmother, as the wife of a Protestant minister, was asked to oversee the dances, to make sure nothing took place between the Canadians and their Dutch girlfriends that might sully the national honor. Her colleague in this endeavor was a Catholic priest called Father Ogtrop, whose name was shouted out by the dancers to the tune of "Hey! Ba-Ba-Re-Bop." I'm not sure what transpired at those dances. But in the words of one Canadian soldier, he had never "met a more willing female population than we did in Holland."[13]

This was just as well, from the point of view of the Allied troops, since their commanders took a dim view of prostitution. Red light areas were "off-limits," even in France, where *maisons de tolérance* had thrived under

German occupation. Some of the older American veterans still had fond memories of Paris in 1918, after World War I, where the brothels of Pigalle ("Pig Alley") had given the doughboys a warm welcome. Even after World War II, the ban on prostitution was not always observed. In at least one recorded instance, in the city of Cherbourg, several brothels were indirectly run by the U.S. Army itself.[14] Some were reserved for black GIs, others for whites only, and American MPs made sure the queues at the brothel doors were orderly. But for the most part, this time, much to the chagrin of those who worried, with excellent reason, about the proliferation of venereal diseases in the absence of organized sexual trade, fraternization was on a strictly freelance basis.

Not that relations between troops and local women were equal. The men had the money, the luxury goods, the cigarettes, the silk stockings and, more important, the food that people desperately needed to survive. And the many expressions of worship for the liberators suggest a potentially humiliating lack of balance. Yet to see the women who were so eager to fraternize as naïve hero worshippers, or powerless victims, would not be entirely accurate. Simone de Beauvoir mentions a young Parisian woman in her memoir whose "main distraction" is "American hunting" (*la chasse à l'Américain*).

Benoîte Groult, who later became a popular novelist, wrote an account, with her sister Flora, of their American-hunting exploits. They called their *Journal à Quatre Mains* a novel, but it is a barely fictionalized diary. Groult spoke English and was one of the French women who volunteered to fraternize through the American Red Cross. But her real stamping grounds were less salubrious. She spent most of her evenings at clubs in Paris that catered to Allied soldiers and welcomed French girls but barred French men, clubs with innocuous names like Canadian Club, Independence, Rainbow Corner.

Groult's detailed physical descriptions of American and Canadian soldiers are as adoring as those by people who thought they were gazing at saints. Except that they are amazingly down-to-earth, and the men are far from saintly. She writes about her conquests in the way some men brag about picking up babes. The clubs she frequents are described as "slave markets." But the slaves, in this instance, are the conquering heroes.

Here is Benoîte Groult on Kurt, an American fighter pilot: "The nose a little short, or rather, a trifle turned up, giving him a childish air common to all Americans; his skin bronzed by the stratosphere; strong hands, the shoulders of an orang-utang . . . perfect hips, straight, correcting the slightly heavy power of the rest of his body . . ." Kurt never reads books, and is interested only in food and airplanes. But what does she care? Indeed, she writes, "I want the arms of an idiot, the kisses of an idiot. He has an adorable smile, the corners of his mouth curling up above those perfect American teeth."[15]

In short, Groult would have been seen by Frenchmen as terribly *hominisé*. She had been married, but lost her husband during the war. Liberation in the summer of 1944 gave her the license, and the desire, to find pleasure in the arms of men she would never see again. This was a precious freedom. In fact, it was Kurt who wanted a more serious relationship, showed her photographs of his parents, and hoped to take her back to the States as his war bride. For Groult, a young Parisian intellectual with literary aspirations, this was naturally out of the question.

Benoîte Groult was perhaps unusually hard-boiled, or pretended to be. But her account illustrates a point made by a French historian of the German occupation. According to Patrick Buisson, the presence of large numbers of young German men in France during the war offered many women a chance to rebel: women stuck in bad marriages, or in oppressive bourgeois families, maids bullied by their employers, spinsters left on the shelf, or simply women of all classes who wished to break away, even temporarily, from the constraints of a conservative patriarchal society. The fact that liaisons with an occupation army also brought material benefits, allowing many such women to live better than others, including in some cases their former masters, sweetened the sense of revenge.[16]

And not just women. Minorities of all kinds often forge alliances with powerful outsiders to get the majorities off their backs. This was a facet of all colonial societies. But the disproportionate number of French homosexuals who either collaborated with the Germans or used wartime Paris as a sexual playground may also have had something to do with a common grievance against the respectable bourgeoisie. The fact that Nazi and Vichy propaganda was itself homophobic was not an impediment. Occupation was not necessarily endorsed; it was an opportunity.

"Fratting" with the Allied liberators was, in any case, more alluring than collaboration with the Germans, for it was not tainted with treachery. It is hard to know how much homosexual fraternizing went on, since this is obviously something people were rather discreet about. One case is beautifully described by Rudi van Dantzig, the dancer, writer, and choreographer of the Dutch National Ballet. He wrote a novel, *For a Lost Soldier,* based on his own experience after being evacuated from Amsterdam to a northern village during the "hunger winter" of 1944/45. When the Canadians reached his village, he was only twelve years old, but had yearnings he himself barely understood. A jeep stops on a country road. A hand is extended. He is hoisted on board. This is when Jeroen, the boy, meets Walt, the Canadian soldier, who would end up seducing him. But the book is not at all an indictment of pedophilia. On the contrary, it is written as an elegy: "The arm around me is warm and comfortable, as though I'm wrapped in a chair. I let it all happen almost with a sense of joy. And I think: 'This is liberation. This is the way it should be, different from other days. This is a party.' "[17]

Benoîte Groult is perfectly well aware of the material benefits of having sex with an American. She makes the link between sexual hunger and hunger for food quite explicit. Lying in bed under Kurt's body, she remarks, is like sleeping with a whole continent: "And you can't refuse a continent." Afterwards, they ate: "My appetite was sharpened by four years of occupation and twenty-three years of chastity, well almost. I devoured the eggs hatched two days ago in Washington. Spam canned in Chicago. Corn ripened four thousand miles from here . . . It is quite something, the war!"

Spam, eggs, Hershey bars could be eaten right away. Stockings could be worn. But Lucky Strikes, Camels, Chesterfields, or Caporal cigarettes could be exchanged on the black market for more food. The GIs were supplied with plenty. This, as much as their broad shoulders, sweet smiles, straight hips, and fine uniforms, was an inestimable attraction. The easy access to cigarettes alone made them into rich men in very poor countries. It was easy to conclude, then, that the women who slept with them were really no better than whores.

This was indeed what many people thought, especially women who barely scraped by, or men who were barred from the dance halls, cinemas, and recreation centers reserved for the liberators and their local girlfriends. The suspicion was heightened by the fact that some of the young women who latched on to Allied servicemen still wore headscarves to hide the evidence of recently shaved heads, the mark of punishment for those who had shortly before taken German lovers.

No doubt some women were freelance prostitutes, especially in the defeated countries where sexual services were the only way to keep oneself, or one's children, alive. But even in the case of women who switched with perhaps unseemly haste from German to Allied lovers, the reasons were not always straightforward or venal. A freshly shaved "horizontal collaborator" from a small town in France told a self-appointed committee of purgers who threatened her with further punishment for her "immoral" behavior: "I don't care if you shave my hair. I am no longer in touch with my husband [a former prisoner of war]. And I won't let that stand in the way of having fun with the Americans, if I choose to." [18]

Reading contemporary accounts and comments in the press, one might get the impression that the summer of '45 was one long orgy indulged in by foreign servicemen and local women, out of greed, or lust, or loneliness. This impression appears to be confirmed by statistics: five times more women were hospitalized in Paris for sexually transmitted diseases (aka VD) in 1945 than in 1939. In Holland more than seven thousand illegitimate babies were born in 1946, three times the number in 1939. High STD rates can be explained by the lack of medical supervision or contraceptives, poor hygiene in poverty-stricken areas, or any number of other reasons. The fact is that many women and men were simply looking for warmth, companionship, love, even marriage. Much as the early months of liberation offered the chance for wild abandon, people also longed for a return to normality. It should not be forgotten that the 277,000

legitimate Dutch births in 1946 constituted the highest figure in the recorded history of the nation.

· · ·

BERGEN-BELSEN WAS LIBERATED ON APRIL 12. British forces commanded by Lieutenant Derrick Sington were ordered to get there as
quickly as they could. The war was not yet over, but conditions in the
camp were so appalling that local people feared that a typhus epidemic—
the same epidemic that had killed Anne Frank just weeks before—might
spread to them. Since the German authorities could not or would not deal
with the risk of a typhus outbreak, they agreed to let British troops enter
Belsen, even though they were still at war.

Driving past piles of corpses and barracks stinking of excrement and
rotting flesh, the soldiers could not quite believe what they were witnessing with their own eyes. Images from Belsen were among the first to be
published in the Western press, and in Britain Belsen became the main
symbol of Nazi mass murder. Brian Urquhart recalled that he had known
about Nazi anti-Semitism: "Even so, the 'final solution,' the actual extermination of millions of people, was simply unimaginable. We were completely unprepared for Belsen."[19] What neither he, nor the other British
soldiers, realized was that Belsen was not even an extermination camp.
Those camps were in Poland, and most had already been destroyed by the
Germans before retreating to the west.

Lieutenant Sington drove on, telling the survivors through a loud-
speaker that they were free. Most were too far gone to respond in any way.
Then he reached the main women's camp, still holding his microphone:

> In a few seconds the car was surrounded by hundreds of women.
> They cried and wailed hysterically, uncontrollably, and no word
> from the loudspeakers could be heard. The compounds of the
> camp were planted with young birch trees and the women
> plucked leafy sprigs and small branches and hurled them on to
> the car.[20]

These women were among the lucky ones. They could still walk. A British medical student, who had volunteered to help, came across the following scene in one of the barracks:

> I was standing aghast in the midst of all this filth trying to get used to the smell which was a mixture of post-mortem room, a sewer, sweat, foul pus, when I heard a scrabbling on the floor. I looked down in the half light and saw a woman crouching at my feet. She had black matted hair, well populated and her ribs stood out as though there were nothing between them . . . She was defecating, but she was so weak that she could not lift her buttocks from the floor and, as she had diarrhoea, the liquid yellow stools bubbled over her thighs.[21]

The doctors and medical volunteers were desperate for more food, drugs, and medical equipment. They were faced with disease and famine on a scale they had never experienced, or even imagined was possible. Hundreds of people were still dying every day, sometimes from eating army rations that were too rich for their shrunken intestines. But the army is not always an efficient institution, and conditions in Germany were chaotic. One day in late April a mysterious consignment arrived containing large quantities of lipstick.

It turned out to be a godsend. The commanding officer of a British ambulance unit, Lieutenant Colonel Gonin, remembers:

> I believe nothing did more for those internees than the lipstick. Women lay in bed with no sheets and no nightie but with scarlet lips, you saw them wandering about with nothing but a blanket over their shoulders, but with scarlet lips . . . At last someone had done something to make them individuals again, they were someone, no longer merely the number tattooed on the arm. At last they could take an interest in their appearance. That lipstick started to give them back their humanity.[22]

Richard Wollheim, later to become a famous British philosopher, was an intelligence officer. Like Urquhart, he was sent briefly to Belsen, in May, when conditions were still terrible, but not quite as catastrophic as they had been. It had been decided somewhere in the army hierarchy that it would be a good idea to organize a dance party for the soldiers and the survivors at Belsen. Wollheim was told to organize the event. It was, alas, a disaster, for as the band of Hungarian camp guards (who had had a reputation for brutality), dressed up in national folk costumes, struck up a dance tune on their concertinas, there was a misunderstanding. Without a language in common, the women bared their arms to show their camp tattoos. The men, literally at a loss for words, grabbed the women's arms hoping for a dance. The women, terrified, started hitting the men, while the Hungarians played faster and faster.[23]

This, however, was an unusual mishap. There was another dance party held around the same time on a square between the barracks, with a Royal Air Force band providing the music. In the account of a British soldier, it was a huge success, even though some of the girls "could hardly walk," while others "looked as though they'd break in two." One very tall Canadian officer held a tiny girl, whose head only came up to his waist. They waltzed together. "She looked so happy, it was hard for those who saw her not to smile or cry."[24]

This was perhaps a more typical story than Wollheim's, for many people who worked in the camps, from American rabbis to United Nations relief workers, remarked with various degrees of approval or disapproval on the speedy recovery of sexuality among the survivors. Like the lipstick, sexual desire restored a sense of humanity to people, who had been left with none.

If the birthrate in Holland was high in 1946, the birthrate in the displaced persons camps was higher. In the American occupation zone alone 750 babies were born every month in the DP camps. Nearly one-third of the Jewish women in the zone between the ages of eighteen and forty-five had already given birth or were expecting babies.[25] Former concentration camps, including Bergen-Belsen, where so many thousands had died under the worst possible conditions, had become sites of feverish sexual activity, as though the survivors couldn't wait to show to themselves and the world that they were still alive, and not just that, but capable of producing life.

Relief workers were sometimes shocked and spoke of DPs, often Jewish, giving "themselves up to debauch without restraint." Some put it down to boredom. What was there to do but drink and have sex? Some were more moralistic. A French doctor working for a charity organization wrote with evident disapproval, "The moral standings of many of these survivors from the concentration camps is very low . . . sexual irregularity has reached appalling proportions." But he concede;d that there were mitigating circumstances. One could not really blame the young girls who had passed through hell, and "are now seized by an irresistible desire for affection and forgetfulness, which they seek to satisfy with the means at their disposal."[26]

Other observers had more elaborate explanations. A Polish relief worker named Marta Korwin believed that concentration camp victims had dreamed that an end to their torment would lead to the dawn of a perfect world: "All their past difficulties would be forgotten, freedom would take them back to a world where nothing had ever gone wrong . . ." When instead they found themselves living in the misery of DP camps, having lost their loved ones, with no hope, they escaped into drink or sex.[27]

All these explanations are perfectly plausible. But there was also a biological dimension. A people in severe crisis had to reproduce itself to survive. Many Jews in the DP camps were not death camp survivors, of whom there were few. Many came from parts of the Soviet Union, where they had found refuge from the Nazis. But most Jews had lost children, parents, siblings, or other relatives. Older people had little choice but to live with ghosts. But young people craved new family ties, others to live for. And biological regeneration was officially promoted by Zionists and other Jewish organizers. Marriages happened within weeks, even days after first encounters. Contraceptives were frowned upon in the Jewish DP camps.

People felt duty-bound to produce as many children as they could. Sex was not just a pleasure; it was an act of defiance against extinction.

· · ·

TO BE A GERMAN or Japanese in 1945 was obviously a rather different experience than being French, Dutch, or Chinese, let alone Jewish. This applies to the encounter with foreign troops too. The *Amis* (German slang for Yanks), or *Ameko* (the same in Japanese), as well as the Canadians, Australians, British, and Soviets came not as liberators, but as conquerors. The same was true, to some extent, even for many Italians, especially in southern Italy, where the Allied invasions made already hard lives even harder. Cities were bombed to pieces, economic conditions were dire. Prostitution was in many cases a necessity.

In Berlin, they were known as *Ruinenmäuschen,* "mice in the ruins," girls and women prowling the rubble of their city trying to pick up a soldier for a bit of cash, some food, or cigarettes. Some girls, barely into puberty, plied their trade in improvised brothels in the ruins, run by black marketers. Boys had their own *Trümmerbordellen* ("ruin brothels"), where they sold themselves to American soldiers, one of whom, known as Tante ("Aunty") Anna, became a notorious figure in the underworld of Frankfurt.

Survival often dissolved class distinctions. Norman Lewis was a young British army officer stationed in Naples. In his wonderful account, *Naples '44,* he describes the visit to his HQ of a grand Italian aristocrat, owner of a palazzo somewhere in the south. He arrived with his sister:

> Both are remarkably alike in appearance: thin, with extremely pale skin and cold, patrician expressions bordering on severity. The purpose of the visit was to enquire if we could arrange for the sister to enter an army brothel. We explained that there was no such institution in the British Army. "A pity", the prince said. Both of them speak excellent English, learned from an English governess. "Ah

well, Luisa, I suppose if it can't be, it can't be." They thanked us
with polite calm and departed.[28]

In Japan, prostitution was institutionalized from the beginning. They
had their reasons. Japanese authorities were terrified that Allied soldiers
would do to the Japanese what Japanese troops had done to the Chinese
and other Asians. When Nanking was sacked in 1937, and Manila more
or less destroyed in a last-ditch battle in 1945, tens of thousands of women were raped, mutilated, and usually killed, if they hadn't died of the
ordeal already. These were two particularly bad instances. There were
many more. In China, rape by Imperial Japanese soldiers was perpetrated on such a massive scale that it became a military problem, by provoking fiercer Chinese resistance. To cope with this difficulty girls were
sometimes drafted, but mostly kidnapped, especially in Korea and other
countries under Japanese control, to serve as so-called comfort women,
meaning sex slaves, in Japanese army brothels.

Government and military propaganda had frightened Japanese citizens with constant predictions that, in the case of defeat, Japanese women
would be raped, tortured, and murdered by foreign soldiers. To prevent
this ghastly and dishonorable fate, Japanese were ordered to fight to the
death, or kill themselves. Women and children in the Pacific islands and
in Okinawa were ordered to blow themselves up with hand grenades or
jump off cliffs. Many did.

And so, on August 18, three days after the Japanese surrender, the
Home Ministry ordered local police officials to set up "comfort facilities"
for the conquering Allies. Women were recruited to "sacrifice their bodies" in the Recreation and Amusement Association (RAA) as a patriotic
duty. The former prime minister, Prince Konoe Fumimaro, who bore a
large responsibility for starting the Pacific War, told the national police
commissioner to "please defend the young women of Japan."[29] Perhaps
the invading foreigners would be appeased by this measure, and so respectable Japanese women might be able to come out of their hiding
places and walk the streets unmolested.

It must have been a sordid business. Recreation and Amusement facilities were set up in such haste that there were no beds to accommodate the soldiers and the sacrificial women. Sexual intercourse took place wherever space could be found, mostly on the floors, or in the halls and corridors of the improvised brothels. It took a few months for the Japanese to come up with more efficient arrangements. A huge, hangarlike brothel was built in Funabashi, outside Tokyo, known as the International Palace, or IP. The IP offered sex on a kind of assembly line, known as "the willow run" after the wartime bomber factory built by Ford near Detroit. Men would leave their shoes at the entrance of the long building, and pick them up polished to a sheen at the other end.

Army billets, such as the Nomura Hotel in Tokyo, were swarming with women, identified as clerks or cleaning ladies, who regularly spent the nights there. Some of them brought their families to escape from the winter cold. A big dance hall in the center of Tokyo had a sign in Japanese that read: "Patriotic Girls! Assist the Reconstruction of Japan by Serving as Dance Partners!"[30] Condoms were sold at the army PXs (special stores selling food, clothing, and other supplies to members of the occupation forces).

In contrast to Germany, there was no strict ban on "fraternization with indigenous personnel" in Japan at first. General Douglas MacArthur, the Supreme Commander for Allied Powers (SCAP), recognized the futility of this rule. He told one of his aides: "They keep trying to get me to stop all this Madame Butterflying around. I won't do it . . . I wouldn't issue a non-fraternization order for all the tea in China."[31]

In the beginning of the occupation there were about six hundred thousand U.S. soldiers in Japan, in addition to Australians, British, and a sprinkling of other nationalities. So there was a great deal of fraternizing. A letter written by William Theodore de Bary, a U.S. Navy officer who later became a distinguished scholar of China and Japan, described what it was like in Sasebo, a large naval base on the island of Kyushu, in October 1945:

Fraternization itself has been a problem. The MPs, in fact, had to forbid any more congregating on the large bridge by our headquarters, so congested had it become with eager marines talk-ing and using sign language to grinning and friendly Japanese. It has been that way from the first.[32]

This went on despite some extraordinarily racist propaganda back home. This, for example, from an article about the occupation of Japan in the *Saturday Evening Post*: "The flat-chested, button-nosed, splayfooted average Japanese woman is about as attractive to most Americans as a 1000-year-old stone idol. In fact, less so. They like to take pictures of the idols."[33]

The author of this article, if we choose to be charitable, had no idea. Most of SCAP's senior officers had secured Japanese mistresses already in 1945. Since there were very few Western women at first, this was to be ex-pected. Things changed only when a new wave of military officers arrived, less tolerant men who often had had no direct experience of combat. Even as restrictions in Germany had been lifted, they decided to impose more discipline in Japan by declaring most public places, such as local restau-rants, hot spring resorts, cinemas, or army hotels, "off-limits."

As a result, fraternization still took place, just more discreetly, and more and more with freelance prostitutes, which did nothing to keep the VD rates down. In the bombed-out streets and city parks prostitutes had their own territories, known as "islands." Some could be had for as little as one dollar, which was roughly the price of half a pack of cigarettes on the black market. This type of business thrived, especially after the Allied administration decided, much against Japanese advice, to ban organized prostitution in 1946.

Japanese like to categorize things neatly. The freelance hookers, known as *panpan* girls, were divided into those who specialized in white foreign soldiers, black foreign soldiers, and Japanese only, even though some of the more enterprising ones refused to make such neat distinc-tions. Some prostitutes, the so-called *onrii* (as in "only one"), managed to latch on to one client. The more than usually promiscuous ones were *batafurais* (butterflies). Certain areas of central Tokyo, such as Hibiya

Park, opposite General MacArthur's headquarters, or nearby Yurakucho station, were typical *panpan* stamping grounds.[34]

The *panpan*, heavily lipsticked and high-heeled, was an object of Japanese scorn, as the symbol of national degradation, but also of fascination, tinged with envy. They were materially better off than most homeless, hungry, impoverished Japanese citizens. These working girls were also the first and most avid consumers of American goods, and more familiar than most Japanese with the popular culture of the victors. Using the peculiar argot of the *panpan*, Japanese slang mixed with broken GI English, they were also closer to speaking the language of the occupiers than most Japanese could manage.

In a sense, the *panpan* fits into a particular raffish Japanese tradition that combines low life with glamour. The prostitutes of premodern Tokyo, then still called Edo, were fashion plates of a kind, publicized in woodblock prints and the Kabuki theater. In the early years of the Allied occupation, the culture associated with the *panpan* was a great deal less refined. Military defeat and liberation from wartime censorship and militarist education revived a commercial sex culture with roots in the past, but with a great deal of American influence. Salacious pulp magazines with such titles as *Lovely, Venus, Sex Bizarre,* and *Pin-Up* flourished. Striptease parlors opened up in the old entertainment districts, often jerry-built shacks constructed around the bomb craters. Pimps, black marketers, and young hoodlums in Hawaiian shirts danced the mambo with their girlfriends in cheap dance halls. Japanese swing bands and jazz singers came alive again, after years of bans on such foreign decadence. There was a craze for boogie-woogie.

Many women turned to prostitution out of necessity. But not all. Surveys of the time show that a large number of women became *panpan* "out of curiosity."[35] And this, more than getting paid for sex, was what earned the *panpan* particular opprobrium. To "sacrifice" one's body to keep a poor rural family going, or from patriotic duty, was all right, perhaps even laudable; to do it out of curiosity, or a desire for cash, cigarettes, or silk stockings, was a disgrace. Organized prostitution had a long tradition and was tolerated. But the *panpan* were condemned for their free enterprise. It made them dangerously independent.

Tawdry and desperate though much of it was, the commercial sex culture in 1945 was, like mambo dancing and boogie-woogie, liberation of a kind, welcomed by some people, and loathed by others. The roughly ninety thousand babies born in 1946 from unmarried women cannot all have resulted from purely commercial transactions.[36] Having been fed with so much negative propaganda about the barbarian rapists and killers, many Japanese women were much relieved when they actually saw the less fearsome Americans. In the words of one woman writing in the utterly respectable women's magazine *Fujin Gaho:* "I find them courteous, friendly, carefree and perfectly at ease. What a sharp and painful contrast to the haughty, mean and discourteous Japanese soldiers who used to live in the barracks near my home."[37]

This is not to say that Allied soldiers were never abusive, particularly at the beginning of the Occupation. According to one estimate, forty women were raped every day in the latter half of 1945, which is probably an underestimation, since many cases would not have been reported, out of shame.[38] Such figures would never have appeared in the censored Occupation press, of course. But most Japanese would still have recognized that the Americans were far more disciplined than they had feared, especially in comparison to the behavior of their own troops abroad.

In an odd way, changing sexual mores fitted into the propagandistic effort by the Americans to "reeducate" the Japanese. To become democratic, so the Japanese were told, women should be treated more equally. *Panpan* girls may not have been quite what the educators had in mind. But Japanese were encouraged to show physical affection more openly, just like Americans. So it was that the first screen kiss, after much American prompting, was shown for Japanese edification in 1946, in a movie entitled *Young Hearts* (*Hatachi no Seishun*). It proved to be highly popular with young audiences.

Of course there is a broad spectrum between streetwalkers picking up GIs in Hibiya Park and the first cinematic kiss, but the public hunger for erotic entertainment and highly sexed popular music suggests that the gap between the liberated and the defeated peoples was actually not as great as one might think. For the Japanese, too, a new sense of liberty came with the sound of Glenn Miller's "In the Mood."

It was the same story in the Western zones of Germany. In areas occupied by Soviet troops, things were rather different, certainly as far as sex was concerned. If "fratting" came to define relations with foreign troops in the West, rape was one of the curses of being defeated by the Soviet Red Army. Of course, rape happened in the Western zones too, especially, but by no means exclusively, under French occupation. In Stuttgart, for example, about 3,000 women were said to have been raped by French troops, many from Algeria.[39] In the American occupation zone, by far the largest, the number of recorded rapes by American troops in the whole of 1945 did not exceed 1,500.[40]

There are several reasons why rape was less common under Western occupation than in the Soviet zone. Allied troops, with the possible exception of the French, were not as vengeful as the Soviets. Nor were they encouraged by their superiors to do as they liked with German women. (Stalin himself notoriously stated that soldiers who had crossed thousands of miles through blood and fire were entitled to "have some fun with women.") Besides, the willingness of German women to "frat" with Allied soldiers was such that rape was hardly necessary. A popular quip among GIs in the summer of 1945 was that German women were the loosest "this side of Tahiti."[41]

This was no doubt an exaggeration, promoted not just by grateful GIs, but by Germans who were outraged by actions they regarded as a further insult to their already shattered sense of national pride. Still, many soldiers claimed that German women, known variously as "frauleins," "furlines," or "fratkernazis," were even more willing to have sexual relations with them than the French women were. One rather brutal, but perhaps not wholly inaccurate, analysis of this phenomenon was given by a GI after he had just returned to the U.S. "At the risk of letting the cat out of the bag," he wrote, "it must be admitted that all the GI wants in Europe is a 'good deal,'" which included "a chance to fraternize as often as possible." He continued: "In Germany, naturally, the GI finds the best deal . . . In France the deal is different. The GI doesn't find the all-out bootlicking of Germany. He can't make France the plaything he heard it was from his Dad and from the liberators in 1944."[42]

And there were of course far more women than men in Germany by about a 16 to 10 ratio, and the men who were left were often old, crippled, or despised. As the young German says in Rossellini's brilliant film *Germany Year Zero*, shot in the ruins of Berlin: "We were men before, National Socialists, now we are just Nazis."

Benoîte Groult in her literary memoir of liberated France could not resist comparing the "beauty of Americans" to "the Frenchmen who all look gnarled, swarthy, and undernourished to me."[43] The demoralization of German and Japanese men was of course worse. Typical was the attitude of a German waitress interviewed by Carl Zuckmayer, the German playwright and screenwriter (*The Blue Angel*) who returned to his native land as a U.S. cultural attaché in 1946. This waitress wouldn't touch German men, she said: "They are too soft, they are not men any more. In the past they showed off too much."[44]

For me, the most memorable account of masculine humiliation is by Nosaka Akiyuki, a novelist who was himself a teenager in 1945, hanging around the black markets of Osaka. His brilliant novella, *American Hijiki* (*Amerika Hijiki*, 1967), concerns masculinity as well as race. The main character is a Japanese of his own age. At school during the war he was told that Western men were taller than Japanese but weaker, especially around the hips, due to their soft habit of sitting on chairs, instead of Japanese tatami floors. They could be physically bested by any tough little Japanese with muscular thighs. The schoolboys were frequently reminded of the squat, bullnecked General Yamashita, "The Tiger of Malaya," who accepted the surrender of Singapore from the British general Percival, whose rather absurd-looking spindly legs were not flattered by his khaki shorts.

But then the Japanese teenager sees the real thing up close, the unforgettable sight of an American soldier, "his arms like logs, his waist like a mortar . . . the manliness of his buttocks encased in shiny uniform pants . . . Ah, no wonder Japan lost the war."[45] Clearly, not all Allied soldiers were so big and brawny, and many Japanese men were far from puny. But the perception, that first impression of a hungry teenage boy, would last as the melancholy memory of a war that had been presented to the Japanese as a racial contest between noble Asian warriors and the arrogant white race. This made the first confrontation after the war between victors and the defeated more shocking in Japan than in Germany.

In Germany, the Western (but not the Soviet) authorities did their best to enforce a nonfraternization policy at first. "Pretty girls can sabotage an Allied victory," announced the American Forces Network. "Soldiers wise don't fraternize," warned *Stars and Stripes*, the military paper, or "Don't play Samson to her Delilah—she'd like to cut your hair off—at the neck."[46] Lifting the ban, said the *Times* of London, "would probably distress a large number of women at home."[47] But none of this was convincing to men on the spot. The "Mistress Army" was a popular expression for the Western Allies at the time. This referred to the many German mistresses attached to American officers (more than to British officers, for some reason; the British appear to have preferred drinking). This, in turn, led to jealousy in the lower ranks, a feeling expressed in bitter jokes such as, "The policy is just to give the brass the first crack at all the good-looking women."[48]

General George Patton, like General MacArthur, saw no merit in the ban. Should well-fed American soldiers really refuse to give candy to hungry kids? Were all Germans truly Nazis? (It should be said that Patton was a great deal more indulgent to Germans, even if they *were* Nazis, than towards the communist allies, or indeed to Jews.) Even the *New York Times*, not always in the vanguard of public opinion, was critical in its reports from the occupied zones. Their local correspondent reported in June that he had "yet to meet a soldier, whether he comes from London, the Mississippi Valley or the Alberta wheatfields, who wants the ban continued." The same reporter revealed the absurdity of measures taken to tighten the ban. In one village in the U.S. zone, a counterintelligence detachment was sent out to watch a security guard who was monitoring a military policeman who had been "flirting with a German girl."[49]

On June 8, General Eisenhower lifted the ban on fraternizing with children, whereupon the common greeting from GIs or Tommies to a young woman was "Good Day, Child!" In August, Allied soldiers were allowed to speak to adults, and even, as long as they were safely out in the open air, to hold hands with grown women. On October 1, finally, the Allied Control Council, the governing body of the four powers' military occupation, lifted the ban entirely. One of the events that nailed it was the arrival of British and U.S. troops in Berlin, where the Soviets were fraternizing quite freely. This divide became intolerable to Western troops, so in a sense the license to frat with Germans was an early consequence of Big Power rivalry. But lifting the ban came with a condition: marriage with Germans, or putting Germans up in army billets, would still be forbidden. This, too, in time became a dead letter, and tens of thousands of German women left with their new husbands to the promised good life of the United States.

Germany had its version of the *panpan* women, the lowest and most desperate being the *Ruinenmäuschen*, the "mice in the ruins." But, as was true in all countries under military occupation, the borderlines between romance, desire, and prostitution were not always clear. Even in the Soviet zone of Berlin, where few women, including the very young and very old, had managed to avoid sexual assault, and where raping was still a common occurrence for months after the war, sexual relations with foreign troops were not always a straightforward matter. The best and most harrowing account is *A Woman in Berlin*, a diary kept by a journalist in her early thirties who finally escaped being serially raped by anonymous soldiers by soliciting the protection of one Russian officer. The gentle Lieutenant Anatole became her regular lover. After all, she wrote, "he's looking more for human, feminine sympathy than for mere sexual satisfaction. And this I'm willing to offer him, even with pleasure . . ."[50]

In the Western zones, women who accepted material goods from their American boyfriends, as most of them would have, were quickly branded as prostitutes, a reputation they would not have acquired so easily by taking gifts from German men. Of course, access to goods from the PX was a matter of survival for many. In the winter months, even the warmth of a well-heated nightclub was a welcome refuge from icy rooms, shared with many strangers, in bombed-out buildings. But those Lucky Strikes, chocolates, and silk stockings, along with the swing music and the easygoing GI manners, also represented a culture to women, and many young men, which was all the more desirable for having been forbidden in the oppressive Third Reich. People hungered for the trappings of the New World, however crude, because the Old World had collapsed in such disgrace, not just physically, but culturally, intellectually, spiritually. This was true of liberated countries, like France and Holland. It was even more true of Germany and Japan, where the postwar Americanization of culture, beginning with "fratting," would go further than anywhere else.

At least one woman saw all this for what it was, a dream, which was bound to disappoint in the end—but not without leaving a few traces. After Benoîte Groult has turned down her American lover Kurt's marriage proposal for the last time, she decides to abandon her game of "hunting for Americans." Now, she writes, "old Europe is all alone. I feel like Europe, very old and desperate. I have just said goodbye to the whole of America this evening. And to you too, Steve, Don, Tex, Wolf, Ian, who came into my life with such a comforting smile, I'll be closing my door . . . It no longer amuses me to fool around with all of you from the Far West: you came from too far away, and you will go back. You have liberated me. Now it is up to me to remake my own freedom."

. . .

NAGAI KAFU, A JAPANESE NOVELIST best known for nostalgic fictions of the seamy side of his beloved Tokyo, wrote the following diary entry on October 9, more than two months after the Japanese defeat: "Had an evening meal at the Sanno Hotel. Observed seven or eight young Americans, who looked like officers. They did not seem to lack a certain refinement. After supper, I saw them sitting at the bar, practicing their Japanese on the young woman serving them. Compared to Japanese soldiers, their behaviour was remarkably humble."[51]

A month before, Kafu noted in his diary that according to the newspapers American soldiers were shamelessly fooling around with Japanese women. Well, he said, "if true, that is payback for what Japanese soldiers did in occupied China."[52]

Kafu was a highly sophisticated eccentric, a Francophile who cared little for conventional opinion. His reaction was, in fact, rare. The more usual view on American fraternization with Japanese women, even among highly educated writers and intellectuals, was a great deal more censorious. Takami Jun, a relatively liberal writer, younger than Kafu, who felt ashamed that he had ever supported, however ambivalently, the militant nationalism of the wartime regime, recalled in his diary something he had seen at the main Tokyo railway station one October evening. Loud American soldiers were flirting with two female station attendants, trying to get them to sit down with them. The girls were giggling, and seemed anything but unwilling. In Takami's words: "They looked as if being flirted with in this way was unbearably pleasurable. Another station attendant came up. Everything about her suggested that she also wanted to be teased. What an indescribably shameful sight!"[53]

This must have been quite typical, both the scene and the reaction to it. But whose shame was Takami really talking about? Was it the flirting he found shameful, or the fact that Japanese girls were flirting with foreigners? Or was it his own shame, as a Japanese male? Disapproval of this type of fraternization was expressed in more violent ways too. Japanese girls hired to work for the U.S. Army in Hokkaido complained that they got beaten up regularly by Japanese men because of their association with foreign troops. Henceforth the army had to escort them home in armed trucks.

Envy no doubt played an important role in male resentment. And there was a great deal of envy to go around: defeated men were envious of the victors, American soldiers of Soviet soldiers (when the U.S. ban was still in force), soldiers of officers, and so on. In *American Hijiki*, Nosaka Akiyuki describes how long this feeling could linger. The teenager in the story grows up and has a family. His wife makes friends with a middle-aged American couple on holiday in Hawaii. They come to visit Japan, a country that brings back fond memories to Mr. Higgins, who served there in the occupation army. Obliged by his wife to be a good host, the Japanese husband decides to entertain Mr. Higgins by taking him to a live sex show in Tokyo. A virile performer, known as Japan's "Number One," promises to show the audience what Japanese manhood can do. Alas, that night, Number One's powers fail him, and once again, the Japanese husband, feeling a vicarious shame, thinks back to that GI he first encountered in the ruins of Osaka, those loglike arms, those tough buttocks encased in shiny gabardine.

Mr. Higgins is white. Wartime Japanese propaganda did not talk about blacks, except as another example of American racism to discredit the enemy further. But occupation by multiracial troops introduced something more disturbing than mere sexual rivalry. A letter from a Japanese woman, intercepted by U.S. military censors, mentions the rumor that there were "twenty thousand women in Yokohama who had intimate relations with Allied soldiers. It has also been brought to the attention of the prefectural office that thirteen thousand halfbreeds are to be born in Kansai. It is enough to make one shudder when one hears that there are three thousand Japanese women with Negro children in Yokohama."[54] The real source of anger here is not immoral behavior per se, or even prostitution, but the pollution of racial purity.

Similar sentiments were voiced in Germany, especially towards the end of 1945, after the fraternization ban was lifted, just as many young German men were beginning to be released from POW camps. As was true in Japan, young army veterans were especially sensitive on the "fratting" issue. Here, a pamphlet circulated in Nuremberg, denouncing "Niggerwomen" (*Negerweibern*): "Painted and tarted up in colors, with red-lacquered nails, a hole in their stockings and a wild, fat Chesterfield stuck in their beaks, strutting around with their black cavaliers."[55] Another word for fraternizing German girls was "chocolate women" (*Chokoladeweibern*), referring both to material greed and a shameless penchant for those colored cavaliers.

It is surely no coincidence that so many Japanese and German films about the occupation period show black American soldiers ravishing native women, as though their race made the humiliation of the defeated even worse. A German pamphlet warned: "We'll tell you right now, we'll shave off your hair, the blacklist is ready, waiting for when times will have changed."[56] In fact, some women received this treatment already in 1945. There was a case, in Bayreuth, of a woman who was set on fire. In Würzburg, three men were arrested for organizing a terror group called the "Black Panthers," who threatened to cut the hair off "all German girls who go walking with colored soldiers."[57] A twenty-year-old former Nazi wrote about the fraternizing women: "Have the German people no honor left? . . . One can lose a war, one can be humiliated, but one need not dirty one's honor oneself!"[58]

Again, like Takami Jun's use of the word "shame," this reference to honor is revealing. The honor of women (let alone their right to decide for themselves whom to consort with) is beside the point. It is the honor of men that is at stake here. They are the ones who feel humiliated. This was, of course, common to all societies traditionally dominated by men. Postwar conditions upset the old order. Women were no longer under male control. Perhaps that was their greatest sin.

One way of looking at these resentments is to link them directly to reactionary political views which the Allies wished to stamp out, if not necessarily in their own countries, then at least in the nations they had just defeated. An American army lieutenant named Julian Sebastian Bach, who later worked as an editor for *Life* magazine, wrote an account of the occupation of Germany. He believed that "The extent to which German men accept 'fratting' is the thermometer which registers the degree to which they accept defeat, contain their national pride and look forward to a new and more congenial way of life. Obviously the sight of a German woman with an American conqueror enrages an 'unreconstructed' German more than a German who is anxious to cooperate with us."[59]

Takami Jun expressed a very similar opinion in his diary, only a few days after his initial reaction to the shameful behavior of those giggling station attendants. The scene is again at a railway station. He watches a Japanese woman, leaning out of the train window, saying *"baibai!"* to her American soldier friend, seemingly oblivious to the hateful stares of other Japanese passengers. Takami sees a special pathos in the situation. In the eyes of the bystanders, including himself, the girl, as he puts it, "came to look like a woman at a 'special comfort facility.'" But the girl, in fact not a hooker at all, doesn't seem to care. Indeed, she looks "proud to behave shockingly with an American soldier." This, Takami predicts, will become a normal sight in Japan. What's more, he says, "It would actually be a good thing . . . Best of all would be a deluge of such sights. It would be good training for the Japanese. For then, in time, more natural, even beautiful social relations will come into being."[60]

What strikes me as humane and even sensible in the case of Takami seems naïve and self-serving in Julian Bach, the U.S. lieutenant in an occupation army. For the jealousies and resentments felt by men, and also women, towards the fraternizers among their own people were hardly confined to unreconstructed fascists. Humiliation was no doubt felt more keenly by the defeated. But it was a common sentiment among the liberated, too, even those who had greeted the young Allied soldiers with flowers when they first arrived as saintly victors.

A popular Dutch song after the war was called *Girl, Watch Out for Yourself.*

Brave boys, proud warriors
Came here from afar
They brought us freedom
So they should have some fun

But many a "Dutch girl"
Soon threw away her honor
For a packet of cigarettes
And chocolate bar . . .

Many who hailed with the Huns
Have already paid the price
Girl, you betrayed the honor of your country
Just as much . . .

No Dutch boy will look at you again
Since you left him in the cold . . .

It is all there: national honor, loose morals, material greed, the local boys spurned. Most revealing is the direct comparison of girls who had relations with the German occupiers and the liberators from Britain or North America. The implication is clear. What mattered was female immorality. That is why some Dutch girls who fraternized with Canadians had their hair cut off by angry mobs, just like the "Jerry whores" (*Moffenhoeren*).

Several things made the moral panic unleashed by foreign occupation, in liberated countries as much as among the defeated, more acute. Misguided occupation policies did little to soften the resentment of local men. Allied troops requisitioned cinemas, cafés, dance halls, and swimming pools for themselves. These were off-limits to the native population, but not to local girls who managed to pick up an Allied soldier. Naturally, this was resented. In the city of Utrecht, a group of young Dutchmen grabbed some girls who had been seen with Canadian soldiers and tried to shave their heads. The Canadians felt protective. Knives were pulled, stones were thrown, guns went off. Nobody got killed in this instance, although several people were wounded.

The ban on organized prostitution by the Allied authorities also contributed to the high rate of venereal diseases. A popular expression among the Americans in Germany, just after the war was finally declared over, was "VD follows V-E." In the American occupation zone in Germany, VD rates are said to have gone up 235 percent between V-E Day and the end of 1945, that is, from 75 per 1,000 soldiers per year to 250 per year.[61] This despite distribution among GIs, at railway stations and Red Cross

Clubs, of "V-packets," containing condoms and potassium permanganate pills. In Holland, VD rates had already gone up considerably during the German occupation, and rose further immediately after the war. The press published scare stories about more than 10,000 women who were supposedly infected with diseases without even realizing it. There were similar scares in France.

In southern Italy, the moral panic, equating the danger of VD with national humiliation, found a typically histrionic expression in a famous book by Curzio Malaparte titled *The Skin*. Malaparte was a fabulist, something he never denied, and was more than a little bit sympathetic to the fascists, but he had a gift for expressing a popular mood, even if details were made up for effect. The Allied invasion is compared in his book to a plague, in which "the limbs remained seemingly intact," but "the soul festered and rotted." During the German occupation, Malaparte explains, "only prostitutes" had relations with the occupiers. But now, under the Americans and British, "as a result of this loathsome plague, which first corrupted the feminine sense of honor and dignity," shame has infected every Italian home. Why? Because such was "the baneful power of the contagion that self-prostitution had become a praiseworthy act, almost a proof of patriotism, and all, men and women, far from blushing at the thought of it, seemed to glory in their own and the universal degradation."[62]

This was probably an exaggeration. But many people, apart from the author, may have felt it that way. Sleeping with the foreign soldier was the same as prostitution. If it was voluntary, so much the worse.

GIs in France were shown a documentary film titled *Good Girls Have VD Too*. One of the humiliations suffered by women in occupied cities, in Amsterdam no less than in Tokyo, was to be regularly rounded up at random for VD checks. No doubt the scarcity of medical facilities in the postwar chaos, the bad hygienic conditions, and the relative inexperience of many young men and women, often raised in socially conservative or puritanical societies, compounded the medical problems. But Malaparte, in his overwrought manner, put his finger on the sorest spot: women, for a variety of reasons, were doing as they liked.

Not everyone disapproved. Some progressively minded people, such as the Dutch gynecologist and sexual reformer Wim Storm, saw merit in fraternization: a breakthrough for female emancipation and a welcome end to such outdated notions as male privilege and wives' submission to their husbands. Women seeking happiness in the "khaki arms" of Canadians, "getting to know a new language, the jitterbug, and love," well, "all these women know exactly what they want." To claim that they are prostituting themselves for a bar of chocolate or a few cigarettes "is a terrible insult."[63] The best solution to the VD problem was to hand out more condoms to women and promote sex education among the young.

But the likes of Storm were a minority, and they would lose the argument, at least for the time being. The voices for moral regeneration, for rebuilding society on a traditional moral basis, were stronger in an atmosphere of moral panic. This was true in the Netherlands, where even a liberal newspaper such as *Het Parool*, founded by the anti-Nazi resistance, fired an editor for printing an article in favor of handing out contraceptives to women: "We see it as our duty to educate our nation's people towards higher moral norms . . . and resist all forms of dissipation."[64] It was true also in France, where the provisional government under General de Gaulle was deeply worried that wartime occupation and liberation had undermined public morals, posing a fatal threat to "the French race."[65] Laws against abortion and adultery in liberated France were as strict as they had been under the Vichy regime, in some cases even stricter.

The puritanical reaction to what was regarded as moral dissolution was by no means confined to religious conservatives or the political right. In France, a large number of men and women in the resistance had joined the Communist Party for romantic or idealistic reasons. Wartime conditions had loosened the rules of conventional morality. But the postwar French communists, under the leadership of Maurice Thorez, put a swift end to this. Dedication to the Party, and a stable family life, were promoted with zeal. "Debauchery" resulting from war and fraternizing with foreign troops was denounced. In Germany, too, where communists tightened their control of the Eastern zones under their Soviet patrons, political repression came with a new moral order. Erich Honecker, leader of the Communist Youth Federation, tried his very best to wean young women from such frivolities as swing music and sex, hoping to gain their support for the communist cause. But he felt frustrated in his efforts. The problem, he said, was clear: "We have to overcome their drive to take pleasure in life [*Drang nach Lebensfreude*]."

Erich "Honni" Honecker—no stranger to life's pleasures himself, having had several affairs with much younger women—needn't have worried unduly. A state of exultation cannot last. The rush of liberation had already begun to fade by the end of 1945. Foreign troops were going home in ever greater numbers, even though large military bases would remain in Germany and Japan, and to a lesser extent in Britain and Italy as well. Moral panic laid the ground for a conservative reaction. Fear of female sexual license, as well as a common desire for bourgeois stability, after years of danger, chaos, and deprivation, would soon restore a more traditional order to life in the liberated as well as the defeated nations. In the 1950s the summer of '45 would already seem like a distant memory. Sexual liberation had to wait for another twenty years, when the birth control pill arrived along with the second wave of Anglo-Saxon hedonism, when the Beatles and the Rolling Stones unleashed something Glenn Miller and Benny Goodman could only have dreamed of.

Even so, the postwar disorder, however temporary, was not without some positive consequence. Benoîte Groult's wish to remake her own freedom did not rest on a complete illusion. Women in France were given the right to vote in March 1944 by the provisional government even before France was liberated—a right born from the dearth of men; the assumption was that wives would represent the views of their absent husbands. The same right came to Italian women in 1945, to Japanese a year later, to women in Romania and Yugoslavia in 1946, and to Belgian women in 1948. No matter how much some people might have wished, the world could never quite go back to the way things had been before.

CHAPTER 2

HUNGER

If the Canadians arriving in May were seen by some Dutch people as gods, there is another, equally exalted image forever associated with liberation in the Netherlands: Operation Manna. Decades later people still spoke with tears of gratitude of the "Swedish white bread" donated by the Red Cross, dropped over Holland in May 1945 by RAF and U.S. Air Force bombers. As a child I envisaged this extraordinary event literally as loaves of white bread raining from the sky. In fact, the Avro Lancaster and B-17 bombers, swooping low over the red-tiled roofs dotted with cheering people waving white kitchen towels, dropped bags of flour, as well as crates filled with chocolate, margarine, corned beef, powdered eggs, cigarettes, coffee, and chewing gum. The British called it Operation Manna, the Americans Operation Chow Hound.

For the American and British bomber pilots, dropping food over Holland was a welcome diversion. One British pilot wrote a note, found among the tins of chocolate and bags of flour:

To the Dutch people.

Don't worry about the war with Germany. It is nearly over. These trips for us are a change from bombing. We will often be bringing new food supplies. Keep your chins up. All the best.

An R.A.F. man.[1]

The people were more than grateful; many of them were starving. In May, just after Liberation, the *New York Times* mentioned a "starvation hospital" in Rotterdam, where "wasted humans" were "receiving six light feedings daily." Men and women of thirty, the report says, "appear twice that age, their sunken eyes, yellowed skin and horribly swollen limbs revealing the extremity of their plight when they were rescued." Meanwhile, there were still restaurants in the city, providing a "well-dressed clientèle" with "elaborate meals and plenty of various beverages." Indignant Dutchmen, "who know the other extreme, quickly retort: 'Black Market.'"[2]

This was the situation in much of the European continent, and many places were worse off than Rotterdam. Millions had died of hunger in parts of the Soviet Union. But there was something particular about Dutch starvation; it was the only western European country subjected to hunger as a deliberate collective punishment. Slavic peoples had been subjected to this treatment, but not western Europeans.

Doing their part to assist Montgomery's disastrous effort to bridge the Rhine at Arnhem in September 1944, Dutch railway workers had gone on strike. In retaliation, the Germans cut off food supplies to the still occupied western part of the country. They also switched off the electricity, flooded fertile land, and banned Dutch citizens from using trains. On top of everything else, the "hunger winter" of '44/45 was unusually cold. Eighteen thousand people starved or died of diseases related to malnutrition. The survivors burned up their furniture to keep warm, and subsisted on pets, if they could still be found, or dead horses, sliced up as soon as they collapsed in the streets, or soup drawn from stinging nettles and fried tulip bulbs.

The problem with starvation is that too much food, or the wrong kind of food, can kill a person too. Even cookies, handed out by friendly Canadian troops, could be catastrophic. They caused an acute thirst, relieved by gulps of cold water, which made the undigested biscuits swell, resulting in burst stomachs, and a quick death.

There was hunger almost everywhere in the world, in liberated countries and in the defeated ones too, where all services had broken down and normal economies had ceased to function. There were other places, apart from Holland, where food had to be dropped from the skies. The teenager in Nosaka Akiyuki's *American Hijiki* watches an American bomber drop a steel drum attached to a parachute. At first, the Japanese villagers think it might be another devastating bomb. They had heard about Hiroshima. There, too, the bomb had allegedly been attached to a parachute. However, when the container fails to explode, hunger and curiosity trump fear. The villagers pry it open and find food parcels, which they guess must have been meant for the prisoners in a nearby POW camp. But charity to strangers is too much to ask in desperate times. The parcels contain bread, chocolate, and chewing gum, which the children chomp on for days, passing on the hardened, tasteless morsels from mouth to mouth. There is also a parcel filled with brownish stuff, which the villagers assume must be seaweed, or *hijiki*, a much prized delicacy in Japan. It tastes so bad, even after boiling, and is so hard to digest, that they wonder how the Americans can stomach it. Still on the assumption that the dark tea leaves are "American seaweed," they eat their way through the whole supply.

The worst cases of hunger in a famished year were in the concentration camps. The Japanese camps in Southeast Asia were appalling. Most camps in Germany, where slave workers and survivors from death marches had been left to rot by the German authorities, were even worse. The filthiest camp, by most accounts, was Bergen-Belsen, built originally as a camp for "exchange Jews," well-connected men and women who might be exchanged for German prisoners. Few exchanges actually took place. Political prisoners and criminals were added to the camp population. Finally, in late 1944, it became a dumping ground for Jewish survivors of the death camps in the path of the Soviet Red Army. One was Anne Frank, who died of typhus less than a month before the camp was liberated. Already cramped from the beginning, Belsen was so overcrowded by early 1945 that people literally slept on top of each other, with no sanitation, deprived in the end of any food or water. Some desperate people, who still had enough strength left, cannibalized the corpses piling up outside the huts. Only the SS guards had plenty of food. The camp commandant, Josef Kramer, had his own private supply of pigs.

Since the British had never seen anything like this, they had little idea what to do. All they could offer the starving people were their own army rations of ham, bacon, baked beans, sausages, and steak and kidney pie. Shrunken human intestines can no longer take such food; it goes right through the body. Even so, people tried to wolf the rations down. About two thousand people died as a result.

The British had encountered starvation on this scale only once before, in Bengal in 1943, when a combination of floods, bad crops, government incompetence, corruption, wartime disruption, and shocking official callousness caused the death of up to three million people. British army doctors, drawing on recent research, used something called the Bengal Famine Mixture, a saccharine gruel of sugar, dried milk, flour, and water. Aside from that, they experimented with nasal drips and injections of amino acids. The Bengal Famine Mixture, for those who could still swallow, and amino acid drips for those who couldn't, were tried at Belsen as well. Both methods failed. The mixture was too sweet. People couldn't keep it down. Injections and dripping techniques had to be abandoned because death camp survivors were terrified of anything resembling a medical experiment. Convinced they were going to die, they whimpered in concentration camp German, "Nix crematorium."[3]

That many survived was due to the extraordinary efforts of British doctors and medical students, as well as doctors who had survived the camps themselves. Through much trial and error, they found the right combinations of food and fluids to nurse people back to life. One of the survivor doctors was Hadassah Bimko, a Polish dentist. Still at Belsen, she married Josef "Yossele" Rosensaft, a tough Polish Jew who had escaped from several transports to Auschwitz and became one of the main Zionist leaders in the camp. We will hear more about him later. Their son, Menachem, was born in Belsen.

. . .

LIFE IN BRITAIN WAS BETTER than in Holland, Italy, Poland, Yugoslavia, or Germany, but it was far from plush. Wartime rations of food in Britain were actually cut in May 1945: less cooking fat, less bacon, and in the following year even bread was rationed. Many people continued to sleep in the tunnels of the London Underground. And heating was so sparse even a year later that the winter of '46/47 was known as "Shiver with Shinwell," after Emanuel Shinwell, minister of fuel and power, and "Starve with Strachey," after John Strachey, minister of food.

The American literary critic Edmund Wilson, on a visit to London in the summer of 1945, went for a walk through the London borough of Holborn with a friend and was struck by a foul smell. Looking around, he saw "a little market, on the shelves of whose open windows were laid out rows and rows of dead crows. That was apparently all they sold in that shop."[4]

In December, the arrival in Bristol of a ship carrying bananas and oranges (as well as four Jamaican stowaways, who jumped overboard) was met by an official welcoming committee led by the city mayor. These were the first bananas seen in Britain since the beginning of the war.

It wasn't just the lack of decent food that made London seem depressed just months after the victory celebrations. Edmund Wilson put the general British attitude in his own words: "How empty, how sickish, how senseless everything suddenly seems the moment the war is over! We are left flat with the impoverished and humiliated life that the drive against the enemy kept our minds off. Where our efforts have all gone towards destruction, we have been able to build nothing to fall back on amidst our own ruin."[5]

France was even more demoralized. The minister of supply, Paul Ramadier, was known as Ramadan, after the Muslim month of fasting, and the meagre daily rations as *Ramadiète*.[6] French farmers refused to sell at fixed prices, since they got rich off the ubiquitous black markets, without which it was impossible for most French people to live in any kind of comfort. Stephen Spender, the poet, spent a few months in France on a break from Germany, where he was writing a report for the British government on the state of culture. In terms of morale, he observed one important difference between Britain and France. In Britain it had always been possible to be fed and clothed without turning to the black market. In France, where Spender did not exactly move among the poor, he kept meeting people like the Sorbonne professor "whose suit was twice too large for him" and who had to explain "with a wry smile that he had been living for two months without recourse to the Black Market."[7]

But at least in France most of the country was still physically intact: the great historic cities, the churches and cathedrals. In Spender's eyes, fresh from the wreckage of Germany, this made everything seem even spookier. France, he wrote, was an "invisible ruin." Like Germany, France had to be "reconstructed from zero," but "although the sense of this pervades the atmosphere, meanwhile the walls stand, the cafés are crowded (although there is no coffee) and there is always the Black Market."[8]

Since the economy had been systematically bled dry by the Germans, the black market had already been operating in France for some years. The main problem, after Liberation, was not just the lack of food, but the difficulty in getting food from the countryside to the hungry cities. Trucks and gasoline were very scarce. Whoever had access to these essential means of transport could become exceedingly rich very quickly. Enterprising U.S. soldiers, some with criminal records back home, deserted from the army and organized gangs in Paris. The scam was to steal army trucks and stock up on gas by forging documents or bribing men at the army petrol-oil-lubricants (POL) depots. These supplies were then sold to French gangsters. Huge fortunes were made, but many of the American racketeers were caught by their own conspicuous consumption. Money transfers to the U.S. would have given them away, so they lived like kings in Paris, which alerted the authorities. To live like a king in continental

Europe was to operate in the semi-criminal world of black market restaurants and nightclubs, where champagne and fine wines still flowed, and all manner of delicacies were on offer.

From London, Edmund Wilson flew to Rome, which looked to him "more fetid and corrupt than ever."[9] He had dinner at an outside table of a black market restaurant with friends from America. Wilson did not notice it at first, engrossed as he was in his food and conversation, but a crowd had gathered behind them "reaching to grab things from our plates." Then a bouncer appeared who knocked down an old woman and drove back the crowd, mostly women and children, "some of whom disappeared, while others, keeping their distance, stood and stared at the diners."[10]

Rome, like Paris, was still physically more or less in one piece. Cities like Palermo and Naples were not. Milan, too, had been badly scarred by Allied bombs and civil war. To Wilson, who visited Milan in May, it "looked like a slice of Hell. Some of the shabby green trams were running and some of the inhabitants were going about their routines, but the whole place seemed stunned and stopped, and the bloodless undernourished people, dressed in any old cloth that could protect their skins, seemed to have been fixed . . . in a condition of permanent strain."[11]

Sándor Márai, the Hungarian novelist, was living in Budapest during the days of liberation. The badly damaged city had been under siege from Soviet troops for more than two months. Liberation by the Red Army in February 1945 was followed by crippling inflation. A dollar or a piece of gold would be worth billions more overnight. Peasants, "who knew their time had come," became rich "by trading a water-bloated, fattened pig for a piano, for Napoleon gold pieces on the market in Pest," while "intellectuals, workers and civil servants waited every day, more pale, more hungry and more hopelessly . . ." During those months of inflation, Márai recalled, "most Budapest inhabitants became as skeletally thin as the sketches of the human structure found in anatomy books, without any flesh and fat."[12]

Compared to Berlin and most other German cities, however, even

Budapest was still in better shape. For all that was left of Berlin, Frankfurt, Hamburg, Bremen, Dresden, and even smaller cities and towns such as Würzburg or Pforzheim, destroyed in 1945 as a kind of afterthought, were smoldering piles of rubble, still reeking of death. The first thing that struck many visitors in the early months after the war was the eerie silence.

Standing in the center of Berlin, between the ruins of the Romanisches Café, once the most fashionable café in Weimar period Berlin, and the gutted Kaiser Wilhelm Memorial Church, the playwright Carl Zuck-mayer recalled that same spot before the war: the incessant din of traffic and car horns, and chattering crowds shopping, drinking, and dining. Now he felt as if he were alone amidst the silent ruins. He heard a soft scraping sound. A thin young boy, in wooden sandals, was dragging a small handcart through the debris of a cobbled street. The wind blew softly through the desolated landscape, and Zuckmayer could hear the sound of his own heart beating.

And yet, he writes, "there was at the same time, in the whole of Germany, a constant sensation of crawling, scratching, groping, like a gigantic ant hill, . . . a ceaseless coming and going, wandering, walking, crossing; the scuffing and grating of millions of shoes. This is the 'Black Market' . . . The world and the march of the homeless, the refugees, the scattered masses, the marauding bands of youths."[13]

Here is Stephen Spender on the German city of Cologne, another urban wreck: "The ruin of the city is reflected in the internal ruin of its inhabitants who, instead of being lives that can form a scar over the city's wounds, are parasites sucking at a dead carcass, digging among the ruins for hidden food, doing business at their black market near the cathedral—the commerce of destruction instead of production."[14]

If Cologne, or Berlin, were bad, Tokyo or Osaka, let alone Hiroshima, was probably worse still. Not to mention Manila, Warsaw, Stalingrad, and other cities laid to waste by the Axis Powers. The chief Orthodox rabbi of England, Dr. Solomon Schonfeld, told reporters about his trip to Warsaw in December. The entire former ghetto of Warsaw, he said, "is literally one vast wilderness of bricks and debris. The streets are as they were on the last day of extermination. Thousands of bodies lie underneath a sea of brick and human bones, some of which I personally picked up."[15]

Destroying the Jewish ghetto of Warsaw was part of a vast criminal enterprise. The motives for bombing Japanese cities were different, but the resulting devastation was not. Japanese dwellings had been largely constructed of wood. The massive area bombings, followed by rapidly spreading firestorms, had left virtually nothing, apart from a few stone chimneys of public bathhouses, which still stood out pathetically in the charred debris. Japan, too, was marked by silence. Sherwood R. Moran, a U.S. Navy lieutenant, wrote a letter to his friend Donald Keene, later to become a great scholar of Japanese literature: "Tokyo, the first war casualty I've seen, is a devastated, immodest mess, but the silence is what gets me most; no honks, yells, clangs—none of the stuff you hate in a town but come to expect. For Tokyo, for all of Japan I suppose, the calamity is past, but everybody is still staring in that god-awful silence."[16]

The prospect of famine, and pandemics, was quite real in the defeated nations. There were already outbreaks of typhoid, typhus, and tuberculosis in German cities. In Japan, more than twenty thousand people died of dysentery in 1945, and by 1948, almost seven hundred thousand had been infected by typhoid, typhus, tuberculosis, cholera, and polio.[17] Life was a little better in rural areas, where food could still be found. But urban conditions were probably worse than in Germany. Germans who were prepared to work received food ration cards. A report from Berlin in *Yank*, the magazine for U.S. armed forces, described the typical daily menu for the family of a manual worker with six children: a cup of tea and a slice of black bread each for breakfast, and a potato soup for dinner made from one onion, one potato, and half a pint of milk, garnished with a tiny bit of cauliflower. Inadequate, to be sure, but enough to stay alive.

The Japanese had already been starving well before the war was over. Government authorities were advising people how to prepare meals from acorns, grain husks, sawdust (for pancakes), snails, grasshoppers, and rats. When soldiers began to return in large numbers after the defeat, a bad situation turned into a crisis. Many of the homeless lived in the underground passages of railway stations, like the narrow, mazelike slums in Victorian London. This Dickensian world included orphaned children collecting cigarette butts to exchange for something edible, or picking pockets, or selling their ill-nourished bodies. Tokyo's Ueno Station was especially notorious as a kind of urban beehive full of the homeless. The bands of hungry children were called "charin kids" (*charinko*), *charin* being the sound of clinking coins.[18] In photographs of these tough little creatures, dressed in rags, dragging on cigarette butts, they look less human than feral. Which is just how a British soldier described their counterparts in Germany, huddling in ruined underpasses, or railway stations, "perfectly camouflaged in filth, so you could not tell they were there." They would scurry away at the sight of a foreign soldier, only to reemerge carrying stones or iron bars, "and their teeth were black and broken," the only clean spots on their bodies being "the whites of their eyes," the eyes of diseased leopard cubs "whose one enemy was man."[19]

To keep this in some perspective, we should also remember what it was like for countless millions of Chinese surviving in the ruins of a devastating war. American soldiers in areas controlled by General Chiang Kai-shek's Nationalists were shocked to see children sneaking into their barracks to pick through the garbage cans for food. One U.S. sergeant recalled how "mothers with young girls came up to our guard stations to offer these little girls of theirs and trade them for candy bars and cigarettes."[20] Meanwhile, Chinese men would crawl under army latrines to catch human excrement through cracks in the floor, which they could peddle to the farmers as fertilizer.

The scale of human misery in the aftermath of the war was so vast, and so widespread, that comparisons are almost useless. Germany had to contend not only with its own citizens and returning soldiers, but also with more than ten million German-speaking refugees from Czechoslovakia, Poland, and Romania who had been expelled from their native lands with the official approval of the Allied governments. Many refugees died, or were killed on their way to Germany, a country many of them had never seen before. Almost all had lost everything they ever possessed. This added huge numbers of people to the drifting masses in search of food and shelter.

Compounding the food crisis in Japan, as well as in Germany, was a terrible harvest in 1945. Agriculture had been damaged badly by the war, with depleted livestock, ruined fields, wrecked machinery, and a shortage of manpower, as well as a spell of appalling weather. In Germany, much of the farm machinery in the Eastern zones had been destroyed, or looted, in the last months of the war. And the foreign farm workers, who had replaced Germans during the war, were leaving. Japan, which once relied on food supplies from its Asian empire, was now cut off.

In October, the Japanese minister of finance told American reporters that without immediate food imports, ten million Japanese might starve to death in the coming winter. Equally catastrophic predictions were made in Germany. A social democratic administrator in Lower Saxony stated that "now one can calculate when the German people will starve if its former enemies do not come to its aid."[21] Reports of the imminent collapse in Germany were discussed in the British Parliament. Arthur Salter, a United Nations relief official, gave a stern warning that "if, as is now thought, millions during this winter freeze and starve, this will not have been the inevitable consequence of material destruction and world shortages of material." Members in the House of Commons were warned of the "greatest catastrophe the human race ever experienced."[22]

This proved to be exaggerated. Some travelers in Germany found that conditions, especially in the Western zones, were no worse than in many other western European countries and were actually somewhat better than in places farther east. But even with some leftover stockpiles of food looted from occupied countries, life in Germany was bad enough. Berlin was especially dismal, and accounts from other parts of Germany were dire as well. An American reporter observed the following scene near Hamburg: "One evening, in a marshy plot of land, an elderly German in a business suit takes his cane and clubs a duck to death. More will be said about the food situation, but that in essence is it."[23]

All this was distressing, of course, but while the former victims of Nazi

Germany were still starving in places like Bergen-Belsen, and prisoners of
the Japanese languished in POW camps, while millions of refugees and
DPs needed to be repatriated, and British, Dutch, French, Poles, and Italians were surviving off meager rations, and Filipinos, Chinese, and Indonesians lived on even less, and while citizens of the Soviet Union still had
very fresh memories of being systematically starved by the German army
and the SS, public sympathy for Germans and Japanese was somewhat
limited. It was difficult enough convincing U.S. congressmen, especially
on the more isolationist Republican side, to fund international relief
organizations, such as UNRRA (United Nations Relief and Rehabilitation Administration), to help the victims of German and Japanese aggression. The idea of spending more tax dollars, or, as was suggested, cutting
British rations, to feed the former enemies, was not an easy policy to
promote.

Yet something had to be done, for practical if not for moral reasons. A
total breakdown in Germany and Japan would put an intolerable strain on
the Allied governments and make any kind of orderly, let alone democratic, reconstruction of the postwar order impossible. The British *Daily
Mirror*, a pro–Labour Party newspaper widely read by soldiers, put the
case for relief under the succinct headline: "Feed the Brutes?" The paper
made it clear that it was not necessary to act out of sympathy for the German people, or even for the destitute German refugees driven out of their
homelands. No, it "was not any feeling of compassion which prompts us
to emphasize the necessity of dealing with the situation." The problem
was this: "The longer Europe is allowed to sink into the bog, the longer it
will take to raise up—the longer the occupation will have to go on."[24]

There were other considerations, too, more persuasive to U.S. members of Congress. Even if UNRRA, with its internationalist ideals, was
suspected of communist sympathies, growing rivalry with the Soviet
Union prompted action, and UNRRA was indispensible. Daniel J. Flood,
a Democratic congressman from Pennsylvania, told his colleagues that
"Hunger, destitution, sickness and disease will breed unrest and the spec-
ter of Communism. Hungry people are fertile fields for the philosophies

of the anti-Christ and for those who would make God of the omnipotent state."[25]

And so some measures were taken. In the British zone of Germany, beginning in late November, General Sir Gerald Templer organized Operation Barleycorn, setting about eight hundred thousand German POWs free to work on farms and rescue what remained of the harvest. To be able to export more food to Germany, British citizens were made to tighten their own belts further; this is why bread was rationed in 1946. The Americans, too, following the 1944 directive from the Joint Chiefs of Staff (JCS 1076) pertaining to "accommodation for prisoners of war captured in northwest Europe," provided enough economic assistance to "prevent disease and unrest." The idea was to keep the standard of German life to a bare minimum. How bare was the question. Politicians who favored a "hard peace" wanted to punish Germany by dismantling its industry and keeping its citizens at subsistence level. The main proponent of the hard line was Henry Morgenthau, Roosevelt's treasury secretary, who planned to turn Germany into a pastoral country, incapable of making war ever again. A harsh directive was given to the Allied administration in Japan as well. Joint Chiefs of Staff directive 1380/15 ordered General MacArthur to limit relief to the Japanese to "the extent . . . needed to prevent such widespread diseases and unrest as would endanger the occupying forces or interfere with military operations. Such imports will be confined to minimum quantities of food . . . fuel, medicinal and sanitary supplies . . ."[26]

Luckily for the Germans and the Japanese, these punitive directives were either ignored or softened by the men who actually had to govern the occupied nations and could see how disastrous such measures would be. The financial adviser to U.S. High Commissioner General Lucius Clay called JCS 1076 the work of "economic idiots." Instead of causing even greater chaos by destroying Germany's industrial economy, General Clay, supported by such powerful figures in Washington as Secretary of War Henry Stimson, soon tried to help the Germans rebuild it. Stimson was more understanding of the Germans' plight than of Treasury Secretary Morgenthau, whom he suspected of being "biased in his Semitic grievances"[27]—echoing an unpleasant but not uncommon sentiment in the upper echelons of the American and British governments. But then, to expect much feeling for Jewish sensibilities would have been to miss the point. What these men were afraid of was that German rage would favor communism, or foster a mood of revanchism. General MacArthur was not inclined to help Japanese industry back to its feet, but was convinced, like Stimson and Clay, that "starvation . . . renders a people an easy prey to any ideology that brings with it life-sustaining food."[28]

The Soviet authorities in the Eastern occupation zones, where much of German agriculture, as well as industry (Leipzig, Dresden, Chemnitz), was located, did nothing to rebuild German economic capacity. What remained of factories and other assets was looted. Machinery, railway cars, tram cars, trucks, all disappeared in convoys headed east. Bank vaults were emptied of gold and bonds, research institutes stripped of archives, and many artworks were confiscated as war reparations. And there was nothing even the German Communist Party leaders, who had just returned from Nazi prisons or exile in Moscow, could do to stop their fraternal Russian patrons.

The same thing happened in Manchuria, now northeastern China, where the Japanese had ruled over a colonial puppet state called Manchukuo since the early 1930s. Manchukuo was the industrial powerhouse of the Japanese empire. The Soviet Union, urged by the United States, had declared war on Japan just before the end, on August 8.

On August 9, three days after the bombing of Hiroshima, Soviet troops invaded Manchukuo. Heavy industrial plants, modern railways, mining operations, built with great ruthlessness to the local population by the Japanese, were systematically stripped and the material transported to the Soviet Union. Entire industrial plants were dismantled and taken away in a steady parade of trains. In the end the trains themselves, and even the wooden railroad ties, were often stolen and moved to the Soviet Union. This happened before the Chinese had a chance to take Manchuria back. Neither the Chinese Communists nor Chiang's Nationalists would in any case have been able to put a stop to this gigantic exercise in asset-stripping.

And the Soviets would no doubt have done the same in northern Japan, if they had had the time to invade, which was one reason why the U.S. had been so keen to end the war in the Pacific swiftly.

Germans in the Soviet zone, including the communists, were in a bind, for even as their economy was being plundered, they were still required to feed the Soviet occupation troops, as well as themselves. In many instances, German workers would try to reassemble pillaged factories with bits and pieces of leftover machinery, only to see them taken apart again. When the workers protested, they would get beaten up. None of this helped to create much sympathy among German workers for the communist cause. A popular ditty of the time went like this:

Welcome, liberators!
You take from us eggs, meat, and butter, cattle and feed
And also watches, rings, and other things
You liberate us from everything, from cars and machines.
You take along with you train cars and rail installations.
From all this rubbish—you liberated us!
We cry for joy.
How good you are to us.
How terrible it was before—and how nice now.
You marvellous people![29]

However, the rations promised to keep Germans alive in the Soviet zone were no lower than in the other Allied zones of occupation: around 1,500 calories a day for a working person; 1,200 calories is generally considered to be the minimum necessary for an adult to stay healthy. In fact, most people in the cities were lucky to get half of that in 1945. Even when there was enough bread, there was little in the way of fresh food. What saved Germans and Japanese from catastrophe in the first year after the war were the military supplies. When Allied troops in Japan were reduced in the fall from 600,000 to 200,000, large amounts of army food, such as corned beef and beans, were handed over to the Japanese government for

distribution. It made for a diet most Japanese were not used to. Some gen-
teel Japanese ladies complained that beans caused embarrassing instances
of flatulence. As one such person complained to a guest, "The new ration
makes one so ill-mannered."[30] But without it, they would have starved. In
the summer of 1946, Tokyo citizens still received only 150 calories from
Japanese sources.[31]

Even with Allied supplies, however, most people in Europe and Japan
still had to rely on that vast criminal network, the black market. The
money economy had been replaced in many places by forms of barter,
with cigarettes as the main currency. For the occupation troops it was an
irresistible opportunity. In the Netherlands, Canadian cigarettes, especially the Sweet Caporal brand, were the most valuable. Black market
dealers bought them for one guilder each, and sold them for five guilders.
A Canadian serviceman could have a thousand cigarettes sent from home
for three dollars, and make almost 1,000 guilders in profit.[32]

And you could buy almost anything with cigarettes: fine antique
watches, opera glasses, diamond rings, Leica cameras, the kind of things
people would gladly exchange for fuel and food. Cigarettes also bought
more essential items. The German writer Erich Kästner was in the Austrian countryside in May, watching an endless trail of German soldiers
walking, limping, hobbling on their way home from eastern battlefronts.
He wrote in his diary: "To get a little cash, they sell cigarettes. The price
varies from one to three marks each. There is a constant demand for civilian clothes. The supply is virtually nil. Someone in the house next door
gets 450 cigarettes for an old pair of trousers. I wouldn't mind exchanging
a pair of trousers for that, but I've only got the one pair I'm wearing. The
trade and the result are immoral. With only one pair of trousers one cannot do business."[33]

Sakaguchi Ango, a sardonic Japanese essayist and short story writer,
often classified together with other writers of the immediate postwar period as the "Ruffians" or "Decadents," noted how quickly young soldiers
and airmen who were trained to die gloriously for the emperor transformed themselves into black marketers. Just so, war widows forgot all

about loyalty to their fallen husbands and found new lovers. That's the way it was, Ango wrote. And that was fine with him. For through degradation, by tasting human greed and desire in its rawest state, the Japanese would rediscover their common humanity. Out with idiotic emperor worship! Out with heroic death in suicide airplanes! "We haven't fallen this low because we lost the war. We fall because we are human, because we are alive."[34]

There is no doubt that many veterans of the Japanese Imperial armed forces found their way to the black market, together with Korean and Taiwanese mobsters, gangs of Japanese outcasts, and all the other flotsam of a broken-down society. A saying at the time was: "Women become *pan-pan*, men become carriers for the Black Market."[35] There were more than fifteen thousand black markets spread across Japan, mostly around railway stations. The remnants of some are still there, such as the Ameyoko-cho, possibly named after the Americans, a teeming strip of small food and clothes stores along the railway line near Tokyo's Ueno Station. People went there to acquire essential items to stay alive, or to eat at one of the thousands of flimsy food stalls offering anything from fried frogs to stews made of offal, taken from a variety of animals if one was lucky; there were rumors that human remains found their way into the stews as well.

Anything was bought and sold, including old hospital blankets stained with blood. In Manchuria, Japanese colonizers, who had been lording it over the Chinese for fifteen years, panicked by the invasion of the Soviet troops and unable to return to Japan (most transport was reserved for armed forces and high-ranking Japanese officials), survived by selling all their possessions on the black market: kimonos, furniture, antiques. And sometimes even their babies. Colonial myths about the native superiority of Japanese intelligence made Japanese babies desirable, especially to Chinese peasants who needed the future manpower. Fujiwara Sakuya, who later became vice president of the Bank of Japan, was a child in Manchuria when the war was over. Both his parents sold their possessions on the black market. He remembers seeing Chinese shouting: "Babies for sale? Babies for sale?" The going price was between 300 and 500 yen.

Sometimes babies were bought and immediately sold again for a higher price.[36]

Much of the black market items in Japan itself came from military supplies, sold by Allied servicemen to Japanese gangsters. I once spoke to a retired Japanese gangster whose eyes misted over with fond memories as he recounted tales of those good old days when he made so much money channeling goods from the American PX stores to the black market that he could drive around in a large American car stuffed to the roof with bills. But he was a minor player compared to far better-placed Japanese, who had managed to conceal 70 percent of military stocks at the end of the war. What remained, including all kinds of machinery and construction materials, was handed over by the Americans to the Japanese government to be used for public welfare. That, too, largely disappeared, along with the looted stuff, and made many Japanese officials, some of them former war criminals, very wealthy.

There were obvious differences between Germans and Japanese regarding culture, politics, and history. But in terms of human behavior under similar circumstances they had much in common. One effect of a criminalized economy, exploiting people's hardship, was a breakdown of social solidarity—part of the "degradation" described by Sakaguchi Ango. It was every man, or more often, every woman, for him- or herself. In the words of Heinrich Böll: "Everyone possessed just their lives and, in addition, whatever fell into their hands: coal, wood, books, building materials. Everyone justifiably could have accused everyone else of theft."[37]

And accusing others is what many people did. In Germany, Jews and DPs were often blamed for the violence and racketeering. In Japan, it was the Koreans, Chinese, and Taiwanese, known as "third country nationals"—neither Japanese nor Americans—who were seen as the worst criminals. Many of them had been shipped to Japan as slave workers. Korean and Taiwanese gangs certainly competed with Japanese for the spoils, just as there were Jews and DPs who engaged in the black market; they, too, had to find a way to survive. Bergen-Belsen became one of the main hubs of black market activities. Many DPs—Jewish, Polish, Ukrainian, and Yugoslavs—were stuck in camps for years, without proper facilities. Carl Zuckmayer, in his report about Germany and Austria, warned that there "was no way to stamp out anti-Semitism in Germany, as long as there is no international solution to the DP problem."[38] Actually, Germans often failed to make distinctions—Latvians who had volunteered for work in Hitler's Reich, or Jews, they were all "foreigners." Sometimes Germans had to go to these "foreigners" to buy goods at exorbitant prices. In fact, however, the majority of racketeers, and certainly the most powerful ones, were not Jews or foreigners at all, but Germans.

Major Irving Heymont was the U.S. military officer in charge of an area of Bavaria that contained large Jewish DP camps, notably Landsberg, the town where Hitler had once served time in prison (and wrote *Mein Kampf*). Heymont observed that "Like many individuals in Germany, the camp people are active in the black market . . . Their activity for the most part consists of simple bartering for comfort items and fresh food."[39] He also noted that the "few big operators" in the black market were former businessmen or criminals. They did what came naturally to them. This was their metier.

Simple prejudice was one reason why Jews, or third country nationals and other foreigners, were regarded as particularly egregious criminals. This common human trait, made worse by harsh conditions, was further sharpened by the common perception that the Allies privileged the foreigners, that American MPs in Japan gave the Koreans free rein, or that the Allied authorities made sure Jews lived lavishly at the expense of innocent Germans. There was a kernel of truth to this, even though very few Jews, let alone those languishing in DP camps, lived lavishly, or even comfortably. But only a kernel. For in fact, Allied officials themselves were not immune to anti-Semitism or racism. General Patton was perhaps a little more extreme than most, or at least more outspoken, in his contempt for Jewish survivors he found at the Dachau concentration camp, whom he described as "lower than animals."[40] Even though General Eisenhower instructed Americans in occupied Germany to give Jewish DPs priority over Germans, this was often ignored. Many Americans seem to have found Germans, as well as former collaborators or refugees from the Baltic states, easier to get on with than the traumatized Jews.[41]

More than anything, blaming the foreigners was part of a wider sense of denial, a refusal to face up to what Germans and Japanese had done to others. It was easier to feel sorry for themselves. A reporter for *Yank* magazine, walking around Berlin in August, saw a German woman in a tattered dress and large men's shoes, sticking out her tongue at a female Russian soldier. "You are well fed and we Germans starve," she said, before spitting on the ground.[42] But there were dissident voices even then. An article in the *Berliner Tagesspiegel* deplored "the erection of walls to shield oneself against the gruesome crimes against Poles, Jews, and prisoners; the stupidly arrogant ingratitude for the gift of foodstuffs received from America and England . . ."[43]

In time, of course, the black market economy was gradually replaced by a more regulated one. But the long-term effects of those lawless times were significant, especially in Germany and Japan. For postwar economic collapse and the ensuing black market were great destroyers of old class distinctions. Women from grand families had to trundle to the countryside to barter family heirlooms for food. Poor peasants suddenly grew cash-rich. It was not rare to see Japanese village women stepping through muddy rice fields in beautiful antique kimonos which had once cost a fortune. Impoverished daughters of the aristocracy were compelled to marry successful, and often far from scrupulous, nouveaux riches. But the postwar chaos also created some freedom to set up enterprises unhindered by more established competitors. In 1945, Masaru Ibuka started a radio repair shop in a bomb-damaged department store in Tokyo. It was the beginning of the Sony Corporation.

It is worth quoting in full an observation made by Alfred Döblin, author of the prewar masterpiece *Berlin Alexanderplatz* (1929). After surviving the war in exile in California, Döblin returned to Germany, where he felt like an exile all over again. This is what he wrote after arriving in the spa town of Baden-Baden:

> The main impression I got in Germany was of people who were like ants running back and forth through a destroyed nest, in a state of excitement and desperate to get to work in the midst of their ruination. Their only worry is that they can't get to work at once without the requisite tools and directives. They are less depressed by the destruction than inspired to want to work even harder. If they had the means, which they lack today, they would rejoice tomorrow, rejoice that their antiquated, badly laid out places have been demolished, offering them the chance to build something first class and modern.[44]

CHAPTER 3

REVENGE

In Czechoslovakia in the summer of 1945, near the town of Budweis (České Budějovice), best known for its fine beer, was a concentration camp with a sign nailed to its main gate which read: "An Eye for an Eye, a Tooth for a Tooth." The camp was now under Czech control. It was filled with German prisoners, most of them civilians. The Czech commandant, a young man with a savage reputation, made the Germans work twelve hours a day on minimal rations, then woke them in the middle of the night and ordered them to the *Appelplatz* where they were made to sing, crawl, beat each other, dance, or any other torment that amused the Czech guards.[1]

The desire for revenge is as human as the need for sex or food. Few people have expressed this more finely, and more brutally, than the Polish author Tadeusz Borowski. After being arrested in 1943 for publishing his poems in the clandestine press—wartime Warsaw was alive with a vast underground culture, including schools, newspapers, theaters, and poetry magazines, all of which exposed participants to the risk of concentration camp or a more immediate death—Borowski survived a Gestapo prison, then Auschwitz and Dachau. Liberated in Dachau, he stayed more or less locked up as a displaced person in a former SS barracks near Munich. His account of this squalid experience in limbo was included in a classic book of short sketches of camp life and death titled *This Way for the Gas, Ladies and Gentlemen.*[2]

One of the stories is called "Silence." A number of DPs spot a former Nazi henchman trying to escape through a window. They grab him and begin "tearing at him with greedy hands." When they hear U.S. soldiers, who are running the DP camp, approaching, they push the man onto a straw mattress under layers of bedding. The senior American officer, a fine young fellow in a freshly pressed uniform, tells them through his translator that he quite understands how much the survivors of Nazi camps must hate the Germans. But it is most important that the rule of law should be observed. The guilty should be punished only after due process. The Americans would see to that. The DPs nod and give the nice American a cheer. He wishes them a good night's rest and "accompanied by a friendly hum of voices" leaves the room to conclude his tour of the barracks. No sooner has he gone than the German is pulled from the bed and kicked to death on the concrete floor.

This was not an unusual incident in the immediate aftermath of Liberation, or, in the case of the DPs, semi-liberation. In other accounts, the liberating soldiers, shocked by the visual evidence of German depravity, were less attached to the rules of due legal process. At Dachau, American soldiers stood by as SS guards were lynched, drowned, cut up, strangled, or battered to death with spades, and at least in one case beheaded with a bayonet lent by a GI to a former inmate for this purpose. Sometimes the GIs took it upon themselves to shoot the German guards. Also at Dachau, one American lieutenant executed more than three hundred guards with his machine gun. His rage was understandable; he had just seen the corpses of prisoners piled up in front of the camp crematorium.[3]

At Bergen-Belsen in April 1945 a British nurse saw what happened when a group of German nurses entered the camp for the first time. Having been ordered to care for the desperately ill survivors, they walked into one of the hospital wards, and in an instant "a shrieking mass of internees, among them even the dying, had hurled themselves at the nurses, scratching and tearing at them with knives and forks, or with instruments snatched from the dressing trolleys."[4]

In this case, the British had to protect the German civilians, whose presence was vital to the survival of the inmates. Dealing with the natural desire for vengeance, for the rough justice of an eye for an eye, was a serious problem for Allied officers, government officials returning from exile, members of welfare organizations, and all others who were interested in restoring some sense of order or normality to the devastated continent. Like the hapless GI in Borowski's story, however, they were often powerless to stop further mayhem, especially in countries torn by civil war. On many occasions, too, they decided to look the other way, or were actively complicit, in far more unsavory ways than the GI who lent his bayonet at the Dachau concentration camp. Indeed, most cases of organized vengeance would not have happened without official encouragement. Just as sexual desire rarely leads straight to orgies, mass violence seldom comes from individual initiatives; it needs leadership, organization.

And it needs the right timing. One of the surprising things about the aftermath of the war is that more Germans didn't attack other Germans. A journalist in Berlin, one of the few Germans who had actively resisted the Nazis, wrote in her postwar diary that people had been "ripe for retribution." During the last months of the war, a time of desperation for many Germans, "even the biggest fool understood how villainously he had been deceived by Nazism . . ." And so, she continued, "If there had been a three-day period between the collapse and the [Allied] conquest, thousands and thousands, disappointed, humiliated and abused by the Nazis, would have wreaked revenge upon their enemies. To each his personal tyrant. 'An eye for an eye,' people swore back then. 'The first hour after the collapse belongs to the long knives!' Destiny had it differently."[5]

She was right; the shared hardship under foreign occupation kept

Germans from each others' throats. Vengeance against Germans would be exacted by others.

Hans Graf von Lehndorff was running a hospital in the old East Prussian city of Königsberg, now a Russian city called Kaliningrad, when it was taken by the Soviet army in April 1945. In his diaries, written in a style both clearheaded and deeply religious, he describes how Soviet troops, blind drunk from a raid on the adjacent liquor factory, stagger into the wards and rape every female they can find, including the very old and the very young, nurses as well as patients, several of them so gravely wounded that they are barely conscious. Some of the women beg the soldiers to shoot them, but this act of mercy is seldom accorded before they have been assaulted many times, rendering an execution superfluous in most cases.

Lehndorff was not a Nazi. Indeed, like many members of his aristocratic family, he abhorred the Nazis. His mother had been arrested by the Gestapo. A cousin was executed for having taken part in the July 20, 1944, plot to assassinate Hitler. Seeing his city burning, while the women are raped, the men hunted down, and the shot-up houses systematically looted, Dr. Lehndorff wonders what it all means: "Does this still have anything to do with natural wildness, or is it vengeance? Vengeance, probably . . . What an effort they make to create a show out of chaos! . . . And these frenzied children, not much older than fifteen or sixteen, throwing themselves on our women like wolves, without having a clue what it's all about. This has nothing to do with Russia, nothing with any particular people or race—this is man without God, a grotesque caricature of humanity. Otherwise all this would not hurt one so deeply—like one's own guilt."[6]

The sentiments are noble, and Lehndorff is surely right that human beings everywhere, given the license to do what they please with other human beings, are quite capable, even willing, to do their worst. But often the worst is done by men who feel that God, or some worldly substitute, *is* on their side. Vengeance is rarely free-floating. It usually has a history, personal or collective. Jews aside, citizens of the Soviet Union had suffered more than other peoples from German savagery. The figures are hard to imagine. More than 8 million Soviet soldiers died, of whom 3.3 million were deliberately starved to death, left to rot in open-air camps, in midsummer heat or wintry frost. The civilian death toll was 16 million. Only the Chinese, who lost more than 10 million civilians under Japanese occupation, come anywhere close. But these are statistics. They don't tell the full story. Murder and starvation went together with constant degradation and humiliation. Russians, like other Slavs, were less than fully human in Nazi German eyes, *Untermenschen*, whose only role would be to work as slaves for their German masters. And those unfit to work as slaves did not deserve to be fed. Indeed, Nazi Germany had a policy, called the Hunger Plan, of starving the Soviet peoples to provide Germans with more living space (*Lebensraum*) and food. If fully carried out, this monstrous economic plan would have killed tens of millions.

But vengeance was not just a matter of rage or indiscipline. Men who are brutally treated by their own officers often take out their suffering on the civilian population too. This is one explanation for the ferocity of Japanese soldiers in China, besides their racist contempt for Chinese people. The ruthless treatment of Soviet soldiers by their military superiors, as well as by the political commissars and secret police, is well known. But quite apart from that, once the Germans were forced to retreat from the Soviet Union, the Red Army troops were explicitly told to do their worst as soon as they entered German lands. Road signs on the border said in Russian: "Soldier, you are in Germany: take revenge on the Hitlerites."[7] The words of propagandists, such as Ilya Ehrenburg, were drummed daily into their heads: "If you have not killed at least one German a day, you have wasted that day . . . If you kill one German, kill another—there is nothing funnier for us than a pile of German corpses." Marshal Georgy Zhukov stated in his orders of January 1945: "Woe to the land of the murderers. We will get our terrible revenge for everything."[8]

Men who had been humiliated for years as *Untermenschen* and had usually lost friends and relatives, often in horrible circumstances, needed little encouragement. There was another factor too. The Soviets had already been fed propaganda about the rapaciousness of bourgeois capitalism. Here was a chance for revolutionary violence. What shocked the soldiers, some of whom had barely seen functioning electricity, let alone such luxury items as wristwatches, was the relative opulence of German civilian life, even in the miserable conditions of bombed cities and wartime shortages. Greed, ethnic rage, class envy, political propaganda, fresh memories of German atrocities, all this served to quicken the thirst for vengeance. As one Soviet officer put it, "the deeper we penetrate into Germany, the more we are disgusted by the plenty we find everywhere . . . I'd just love to smash my fist into all those neat rows of tins and bottles."[9]

Even when not fueled by a desire for revenge, this feeling could lead to serious aggression. When the Soviet Red Army invaded northeastern China, or Manchuria, in August, less than a week before the Japanese surrender, their troops went on a rampage in such major cities as Harbin, Mukden (Shenyang), and Shinkyo (Changchun). There was no reason for vengeance against the large Japanese civilian population in these cities, let alone against the Chinese. Japan had never invaded any part of the Soviet Union, even though the Japanese did inflict a humiliating defeat on Russia in the Russo-Japanese War of 1905–6, fought over the very same Manchurian territory. On the one occasion when Japan foolishly attacked the Soviet Union, in 1939, on the Mongolian border, the Japanese were decisively beaten. And yet the behavior of Soviet troops in northeastern China was like that of fifteenth-century conquistadores.

Like the German populations in eastern Europe, Japanese civilians were totally vulnerable, for the same reason: just as most German SS men, military officers, and senior Nazi officials had fled to the west, Japanese army officers and government officials had hogged the last trains bound for the ships that would take them back to Japan, leaving the mass of civilians behind to fend for themselves. This meant that almost two million Japanese were trapped without any protection. Many of them had moved to the continent since 1932, when Manchuria became Manchukuo, the Japanese puppet state; emigration was actively promoted by the Japanese government seeking *Lebensraum* for its rural citizens. In the cities—Mukden, Shinkyo, Kirin, Harbin—an entire Japanese society emerged of banks, railways, department stores, schools, art academies, cinemas, restaurants, all run by Japanese for Japanese. In rural areas Chinese had been kicked off their land to make room for Japanese settlers. All this was justified by official Japanese propaganda about Asia for the Asians, a brave new Orient, more modern, more efficient, more just than the old Western imperial order, ruled by the Japanese masters.

Some Chinese took advantage of Japanese defeat by robbing Japanese civilians. They had reason to feel aggrieved. For in Manchukuo, set up and controlled by the Japanese Kwantung Army, Chinese were treated as third-class citizens, lower even than the Koreans, at the mercy of almost any Japanese. Yet in many Japanese memories, the Soviets were far worse than the Chinese. In one account: "They would break into Japanese homes, firing off their pistols, and not only grab any object that caught their fancy, but rape any woman they liked as well."[10]

Japanese who fled farther south, mostly on foot, to escape the Soviet troops often fared little better. Food ran out. Typhus broke out on lice-infested bodies. Babies were stifled to death to stop their cries from alerting vengeful Chinese, Koreans, or Soviet soldiers. Small children were handed over to Chinese peasants in the hope that they might at least survive that way. All in all, more than eleven thousand Japanese settlers lost their lives in these ordeals, about one-third by committing suicide.

Stories of Soviet violence spread fast, provoking odd measures to appease the Red Army troops. In the city of Andong, on the border of Manchuria and Korea, the Japanese community decided to greet the Soviet troops with a welcoming committee. Japanese children were issued with little red flags, an arch was erected at the railway station, festooned with more red flags and slogans expressing the deep feelings of friendship for the Soviet Union, and the local Japanese notables had prepared effusive speeches of welcome. They waited, and waited, and waited. The children fell asleep, still clutching their flags. It was already late at night when the Japanese finally heard that the Red Army had decided to take a different route, and would not be coming to Andong just yet.

Japanese accounts tend to leave out the suffering of Chinese at the hands of Soviet troops, but it is true that Japanese civilians suffered more. Their wealth, or assumed wealth, was clearly an incentive. The witness quoted earlier related: "Soviet soldiers swaggered about town, as though they owned it, with wrist watches on both arms, cameras dangling from their shoulders, fountain pens stuck in rows in their coat pockets."[11] As was the case of Soviet troops in Germany, many soldiers were unfamiliar with the trappings of the modern world. When watches stopped working, because their new owners had failed to wind them up, they were angrily tossed away—only to be picked up by Chinese urchins who sold them on the black market. Electric ceiling fans filled some soldiers with such fear that they would shoot their guns at them.

Still, the looting of civilians by Soviet soldiers would not have been on anything like this scale were it not for official encouragement, or indeed example. What is stealing a few watches compared to the wholesale looting of Japanese factories, mines, railways, and banks? The only way the Soviets could justify this—not that they tried very hard to do so—was by treating it as a right in the people's war against fascism, which was, in communist propaganda, simply an extension of capitalism. Theft was part of the revolutionary project. In any case, humiliation, unless it is the humiliation of the poor thrust into a world of the relatively rich, cannot really account for Soviet behavior in northeastern China. Germany was a different matter. And there Soviet violence was even worse.

The surest way to repay humiliation with humiliation is to rape the women, in public, in front of the men, who are helpless to do anything about it. It is the oldest form of terror in human conflict, and not specific to Russians. Dr. Hans Graf von Lehndorff was right about that. But the justifications people use for their savagery are not always the same. The disparity in wealth, as well as racialism, created a vicious circle of mutually hostile propaganda that made Soviet behavior in Germany especially brutal. Germans were told to fight to the death, rather than to see their women fall prey to the "Asiatic" or "Mongol" barbarians. The harder the Germans resisted, the more the "barbarians" wanted to exact their price for brutality that had been far greater in scale than anything they did to the Germans. But here too vengeance was related to the war against capitalism. German women were not just depicted in Soviet propaganda as Nazis, just as bad as the men, but as fat, pampered, rich Nazis. In one Russian cartoon, a wealthy German woman, her daughter, and her maid, surrounded by loot from Russia, frantically look for something to use as a white flag of surrender. Ironically, a caricature of a German woman ("Miss Veronica Dankeschön") in a U.S. Army magazine, plump, blond, her skirt embroidered with swastikas, looks identical. The only difference is that the GIs were warned to stay away from Miss Veronica to avoid VD, while the Soviet soldiers were invited to seize what was their due. As the Russian ex–slave worker says to her former mistress in another Soviet cartoon: "Now you'll see, Frau. I've come to collect."[12]

And collect they did. The anonymous author of A Woman in Berlin described in harrowing detail the humiliation visited on women, which showed the kind of disgust expressed by the soldier who wanted to smash his fist into all those neat little gewgaws in bourgeois German homes. On one of the many occasions that she is raped by a soldier, while others await their turn, she notes how her attacker barely seems to notice her. She is an object too, "which makes it all the more frightening when he suddenly throws me onto the bed . . . I feel fingers at my mouth, smell the reek of horses and tobacco. I open my eyes. Adroitly the fingers force my jaws apart. Eye looks into eye. Then the man above me slowly lets his spittle dribble into my mouth . . ."[13]

Raping German women, especially those who appeared to have unlimited wealth, and especially in front of the emasculated ex-warriors of the "master race," made the despised Untermenschen feel like men again. In the words of a senior Soviet officer in Berlin, "in the first flush of victory our fellows no doubt derived a certain satisfaction from making it hot for those Herrenvolk women."[14] However, it went on well beyond that first flush of victory. In its wild form, freed from any official restraints, the raping of German women continued through the summer of 1945. After that, Soviet military and civilian officials tried to crack down, at least sporadically, sometimes with draconian measures, including the death penalty. In fact, the risk of being raped by a Soviet soldier ceased only once the troops were confined to their barracks in 1947.

. . .

IF THE WISH TO OVERCOME humiliation and restore masculine pride is one plausible explanation for the violence of Soviet soldiers in German lands, it might also explain the vengeful behavior of men who had suffered far less than the Soviets. During the so-called wild purge (*l'épuration sauvage*) in France, which took place in 1944, before the war was even over, about six thousand people were killed as German collaborators and traitors by various armed bands with links to the resistance, often communists. Double that number of women were paraded around, stripped naked, their heads shaven, swastikas daubed on various parts of their anatomy. They were jeered at, spat on, and otherwise tormented. Some were locked up in improvised jails, and raped by their jailers. More than two thousand women were killed. Similar scenes, though not nearly on the same scale, took place in Belgium, the Netherlands, Norway, and other countries liberated from German occupation. Sometimes, the naked women were tarred and feathered in the traditional manner of vengeful mobs.

Female collaboration with the enemy was mostly about sex. Unlike treason, this was not a crime that existed in any legal code before. One could call it tactless, selfish, indecent, an affront, but not a crime. So a new law was devised in France, in 1944, to deal with such cases. People who had undermined the national morale by unpatriotic behavior, such as sleeping with the occupiers, were guilty of "national unworthiness" (*indignité nationale*) and stripped of their civil rights.

All kinds of people, men and women, were purged, often with extreme violence, after May 1945 in France. About four thousand people lost their lives. Many had been guilty of treason; others were purged for reasons of personal vengeance, or for political reasons, if they stood in the way of the Communist Party, for example. But popular wrath fell disproportionately, and most publicly, on women accused of "horizontal collaboration." This, too, can be explained at least partly through a common sense of humiliation. The submission of France by superior German force was often described in sexual terms. The rampant German army, representing a powerful, virile nation, had forced weak, decadent, effeminate France to submit to its will. Horizontal collaboration, the giggling young *française* perched on the knees of the Boche, swilling fine French champagne, was the most painful symbol of this submission. And so it was the women who had to be punished with maximum disgrace.

Already before national liberation, and the wild purge, Frenchwomen had been given the right to vote for the first time, in April 1944 to be exact. The following sentences, from *Le Patriote de l'Eure*, a resistance newspaper, published in February 1945, reveal a great deal about contemporary attitudes to the women who had strayed into the wrong arms:

> Soon we shall see these women voting side by side with our valiant ordinary French women, good mothers, wives of prisoners of war. But surely we should not allow those who sniggered at us, who threatened us, who swooned in the arms of the Boches, to have any say in the destiny of France reborn.[15]

Contrast the sniggering, swooning floozies with those virtuous mothers and POW wives, and one senses the shame, as well as the strong puritanical streak. The horizontal collaborators were not only unpatriotic, but also threats to bourgeois family morals. Add to this the always toxic element of economic envy, and righteous indignation becomes truly explosive. From the indictments of the wicked women it is not always clear which was considered worse, the sexual immorality or the material benefits that came with it. Sleeping with the enemy was bad enough, but living better than everyone else made it a far graver crime. The case of one Madame Polge, wife of a well-known football player in Nimes, serves as a grim illustration.

During the occupation, Mme Polge became the mistress of the local

German commander, whose French family name was Saint Paul. In exchange for her services, she received all manner of material benefits. In the words of a contemporary newspaper, *Le Populaire*, Mme Polge "admitted to having two or three liters of milk delivered every day, as well as fresh game, twice or three times a week, from the Boche commandant. She was also able to keep her house nice and warm, as well as having her hair done, and all that without paying a centime . . . And meanwhile working-class people and their children were dying of hunger . . ."[16] Mme Polge was sentenced to death. Shaven and stripped, she was driven through the streets to the execution ground. After she was shot, her corpse was displayed to the good people of Nimes, who covered it in spit, and prodded it with a broomstick, the final indignity befitting a modern witch.

The most enthusiastic persecutors of *filles de Boches* were usually not people who had distinguished themselves in acts of courage during the war. Once Liberation came to formerly occupied countries, all kinds of men managed to present themselves as members of resistance groups, strutting around with newly acquired armbands and Sten guns, disporting themselves as heroes as they hunted for traitors and bad women. Vengeance is one way of covering up a guilty conscience for not standing up when it was dangerous. This too appears to be a universal phenomenon, of all times. As the truly heroic Polish dissident Adam Michnik once put it, when he protested against purging former communists after 1989, he had nothing to be ashamed of before, so he had no need to prove that he was a hero by pointing fingers at others now. This humane attitude, always rare, was not exactly common in 1945.

Greed, prejudice, and a guilty conscience might help us understand the most perverse form of revenge in 1945, the persecution of Jews in Poland. The ancient Jewish community in Poland was almost annihilated. Three million Polish Jews were murdered during the Nazi occupation, either shot or gassed, mostly on Polish territory. Ten percent managed to survive, hidden by Polish Gentiles, or living in exile in far-flung parts of the Soviet Union. The physically and mentally wounded survivors who came staggering back to their hometowns and villages, after having lost all

or most of their friends and relatives, usually found that they were no longer welcome. Worse than that: they were often threatened and driven out
of town. Other people had moved in to their houses. The synagogues
were destroyed. What possessions they might have left behind had long
ago been stolen by others, frequently former neighbors. And it was a rare
person who was willing to give anything back.

This happened in other parts of Europe as well. Quite a number of
Jews returning home to Amsterdam, Brussels, or Paris found that they had
no home left there, either. But in Poland, especially outside the main cities, Jews were in physical danger. There were cases of families being
pulled off trains, robbed of all their possessions, and killed on the spot.
More than a thousand Jews were murdered in Poland between the sum-
mers of 1945 and 1946. Even in the cities, they were not always safe.

In August 11, 1945, a rumor started in Krakow that Jews had killed a
Christian child in the synagogue. This was an updated version of an age-
old anti-Semitic canard. People spoke darkly of Jewish survivors using
Christian blood to revive their ravaged health. Soon, a mob gathered, led
by policemen and militiamen. The synagogue was attacked, Jewish homes
were plundered, and men, women, and children were beaten up in the
streets. Several people (the exact number is not known) were murdered. It
was a bloody pogrom against people who had only just survived a genocide. Badly wounded Jews were taken to the hospital, where some of them
were assaulted again while awaiting surgery. One female survivor recalls
"the comments of the escorting soldier and the nurse, who spoke about us
as Jewish scum whom they had to save, and that they shouldn't be doing
this because we murdered children, that all of us should be shot." Another
nurse promised to rip the Jews apart as soon as surgery was over. A railway
man at the hospital remarked: "It's a scandal that a Pole does not have the
civil courage to hit a defenseless person."[17] This man, true to his word,
proceeded to beat a wounded Jew.

Poles, too, suffered horribly under German occupation. *Untermenschen*, like the Russians, they were enslaved, their capital city was razed,
and more than a million non-Jewish Poles were murdered. Poles could not

be blamed for the German decision to build the death camps on their soil. And yet it is as though the Poles took out their own suffering on the one people who had suffered even more.

A common account is that Polish vengeance was based on the perception that Jews were responsible for communist oppression. When Soviet troops had occupied different parts of Poland, some Jews hoped that they would protect them from Polish anti-Semites, or from the even more lethal Germans. Communism as an antidote to ethnic nationalism had long had a natural appeal to members of a vulnerable minority. But while many communists were Jews, most Jews were not communists. So vengeance against Jews for what was called "Judeo-Communism" was at best misplaced, and politics may in fact not have been the main source of revenge at all. For most Jews were not attacked after the war for being communists, but for being Jews. And Jews were associated not only with bolshevism in popular anti-Semitic lore, but with capitalism too. They were assumed to have money, to be better off than other people, even privileged. Communists were not above exploiting anti-Semitism themselves, which is why most Jewish survivors in Poland ended up leaving the country of their birth.

Although the majority of Polish Jews were in fact poor, the perception of superior wealth lingered. This had something to do with a guilty conscience, sometimes eased in a bizarre way by communist propaganda against Jewish capitalists. Poles certainly bore no responsibility for the German plan to exterminate the Jews. But many of them did stand by at the edge of the ghetto, with horse carts, waiting for their chance to plunder once the Jews had been conveniently disposed of. Others—like so many European citizens—were also happy to move into houses and apartments, whose rightful owners were taken away to be murdered.

In some places, especially in northeastern villages around Bialystok, Poles did some of the killing themselves. In July 1941, the Jews in Radzilow were locked up in a barn and burned alive while their fellow citizens ran around filling their bags with loot. An eyewitness remembers: "When the Poles started rounding up and chasing Jews, the plundering of Jewish houses began instantly ... They went mad, they were breaking into houses, tearing up quilts; the air was full of feathers, and they'd just load up their sacks, run home and come back with an empty sack again." One family, the Finkielstejns, managed to run away. After they returned, they asked the priest to convert them so they might have a better chance to survive. The daughter, Chaja, recalls the village conversations: "They would always talk about one thing: who had plundered how much and how rich the Jews had been."[18]

It should never be forgotten that other Polish Gentiles behaved very differently. Hiding or helping Jews to survive carried huge risks, not just for the helper alone, but for his or her family. If caught in a western European country, a person might be sent to a concentration camp for helping Jews. In Poland it could mean death by hanging. Yet some Jews did survive thanks to the bravery of Polish Gentiles. Children were adopted, families hidden. In one famous case, several Jewish families were hidden for more than a year in the sewers of Lvov by a petty thief named Leopold Socha. More than twenty people survived underground, eating Socha's crusts of bread while fending off rats in the dark, and at least once almost drowning after a heavy rainstorm flooded the sewer. When they emerged from the manhole, pale, emaciated, covered in excrement and lice, the people aboveground were astonished to see a Jew still alive. Several months later Socha died in an accident, run over by a drunken Soviet army truck driver. The neighbors whispered that this was God's punishment for helping the Jews.[19]

This is perhaps the most shocking thing about the postwar Polish story. People who had protected Jews from being murdered were well advised not to talk about it. Not only because of God's wrath for helping "the killers of Christ," but because of the suspected loot. Since Jews were assumed to have money, and their saviors were expected to have been richly compensated, anyone who admitted to have hidden Jews was vulnerable to plunder.

Even after they were long dead, Jews were still thought to have something worth taking. In the autumn of 1945, the former death camp of

Treblinka, where more than eight hundred thousand Jews had been murdered, was a muddy mass grave. Local peasants started digging in search
of skulls from which they might still be able to extract some gold teeth
overlooked by the Nazis. Thousands worked the site with shovels, or sifted
through the mounds of ashes, transforming the mass grave into a huge
field of deep pits and broken bones.

The Poles, it must be emphasized again, were not unique. Greed was
the common result of barbarous occupation, which affected countless Europeans. The historian Tony Judt observed: "The Nazis' attitude to life
and limb is justifiably notorious; but their treatment of *property* may actually have been their most important practical legacy to the shape of the
post-war world."[20] Property up for grabs is a great incitement for brutality.
What is unusual about Poland is the *scale* of plunder. A whole new class
had come up from the war which essentially took over the assets of those
who had been killed or driven out. A lingering sense of guilt can have
perverse consequences.

A contemporary Polish weekly paper, *Odrodzenie*, put it succinctly in
September 1945: "We knew in the country an entire social stratum—the
newborn Polish bourgeoisie—which took the place of murdered Jews, often literally, and perhaps because it smelled blood on its hands, it hated
Jews more strongly than ever."[21]

This explains the sometimes bloody vengeance against the main victims of Hitler's Reich better than anything. Plundering the Jews, in a way,
was part of a larger social revolution. And this type of revenge, too, would
not have happened without the sometimes tacit, but often active, connivance of powerful opportunists in the Polish bureaucracy and police. It was
not the official policy of the communist-dominated Polish government in
1945 to go after the Jews, but encouragement from the middle ranks was
often quite enough.

. . .

THAT POLES WOULD WISH to direct their revenge against Germans is
more comprehensible. But that, too, was partly driven by class warfare.

For centuries Germans had lived in areas such as Silesia and East Prussia that are now part of Poland. Major cities, like Breslau (Wrocław) or Danzig (Gdańsk), were largely German. German was the language of the urban elites, the doctors, bankers, professors, and businessmen. In 1945 more than four million Germans were still living in former German lands invaded by Soviet troops. Roughly the same number, terrified of what they had been told about Russian behavior, had fled to the west. Plans to expel the rest of the German population were already clear well before May 1945. In 1941, General Sikorski, the Polish prime minister exiled in London, declared that "the German horde, which for centuries had penetrated to the east, should be destroyed and forced to draw back far [to the west]."[22]

This policy had been endorsed by the Allied leaders. Even worse, Stalin advised the Polish communists to "create such conditions for the Germans that they would want to escape themselves." And Churchill had told the House of Commons in December 1944, "Expulsion is the method, which, so far as we have been able to see, will be the most satisfactory and lasting."[23]

As long as the Red Army was in control, the Poles more or less held themselves back. Libussa Fritz-Krockow, scion of a noble Pomeranian landowning family, remembered how they had actually felt protected by the Russians at times, even though those same Russians "were responsible for the vast majority of the rapes and the lootings." Yet, she observed, "their violence was somehow comprehensible to us, whether we explained it as the principle of an eye for an eye, sheer exuberance, or conquerors' rights. The Poles, on the other hand, were merely camp followers. Their seizure of power had a different character. There was something cold and furtive about it, almost sneaky, which made it seem far more sinister than naked force."[24]

The Krockows were not Nazis. Christian von Krockow, who wrote up his sister Libussa's memoirs, was a liberal who understood very well that their suffering was "the result of our own German madness."[25] But there may be a hint of anti-Polish bias or bitterness in Libussa's statement, even perhaps a sense of betrayal. This was not an unusual sentiment. A German Protestant minister, Helmut Richter, expressed the same thing. He had always expected the Poles to be good people. After all, hadn't Germans treated them well in the past? But now he realized "the awful nature of these eastern peoples." For a long time, they had behaved themselves as long as they felt "a fist hovering over their heads," but they turned "barbaric when they have the chance to wield power over others."[26] This is the way colonizers always talk about the natives. The difference with most European colonies in Africa or Asia, however, is that in this case many of the former colonizers had been natives themselves, albeit natives of a privileged class.

In any case, the Poles did not want Soviet troops to spend a moment longer than necessary in the conquered lands that were now officially part of Poland. And the cruelties that went with massive expulsions and population transfers decided by the Big Powers at the Yalta Conference in February 1945 were not just the result of Polish vengeance. More than two million "Congress Poles" from the east of the Polish Soviet border, now part of Ukraine, were moved to Silesia and other areas that had been more or less swept clean of the Germans. So they took German homes, German jobs, and German assets, a process that was rarely gentle.

Of course, ethnic cleansing did not begin in 1945. Hitler had expelled Poles and murdered Jews to make room for German immigrants in Silesia and other border areas. But bitterness over disputed homelands went back further than that. As so often with bloody ethnic revenge, a history of civil war preceded it. With the defeat of Germany and the Austro-Hungarian Empire in 1918, the fate of their holdings in Silesia had to be decided. Bits went to Austria, bits to Czechoslovakia, and bits to Poland and Germany. Upper Silesia, however, remained in dispute. There was a strong Upper Silesian independence movement, supported by local Poles and Germans. But the Allies decided in 1919 that a plebiscite should decide whether the territory should go to Poland or Germany. This decision led to serious violence. Armed Polish nationalists assaulted Germans, especially in the industrial area around Kattowitz (Katowice), not far from

Auschwitz (Oświęcim). These attacks provoked even bloodier reprisals by thuggish German adventurers in the ultranationalist, paramilitary Freikorps, a breeding ground for the future Nazi movement that was formed in late 1918 after Germany's defeat. "Black-Red-Gold! Smash the Poles!" was one of their charming slogans. The majority voted for Germany to govern Upper Silesia, a decision that caused more violence. In the end, part of Upper Silesia went to Poland after all. But memories were still raw in 1945, all the more so because of the treatment of Poles under Nazi occupation.

The family of Josef Hoenisch had lived in Upper Silesia for many generations. Because he had never joined the Nazi Party, he decided that it would be safe to stay home in 1945. A bad decision. He was arrested by the Polish Militia, which had replaced Soviet troops. Asked by Militia interrogators whether he had been a Nazi, Hoenisch replied that he had not, and was booted in the face. This went on for some time, until he was dragged, covered in blood, into a six-by-nine-foot cell filled with nine other German prisoners who had barely enough room to stand, let alone sit. Polish militiamen, he recalls, had their fun by making prisoners, men as well as women, strip and beat one another. After eight days of this, Hoenisch was confronted by a former schoolmate, a Polish wheelwright named Georg Pissarczik, who had fought against the Germans over the fate of Upper Silesia in 1919. This was Pissarczik's chance for revenge. Now, at last, the German would get his just deserts. The story has a further Silesian twist, however. The two men met again, and Pissarczik was reminded by his former schoolmate that Hoenisch's father had helped Pissarczik's father get a job in the early 1920s, when no German would employ him. Could Pissarczik not help him in return? Four weeks later, Hoenisch was released.

Unfortunately, Hoenisch's story, like many recollections of German victims, is marred by a peculiar obtuseness about the suffering of others. He remarks how lucky he was not to have been sent to Auschwitz after his release, one of those "famous Polish death camps [after the war], from which no German came out alive."[27] This same language creeps into other accounts by German conservatives. In his diary of 1945, the soldier-writer Ernst Jünger mentions Russian "extermination camps" and compares "anti-Germanism" to anti-Semitism. Newspapers, he notes, are "indulging" in anti-German sentiment, "like an orgy."[28]

There is little evidence even in the most self-pitying of German accounts that many Poles indulged in collective retaliation spontaneously. But clearly many innocent German civilians were falsely accused of having been Nazis, or in the SS, and suffered horribly. The detention camps, often in former Nazi concentration camps, were very brutal. And Germans in Silesia lost their civil rights if they opted not to be citizens of Poland, which was in any case impossible if they could not speak Polish. Without rights, people were at the mercy of any militiaman or petty official. Simply being unable to follow a roll call in Polish in a camp could mean a rain of fists, clubs, or worse.

Libussa Fritz-Krockow was about to sell a carpet from her family home to the Polish mayor's wife, who had paid her a pittance on several occasions before for valuable items. She was caught in the act by a militiaman. Germans were not allowed to sell their possessions. For this crime, Libussa was shackled in a pillory so people could spit in her face. But, she relates, "the Poles generally just cleared their throats, or spat on the ground, while the Germans crossed to the other side of the street."[29]

The worst cases of anti-German violence were no doubt committed by the Militia. They ran the concentration camps, tortured prisoners, killed at random, and put people in pillories, sometimes for no reason at all. Hastily pulled together, the Militia found many of its recruits among the most unsavory Poles, often very young criminals. One of the most notorious killers, Cesaro Gimborski, the commandant of the Lamsdorf camp, was just eighteen. More than six thousand people, including eight hundred children, were murdered under his command. Like a child amusing himself by tearing wings from a fly, Gimborski, by all accounts, took pleasure in his power.

Some of the most ferocious militiamen had survived German camps, so vengeance was surely a factor. But once again, bloodlust was inflamed by material and class envy. Teachers, professors, businessmen, and other members of the upper bourgeoisie were popular targets. The Polish guards, ably assisted by German turncoats, found particular enjoyment in torturing prisoners of high status. A professor imprisoned in Lamsdorf was beaten to death for the simple reason that he wore "intellectual glasses." One is reminded, both by the guards' youth and their favored victims, of the Cambodian Khmer Rouge, or the Red Guards in China. Setting teenagers upon teachers and other authority figures is never very difficult. In this case, a history of ethnic conflict made the sadism even keener.

More or less the same things happened in other parts of the old Austro-Hungarian Empire, filled with German-speaking citizens who were first handed to non-Germanic governments in 1919, then became privileged citizens of Hitler's Reich, and finally were kicked out by former neighbors, employees, or sometimes even friends. Germans subjected to the full force of revenge in Czechoslovakia agreed that the greatest menace came from teenage boys, encouraged by the adults, some of whom had good reasons to be vengeful. Many Czechs and Slovaks had suffered after Hitler annexed the Sudetenland in 1938; some had survived Dachau, Buchenwald, and other German concentration camps. As was true in Upper Silesia, the bad blood had a history, going back as far as the seventeenth century when the Protestant Bohemian nobility was wiped out by the Catholic Holy Roman Emperor. Since then, Germans had had the upper hand over Czechs and Slovaks. Non-Germans were the servant class and the peasants. So there, too, the summer of 1945 was the time for class, as well as ethnic, revenge. And there too, encouragement came from the top.

The Czech president in exile during the war, Edvard Beneš, a Czech nationalist who once had had dreams of a harmonious multiethnic Czechoslovakia, now decided that the German problem should be solved once and for all. In a radio broadcast in 1945, he declared: "Woe, woe, woe, thrice woe to the Germans, we will liquidate you!"[30] In April, May, and June, various decrees deprived Germans of their property rights. "Extraordinary People's Courts" were created to judge Nazi criminals, traitors, and supporters. In October, all those who had acted against "national honor," which might almost have applied to all Germans, were to be punished as well.

Czechs, like other human beings, will do their worst if they are officially set upon defenseless people. Torture prisons were established in Prague and other cities. Suspected SS men were strung up from lampposts. More than ten thousand German civilians were packed into the Strahov football stadium, where thousands were machine-gunned just for sport. The Revolutionary Guards (RG) were the Czech equivalent of the Polish Militia, young hoodlums given official license to act out their violent fantasies. They led the mobs, stoning Germans in the streets, and otherwise molesting citizens who had once been privileged, or wore "intellectual glasses." But they had the support of the army, and the newly liberated country's top officials, too.

One story—by no means the most horrific—will have to suffice to give an impression of what it was like during those wild summer months, before the violent orgy, like the sexual abandon in other parts of Europe, petered out, and a new order was imposed. It is the story of a German actress named Margarete Schell. Born in Prague, Schell was famous before the war for her performances in the theater and on the radio. On May 9, she was arrested by four Revolutionary Guards, one of whom was her local butcher. Along with other German women, she was taken to the railway station to sweep away the rubble left by an air raid. Made to carry heavy paving stones, she was struck with rifle butts and kicked with heavy army boots. The mob cried: "You German pigs! Fattening yourselves all those years, well, you have your Führer to thank for this!"

Things escalated quickly from there: "I had nothing to cover my head, and my hair seems to have annoyed the crowd . . . Some recognized me and screamed: 'She was an actress!' Unfortunately I had manicured and lacquered nails, and my silver bracelet put the mob into an even greater frenzy."[31]

German women were made to eat pictures of Hitler. Hair hacked off their own heads was stuffed into their mouths. Schell was sent to a slave labor camp where she was flogged by Revolutionary Guards for no reason she could discern. Yet, she was less obtuse than some other Germans in central and eastern Europe. Not all the Czech guards behaved badly. One Guard, seeing that she could barely walk anymore, let alone work in her ruined shoes, offered to find her a pair of sandals. And Schell noted: "When I hear this RG man's description of spending seven months in a German concentration camp, we really shouldn't be surprised by the way we are treated."[32]

Schell understood the true nature of Czech resentment too. Still wondering why she was singled out for a specially savage beating one day, she remembered how people had told her that the commandant found her "too refined." In the diary entry of the same day, August 8, she mentions a vicious female guard in the camp kitchen. "The women," she observes, "are the worst everywhere. It clearly has to do with their rage, because they can see perfectly well that, despite our current labor as servants, we still remain what we always were."[33]

Edvard Beneš was not a communist. But he tried to be friendly with Stalin, and, mindful of the way his country had been let down by the Western democracies before, he unwisely forged an alliance with the Soviet Union. This devil's pact would end in a Communist Party takeover of Czechoslovakia in 1948. But the seeds of revolution had already been sown, in the kind of rage so acutely observed by Margarete Schell in the kitchen of her concentration camp. The year 1945 in Czechoslovakia, especially in those areas that had been dominated by Germans for centuries, was like the Terror, except that, unlike in France two centuries before, it came before the Revolution.

. . .

ONE OTHER THING IN SCHELL'S DIARIES is worth mentioning. She describes how she was taken to a house that used to be occupied by Gestapo agents. Her group of prisoners was ordered to clean up after the house painters and move in new furniture. The man overseeing their labor happened to be a Jew. Yet he treated Schell and her fellow German prisoners decently. "Having spent five years in a concentration camp, he said, where he lost both his parents and his sisters, he didn't wish to abuse any-one. He knew what being a prisoner was like. Although he had a perfectly sound reason to hate all Germans, he didn't take it out on us."[34]

This may be untypical, a rare instance of compassion at a time of li-censed inhumanity. But in fact, while vengeance was being taken all over Europe, on Germans, on traitors, on women who had offended against national dignity, on class enemies, and on fascists, the people who had suffered most showed extraordinary restraint. This was not because Jews lack the base instincts that drive other people to revenge. It was certainly not because Jews in 1945 had any fond feelings for the people who had tried to exterminate them. To be sure, most survivors of the camps were too sick, or too numb, to feel up to any act of vengeance. But there were cases of crude justice in some of the camps. And some Jewish-American interrogators of suspected Nazis might have shown more than professional enthusiasm for the task. An inquiry investigating rather severe treatment of German SS officers in a prison near Stuttgart revealed that 137 of them "had their testicles permanently destroyed by kicks received from the American War Crimes Investigation Team."[35] Most of the interrogators had Jewish names.

But these were individual cases. There was no organized attempt by Jews to get their eye for an eye. The reason, again, was not for the lack of desire; it was political. The desire in 1945 was very much alive. In 1944, a Jewish Brigade was formed inside the British Army. After the German defeat, the Brigade was stationed in Tarvisio, on the border of Italy and Austria, and then added to the occupation forces in Germany. To stop individual acts of revenge on Germans, a natural temptation among men who had lost their families in the Holocaust, the Brigade issued a com-mandment: "Remember the blood feud is everyone's, and every irrespon-sible act causes everyone to fail . . ." Another commandment reminded the troops that the display of the Zionist flag in Germany was a sweet enough revenge.[36]

Instead of allowing individuals to exact rough justice, the Brigade formed its own group of avengers, known as the Lick My Ass Business, or

Tilhaz Tizi Gesheften (TTG), led by a man named Israel Carmi. Acting on information extracted from prisoners or military contacts, members of TTG would leave Tarvisio at night on missions to assassinate notorious SS officers and others who were thought to be responsible for murdering Jews. Once the British Army caught on to these activities, the Brigade was moved out of Germany to less inflammatory territories in Belgium and the Netherlands. We don't know exactly how many Nazis they killed, but the number was probably not more than a few hundred.

One man who refused to give up on his desire for vengeance was Abba Kovner, a Lithuanian Jew whose soulful eyes and long curly hair made him look less like a killer than a romantic poet, which he also was. Indeed, in Israel he is still known chiefly for his poetry. Born in Sebastopol, Kovner grew up in Vilna (now Vilnius, Lithuania), where he joined the socialist wing of the Zionist movement before the war. In 1941 he managed to escape from the Vilna ghetto and hid in a convent before joining partisans in the forest. After Germany's surrender, Kovner and some other survivors, mostly Polish and Lithuanian Jews, were convinced that the war was not actually over, indeed should not be over. They formed a group named *Dam Yehudi Nakam*, Jewish Blood Will Be Avenged, Nakam for short. One of their principles, devised by Kovner, was: "The idea that Jewish blood can be shed without reprisal must be erased from the memory of mankind." Without proper vengeance, Kovner believed, someone would attempt to annihilate the Jews again. "It will be more than revenge," he wrote. "It must be the law of the murdered Jewish people! Its name will be DIN [Hebrew acronym for 'The blood of Israel is vengeful'] so that posterity will know that in this merciless, uncompassionate world there are both judges and judgment."[37]

Kovner's bleak Old Testament view in 1945 went far beyond secret assassinations to get rid of a few SS men. This would be a score settled between nations. Only the death of six million Germans would be a sufficient price for what the Germans had done to the Jews. Years later, living on a kibbutz, Kovner admitted that his scheme showed signs of derangement. As he said, "it was an idea that any sensible person could see was mad. But people were almost mad in those days . . . and perhaps worse than mad. It was a terrible idea, born of despair, with something suicidal about it . . ."[38] What is interesting is how and why Kovner's notion of "an organized, unique vengeance" failed.

The plan was to put deadly chemicals into the water supplies of several major German cities. To secure the poison, Kovner visited Palestine. There was some sympathy for his feelings, but he found little enthusiasm for mass murder, even of former Nazis. The priority of Ben-Gurion and other Zionist leaders was to build a new state for the Jews, and they needed the goodwill of the Allies. Rescuing the remnants of European Jewry and transforming them into proud citizens of Israel was the goal. There was no chance of going back to normal life in Europe. Europe represented the past. Getting caught up in schemes to murder Germans was a waste of time at best. And so, even though Kovner never divulged the full scale of his plans, the paramilitary arm of the Zionist movement, the Haganah, had no interest in helping him.

The rest of the story was almost farcical. Despite the lack of official cooperation, Kovner did manage to procure poison from a chemical laboratory at Hebrew University in Jerusalem. Two brothers, named Katzir, one of whom, Ephraim, later became Israel's fourth president, worked as laboratory assistants there. Thinking that Kovner would only use the poison to kill SS officers, an objective few people would have quarreled with, they gave him a particularly lethal substance; one milligram could kill a substantial number of people.

Carrying a duffel bag filled with the cans of poison labeled milk powder, in December 1945 Kovner and a comrade named Rosenkranz boarded a ship bound for France. They had forged identity papers and posed as British army soldiers, even though Kovner spoke no English. Kovner was seasick for much of the time. Just as they were nearing Toulon, Kovner's name was announced on the ship's public address system. Thinking that he had been identified and his mission was compromised, Kovner threw half the "milk powder" cans overboard and told Rosenkranz to destroy the rest if things should go wrong.

In fact, Kovner had not been identified at all, nor was his mission detected. He was arrested on the correct assumption that he was travelling on forged papers. But the poison never reached Europe. In a fit of panic, Rosenkranz had thrown the rest overboard. The water supplies of Nuremberg, among other places, were safe, and hundreds of thousands of German lives were spared. There was a halfhearted attempt by some of Kovner's friends to poison the food in a detention camp for Nazis. Even this came to nothing much. A few men got ill; no one died.

Jewish revenge, then, was never carried out, because there was no political support for it. The Zionist leadership sought to create a different kind of normality, of heroic Israelis tilling the desert land and fighting their enemies as proud citizen-soldiers, far from the war-bloodied lands of Europe. They looked self-consciously to the future. That, too, would be full of bloodshed, and ethnic and religious conflict, but it would not be German blood. Abba Kovner never could adapt to a life of the future. Haunted by the past, he wrote tragic poems, and woke up screaming most nights.

He wrote about his sister:

From the promised land I called you,
I searched for you
among heaps of small shoes.
At every approaching holiday.

And about his father:

Our father took his bread, bless God
forty years from the same oven. He never imagined
a whole people could arise from the ovens
and the world, with God's help, go on.[39]

• • •

SPEAKING ABOUT FRANCE during the war, Tony Judt wrote that for active resisters or collaborators, "their main enemy, more often than not, was each other: the Germans were largely absent."[40] The same thing could be said about many countries under foreign occupation: Yugoslavia, Greece, Belgium, China, Vietnam, Indonesia. Occupation forces, like all colonial governments, exploit tensions that existed before. Without the Germans, Vichy's reactionary autocrats would not have come to power, and neither would Croatia's murderous Ante Pavelić and his fascistic Ustaša. In Flanders, the Flemish National Union worked with the Nazi occupiers in the hope of emancipating themselves from the Francophone Walloons in a German-dominated Europe. In Italy and Greece, fascists as well as other right-wingers collaborated with the Germans for their own gain, but also to fend off the left.

And in China? When the Japanese prime minister Tanaka Kakuei, in 1972, apologized to Chairman Mao for what his country had done to the Chinese during the war, Mao, who was not without a macabre sense of humor, told his foreign guest to relax: It is us who should thank *you*, he said; without you we would never have come to power. Mao was right. What happened in China was the most dramatic example of unintended consequences. The Japanese shared with Chiang Kai-shek's Nationalists a horror of communism; there were even some attempts at collaboration; one faction of the Nationalists did, in fact, collaborate. But by fatally wounding the Nationalists, the Japanese helped the Communists win the civil war which was simmering in 1945 and came to a climax soon after.

The civil war in China, as in Greece, had begun well before the invasions by foreign armies. In France and Italy civil war was not far under the surface. And the European practice of divide and rule in Asian colonies created enough bad blood for any number of social conflicts to erupt. But by exploiting these divisions, the Germans and Japanese made them lethal.

Communists and leftists had played a major role in anti-Nazi, or antifascist resistance, while the German and Japanese efforts at empire-building tainted many figures on the right with collaboration. The French Communist Party, proud of its resistance record, called itself "*le Parti des Fusillés*," the party of the executed. Even fellow leftists who resisted the Stalinist line adopted by the Party were denounced by communists as unpatriotic or even as collaborators—"Hitlerotrotskyists." The history of armed resistance of the left, not unreasonably, led to revolutionary demands for a new order. After the war, the Soviet Union exploited these demands, at least in countries within its sphere of influence, while the Western Allies disarmed and helped to crush some of the very forces who had fought on their side against Germany and Japan. Not only that, but it was with Allied help that some members of the old collaborationist elites came back to power. These were the seeds that would later develop into the Cold War.

Collaboration was not always a straightforward matter, however. In Yugoslavia, Tito's communist Partisans negotiated in 1943 with the Germans, because Tito wanted a "free hand" to attack the Serbian royalist Chetniks (or Četniks). In the autumn of the same year, the Chetniks collaborated with the Germans to fight off Tito's Partisans. The Bosnian Muslims cooperated with anyone who would protect them: the Croatian fascists, Serbian Partisans, even the Nazis. And all these temporary alliances were made in opposition to domestic, not foreign, enemies.

In France, most collaborators did not work directly for the German occupiers, but for a French government under Marshal Philippe Pétain. With German help, the Vichyistes thought they would restore France, the true France, of Church, family, and patriotism, shorn of liberals, Jews, Freemasons, and other blots on *La France profonde*. Italian fascists could not really be called collaborators until 1943, when Italy was occupied by German troops, and the authority of Benito Mussolini's fascists was reduced to a tiny Nazi puppet state on Lake Garda. But the previous twenty years of Italian fascism had engendered enough loathing for the left to embark on a ferocious campaign of vengeance once the Germans started leaving.

Harold Macmillan, the later British prime minister, was Churchill's plenipotentiary for the Mediterranean countries. In April 1945, he was driven to Bologna in an army jeep for a meeting with the Allied military commander, who had just installed himself in the splendid and undamaged Municipio, or town hall. He found the bodies of two well-known local liberals lying in state, with tearful crowds passing by to pay their last respects. The two liberals had been shot by members of the fascist Black Brigade, who had fled town just a day before. "The coffins were open,"

Macmillan noted in his diary, "so that friends and admirers could see the faces of their leaders for the last time. They had been shot against the wall of the Municipio—the bloodstains were clear. Above the place where they had stood were already flowers and—pathetically—photographs of men and women of all ages who had been put to death during recent months by the Fascist Black Brigade."

After quoting this passage from his diary, Macmillan goes on to say: "The Prefect—a Fascist—had failed to make his escape in time. He had been shot by the partisans next to his last victim. You could see the brains spattered against the brick and the blood on the ground."[41] Macmillan then went off to have lunch, and observed that the Italian cooks who had previously served Italian food to German officers now served American food to the Allied officers. "There was a moral in this," he wrote, without quite divulging what that moral might have been.

Among the victims of the partisan reprisals in April 1945 were Mussolini himself, with his mistress, Clara Petacci. They were caught while attempting to escape to Austria with German soldiers from an antiaircraft unit. When they were stopped at a roadblock manned by partisans, the Germans were told to go on their way; the partisans had no more interest in them. But the Italians had to stay behind. Mussolini, despite wearing a German army greatcoat over his red-striped Italian general's riding trousers, was recognized. On April 28, he, Clara, and fifteen fascists picked at random were machine-gunned in front of a country villa on Lake Garda. The following day, they were hung, like game, upside down from a girder at an Esso gas station on a shabby square in Milan, exposed to the wrath of the mob. Soon their faces were barely recognizable.

Edmund Wilson was shown the spot where it happened a month later. The names of the executed were still daubed in black on the girder of the now abandoned Esso station. Wilson wrote: "Over the whole city hung the stink of the killing of Mussolini and his followers, the exhibition of their bodies in public and the defilement of them by the crowd. Italians would stop you in the bars and show you photographs they had taken of it."[42]

But this was just one instance of possibly twenty thousand killings of fascists and collaborators in the north of Italy between April and July. Eight thousand in Piedmont. Four thousand in Lombardy. Three thousand in Emilia. Three thousand in Milan province.[43] Many were summarily executed by partisans, dominated by communists. Others were quickly tried in makeshift people's courts, the so-called justice of the piazza. The killings were swift and sometimes involved innocents. Known fascists were gunned down together with their wives and children. Most recipients of rough justice were police officers and fascist government officials. Even those already in prison were not safe. On July 17, the Schio prison near Vicenza was raided by masked partisans, who murdered fifty-five incarcerated fascists. Some of these avengers were hardened resistance fighters. Some were the kind of last-minute heroes who swelled the ranks of the resistance everywhere, once the real fighting was over. Some were criminals who used their new "patriotic" status to blackmail rich businessmen or landowners, or loot their properties.

In Italy, too, however, revenge often had a political agenda; it was a revolutionary settling of scores. Communist partisans saw the purges as a necessary struggle against capitalism. Since big corporations, such as Fiat in Turin, had worked with Mussolini's regime, they were seen as legitimate targets. Even though the most powerful businessmen from Turin or Milan had usually managed to save their skins by crossing the Swiss border, or buying potential killers off with black market goods, the corpses of lower-ranking figures did have a way of ending up dumped in front of the gates of local cemeteries.

Seriously worried about a communist revolution in Italy, the Allied Military Government quickly tried to disarm the partisans, many of whom had fought bravely against the Germans. Conservative Italian politicians supported this effort, not surprisingly, since some of them had been close to the fascists themselves. Indeed, the slowness of the provisional Italian government in Rome to punish the fascists was one reason why the "justice of the piazza" came about in the first place.

As a sop to the pride of former partisans, parades were organized in various cities, with Allied commanders, flanked by Italian notables, taking the salute of partisan military units decked out in scarves denoting their different allegiances: red for the leftists, blue for the Christians, green for the *autonomi*, mostly deserters from the Italian army. Many had given up their weapons, but by no means all. The radical left remained strong, and sometimes armed. Still, as it turned out, conservatives needn't have worried. There was to be no revolution in Italy. In return for extending his empire to central Europe, Stalin agreed to leave the Mediterranean to the Western Allies. But murderous reprisals still went on, and the fear of communism in Italy, as well as a bitter sense of betrayal on the left, would continue, in some cases well into the twenty-first century.

Edmund Wilson, whose sympathies were always on the left, viewed these proceedings with distaste. The main American contribution to Italy's postwar democracy, he noted, was "calling one of our telephone exchanges Freedom; and, after our arming and encouragement of the Partisans through the period when they were serving our purpose, we are now taking their weapons away from them, forbidding them to make political speeches, and throwing them in jail if they give any trouble." He was aware that the hands of the left, too, were bloody, but, he argued, "the new Italian revolution was something more than a savage vendetta, and it is hardly, I believe, a movement whose impetus can be curbed at this point."[44]

The leftist impetus, however, was curbed, just as it was in southern Korea, in France, in southern Vietnam, in Japan, and in Greece, where Wilson arrived in the summer of 1945. He stayed in Athens at the Hotel Grande Bretagne on Constitution Square. The service was surly, to the point of hostility, and Wilson noticed bullet holes in the walls of his room. There was a reason for the surliness, for there was a stink hanging over Athens too, the stink of another betrayal.

The bullet holes need some explaining. There had been a large demonstration the previous December held by supporters of the National Liberation Front, or EAM, the partisan organization controlled by communists. The British Army was formally in charge of liberated Greece. Athens was held by a Greek provisional Government of National Unity which contained conservatives and royalists, as well as some leftists. Much of the rest of the country was still in the hands of the EAM, and its armed forces, ELAS. Having fought the Germans, EAM/ELAS had expected to take over the government and revolutionize Greece. Conservatives, backed by the British, wanted to stop this at all costs, and this is what sparked the demonstration of December 3, 1944, the day, according to Harold Macmillan, when "the civil war began."[45]

Actually, as Macmillan surely must have known, the civil war had already started a long time before. Greece was deeply split during World War I, when the prime minister, Eleftherios Venizelos, wanted to back the Allies, while King Constantine I and his military commander, Ioannis Metaxas, did not. Years of bitter opposition between royalists and "Venizelists" followed. In 1936, Metaxas became a dictator with the face of a banker and the brutality of a fascist caudillo. An admirer of Hitler's Third Reich, Metaxas "united" Greece, as the Father of the Nation, by banning all political parties, and throwing communists and other opponents of his regime in jail. To the relief of most Greeks, Metaxas died in 1941.

Then the Germans invaded. Supporters of the old Metaxas regime mostly collaborated, and the resistance was led by communists who had emerged from Metaxas's jails. Greek fascist battalions, egged on by the Germans, fought left-wing guerrillas who were helped initially by the Allies. There was much brutality on both sides. Many of the victims were innocent people caught in the crossfire.

But Macmillan was right: as far as the British were concerned, the real action began only in 1944, when British soldiers, reinforced by extra troops from Italy, fought the left-wing partisans who had fought the Germans just months before. Edmund Wilson's disapproval of this was widely shared, especially in the United States, where it was seen as another typically British imperialist intervention. But many people in Britain felt the same way; Churchill, though revered for his leadership against the Germans, was distrusted for his bellicosity against the communist partisans.

Harold Macmillan noted that in Greece, as in other places, "the resistance movements had been presented by our propaganda as bodies of romantic idealists fighting with Byronic devotion for the freedom of their country."[46] The most Byronic hero was a man named Aris Velouchiotis. Aris rode through the mountains with his black band of partisans—black berets, black jackets, black beards. The romantic hero, who broke with the communists in 1945, was also a killer. Mass graves have subsequently been dug up in his areas of operation and have been found to contain the scattered bones of his political enemies.

The real issue after liberation, as in Italy (and China, and many other places), was the monopoly on the use of force. The National Liberation Front (EAM/ELAS) in Greece had agreed, after much negotiation, to lay down their arms, as long as right-wing armed militias such as the notorious Security Battalions, set up under Nazi occupation, did the same. The government's aim was to incorporate the best elements from both sides in a national army. According to EAM/ELAS, the government failed to stick to its bargain; even as the left demobilized (up to a point), the right was allowed to retain its firepower. Quite understandably, this is remembered by many former ELAS fighters as a rank betrayal. One partisan recalled rounding up a group of collaborators in 1944. Instead of killing them, however, they were handed over to the police. A bad move, as the police proceeded to give them guns and let them go. For the partisans, defeated in 1945, the moral was clear: "Those who had said 'kill them' were able to point out that the second round of fighting, the Civil War, wouldn't have happened if we had killed all the fascists."[47]

This, then, was the febrile atmosphere in Athens, whose traces Edmund Wilson still noticed in his hotel room in 1945. On December 3, 1944, crowds on Constitution Square, with women and children marching in front, approached the Hotel Grande Bretagne, where the provisional government was holed up. It is claimed that they were about to storm the hotel. The view Wilson received from left-wing sympathizers, shared by most Greeks at the time, is that the majority of peaceful protesters kept marching on while the royalist police opened fire and killed and wounded about a hundred people. The next day, when the protesters filed past the hotel again, in a funeral procession this time, royalists killed up to two hundred more unarmed citizens by firing guns from the hotel windows.

Macmillan had a somewhat different take, as one might expect. The "so-called civilian crowd," he recalled, "contained many fully-armed ELAS guerillas," and the fatal shots were probably fired by a communist agent provocateur.[48]

Even if the truth of the tragic event remains elusive, two things are hard to dispute. The communist-led partisans were very ruthless operators who had already killed a large number of real or alleged collaborators and "class enemies" before Greece was freed from the Germans in October 1944, and continued to purge and kill for some time after that. The second truth is that the Greek left had ample reason to feel betrayed.

Communists and leftists were the backbone of anti-Nazi and anti-fascist resistance in many countries. In Greece they monopolized the resistance by violently purging everyone else. In the countryside, EAM/ELAS had set up a kind of guerrilla state, with people's courts to deal with all enemies of the revolution. A British officer stationed in Greece in September 1944 wrote about the communist "reign of terror" in Attica and Boeotia. "Over 500 have been executed in the last few weeks. Owing to the stench of rotting corpses, it is impossible to pass near a place by my camp. Lying unburied on the ground are naked corpses with their heads severed. Owing to strong reactionary elements among the people [ELAS has] picked on this area."[49]

So there was a good reason to fear the consequences of a revolution in Greece. Bringing back King George II, a pet project of Churchill, whose monarchist lectures irritated even some Greek conservatives, was not the best idea. George II's short reign in the late 1930s coincided with the brutal right-wing dictatorship of Ioannis Metaxas, and there was little popular nostalgia for that.

But given the fear of communism, the British felt that they had no choice but to help the government in Athens fight the leftist partisans. The fighting lasted five weeks at the beginning of 1945. Up to twenty thousand "class enemies" were deported by ELAS, and often murdered after forced marches into the mountains. On the other side, many suspected leftists were deported by the British to camps in Africa. The fighting was so vicious on all sides that a negotiated peace in February was greeted with great public relief. Churchill appeared on the balcony of the Hotel Grande Bretagne, with the archbishop of the Orthodox Church, and spoke to a huge, cheering crowd: "Greece for ever! Greece for all!"[50]

It was but a lull in the action. The Greek civil war would resume the following year and last for another three years. But even before that, almost as soon as Churchill had finished his rousing speech, another form of revenge began, a counter-revenge, this time against the left. Right-wing paramilitary forces and gendarmes went on a rampage. Communists, or suspected leftists, were arrested without warrants, beaten up, and murdered or locked up in huge numbers. The National Liberation Front issued an appeal drawing the world's attention to "a regime of terror even more hideous than that of the Metaxas dictatorship."[51] By the end of 1945, almost sixty thousand EAM supporters were in prison. These included women and children, so many indeed that special detention camps for women had to be built. The common charge was crimes committed during the occupation. But crimes committed by former Nazi collaborators, or the right-wing security battalions, went largely unpunished.

Harold Macmillan and Edmund Wilson came to Greece from very different perspectives, one as the British minister resident, the other as an American literary journalist, but on one thing they agreed. Greater efforts should have been made to split the democratic left from the communist revolutionaries. Macmillan thought that "a moderate, reasonable, progressive policy" could have peeled off "the vague, radical element from the hard, Communist core."[52] In Wilson's view, England should have "helped the leaders of EAM to detach themselves from the Soviet entanglement and keep in order those wilder elements whose fierceness, in the days of the Resistance, the British had been only too glad to abet."[53] The pity is that any such efforts, even if the will had been there, were quickly smothered in a thirst for vengeance, encouraged by political forces seeking their advantage in stirring it up.

. . .

LIBERATION IS PERHAPS not the right word to describe the end of the war in colonial societies. Most Asians were more than happy to be rid of the Japanese, whose "Asian liberation" had turned out to be worse than the Western imperialism it temporarily replaced. But liberation is not quite what the Dutch had in mind for the Dutch East Indies in 1945, or the French for Indochina, or the British for Malaya.

American plans for the Philippines were more accommodating, and Lord Louis Mountbatten, Supreme Allied Commander in Southeast Asia, had some sympathy for Asian aspirations towards national independence. But the Dutch and the French wanted to restore the prewar colonial order as soon as possible. Even Dutch socialists, who were not unsympathetic to the Indonesian desire for independence, were afraid that the Dutch economy, badly damaged by the German occupation, would collapse without the Asian colonies. In the popular slogan of the time, "Disaster will be our cost, if the Indies are lost" (*"Indië verloren, rampspoed geboren"*). The most the relatively progressive Dutch government would concede to the Indonesian nationalists was a degree of autonomy under the Dutch crown. And there could be no truck with Indonesians who worked with the Japanese.

This made the question of collaboration and revenge rather complicated, for there had been considerable enthusiasm among Southeast Asians, at least in the early years of the war, for the Japanese propaganda of "Asia for the Asians." To activists such as Sukarno in Indonesia, working with the Japanese was the best way to get rid of the Dutch colonial masters. But in Dutch eyes, this made Sukarno a collaborator with the enemy. There was no question of negotiating Indonesian independence with him after the war; on the contrary, the Dutch were convinced that he should be punished as a traitor.

Asians, too, were consumed by a rage for vengeance in 1945, but this was not always directed at the European colonialists. Vengeance was often more indirect, aimed at other forms of collaboration that preceded the

Japanese occupation. As was the case in parts of Europe, the victims of Asian vengeance were often unpopular minorities, especially if they were thought to be privileged, richer, and in league with the Western colonial powers.

The Chinese, often called "the Jews of Asia," took the brunt of Japanese ferocity in Southeast Asia. In Malaya, for example, the Malays were preferred to the Chinese, whom the Japanese distrusted. Chinese merchants benefited from Western colonialism, or so it was thought. And so the Chinese had to be crushed, while the Malay elites were promoted in the civil service and the police. Not that Malay or Indonesian peasants and workers were necessarily well treated; Indonesians forced to work on Japanese military projects died in huge numbers in even more miserable circumstances than most Western POWs. The countryside was often ravaged, leaving millions of peasants destitute; the cities were plundered, deprived of minimal services, the streets ruled by criminal gangs.

Japanese rule in Southeast Asia was brutal, and yet a new assertive spirit had seeped into people who had tended to adopt an attitude of surly colonial submission before. Western powers had been humbled by Japan and shown to be vulnerable. Hundreds of thousands of young Malays and Indonesians were trained by the Japanese as soldiers in auxiliary forces, militias, and various militant youth organizations. This gave them a quite unaccustomed sense of pride. Exploiting the common sense of humiliation and inferiority among colonized peoples, the Japanese deliberately stirred up anti-Western, as well as anti-Chinese, feeling.

Much of the anti-Japanese resistance in Malaya during the war came from the Chinese. Inspired by the Communist Party in China, but also perhaps by the internationalism that made communism attractive to minorities elsewhere, resistance was led by the Malayan Communist Party. Although the MCP was not particularly anti-Malay, almost all its members were Chinese. Its military arm was the Malayan People's Anti-Japanese Army (MPAJA) which, in August 1945, had about ten thousand men under arms who controlled much of the countryside, forming a state within a state, with its own rules and laws and given to widespread purges of unsympathetic officials, rather like the communist guerrillas in Greece.

After the war, revenge was swiftly taken by members of the Anti-Japanese Army on local collaborators with the Japanese, most of whom were Indians and Malays; mayors, policemen, journalists, informers, former mistresses of Japanese officials, and other "traitors and running dogs" were dragged through the streets, displayed in cages, summarily tried in "people's courts," and publicly executed. This put the fear into many Malays. And when the British colonial government, which had worked closely with the MPAJA against the Japanese, decided in October that Chinese should be granted equal citizenship, Malays, understandably, were frightened of losing control over their own country, a fear that has been exploited by Malay politicians to this day.

Malays decided to strike back at the Chinese. The leading figure was a fierce-looking former gangster boss in a turban, named Kiyai Salleh. He emerged after the war as the chieftain of a group named the Red Bands of the Sabilillah (Holy War). Their goal was to protect the Muslim faith against Chinese heathens and to avenge the Malays whom the Chinese had humiliated and killed after the Japanese defeat. Although the jihad against the Chinese was ostensibly Islamic—Koranic texts were read, Sufi saints invoked—Salleh modeled himself after Malay mystics, claiming to be invulnerable to harm: "He cannot be killed by bullets; he can walk dry-shod across rivers; he can burst any bonds that are put on him; his voice can paralyze his assailants."[54] His followers believed that they were blessed with similar powers, after pricking themselves with golden needles and drinking potions blessed by the holy warrior chief.

The Red Bands' favorite method of killing was by machete, or the Malay dagger called *kris*, a weapon imbued, like the warriors themselves, with mystical powers. In one typical incident, on November 6, a band of Malay jihadis swooped down on a Chinese village at Padang Lebar and hacked five men and thirty-five women and children to death with their daggers and machetes. The corpses of the children were thrown down a well. Malay politicians did not exactly support this kind of thing, but they did little to stop it. According to a British military intelligence report, "there appears to be an appreciable concern among educated Malays regarding the future status of Malays in Malaya and there is a fairly widespread belief that the Chinese are securing an economic grip of the country, which, if unchecked, may eventually lead to political control."[55]

This same fear haunted Indonesians, so it was not by chance that the Malay chieftain's three main lieutenants were Indonesian nationalists from the Dutch East Indies, where the situation in the autumn of 1945 was a good deal worse than in Malaya.

G. F. Jacobs, a South African major in His Majesty's Royal Marines, was one of the first Allied soldiers to be parachuted into Sumatra in August 1945. His task was to establish contact with the Japanese military authorities and prepare the way for their surrender and Allied troops to land. Jacobs was also one of the first to see the state of Japanese POW camps holding thousands of diseased, emaciated, beaten, and starved civilians. Dutch prisoners couldn't understand why Jacobs would not let them exact rough justice: "Why did you stop us . . . can't you see we want to fix these little yellow bastards?"[56]

The reason why Major Jacobs had to stop the POWs from lynching their guards was his fear of a far greater threat. Indonesians were roaming the country with guns, daggers, and pointed spears, screaming *"bunuh Belanda!,"* "Death to the white man!" Japanese were needed to guard their former prisoners.

On the morning of August 17, two days after the Japanese surrender, Sukarno read a short, typed declaration to a smallish crowd in Batavia (Jakarta): "We the people of Indonesia hereby declare the independence of Indonesia. Matters concerning the transfer of power etc., will be carried out in a conscientious manner and as speedily as possible."

The declaration had been drafted by Sukarno, self-appointed president of the new Republic of Indonesia, and his vice president, Mohammed Hatta, in close consultation with the Japanese army and navy commanders. When defeat looked inevitable in the summer of 1945, the Japanese decided that an independent, anti-Western Indonesia would be their best option. Most Japanese, after all, took the slogan "Asia for the Asians" seriously, even if they had hoped to rule over other Asians as the superior race. Many Indonesians, tired of violence, brutalized by the Japanese, hungry and vulnerable to diseases brought back by survivors of forced labor on the Thailand–Burma Railway and other hellish Japanese projects, were not sure yet what to think. There was little hostility to Dutch civilians in the first weeks after the Japanese surrender. Sukarno, Hatta, and other leaders such as Sutan Syahrir, a Dutch-educated socialist who had never cooperated with the Japanese, did their best to contain potential violence in an archipelago over which they did not yet have much control.

The new Indonesian leaders certainly had little sway over the large numbers of young toughs, who had been radicalized and trained as auxiliaries in the Japanese army. These boys were in a mood to fight. Weapons were acquired from sympathetic Japanese officers, sometimes bought, sometimes stolen from Japanese depots. In one estimate, the fighters obtained more than fifty thousand rifles, three thousand light and heavy machine guns, and a hundred million rounds of ammunition.[57] What the Dutch should have done, and were encouraged to do by their Western allies, was to negotiate with Sukarno and the other Indonesian leaders who had no interest in revolutionary violence. In Mountbatten's wishful words: "Our only idea is to get the Dutch and the Indonesians to kiss and make friends and then pull out."[58] Instead, the Dutch petitioned the British Foreign Office, comparing the "so-called Sukarno government" to the pro-Nazi Quisling regime, and the young Indonesian fighters for independence to the Hitler Youth and the SS. Sukarno's proclamation of independence was portrayed as a Japanese plot to continue a fascist regime in the Dutch East Indies.[59]

About Sukarno's collaboration with the Japanese there can be no doubt. He had spent much of the 1930s in Dutch colonial prisons, or in exile on a remote island. The Japanese had treated him with more respect than the Dutch had done. It was in any case not unreasonable for Sukarno to see Japan as the quickest route to national liberation. "For the first time in all my life," he said, in 1942, "I saw myself in the mirror of Asia."[60]

But Sukarno's collaboration went too far even for many Indonesians. His support of Indonesian forced labor for the Japanese war effort tarnished his reputation, and the young radicals were angry that he had involved the Japanese in the declaration of independence. They wanted nothing to do with the Japanese. But no one disputed Sukarno's credentials as an Indonesian nationalist.

Rather than deal directly with Sukarno, however, the Dutch issued vague promises of Indonesian autonomy in a Dutch-led commonwealth. Meanwhile, starting in September, veterans of the Dutch East Indies Army swaggered around Indonesian villages and neighborhoods, shooting their guns, tearing down red and white Indonesian flags, and threatening people, all in the way of showing who was boss. The most notorious vigilantes were a group called Battalion X, led by Dutch and Eurasian commanders, but mostly manned by dark-skinned Ambonese Christians, Medanese, and other minorities, who were more afraid of being dominated by other Indonesians than by the Dutch, and who had been loyal servants of the colonial system. When news came of the arrival of Dutch and British battleships carrying Allied troops, mostly Indians, and agents of the Netherlands Indies Civil Administration (NICA), bent on restoring the old order, the scene was set for the bloodiest violence in Southeast Asia, violence that was part revolution, part vengeance, and part criminality, the same lethal brew that exploded in central Europe earlier in the year.

The bands of armed extremists that unleashed the wave of terror in October and November 1945, a wave known as *bersiap* ("Get ready!"), consisted mostly of former members of Japanese-led militias and street toughs, often teenagers recruited from gangs in Jakarta, Surabaya, or other cities. But the youth groups, or *pemuda*, also included students, factory workers, and villagers. Some of their leaders were gangster bosses, whose reasons for robbing and killing the rich and powerful had less to do with politics than with greed. Some were charismatic figures, such as the bandit chief named Father Tiger, who sold amulets to his men for invulnerability. The mixture of Javanese mysticism and Japanese indoctrination about the warrior spirit imbued young fighters with a reckless sense of heroism: "*Merdeka atan mati!*" ("Freedom or death!"). There were instances of youths battling tanks with nothing but machetes and bamboo spears.

The main victims of revolutionary vengeance were the Chinese, associated with business and suspected of treachery, and the Eurasians, or "Indos," as well as other minorities who had often sided with the Dutch. Then there were those often imaginary creatures called NICA spies. The definition of a NICA spy could be quite arbitrary; a person with too much red, white, and blue (the Dutch national colors) in his sarong could be picked up as an agent for the Dutch administration.

Chinese, Indos, or Ambonese knew trouble was coming when they heard the sound of bamboo spears being banged like drums of war against the hollow metal lampposts of Jakarta. The armed Japanese soldiers who were ordered to protect civilians in the absence of Allied troops often slunk away when the banging started. Shops were raided and houses set on fire. The families inside were hacked to death by frenzied youths, drunk with violence, literally in love with their daggers, and sometimes given to drinking the blood of their victims. In one area near Jakarta, there was no more fresh water, because the wells had been stuffed solid with putrefying Chinese corpses.

The Indo-Dutch phrase for the most common kind of killing was *getjintjangd*. *Tjintjang* meant slashing a person with a *kris* or machete. Dutch civilians, foolish enough to leave the camps still guarded by Japanese, were frequently *tjintjanged*, as were Japanese soldiers who resisted demands to help the rebels or hand over their weapons. Even though the old concentration camps, huge squalid villages full of sick and hungry people, were also targeted for attack, they were still the safest places to be, as long as the Japanese guards stayed at their posts.

One young man, named Peter van Berkum, born in Indonesia like many Dutch civilians, was picked up at random one night in Surabaya by a group of wild teenagers with sharpened bamboo spears. He was taken by truck to a local prison: "As the truck slowed it was surrounded by this mass of screaming people. I saw only a blur of brown, sweaty faces with contorted, wide-open mouths. They were shaking clenched fists and brandishing all sorts of weapons." Amidst screams of "Death to the whites!" the prisoners were pushed out of the truck. "Immediately the crowd started in on them, beating, hacking, stabbing with sticks and bayonets, using axes, rifle-butts, and spears."[61]

Bersiap, never wished for by the Indonesian leaders, was now utterly beyond their control. Battles broke out all over Java and Sumatra, not just acts of vengeance against colonials and their alleged helpers, but between rebels and Japanese as well, in a bloody cycle of revenge and retaliation. In Semarang, a Japanese unit led by Major Kido Shinichiro clashed with *pemuda*, who believed the Japanese were sabotaging the water supply. The Japanese, in a brutal form of intimidation, killed a number of Indonesian militants. Indonesians then murdered more than two hundred Japanese civilians locked up in the city jail. A British army report noted: "Some corpses were hanging from the roof and from the windows, others had been pierced through and through with bamboo spears . . . Some had tried to write last messages in blood on the walls."[62] More than two thousand Indonesians were butchered in retaliation by the enraged Japanese.

The worst violence engulfed the industrial city of Surabaya, which was entirely in the hands of the Indonesians by the end of October. The jails had been emptied. Crowds of *pemuda* freedom fighters, petty mobsters, and romantic youths fired up by tales of traditional Javanese derring-do broadcast on "Radio Rebellion" by a charismatic long-haired figure known as Brother Tomo, ruled the streets. Chinese, Ambonese, and Indos, accused of being NICA spies, were assaulted with daggers and spears. And the Japanese, worried about their own lives, happily supplied the mobs with more lethal arms.

Peter van Berkum's sister, Carla, arrived with other Dutch refugees from a nearby concentration camp: "We were stormed by a mob of

natives. They stuck their bamboo spears at us aggressively. And they kept
screaming: *merdeka! merdeka! merdeka!* [freedom]. They were dressed in
rags. Their dark eyes had a terrifying look. I was scared."[63]

The Allies decided to act. P. J. G. Huijer, a Dutch navy captain, was
sent into the city to prepare the way for an Allied landing. Quite naturally,
his arrival was seen as a further provocation. Arms kept flowing from Japanese arsenals to the *pemuda* fighters. On October 25, about four thousand
British troops, mostly Indians and Nepalese Gurkhas, came ashore. Rumor had it that these soldiers were Dutchmen in blackface. They were
attacked by a ragtag army of Indonesians. Afraid that their troops would
be massacred, the British asked Sukarno and Hatta to come down and
control the mobs. They complied, and had some success. The cease-fire
held, more or less, until October 31 when the British commander, Brigadier General A. W .S. Mallaby, trying to intervene in a fight, was shot by
Indonesians.

This time it was the British who sought retribution. For the next three
weeks, beginning on November 10, Surabaya was bombed, shelled, and
strafed. An eyewitness described the scene in the center of the city:

> Bodies of men, horses, cats and dogs, lay in the gutters, broken
> glass, furniture, tangled telephone lines cluttered the roads, and
> the noise of battle echoed among the office buildings . . . The In-
> donesian resistance went through two phases, first fanatical self-
> sacrifice, with men armed only with daggers charging Sherman
> tanks, and later in a more organized and effective manner, follow-
> ing closely Japanese military manuals.[64]

By the end of November, Surabaya had been pacified at the cost of
being reduced to a bombed-out battleground reeking of the corpses of
Indonesians, Indians, British, Dutch, Indos, and Chinese. It would not be
until 1949, after further acts of vengeance, not least from the Dutch, who
in 1946 sent death squads led by Raymond "Turk" Westerling into South
Sulawesi, where thousands of civilians were murdered, that Indonesia

achieved full independence. (Westerling, incidentally, who had fought the Germans in North Africa during World War II, later became a devout Muslim.)

Blood, however, will have more blood. In addition to accusing Sukarno of treachery, the Dutch saw him as a front man for the communists. Exactly twenty years after the Battle of Surabaya, officers in the Indonesian Army ousted Sukarno in a military coup, supposedly to prevent the communists from taking over Indonesia. This marked the beginning of a nationwide purge of communists. Muslim vigilantes, armed youths, army battalions, Javanese mystics, and ordinary civilians all took part in the killing of half a million people, many of whom were Chinese. The leader of the coup, and the future president of Indonesia, was a Major General Suharto. Trained by the Japanese military, and thoroughly indoctrinated against Western imperialism, Suharto had fought against the Dutch in 1945. His presidency would last for thirty-two years. During that time, as a staunch opponent of communism, he enjoyed the warm and unwavering support of all Western powers, including, of course, the Netherlands.

. . .

THE FRENCH WERE AS FEARFUL as the Dutch of losing their colonial possessions in 1945, and, if anything, felt more humiliated, not just because of their defeat in 1940, but also because of their history of official collaboration. French Indochina continued to be administered by a Vichy-oriented colonial government during what was, in fact, a Japanese occupation. The Japanese used the colony as a military base, while the French carried on drinking their apéritifs at Saigon's Cercle Sportif and generally minding their own business. But this sweet life came to an end in March 1945. Once France was liberated, French collaboration with Japan could no longer be taken for granted, so French troops and officials were swiftly imprisoned in Saigon and Hanoi.

When defeat was almost certain in the first week of August, the Japanese transferred political authority to the royal government of Vietnam, while the communist Vietminh (League for the Independence of

Vietnam) took control of the north. A few weeks later, with Chinese troops pouring across the northern border and the arrival of British troops imminent in the south, both the emperor of Vietnam, Bao Dai, and the Communist leader Ho Chi Minh made it quite clear that whatever happened, the resumption of French rule was unacceptable. Statues of French colonial dignitaries were already being pulled down in Hanoi. On September 2, more than three hundred thousand Vietnamese gathered on Ba Dinh Square, near the former French governor-general's palace, to hear Ho Chi Minh declare national independence. Bands played communist marches, including harsh words about "drinking French blood." Vietminh soldiers, armed with pistols, guarded the speaker's platform, festooned with red flags. A royal umbrella was held over "Uncle" Ho's head, as he softly spoke into the microphone: "Countrymen, can you hear me?" The crowd hollered back that they could.

A U.S. intelligence officer who witnessed this event reported to his superiors in the southern Chinese city of Kunming: "From what I have seen these people mean business and I am afraid the French will have to deal with them. For that matter we all will have to deal with them."[65] He couldn't have known quite how prophetic his words would turn out to be.

If the French, many of whom remained in their prisons, still guarded by Japanese soldiers, were spooked by these events, French colonizers in Algeria were panic-stricken. Both Algeria and Indochina were experiencing serious famines in early 1945, the result of droughts as well as the diversion of food supplies for military purposes. In Indochina more than one million people died of hunger. In Algeria, hunger was fueling a popular rage that was seen by frightened Frenchmen as the beginning of a violent revolution.

In fact, despite some agitation among Algerian communists and radical nationalists, most Algerians simply wanted equal rights. But every time a Muslim stone was thrown at a French settler, the French thought that the "Arab revolt" was at hand. The new colonial administration in 1945 was led by French leftists, many of whom had actively resisted the Germans. Many of the settlers had been pro-Vichy, and were fiercely anti-Semitic. (Often the only ones who had defended the rights of Jews under French rule were Algerian Muslims.) Yet the Muslims who called for Algerian independence or equal rights were quickly branded as "Nazis." This was like calling Indonesian and Vietnamese demands for national independence part of a Japanese fascist plot. It made it easier for leftist colonial authorities, as well as former Vichyistes, to crack down on them.

Violence had been mounting steadily in Algeria, especially in the famine-stricken areas around the town of Sétif in the northeast. Settlers clashed with nomads, arrogant police officers were chased out of villages, right-wing European youths taunted Muslims in Algiers with cries of "*Vive Pétain!*" or even "*Vive Hitler!*", and French policemen shot into a crowd of Muslims who wished to take part in a May 1 demonstration.

Sétif, the center of Muslim agitation and Algerian nationalism, was a logical place for serious violence to explode. On May 8 the French, despite their former allegiances, decided to celebrate the Allied victory over Germany with full patriotic pomp. Early that same morning, Muslims, mostly rural people, men as well as women and children, gathered in front of the main mosque. Some men carried traditional daggers under their jellabas. Some had pistols. Leaders of the AML (Amis du Manifeste et de la Liberté, or Friends of the Manifesto and Liberty), the Muslim organization for equal rights, assured the authorities that this was not a political demonstration. There would be no nationalist banners.

By eight o'clock the crowd had grown to about three thousand and began to march along the Avenue Georges Clemenceau to lay a wreath at the war memorial. Despite promises to the contrary by the AML, banners were unfurled by some nationalists, reading: "We want the same rights as you." When policemen at a roadblock saw a banner that said "Long live Algerian Independence," they tore it from the hands of a poor Algerian, who was killed on the spot. Whereupon French civilians, as though they had waited for this moment, started firing submachine guns into the crowd from their balconies and the windows of the Café de France. Between twenty and forty people were killed. Terrified by the shooting,

Muslims rushed into the side streets, using their pistols and daggers to attack Europeans. The French communist leader Albert Denier was so badly cut that his hands had to be amputated.

A French teacher recalled having a drink at a café opposite her school, when "a flood of screaming natives appeared from all sides, with daggers in their hands. They were running towards the Arab market. Atrocities had been committed. I saw about fifteen of them beat an old friend of the Arabs, Mr Vaillant, with clubs . . . It's terrible when you think about it. The odd thing is that most of the victims were Arabophiles."[66]

News of the killings swiftly reached the villages. Vengeance was sporadic, but brutal: "We were armed with knives and rifles. It was my father who killed the baker because he was French. We broke down the doors, burning down the houses with the oil and petrol that we found."[67] French settlers fled to local police stations. Some who were caught were mutilated with knives, had their breasts slashed or their genitals stuffed into their mouths. About one hundred Europeans were killed in three days.

Instead of urging calm, the socialist governor-general Yves Chataigneau called for ten thousand troops: Moroccans, West Africans, and Foreign Legion units. This would not just be an exercise to restore order. A lesson had to be taught. The killings of French citizens had to be avenged.

French settlers formed militia units and started assaulting the local population. One of the toughest infantry regiments, manned by Algerian soldiers, was shipped back from Germany where they had fought hard to defeat Hitler. In their native country, they were sent into the hinterlands to hunt fellow Algerians. By the end of June the countryside was petrified into an awful silence. Villages and towns had been bombed for weeks from the air and shelled from cruisers; thousands had been arrested, often tortured, and executed. The exact number of Algerian dead is not known. Some say up to thirty thousand. With murder came deliberate humiliation. A nineteenth-century practice of making natives submit ceremonially to their conquerors was revived. Thousands of famished peasants, who could no longer stand the bombings, were made to kneel before the

French flag and beg for forgiveness. Others were pushed to the ground and made to shout: "We are Jews. We are dogs. Long live France!"

To some Frenchmen it may have looked as though normality had finally returned to Algeria. But the more sophisticated ones, including General de Gaulle, knew perfectly well that mass-murdering native populations was an embarrassing blot on *La France éternelle*, which, in official mythology, had so bravely resisted the Nazi menace. So what happened in Sétif and surrounding areas was smothered in official silence for many years.

The French in Saigon, however, read Sétif as a warning of what could happen to them if aspirations for Vietnamese independence were not quickly stifled. In August things did not look good for the French. Many were still in Japanese prisons. The Vietminh were given, or simply took, more and more Japanese arms. Some Japanese military officers were joining the Vietminh, either out of conviction ("Asia for the Asians") or because they needed a place to hide from prosecution for serious war crimes. French imperial designs were not popular with the Americans, even though the Chinese, still under Chiang Kai-shek's Nationalists, had no objections to French rule in Indochina. The only ones who were entirely on the side of the French, not so curiously, were the British.

Mob violence often begins with a rumor. So it was on September 20 in Hanoi, when people spoke of a French plot, assisted by Vietnamese members of the French colonial security police, to regain control. Caches of arms were supposed to have been found. There was talk of poison gas. French soldiers had been released from prison by the Japanese, and even rearmed. To foil these dark French designs, thousand of Vietnamese, armed with knives, spears, and machetes, ransacked French homes and molested any French people found in the streets. Japanese soldiers mostly just stood by.

The waiters in the best hotel in Hanoi, the Metropole, attacked the guests in their rooms and barricaded them in the dining room. A Frenchman who managed to escape asked the Japanese to relieve the French prisoners and restore order.

Françoise Martin was a young French woman who had arrived in Hanoi "not to make money in this country, but, on the contrary, filled with
humanitarian idealism." She felt nothing but "respect for the Sino-
annamite culture." Yet her sentiments about the Vietnamese who demonstrated in the streets for independence were probably typical of most
French colonials: "It is possible that there were *real* patriots among
them . . . But so far as this mob of criminals and imbeciles bustling about
town with their flags is concerned, the sight of half a dozen guns would
send them scurrying back to their rat holes. Unfortunately, we don't have
half a dozen guns, nor would we have them soon."[68]

In August, there had been more rumors about stockpiles of arms found
in a French villa. Demonstrators denounced French imperialism. But
apart from some murders in the countryside, Vietnamese violence against
the French did not amount to much. The French were terrified nonetheless, all the more because they were still so helpless, despite brave words
from France, where General de Gaulle spoke of developing Indochina as
"one of the principal goals of [France's] activity in her reborn power and
rediscovered grandeur."[69]

"Everyone is armed to the teeth," recalled Françoise Martin about the
situation in Hanoi, "Americans, Chinese, Annamites; only the French
have nothing to defend themselves with except sticks and empty bottles . . ."[70] Her analysis of the Vietnamese fight for independence was as
typical of her place and time as her views of the "imbecilic" demonstrators. It was all a plot: "Officially, Japanese had laid down their arms, but
continued to wage war in a different manner, impeding any revival of
Europeans in Indonesia and Malaya; everywhere their methods were the
same: a perfidious plan, admirably prepared, carefully carried out . . . An
admirable and new example of Asian duplicity, which never fails to fool
the White man."[71]

When violence finally broke loose, however, it wasn't in Hanoi, but in
Saigon. The first sign of serious trouble was remarkably similar to events
in Algeria. On September 2 hundreds of thousands of Vietnamese, or
"Annamites" as they were called in the Western press, many from the

countryside, gathered in Saigon to hear Ho Chi Minh's declaration of independence on the radio from Hanoi. Earlier that morning, armed Vietnamese youths had staged a demonstration at the gate of a military camp where French soldiers were still interned. The French replied to Vietnamese taunts by shouting insults back and singing the "Marseillaise." Because of a technical problem, the crowds never heard Ho Chi Minh's speech on the radio. Suspicions of French sabotage made the crowds even angrier. Just as the marchers reached the cathedral, shots were fired. The crowd panicked, and mobs, suspecting the French of the shooting, attacked every French person in sight. Chinese and European shops were looted, priests were killed, women had their teeth kicked in.

The French blamed Vietnamese provocateurs for the shots that caused the mayhem. A little over two weeks later, they convinced the British general Douglas Gracey that it was time to kick out the Vietnamese from police stations and public offices and rearm the French. And the British, in a spirit of colonial solidarity, complied. On September 23 it looked as if order had been restored to Saigon: the French were in charge once more. The humiliation and helplessness felt over weeks, months, perhaps even years, turned French celebrations of their triumph into a rampage: now it was the turn of Vietnamese to be lynched by mobs of Frenchmen. A British officer reported that there "were wild shootings and Annamites were openly dragged through the streets to be locked up in prisons."[72]

Revenge was not long in coming. The next day, Vietnamese entered French houses and assaulted the inhabitants. People were tortured on the riverbanks. Vietnamese wives of Frenchmen were mutilated with knives. In one account, an eight-months-pregnant woman was disemboweled. Battles raged in Saigon for almost two months, with the British, the French, and the Japanese fighting the Vietnamese. Some Japanese went over to the Vietnamese side. The French Foreign Legion included in its ranks Germans who had fought the Allies in North Africa, and possibly some former SS officers too. Thousands of Vietnamese were tortured in prisons and received harsh prison or death sentences after "trials" that lasted all of five minutes.

By the middle of November, the French could enjoy their apéritifs at the Cercle Sportif once more, assured that life would soon return to normal. This illusion would last for a while, in the south until 1949, when South Vietnam became independent, with Saigon as its capital, and in the north until 1954, when Ho Chi Minh's Communists were recognized as the rulers of the Socialist Republic of North Vietnam, whose capital was Hanoi. But nowhere have the words spoken by Macbeth to his wife about blood willing more blood been more true than in that narrow Southeast Asian country that was once thought of as three, then as two, and finally as one.

PART 2

CLEARING
THE RUBBLE

CHAPTER 4

GOING HOME

M y father was one of more than 8 million "displaced people" stuck in Germany in May 1945, waiting to be transported home. There were roughly 3 million more in other parts of Europe, some who longed for home, some who wanted to go anywhere but back, and others who no longer had a home to return to: Poles in the Ukraine, Serbs and Croats in Austria, White Russians in Yugoslavia, Jewish refugees in Kazakhstan, and so on. The figures in Asia are just as staggering: 6.5 million Japanese were stranded in Asia and the Pacific, half of them civilians. More than a million Korean workers were still in Japan. And thousands of Australian, European, and American POWs were marooned in China, Japan, Taiwan, and Southeast Asia, as well as Indonesians and other Asians forced to work on Japanese military projects around the region. Up to 180,000 Asians had worked on the Thailand–Burma Railway; about half of them survived.

All wars displace people; the war in Iraq, beginning with the U.S.-led invasion in 2003, severed up to 5 million people from their homes. The scale of displacement because of World War II was especially horrendous because so much of it was deliberate, for ruthlessly practical as well as ideological reasons: slave labor programs, population exchanges, "ethnic cleansing," shifting national borders, emigration in search of *Lebensraum* for the German and Japanese master races, the civil wars ignited, entire populations deported to be killed or to languish in exile, and so on. The main culprits in Europe were the Germans, but Stalin's policies in the Soviet Union and its periphery were often as murderous as Hitler's.[1]

For my father, the idea of going home was not complicated. Although correspondence with his family had ceased in 1944 when the Allies liberated part of the Netherlands, cutting off his hometown from communications with Germany, he had a home to go back to. In the summer of 1945 he was transported to the Dutch border from a British DP camp in Magdeburg by British army trucks, by train, and by bus. The reception committee at the Dutch border town of Enschede questioned him and other returnees on whether their work in Germany had been voluntary or not. Those who were suspected of voluntary labor forfeited their right to food rations, and the trouble they faced was but a small harbinger of an issue that would obsess the Dutch for decades, like a national scab that had to be picked over and over: who had been "good" and who "wrong," brave or cowardly, collaborator or resister, hero or villain. (In fact, of course, few people fell neatly into either category.) It was a tedious way to be welcomed back. But my father was impressed by the politeness of his interlocutors: he was no longer used to meeting officials who weren't barking at him.

By the time he arrived in his hometown, Nijmegen, my father's feelings were more complex. He had left Berlin as an utterly ruined city. So he was used to destruction. It must still have been quite disorienting to walk through the old center of Nijmegen, many of whose handsome buildings, some dating back to the Middle Ages, were gone too, demolished by an accidental American bombing raid in 1944. After years of longing to go home, my father suddenly had cold feet. He could not bring himself to walk the fairly short distance to the family house. The reasons are no longer clear in his memory. Perhaps it was because he could not be sure that his parents were still alive, or that the house would still be there. Or perhaps he feared that the longed-for reunion might be awkward; so much had happened in the meantime.

In the event, he did go home. The whole family had survived. The reunion was joyous. He soon found his old place in society; he fitted back in. He was one of the lucky ones.

For others, displacement was a more lasting condition, and coming home was a disappointment, or worse. Extreme experiences created chasms of incomprehension between people. Everyone felt that they had a story to tell. How could someone who survived Auschwitz possibly convey what he or she had lived through to people back home who had barely even heard of death camps?

The Hungarian writer Imre Kertész wrote an account of this incomprehension in his novel *Fateless* (1992).[2] The author himself, an assimilated Budapest Jew, had been a prisoner in Auschwitz and Buchenwald. Only fourteen when he was deported, he came of age, as it were, in the camps. His fictional alter ego, György, returns to Budapest, still dressed in the ragged striped jacket of Buchenwald, his face pinched and blotched like that of an old man. Strangers are living in his old family apartment now, unfriendly, suspicious people who slam the door on him. This was not an unusual experience for camp survivors, especially Jews, who were not expected to come back, and were often resented if they did. In a way, however, the reunion with old Jewish neighbors who had managed to stay in Budapest is even more painful. They tell him that "life wasn't easy at home either." Hearing where he had been, they give him friendly advice: he should simply "forget the terrors," only think of the future. This was like something another solicitous person, a "democratic" journalist whom György had just met on the tram, had said: the important thing was that the "Nazi pits of hell" were over, finished.

What György failed to make people understand is that he hadn't been to hell; his experience was not metaphysical; he had been in concentration camps. How could he forget and just think of the future, as though his past life had been a bad dream or a horror film? Life in the camps was neither voluntary nor pleasant, but it was still life, *his* life. You could not ignore continuity. The problem was that people who had not experienced anything similar could not possibly imagine what it had been like, nor did they wish to, hence the flight into abstractions, "hell," or "the terrors," which should be forgotten as quickly as possible.

The people described at the end of Kertész's novel, the journalist and the neighbors, Mr. Steiner and Mr. and Mrs. Fleischmann, meant well. This was not always the case when people who spent the war at home were confronted with camp survivors, or others who came back, such as POWs, or foreign workers in the Third Reich. Suffering is a personal matter. Most of us like to have our own suffering recognized. The suffering of others, especially if it was clearly worse, can be a source of irritation, and perhaps even guilt: "Life wasn't easy at home either."

The sometimes frosty reception of Jewish survivors coming home, not just to Poland and other blood-soaked nations in central Europe, but to western European countries such as the Netherlands, too, owed something to a vague and not wholly repressed guilty conscience, as well as anti-Semitic prejudices which had, if anything, been strengthened by the years of German occupation—propaganda sticks.

This was by no means only true of collaborators or Nazi sympathizers. When a young woman named Netty Rosenfeld emerged from hiding after the liberation of the southern Netherlands in 1944 and applied for a job at a radio station run by the Dutch resistance, she was told that Rosenfeld was not a suitable name for public broadcasting. After all, she had to understand that there were already enough Jews working for Radio Herrijzend Nederland (Netherlands Reborn). The station had been nicknamed "Jerusalem Reborn." One lesson Jews surely should have learned from their unfortunate experience was not to push themselves to the front of the queue and presume to dominate society again. And this was meant as friendly advice.

A man named Siegfried Goudsmit wrote the following story in September 1945 in *Paraat*, a left-wing newspaper founded by the Dutch resistance:

A bus stop. Passengers waiting for the bus to Amsterdam. Among them two Jews. One of whom sits down on the bench . . . A non-Jewish "lady" does not approve and tells him that he should remain standing. "Other people have a right to this seat." Yes, madam, in other circumstances I would have stayed standing, but I just got out of hospital where I was taken in a state of exhaustion after my return from a German concentration camp and, as you can see, I am still rather weak. "If only they'd kept you in the concentration camp. We've got enough of your kind here as it is" . . . [3]

Other survivors of the Nazi camps were reminded that they were not the only ones who suffered; Dutch people went hungry too, or lost their bicycles, or whatnot. Jews were told not to make too many claims, to not be too assertive. They should know their place, and above all show gratitude.

A former resistance paper, called *De Patriot*, published a letter about the problem of anti-Semitism in postwar Holland. This appeared on July 2, 1945:

There can be no doubt that the Jews, specifically because of German persecution, were able to enjoy great sympathy from the Dutch people. Now it is appropriate for the Jews to restrain themselves and avoid excesses; they should be constantly mindful of their duty to be grateful and that this gratitude should be primarily expressed by redressing that which can be redressed for those who fell victim on the Jews' behalf. They can thank God that they came out alive. It is also possible to squander this sympathy [from the Dutch people] . . . The [Jews] are truly not the only ones who suffered . . . [4]

No wonder, then, that most Jewish survivors chose to remain silent. Silent about the fact that 75 percent of the roughly 150,000 Jews living in the Netherlands in 1940 did not survive. Silent about the mere five thousand who returned from the camps. Silent about the able assistance given to the Nazi killers by Dutch bureaucrats, policemen, and jurists. Silent about the silence, while the deportations went on, train after train after train.

The early postwar years saw a flurry of war monuments in the Netherlands, monuments to resistance fighters, to fallen soldiers, to national suffering, to the sacrifice of brave individuals. The first monument to the Jewish catastrophe was erected in 1950, in Amsterdam, near the old Jewish market, the seventeenth-century Portuguese synagogue, and the abandoned and subsequently gutted houses of Jews who had been dragged from their homes. Made of white stone, the monument has a star of David on top and five reliefs carved into the surface, depicting the love, the resistance, the fortitude, and the mourning of the Dutch Gentile population. It is called the Monument of Jewish Gratitude.

The fact is, Jewish survivors were an embarrassment. They did not fit the heroic narrative that was being hastily constructed in the wreckage of the war, in the Netherlands, in France, or indeed in any country where people sought to forget inconvenient, painful truths about the past. Men and women who had survived the humiliations of wartime occupation as best they could, by keeping their heads down and looking the other way when bad things happened to others, pretended to have been heroes all along. I grew up, at primary school in the 1950s, with proud stories from teachers of petty acts of resistance, such as sending German soldiers the wrong way when they asked for directions, and so on.

My favorite boyhood author was named K. Norel, whose books were full of tales of brave deeds by young resisters, with such plucky titles as *Driving Out the Tyranny; Stand By, Boys;* or *Resistance and Victory.* There was no place for Jews in the roster of real or imaginary heroes. The old prejudices had not died. Here is a passage from Norel's *Driving Out the Tyranny*: "The Jews may not be heroes, but they are certainly shrewd. Only once the Nazis started grabbing Jewish money and possessions, did the Jews wake up. And with a vengeance. With great cunning they managed to withhold millions from the enemy."

. . .

IN FRANCE, where the Gaullist government tried, after a time of wild reprisals, to close the deep fissures in society by acting as if most citizens had stood up bravely against the German foe, returning POWs did not fit the mood of self-serving though perhaps necessary make-believe, either. There were no celebrations at the homecoming of shabby-looking men, in threadbare old-fashioned uniforms, held responsible for the shameful defeat in 1940. In "the France that fought, the only France, the real France, the eternal France" (de Gaulle's words on the day after the liberation of Paris), there was no room for these men. All they could hope for was a food ration coupon, some cash, a doctor's checkup, and a few bars of the "Marseillaise" (if the group was large enough to merit a musical welcome).

That Vichy propaganda had chosen to depict the POWs as brave combatants who were enduring imprisonment for the greater glory of France didn't help after the war, either. Roger Ikor, later to become a celebrated writer, was taken prisoner in May 1940 and, despite being of Jewish origin, was incarcerated with other French POWs in Pomerania. In his memoir, he writes: "Mute, incapable of protesting, we represented the perfect partisans for Pétain and his gang. Wasn't it natural for him to associate us with the purest blood of France? For exactly the inverse reason, the Gaullists held us in contempt. Two million prisoners, and prisoners tainted with Pétainism at that, this embarrassed the cocks-of-the-walk and their certain idea of France. Hadn't we let ourselves be captured instead of resisting bravely like they did? So we had to be cowards, not of the purest blood, but the most polluted."[5]

And so, on their return, the POWs were commonly treated with cold formality and silent disdain, or at best, condescension. They were met at repatriation centers by bossy officials in uniform, often women, who sometimes outranked these men who had spent their war behind barbed wire and were not shy about showing it.

The author Marguerite Duras, herself in the resistance, wrote a description of this in her memoir *The War*:

> People keep on arriving. Truck after truck . . . The prisoners are dumped at the center in groups of fifty . . . The poor boys look at the hall, they all smile. They're surrounded by repatriation officers. "Come along, boys, get in line!" They get in line and go on smiling . . . These last few days I was at the Gare de l'Est, where one of the women rebuked a soldier from the Legion and pointed to her stripes. "No salute, my boy? Can't you see I'm a captain?"[6]

Duras was very much on the left, and had a special loathing for the kind of rank-pulling officials she described. They were reactionaries, who, in the words of Dionys Mascolo ("D."), her lover and comrade in the left-wing resistance, will "be against any resistance movement that isn't directly Gaullist. They'll occupy France. They think they constitute thinking France, the France of authority."[7] They would construct the heroic narrative of "eternal France" to their own advantage.

There is another more harrowing description in Duras's memoir. Her husband, Robert Antelme, also a left-wing resister, had been arrested and deported to Buchenwald. Although she had already taken up with "D." during the war, Duras still longed to see her husband alive. That is why she had been going back and forth to the repatriation centers and the Gare de l'Est train station, anxious for any news of his survival. When Antelme was found by chance in a German camp by the later president François Mitterrand, he could barely speak, let alone walk. But the longed-for reunion in Paris occurred at last:

> Beauchamp and D. were supporting him under the arms. They'd stopped on the first floor landing. He was looking up.
>
>   I can't remember exactly what happened. He must have looked at me and smiled. I shrieked no, that I didn't want to see. I started to run again, up the stairs this time. I was shrieking. I remember

that. The war emerged in my shrieks. Six years without uttering a cry. I found myself in some neighbor's apartment. They forced me to drink some rum, they poured it into my mouth. Into the shrieks.

Then, a short while later, she sees him again, still smiling:

It's from this smile that I suddenly recognize him, but from a great distance, as though I was seeing him at the other end of a tunnel. It's a smile of embarrassment. He's apologizing for being here, reduced to such a wreck. And then the smile fades, and he becomes a stranger again.[8]

My father was not in Buchenwald. Nor did he have a wife in the Dutch resistance who had taken a lover and would soon divorce him. His return home was far less dramatic. But something in this passage from Duras's memoir hints at the source of his fear of going home too, the fear of being a stranger.

· · ·

IF HOMECOMING WAS DIFFICULT FOR FRENCH POWS, this was even more true of Germans or Japanese. Their shoulders bore not just the burden of a national defeat, which would have been hard enough, but they faced the contempt and even hatred of their own people for having been responsible for a calamitous war, for committing unspeakable crimes, for having lorded it over the nation as arrogant warriors, and coming back as abject losers. This was not entirely fair, of course. Other people, including millions of women, had cheered them on their way to war, waving flags, singing patriotic songs, and celebrating their victories, some real, some the fictions of government propaganda. The common soldier in a highly authoritarian state whipped into a frenzy by official hysteria was no more responsible for the consequences than the ordinary civilians who had vociferously cheered him on. In Germany, at least, the Nazis could be blamed for everything. The Japanese, lacking their own version of the Nazi Party, blamed their catastrophe on "the militarists," and, by extension, on anyone associated with the armed forces. This was also the view promoted in postwar U.S. propaganda, faithfully echoed in the Japanese press.

As the Japanese essayist Sakaguchi Ango wrote, the kamikaze pilots (*Tokkotai*) "are already black market hoodlums today."[9] This fall from grace, this mass awakening from a national delusion, was blamed squarely on the men who were sent to die for the emperor and had the shameful misfortune of coming back alive. There was a Japanese expression current just after the war, *Tokkotai kuzure*, "degenerate kamikazes" —young men whose morbid idealism had collapsed into a binge of whoring and drinking.

Resentment against Japanese soldiers' throwing their weight around was already there before the defeat in 1945, even though voicing it would have been extremely risky. When people saw the quick shift from wartime violence to criminal behavior in peacetime, the proud image of the Imperial armed forces was tarnished even further. At the end of the war military warehouses were still full of goods, anything from weapons to blankets and clothes, essential items for a destitute population. After large-scale organized looting by senior military officers and their civilian cronies, often gangsters with sinister wartime histories, they were empty. Slowly the goods found their way onto the black market, where they went for prices most people could ill afford.

Bringing back millions of young men, trained to kill for their country, into civilian life is never a smooth process. The shameful odor of defeat only makes it harder. It seems entirely fitting that a radio program that was started in the summer of 1946 to provide information about missing persons should have included a special segment, broadcast twice daily, especially for disoriented veterans, called "Who Am I?"[10]

The demoralized warriors, already emasculated by military failure, faced more blows when they came back to homes that were destroyed, or to marriages gone sour. One of the common themes in German or

Japanese films and books about the immediate postwar period is the rift between returning soldiers and wives who had taken lovers in order to relieve loneliness or simply to survive. The theme is as old as war itself: on his return from Troy, Agamemnon is murdered in his own house by his wife, or her lover, or both, depending on which version of the story you read. Rainer Werner Fassbinder's film *The Marriage of Maria Braun* (1979) is one of the finest German examples: Maria's husband, fresh from the horrors of the eastern front, literally finds his wife naked in the arms of a black American soldier. In this case, it is the lover who dies. A much less well-known Japanese example is Ozu Yasujirō's film *A Hen in the Wind* (1948). Quite uncharacteristically for Ozu, the movie ends in high melodrama, with the jealous husband throwing his wife down the stairs for having had sex with another man in his absence. Limping from her injury, the wife still pleads for his forgiveness. And finally all ends well in a gush of tears.

The story preceding this overwrought finale is wholly typical of the times. The wife, Tokiko, not knowing whether her husband is still alive, tries to feed herself and their little son with the pittance she earns as a seamstress. When the son becomes seriously ill, she has no money to pay for the hospital, and so decides to sell herself for one night to a stranger. When her husband, Shuichi, finally comes back, Tokiko confesses her one lapse into prostitution. Enraged about his wife's infidelity, Shuichi becomes obsessed. But fidelity is not really the main point: it is the defeated soldier's struggle to regain a sense of self-respect that drives his fury. The movie is highly realistic, except that in real life the marriage may not have been saved in a tearful reconciliation.

Letters submitted to the newspapers show how deep the problems of repatriation were. The celebrated novelist Shiga Naoya published a letter in the *Asahi* newspaper on December 16, 1945, in which he suggested that the government had a duty to reeducate former kamikaze pilots. How could young men, taught how to commit suicide for the glory of the nation, possibly be equipped to rebuild their lives in the cynical, dog-eat-dog world of 1945? The only way to prevent them from sinking into despair and being called degenerates was for the state to initiate a special education program. A letter in response agreed, but pointed out that Japanese society itself was badly in need of reeducation. One letter writer, a man who had been trained to be a suicide pilot himself, stated that the wartime training and spirit of the *Tokkotai* were precisely what was needed in the degenerate culture of postwar Japan.

One of the most poignant letters to the *Asahi* was by another ex-soldier, published on December 13:

> Fellow veterans! Now we are free. We returned from the dark and cruel military life, from the bloody fields of battle. But awaiting us back home were the sharp eyes of civilians filled with loathing of the militarists, and we found our home towns destroyed by the fires of war . . . The bloody battles are over, but life's real battle has only just begun . . .[11]

In fact, he writes, his youthful illusions had already been dashed by life in the army, with its selfish and bullying officer corps whose pompous preening about loyalty to the nation and other high-flown ideals was shown to be utterly vapid. The common soldier was reduced to a machine. And now, he writes, "the veteran soldier has become synonymous with the bad guy . . ."

"What are the true feelings of the people towards us veterans?" asks another writer on the same day. "People think a soldier is the same thing as a militarist. Of course, the militarists should take responsibility for our defeat in war. But the ordinary soldier was not like that. He was just a patriot fighting for his country. Do you really believe that we cast away our young lives to fight on the battle fields or in the Pacific just for our own profit or desire? I would really like people to show more warmth towards us veterans."[12]

Such sentiments would surely resonate with American veterans of the Vietnam War. But even the victors in a war that was almost universally regarded as just had problems readjusting to civilian life when they came back home. William "Bill" Mauldin was the most popular cartoonist in the U.S. Army. His irreverent drawings in the *Stars and Stripes* of Willy and Joe, two GIs coping with army life on the European front, made him a hero among the GIs, or "dogfaces." Willy and Joe talk like regular soldiers, and think like them too. What they thought was often not flattering to superior officers, which earned Mauldin a dressing down from General Patton, who threatened to have his "ass thrown in jail." In June 1945, Willy was on the cover of *Time* magazine, looking tired, unshaven, disheveled, a cigarette dangling from the left corner of his mouth, far from the heroic image of the warrior.

Back Home (1947) is Mauldin's account in words and cartoons of Willy and Joe's homecoming. The troubles they face, shown in Mauldin's drawings, and the attitudes they convey are softer versions of some of the sentiments expressed by veterans in the letters to the editor of Japanese newspapers. The resentment of the upper ranks, for example: Willy and Joe in loose-fitting civilian suits are standing at a hotel desk waiting to be checked in as a sullen-looking porter in an outfit of striped trousers, cap, epaulettes, and gold buttons is carrying their suitcases. Joe: "Major Wilson, back in uniform, I see."

Willy and Joe's ill feeling does not burn quite as fiercely as the hatred felt by Japanese soldiers toward the officers who sent tens of thousands on suicide missions, or killed them to consume their flesh when food ran out under enemy fire in New Guinea or the Philippines. But Mauldin's point that a bad soldier mostly does damage to himself while "a bad officer can cause a considerable amount of misery among his subordinates" would have rung equally true.[13]

Closing the gulf between military and civilian life was a painful process, for battlefield heroes as much, if not more, as it was for men of no great fighting distinction. To wives and girlfriends, the returned soldiers did not always seem heroic enough. In one cartoon, Willy is shown dressed in a scruffy business suit, rather awkwardly carrying the wartime baby he had never seen before. His wife, in dressy hat and gloves, remarks: "I was hoping you'd wear your soldier suit, so I could be proud of you." In Mauldin's words: "Mrs Willie, who had been in college when Willie met her, had shared with her feminine classmates a worship of fancy uniforms during the early and glamorous stages of the war. She had always felt a little disappointed in Willie because he hadn't become an officer with a riding crop and pink trousers." He didn't even have medals. So, Mauldin continues, not only "was she deprived of the pleasure of strutting with his medals, but she suddenly realized that she had never seen him in civvies before, and he did look a little baggy and undistinguished." [14]

It is not surprising that some veterans, disillusioned or unequipped for civilian life, or traumatized by battlefield brutality, would commit violent acts. This happens after all wars. But in the first year after World War II these acts were given exaggerated attention in the press. Willy's wife is shown reading a newspaper, headlined "Veteran Kicks Aunt," while a dejected Willie sits in his armchair nursing a glass of whiskey. The caption reads, "There is a small item on page 17 about a triple ax murder. No veterans involved." [15] Mauldin points out the sad fact that such lurid headlines "gave added impetus to the rumor that always appears in every country after a war—that the returning soldiers are trained in killing and assault and are potential menaces to society."

Compared to veterans in Germany or Japan, the problems of returning GIs, though similar in certain respects, might appear to be minor. They were heroes coming back to the richest country on earth, basking in their victory, soon to benefit from government-sponsored education programs made possible by the magnificent GI Bill. But even in America, the men in uniform often failed to live up to the heroic narrative. There was one important difference, however, between the victorious nations and the defeated, the effect of which lasted much longer than the hardships that follow any devastating war. Germans and Japanese were disenchanted with the heroic ideal. They wanted nothing more to do with war. British and Americans, on the other hand, could never quite rid themselves of nostalgia for their finest hours, leading to a fatal propensity to embark on ill-advised military adventures so they and their nations could live like heroes once more.

· · ·

WHAT ABOUT THOSE MEN who didn't want to go home?

The Drau Valley in Carinthia, a rural part of Austria known for its stunning Alpine scenery of cool mountain lakes and lush green meadows covered in pine trees and flowers, must have looked like a vision of Eden to the Slovene refugees from Yugoslavia who emerged from a pitch-dark, waterlogged mountain tunnel dug by slave workers for the German army. Others arrived after slogging across rocky, freezing mountain passes. One of them recalled: "It seemed, in this wonderful region, that the majestic, glittering word LIFE shone out and resounded on all sides."[16]

A closer look, in the beautiful spring of 1945, at this blessed landscape of picturesque villages and country churches, would have revealed something stranger and more disturbing. The Drau Valley was filled with camps and shantytowns, the makeshift quarters of tens of thousands of people, former soldiers, as well as women and children, together with their horses, oxcarts, and even camels. There were proud Cossacks in tall sheepskin hats; Slovenian peasants; Serbian Chetniks, some royalist, some fascist, some a bit of both; Croatian fascists from the dreaded Ustaša; Ukrainians; Russians; ex-POWs from various European countries; and even a few Nazi mass murderers hiding in mountain shacks, such as Odilo Globocnik ("Globus" to his comrades), a Slovenian German who had been responsible for, among other things, setting up the extermination camps in Poland. A reporter from the *Times* of London compared this crowd of exhausted refugees, mostly fleeing from Tito's communist Partisans, or from the Soviet Red Army, to "a mass migration like that of the Ostrogoths 1,500 years earlier."[17] In the words of Nigel Nicolson, a British intelligence officer and later a well-known London publisher, Carinthia was "the sump of Europe."[18]

Carinthia, occupied by the British Army, was a fitting venue, in a way, for the miseries of mass migration, since its own recent politics had been so typical of the kind of ethnic nationalism that had caused a human and cultural catastrophe in Europe. Much of the population in the south of Carinthia was Slovenian. The Gauleiter (Nazi regional governor) during the war, a German-speaking Carinthian named Friedrich Rainer, had tried to "Germanize" the south by forcing people to speak German, or by simply deporting the Slovenes and replacing them with people of Germanic stock. At the end of the war, Tito's Partisans invaded the area and claimed it for Yugoslavia, until they were pushed back by the British Army.

But this was just a small part of the problem in "the sump of Europe," filled with people, civilians, and soldiers who either did not wish to return to their countries, or had no home to go back to. Nigel Nicolson observed:

> There seemed to be no limit to the number of nationalities which appealed to us for our protection. The Germans wanted to be safeguarded against Tito, the Cossacks against the Bulgarians, the Chetniks against the Croats, the White Russians against the Red Russians, the Austrians against the Slovenes, the Hungarians against everybody else, and vice versa throughout the list . . . Not only was [Carinthia] the last refuge of Nazi war-criminals, but of comparatively inoffensive peoples fleeing from the Russians and Tito, unwanted and all but persecuted wherever they went.[19]

Worse than persecuted, in many cases. The Slovenes, Croats, and Serbs who had fought Tito's communists, sometimes on the side of the Germans, sometimes not, expected torture and death if they were delivered to their archenemy in Yugoslavia. Cossacks, many of whom had already fought the communists once in the civil war after 1917 and spent their lives since then as waiters, taxi drivers, or writers for obscure émigré journals in various European capitals, knew that execution or slow death in the gulag awaited them in the Soviet Union. Similar fears haunted Ukrainians who had foolishly—but not inexplicably—latched on to Hitler in the hope of getting rid of Stalin. These fearful expectations would all come true. What they hadn't expected was that the British, whom they thought of as the most gallant, decent, generous people in Europe, would force them on their way.

In the Austrian town of Bleiburg, on the Yugoslav border in southern Carinthia, Brigadier T. P. Scott, commander the 38th (Irish) Brigade, received a report on May 14 that two hundred thousand men from the Croatian army, accompanied by half a million Croatian civilians, were approaching the British lines. Meeting their representatives, Scott, by all accounts a compassionate man, had to tell them that they could not possibly be allowed to enter Austria. There was no room for them. They would starve. All right, some replied, then they would starve. Others wondered whether they might not be able to move to Africa, or America. No, that would not be possible, either. Then they "would rather die where they were, fighting to the last man, than surrender to any Bolsheviks."[20]

It took a lot of persuasion, but eventually the Croats, thirsty, unfed, at the end of their tether, agreed to surrender to the Titoists (or "Tits" as the British called them). They were promised that the men would be treated properly as POWs, and the women would be returned to their homes in Croatia. Brigadier Scott could rest assured.

The precise facts of what actually happened might never be known. Accounts from the few survivors are bitter, and possibly exaggerated. But they offer a flavor of how they were treated. On May 15 and 16, according to some accounts, ten thousand soldiers and officers were gunned down on the Yugoslav side of the border and thrown into ditches. On May 17 a "death march" began along the Drau (or Drava) River towards Maribor in Slovenia. In one version of the story, "tens of thousands of Croatians were grouped in a number of columns, their hands tied with wire . . . Then starved, thirsty, emaciated, disfigured, suffering and agonizing, they were forced to run long distances alongside their 'liberators,' who were riding on horses and in carts. Those who could not endure such a running 'march' were stabbed, beaten to death or shot, then left on the roadside or thrown into a ditch."[21] Another account estimates that "about 12,000

Croatians" were buried in the ditches. "Because the blood started to soak through the ground, and the ground itself started to rise due to the swelling of dead bodies, the partisans covered the soil with an alkaline solution, more soil, and then leveled the ground with tanks."[22]

Even if these stories are discolored by hatred, there is no doubt that large numbers of people were murdered by Tito's Partisans, not just Croats on their death marches, but Serbs and Slovenes, too, who were machine-gunned in the dense and beautiful forest of Kočevje, where the wild boar, lynx, and red deer still roam. They had arrived there, as prisoners of the communists, because the British had put them on trains to Yugoslavia, telling them they were bound for Italy. Revealing their real destination would have created the kind of pandemonium that the British troops tried everything to avoid.

The British justified their policy of handing Russian and other anti-communists back to their enemies, by subterfuge if necessary, and sometimes by force, by telling themselves that these Croats, Serbs, Slovenes, White Russians, and Ukrainians were, after all, traitors, men who had fought on the side of the Germans. In short, they were enemies not just of the Soviet Allies, but of the British too. Aside from the fact that women and children could hardly be classified as enemy combatants, things were never quite so simple.

It is true that up to 10 percent of the soldiers in German uniform captured in France after the Normandy invasion were Russians. But these Russians, most of whom didn't speak a word of German, and were happy, indeed relieved, to surrender to the British, had rarely been motivated by any enthusiasm for Hitler's cause. Many had been POWs captured on the eastern front. Those who had survived the deliberate German policy of starving Soviet prisoners to death were given a brutal choice in 1943, when the Germans were desperately short of manpower: either join the German army in special foreign battalions or die.

The case of the Cossacks was more complicated. Their senior officers, veterans of the Russian Civil War, now in their sixties, saw the Nazi invasion of the Soviet Union as their last chance to reclaim traditional

Cossack lands, where they could live as their grandfathers did, as a kind of eighteenth-century warrior caste. The Germans promised to help them if they would fight on the German side, and so they did, as a ferocious band of soldiers, bearing the bejeweled daggers and curved swords of their fore-bears. It was a romantic, misguided, and often savage quest to restore a way of life that was probably lost forever. They fought in the Soviet Union, and when forced to retreat, in Yugoslavia, they were accompanied by thousands of civilian refugees who could no longer stand to live under Stalin. At the end of the war, when the Germans—like the Japanese in Southeast Asia—were handing out territories to collaborating regimes as last-minute bribes to keep fighting, the Cossacks were told they could es-tablish "Cossackia" in the Italian Alps. Once the British arrived, the Cos-sacks, declaring that the Soviet communists were their enemies and not the British, decided to abandon Cossackia and cross into the idyllic valleys of Carinthia.

It is claimed that the behavior of the Croatian fascists, led by the stony-faced Ante Pavelić, was so atrocious that even the Germans were shocked. The Italian journalist Curzio Malaparte, whose accounts were often col-ored by a vivid imagination, reported an interview with Pavelić during which he spotted a wicker basket on the dictator's desk, filled with small, round, slimy objects, juicy mussels perhaps, or oysters. Asked whether these were indeed the famous Dalmatian oysters, Pavelić replied with a thin smile that they were forty pounds of Partisans' eyes gifted to him by his loyal Ustaša.

The Ustaša were extraordinarily brutal, as were Tito's Partisans, the Slovenian Home Guard, and the Serbian Chetniks. But their war cannot be neatly slotted into a war between Allies and Germans, democrats and fascists, or even communists and anticommunists. They were parties in several civil wars going on at the same time fought along ethnic, political, and religious lines: Croatian Catholics versus Orthodox Serbs versus Mus-lim Bosnians versus Serbian royalists versus communist Partisans versus Slovenian Home Guardsmen versus Slovenian communists. Ideology—fascist, communist, Nazi—was only part of the story. All sides made deals with outside powers, including the German invaders, as long as it suited their domestic purposes. How was a British soldier, faced with former Chetniks and Partisans, both of whom had been allies against the Germans at one point or another, to know whom to treat as a friend or enemy?

In the end this choice too was decided by force. Harold Macmillan, the British plenipotentiary in the Mediterranean, put it like this: "By December 1943, the most informed British opinion was that the Partisans would eventually rule Yugoslavia and that the monarchy had little future and had ceased to be a unifying element. At the same time the area was of the greatest military importance; for Tito's forces, adequately supported, were capable of detaining a very large number of German divisions, greatly to the advantage of the Italian and later the French front."[23] The Chetnik royalists had the misfortune of being on the losing side of the civil war.

If Tito was considered an important Western ally in 1945, then so was Stalin, still fondly known to many people in Britain and the United States as "Uncle Joe." So it was not such a stretch for the British foreign secretary Anthony Eden to promise his Soviet counterpart at a Moscow conference in September 1944 that all Soviet citizens would be returned "whether they were willing to return or not."[24] Not only was it thought to be essential to maintain good relations with wartime allies, but Britain did not wish to do anything to jeopardize the fate of thousands of British POWs in territories occupied by the Soviets.

Other members of the British government, including Winston Churchill, felt some scruples about a policy the consequences of which they were well aware of. Lord Selbourne, minister of economic warfare, wrote to Churchill that handing these people back to Russia "will mean certain death for them." But Eden wrote to the prime minister that "we cannot afford to be sentimental about this." After all, he said, the men had been captured "while serving in German military formations, the behavior of which in France has often been revolting." He added something else, something more to the real point of the matter: "We surely don't want to be permanently saddled with a number of these men."[25] And so it was formally confirmed at the Yalta Conference in February 1945 that they would all be handed back.

The fact that many Russians had worn German uniforms under duress, that the women and children, brought to Germany as slaves or lowly workers, had never worn German uniforms, or that a large number of Cossacks had never even been citizens of the Soviet Union and thus were not legally obliged to be "returned" at all, bothered neither Eden nor the Soviet leadership. In the latter case, this had something to do with heroic narratives too, though not quite in the same way as in France or the Netherlands. The idea that so many Russians and other Soviet citizens had fought the Soviet Union, some quite willingly, and that others might have chosen to work in Germany just to survive, was an embarrassment. In the official story, all citizens of the Soviet workers' paradise had resisted the fascist enemy. To surrender was a crime. Those who fell into German hands *had* to be traitors, and would be dealt with as such.

There was one other complication. Tito's Partisans may have been allies against the Nazis, much romanticized in the British imagination as noble peasant heroes, but their claims on parts of Italy and southern Austria were becoming a serious nuisance. The last thing the Western Allies needed was a war with old comrades in arms. But to make absolutely sure that a Titoist advance could be thwarted, Field Marshal Harold Alexander, already burdened with a million POWs, demanded the right to first "clear the decks" in Austria. This meant handing over Yugoslavs back to Yugoslavia, and Russians back to the Soviet Union as swiftly as possible.

Terrible scenes were the direct result of this deck-clearing. If trickery was not sufficient to lull people into acquiescence, battle-hardened British soldiers, sometimes in tears themselves, had to force them onto cattle cars and trucks, prodding, beating, and sometimes using bayonets. Wailing women would throw themselves at their feet, children got trampled by terrified mobs, some people got shot, and some people, rather than face deportation, preferred to stab themselves in the neck, or jump into the Drau River.

The Cossacks were perhaps the saddest case. Their delusions—of being sent to Africa as soldiers of the British Empire, or to Asia to fight the Japanese—were deliberately fostered; anything to keep them calm before their inevitable fate was sealed. They entertained themselves, and their British captors, with great displays of horsemanship. Even their disarmament was a form of trickery; the soldiers were promised newer, better arms if they gave up their old ones. The British realized that Cossacks were less likely to resist their orders in the absence of their officers. At the end of May, the officers, fifteen hundred of them, were told to attend a "conference" to decide their future. They would be back with their families in the evening. In reality, they were never seen again. After being handed over to the Soviet army, those who were not executed immediately were sent to the gulag, where very few survived.

The other Cossacks, frantic with worry about the officers who failed to come back, were getting more suspicious of the British. Time had come for harsher measures. The unpleasant task to force unarmed people to give themselves up to their mortal enemies was given to the Royal Irish Inniskilling Fusiliers, because Major-General Robert Arbuthnot decided that they were less likely to object than English troops. In fact, the soldiers were so disturbed that they came close to mutiny. Their commanding officer, David Shaw, related: "The men moaned like anything, but in the end they obeyed orders too. It was terrible. I remember these women— some of them pregnant—lying on the ground rolling and screaming. My men were putting their rifles on the ground and lifting the women onto the train, then locking the doors and standing there as the train pulled out with women screaming out of the windows."[26]

At another Cossack camp on the banks of the River Drau, on June 1, after being ordered to board the train, thousands of people were gathered together in a massive huddle by their priests in full Orthodox regalia, praying and singing psalms. Inside the human mass, kneeling and locking arms, were the women and children; outside were the younger men. All around were pictures of religious icons, black flags, and an altar with a large cross. The idea was that soldiers would surely not assault people at prayer. Something had to be done. Major "Rusty" Davies, who had befriended many Cossacks, remembers: "As individuals on the outskirts of the group were pulled away, the remainder compressed themselves into a still tighter body, and, as panic gripped them, started clambering over each other in frantic efforts to get away from the soldiers. The result was a pyramid of screaming, hysterical human beings under which a number of people were trapped."[27]

A young woman, whose legs were badly cut by broken glass when she was pushed through a window by the crush, describes what happened when the fence on one side of the human mass gave way:

> People were rushing past . . . , scared out of their wits. Everything was mixed up: the singing, the prayers, the groans and screams, the cries of the wretched people the soldiers managed to grab, the weeping children and the foul language of the soldiers. Everyone was beaten, even the priests, who raised their crosses above their heads and continued to pray.[28]

In the end the job got done. Some drowned themselves with their children in the river. A few people hanged themselves from pine trees outside the camp. But most of the remaining Cossacks ended up in sealed cattle wagons, with one small window and one bucket for all to use as a toilet. Brigadier T. P. Scott had told his commander that the whole thing "was a damned bad show." Major "Rusty" Davies said: "I still regard it with horror."[29]

The Cossacks were just one of the orphaned peoples, battered and in the end decimated by history. In fact, "history" is too abstract. They were destroyed by men, who acted on ideas, of revolution, of purified ethnic states. There were others who fell victim to these ideas, some of whom may have been among the believers themselves.

· · ·

THE WORDS DECIDED UPON by the three victorious Allies—Britain, the United States, and the Soviet Union—at the Potsdam Conference in the

oppressive heat of July 1945 sounded reasonable enough, even a trifle ano-
dyne. On the matter of expelling the German inhabitants from eastern and
central Europe, they concluded the following: "The three governments,
having considered the question in all its aspects, recognize that the transfer to Germany of German populations, or elements thereof, remaining
in Poland, Czechoslovakia, and Hungary, will have to be undertaken.
They agree that any transfers that take place should be effected in an orderly and humane manner."

This sounded fair enough. The agreement, following decisions already made by Churchill, Roosevelt, and Stalin two years earlier at a conference in Teheran about shifting a large slice of eastern Poland to the
Soviet Union, was in keeping with an atmosphere of peculiar bonhomie,
especially between U.S. president Harry Truman and Stalin. (Truman
liked Churchill less; the British prime minister had tried to "soft-soap"
him with unwelcome flattery.) When Truman played Paderewski's Min-
uet in G for Stalin and Churchill at the presidential "Little White House"
in Potsdam, Stalin declared, "Ah, yes, music is an excellent thing, it drives
out the beast in man."[30]

Truman's warm sentiments towards Stalin seem to have been shared
by many American soldiers at the time. Stalin, the U.S. Army paper *Yank*
reported about Potsdam, "was easily the greatest drawing card for soldiers'
interest that this galaxy of VIPs presents. And this was so before the rumor
that Joe had Japan's surrender in his hip pocket. Cpl. John Tuohy of Long
Island, NY, who used to be a booker for Paramount Pictures and who now
stands guard in front of the celebrity-packed Little White House, describes
Stalin as 'smaller than I expected him to be, but an immaculate man who
wears beautiful uniforms.'"[31] In the *New York Times*, the three victorious
leaders conferring in the ruins near the German capital were described as
"three men walking in a graveyard; they are the men who hold in their
hands most of the power in the world."[32] And this included, of course, the
fate of more than eleven million German-speaking peoples, many of
whom had deep roots in areas now claimed by Poland, Czechoslovakia,
Hungary, and Romania.

Behind the bland rhetoric of Potsdam were sentiments expressed in far more brutal terms. Millions of Germans had already been driven from their homes in the Sudetenland, Silesia, and East Prussia. Just before the Potsdam Conference, Stalin had reassured the Czechoslovak prime minister Zdeněk Fierlinger: "We won't disturb you. Throw them out."[33]

When Churchill told Stalin at Yalta that he was "not shocked at the idea of transferring millions of people by force," Stalin reassured the British prime minister too: "There will be no more Germans [in Poland], for when our troops come in the Germans run away and no Germans are left." Whereupon Churchill said: "Then there is the problem of how to handle them in Germany. We have killed six or seven million and probably will kill another million before the end of the war." Stalin, who liked precise figures, wanted to know: "One or two?" Churchill: "Oh I am not proposing any limitations on them. So there should be room in Germany for some who will need to fill the vacancy."[34]

A number of these Germans had been ardent Nazis, even war criminals. Many, perhaps even most, German civilians in the fringes of the German Reich had been well disposed towards the Nazi Party and its local affiliates, especially in the Sudetenland, where Germans, despite their superior wealth, felt that they had been treated by the Czechs as second-class citizens before 1938. Even so, many had held no truck with the Nazis. Some had been actively anti-Nazi. But neither Churchill nor Stalin was inclined to make such fine distinctions. All Germans had to go: criminals, Nazis, anti-Nazis, men, women, and children.

Population transfers, mass expulsions, and shifting borders were commonplace in the policies of Stalin and Hitler. But Churchill had a different precedent in mind: the Treaty of Lausanne of 1923, when it was agreed to move Greek Muslims to Turkey and Greek Orthodox Turkish citizens to Greece. In fact, much of the exchange had already taken place by 1923, as it were spontaneously, as a consequence of the Greco-Turkish War. The official exchange was a relatively bloodless affair. But what happened in eastern and central Europe in 1945 and 1946 was on a wholly different scale. There was an exchange of a kind, to be sure: Poles from eastern

Poland, which became part of the Ukraine, moved to Silesia, once part of Germany and now vacated by the Germans. But what really happened is that around eleven million people were kicked out of their homes, only very rarely in an orderly or humane manner.

Hans Graf von Lehndorff, the doctor from Königsberg who believed that humans behaved like savages because they had turned away from God, tried at one point to leave his bombed, burned-out, thoroughly looted native city by foot. He reckoned that squeezing himself into a west-bound train, usually a coal or cattle car, was too dangerous. And so he walked in the cold rain through "a land without people":

> [past] unharvested fields . . . bomb craters, uprooted trees, army vehicles in ditches, and burned out villages. I looked for some shelter from the rain and the wind in a broken down house. I felt something moving. There was a sound of scraping on the brick floor. A few people in tatters were standing about staring into space. Among them were three children, who scrutinized me with some hostility. Apparently they had tried to get away from Königsberg too and got stuck here. Seized by the Russians, they weren't allowed to go anywhere, neither forward nor back. The last thing they ate were a few potatoes from a Russian truck that made a temporary halt. I didn't ask what price had been extracted. From the way they talked, it was clear that the women had to pay once again. My God, who can still derive any satisfaction from such ghosts?[35]

Far worse things happened. But this story, more than many other tales of sadistic violence, murder, and starvation, tells us something about the sense of helplessness of people who suddenly have no home. They could go neither forward, nor back; they were stuck in limbo in a depopulated land which was no longer theirs.

Lehndorff was right to be wary of trains. Not only would one be stuck for days in overloaded goods wagons, pressed together with many others, with no food, drink, or sanitary facilities, exposed to all weather, but one was liable to be taken away to forced labor camps, or at the very least to be robbed on the way. Paul Löbe, a social democrat journalist arrested before by the Nazi regime, described what this was like on a trip through Silesia:

> After the Russians disconnected the locomotive, we were detained for twenty-two hours. Similar stoppages happened several times . . . The train was plundered four times, twice by Poles, twice by Russians. This was a simple procedure. As soon as the train slowed down because of rail damage, the robbers climbed onto the wagons, snatched our suitcases and rucksacks, and threw them onto the embankment. After half an hour they jumped off and collected the spoils.[36]

In this time of lawlessness, when policemen and other officials often joined the looters, railway stations were the most dangerous places to be. Gangs of robbers preyed on anyone unfortunate enough to have to spend the night there. Women of all ages were also liable to be raped by drunken soldiers in search of diversion. One of the horrors of homelessness and the total loss of rights is that others are given the license to do anything they wish with you.

In some respects, what was done to the Germans in Silesia, Prussia, and the Sudetenland was a grotesque mirror image of what Germans had done to others, particularly to the Jews. They were barred from many public places; they had to wear armbands with the letter N (for *Niemiec*, German); they were not allowed to buy eggs, fruit, milk, or cheese; and they could not marry Poles.

Of course, this parallel has its limits. A friend of Ernst Jünger, the conservative writer and diarist, wrote to him from her prison in Czechoslovakia: "The tragedy of what is happening in the German, as well as the Hungarians parts of Czechoslovakia can only be compared to what happened to the Jews."[37] This is nonsense. There is still much dispute about the number of Germans who died in the deportations. Some German historians have claimed that more than one million died. Counterclaims have been made for roughly half that number.[38] Which is bad enough. There was, however, no systematic plan to exterminate all Germans. And sometimes, native Silesian or Sudeten Germans were given the choice to become Polish or Czech citizens, not an option that was ever open to Jews under Nazi rule.

German women, subjected to random sexual assaults from Soviet troops, Poles, or Czechs, described themselves as *"Freiwild,"* fair game. That is pretty much what all homeless people without any rights become. Silesia was known in the summer of 1945 as "the wild west." The provisional head of the new Polish administration of Gdańsk, formerly the German city Danzig, spoke of a "gold rush": "On all roads and with all means of transport, everyone from all regions of Poland is heading for this Klondike, and their sole aim is not work but robbery and looting."[39] German houses, German firms, German assets of any kind, including the Germans themselves, were ripe for the plucking.

The ethnic cleansing of 1945 went further, however, than deportations, or turning people into slaves. Herbert Hupka, a half-Jewish inhabitant of Ratibor (Racibórz) in Upper Silesia, recalls being marched in the rain past his old school, where his father had taught Latin and Greek. He noticed a heap of torn and soggy books, by Thomas Mann, Alfred Döblin, Franz Werfel, and other authors who had been banned by the Nazis. The books had been confiscated by the Nazi government and tossed into the Jewish cemetery. Somehow they ended up in the street, in Hupka's words, "ownerless, lying in front of the Gymnasium."[40]

What was being systematically destroyed in 1945 was German culture, along with many of the people who lived it. Old parts of the German Reich and the Austro-Hungarian Empire, some of whose great cities— Breslau, Danzig, Königsberg, Lemberg, Brünn, Czernowitz, Prague— were centers of German high culture, often carried by German-speaking Jews, now had to be "de-Germanized." Streets and shop signs were painted over, place names changed, German libraries pillaged, monuments demolished, inscriptions, some of them very old, erased from

churches and other public buildings; the German language itself had to
be abolished. A report from Prague in *Yank* noted:

> If you ask directions in German (in case you don't speak Czech),
> you'll get nothing but a fishy stare . . . It's not that the Czechs don't
> understand. German has been practically a second language with
> them for years. A Czech who was forced to work for the Germans
> in a Prague factory . . . puts it this way: "Please do not speak Ger-
> man here. That is the language of the beast."[41]

There were various motives for erasing not just Germans and their
culture from eastern and central Europe, but even memories of their presence. For communists it was a revolutionary project to get rid of a hated
bourgeoisie. For noncommunist nationalists, such as President Edvard
Beneš, it was a revenge for treachery: "Our Germans . . . have betrayed
our state, betrayed our democracy, betrayed us, betrayed humaneness,
and betrayed mankind."[42] A highly placed cleric in the Czechoslovak
Catholic Church declared: "Once in a thousand years the time has come
to settle accounts with the Germans, who are evil and to whom the com-
mandment to love thy neighbor therefore does not apply."[43] But the sentiment all shared was articulated by Poland's first communist leader,
Władisław Gomułka, at a Central Committee meeting of the Polish
Workers' Party: "We must expel all the Germans because countries are
built on national lines and not on multi-national ones."[44]

In this way Hitler's project, based on ideas going back to the first decades of the twentieth century, or even well before, of ethnic purity and
nationhood, was completed by people who hated Germany. Even if we
take all the horrors of postwar ethnic cleansing in Poland, Czechoslovakia, Hungary, and Romania into account, we shouldn't forget that the real
destroyers of German culture in the center of Europe were the Germans
themselves. By annihilating the central European Jews, many of whom
were fiercely loyal to German high culture, they started the process.

Kicking the Germans out after the war was the quickest way for Poles and Czechs to finish the job.

. . .

IT WAS NOT OUT OF LOVE for Germany that so many Jewish survivors found themselves in German DP camps in the summer and fall of 1945; it was because they felt safer in Germany, the country that had just done its best to murder them all—safer, at any rate, than in some of their native countries, such as Lithuania and Poland. At least they were unlikely to be persecuted in the DP camps under American and British guard. Tens of thousands of Jews who had survived the camps in Poland, fought with the partisans, or returned from exile in the Soviet Union, streamed into Germany during the summer. Naturally, even if the DP camps in Germany offered a temporary refuge, they were still far from home. But what was "home" anymore? Most survivors had no home, except perhaps in the imagination. Home had been destroyed. As some DPs put it: "We are not in Bavaria . . . we are nowhere."[45]

The remnants of European Jewry were in many cases too battered to take care of themselves, and too frightened and angry to accept the help of others, especially if the helpers were Gentiles. The DP camps, which Jews usually shared with non-Jews to begin with, and even with former Nazis in some notorious cases of bureaucratic muddle and indifference, were squalid beyond belief. How could people who had been treated worse than the lowest of beasts suddenly recover their self-respect? It was one thing for General Patton, not known for his philo-Semitism, to call the Jewish survivors "lower than animals." But even tough Palestinian Jews who arrived in Germany to help them could not hide their shock. In Hanoch Bartov's autobiographical novel *Brigade,* a soldier of the Jewish Brigade remarks: "I kept telling myself that these were the people we had spoken of for so many years—but I was so far removed from them that the electric wire might have separated us."[46] An American soldier wrote a letter home about his encounter with a Polish Jew "fresh out of Dachau." The man "was crying like a child," cowering in the corner of a public toilet in Munich. "I didn't have to ask him why he cried; the answers were all the same anyway, and go like this: parents tortured to death; wife gassed to death and children starved to death, or any combination of such three."[47]

If any people were in desperate need of a heroic narrative, it was the Jews, the worst victims among many victims—something, by the way, that was not yet widely acknowledged. The full horror of the Jewish genocide was still incomprehensible even to many Jews themselves. Dr. Salomon Schonfeld, chief Orthodox rabbi of England, reporting on the conditions of Jewish survivors in Poland in December 1945, could still come up with the following sentence: "Polish Jews agree that death at Oswiecim [Auschwitz] (with bathrooms, gas and some Red Cross services) was more humane than anywhere else."[48] *Humane!*

An attempt had already been made during the war in the Jewish press in Palestine to equate the heroism of the Warsaw Ghetto Uprising in 1943 with Masada, hallowed place of the suicidal last stand of the Jewish Zealots against the Romans in 73 CE. The headline of *Yediot Ahronot* on May 16, 1943, read: "The Masada of Warsaw Has Fallen—the Nazis Have Set Fire to the Remnants of the Warsaw Ghetto." In fact, the Ghetto Uprising only really came into its own as a founding myth of the new state of Israel in the 1970s. Yet there were attempts immediately after the war to restore Jewish morale with heroic gestures. And they were all tightly connected with Zionism, a dream of a home promoted to inspire a broken people. Mention has already been made of the Jewish Brigade rolling into Germany from Italy with trucks announcing: *"Achtung! Die Juden kommen!"* ("Watch out! The Jews are coming!"). On July 25 Jewish representatives from camp committees all over western Germany issued a proclamation demanding entry to Palestine. The place they chose for this stirring event was the same Munich beer hall where Hitler had staged his failed coup in 1923.

The link between Jews in the Holy Land and the Diaspora was still tenuous, hence the need to compare Warsaw and Masada, as though Mordechai Anielewicz and the others had died in the ghetto for the good of

Eretz Yisrael (Land of Israel). But Zionist youth groups had actively forged those links during the war, and afterwards too, in the camps, where Jewish survivors were quickly organized in kibbutzim. Major Irving Heymont, the U.S. official in charge of the Landsberg DP camp, was Jewish himself. Even so, he was unsure what to make of the kibbutzniks in his camp: "To add to my problems, I learned today that the young and best elements in the camp are organized into kibbutzim. It appears that a Kibbutz is a closely knit, self-disciplined group with an intense desire to emigrate to Palestine. There . . . they intend to organize their lives along the lines of idealistic collectivism. Each Kibbutz is very clannish and little interested in camp life."[49]

Quite a few survivors actually dreamed of the United States as a new home. The streets in Föhrenwald, one of the largest Jewish DP camps in Bavaria, were given such alluring names as "New York," "Michigan," or "Wisconsin Avenue."[50] But however attractive, the United States did not welcome what was left of European Jewry, certainly not straight after the war. And it was the youth, the relative fitness, the discipline, the high morale, the idealism, the stress on sports, agricultural work, and self-defense, that gave the young Zionists from central Europe such cachet among the survivors. Ten days after the German defeat, Rabbi Levy, the British army chaplain, wrote a letter to the London *Jewish Chronicle* praising the Zionists in Belsen: "Shall I ever forget . . . those meetings within the huts when we sat and sang Hebrew songs? Will the world believe that such a spirit of obstinacy and tenacity is possible? Two days ago I met a group of young Zionists from Poland. They were living in one of the filthiest of the blocks but their own corner was spotless."[51]

The toughest of the tough guys in Belsen was a small, wiry man named Josef Rosensaft. He fit the image of the Jewish hero. Born in 1911 in Poland, he rebelled as a young man against the religious strictures of his Hasidic family and became a left-wing Zionist. In July 1943, he was rounded up with his wife and stepson in the Będzin ghetto and shoved into a train bound for Auschwitz. Somehow he managed to escape from the train and jumped into the Vistula River under machine-gun fire.

Rearrested in the ghetto, he managed to escape once more, only to be caught again and sent to Birkenau, the death camp connected to Auschwitz. After two months of slave work in a stone quarry, he was transported to another camp, from which he escaped in March 1944. Captured again in April, he was tortured for several months in Birkenau, without revealing who had helped him to escape. By way of a stint in Dora-Mittelbau, where prisoners were worked to death in dank underground tunnels constructing V-2 rockets for the German military, he ended up in Bergen-Belsen.

Rosensaft was not a member of the educated urban Jewish elite. He could only speak Yiddish, but that was not the only reason why he insisted on Yiddish as the language of negotiation with the Allied authorities—much to the annoyance of his British interlocutors. It was a matter of pride. As the leader of the Central Committee of liberated Belsen Jews, he wanted Jews to be treated as a distinct people with a common home, which in his mind could only be Palestine. Jews needed to be separated from prisoners of other nationalities, should be allowed to run their own affairs, and should get ready to move on to the land of the Jews.[52]

Similar sentiments were voiced in other camps too. Major Irving Heymont was often irritated by the demands of the Jewish committee in Landsberg. But in a letter home, he quotes from a speech by one of the camp representatives, an agronomist from Lithuania named Dr. J. Oleiski, which he finds "very illuminating." Dr. Oleiski recalls his time in the ghetto when the Jews, "looking through the fences over the Vilna to Kovno and other Lithuanian towns," sang "I Want to See My Home Again." But today, Oleiski continued,

> after all that, after the concentration camps in Germany, after we stated definitely that our former home was changed into a mass grave, we can only grope and clasp with our finger tips the shadows of our dearest and painfully cry: I can never more see my home. The victorious nations that in the 20th century removed the black plague from Europe must understand once and for all the specific

Jewish problem. No, we are not Polish when we are born in Poland; we are not Lithuanians even though we once passed through
Lithuania; and we are neither Roumanians though we have seen
the first time in our life the sunshine in Roumenia. We are Jews!!

Heymont was neither a Zionist nor, it seems, a religious man. In fact,
he never divulged his family background, since he feared this might com-
plicate his delicate task in Germany. But despite his many irritations, he
was not unsympathetic to Dr. Oleiski's aspirations, including the goal of
"BUILDING A JEWISH COMMONWEALTH IN PALESTINE"
(capital letters in the original text). Indeed, wrote Heymont, "the more I
think about this, the less angry I become with the committee. As a group,
the committee is vitally interested in protecting the rights of the people
and in getting them out of Germany. By rights of the people, I mean their
treatment as a free people and not as wards or charity cases."[53]

The idea of transforming Jews from being a persecuted minority, abject
and eager to please the majorities amongst whom they lived, tempted into
hopeful assimilation yet forever looking over their shoulders, from "charity
cases" into a proud nation of warriors working their own sacred soil—this
ideal existed long before the Nazi genocide. The ideal came in many vari-
eties, socialist, religious, even racialist. And the different factions were in
constant and sometimes acrimonious competition. As soon as people were
well enough to vote, political parties were formed in Belsen and other
camps. David Ben-Gurion, another Polish tough guy and leader of the Zionist movement in Palestine, saw early on how Jewish suffering could help
the project he so fervently believed in. In October 1942, he told the Zionist
Executive commission in Palestine: "Disaster is strength if channeled to a
productive course; the whole trick of Zionism is that it knows how to channel our disaster not into despondency or degradation, as is the case in the
Diaspora, but into a source of creativity and exploitation."[54]

This sounds more than a little ruthless, the earliest instance of "instru-
mentalizing" the Holocaust. A firm rejection of softness was certainly part

of Ben-Gurion's style, necessary perhaps to foster a new heroic story for the Jews. A practical man, he saw displays of sentiment as unproductive. But in 1942, Ben-Gurion, too, was still unaware of the scale of the Jewish catastrophe in Europe. Very few people were. One of the first men who seemed to have understood was a Zionist member of the Rescue Committee for European Jewry named Apolinari Hartglass. Already in 1940, he warned that the Nazis were "exterminating the [Jewish] population in Poland." However, even Hartglass, when refugees from Poland confirmed his worst suspicions in 1942, responded: "If I believed everything you're saying, I'd kill myself."[55] Ben-Gurion knew facts. Like most people, he could not yet imagine the truth.

Even so, both Hartglass and Ben-Gurion could be accused of exploiting human misery to their own political ends. In a memorandum to the Rescue Committee in 1943, Hartglass stated that seven million European Jews would probably be killed, and that there was nothing much the Jews in Palestine (the *Yishuv*) could do about it. However, he wrote, if only a handful of Jews could be rescued, "we must at least achieve some political gains from them. From a Zionist point of view we will achieve this political gain under the following conditions. A: If the whole world knows that the only country that wants to receive the rescued Jews is Palestine and that the only community that wants to absorb them is the *Yishuv*."[56]

In October 1945, Ben-Gurion decided to see the former concentration camps in Germany for himself. He made short, dry, factual notes in his diary. About Dachau: "I saw the ovens, the gas chambers, the kennels, the gallows, the prisoners' quarters, and the SS quarters." In Belsen: "Until April 15 this year 48,000 Jews were here . . . Since then 31,000 have died . . . (of typhus, tuberculosis)"[57] Ben-Gurion's goals, according to the biographer Shabtai Teveth, were more in the heroic mold. He envisaged "the survivors of the death camps fighting their way onto the shores of Palestine, breaking through a blockade of British soldiers." Teveth remarks drily, "His examination of the skeletal survivors must have been like that of a commander reviewing his troops before battle."[58]

Word of Ben-Gurion's tour soon got around, and he was mobbed by DPs wherever he went. Heymont knew he was in Landsberg only when he "noticed the people streaming out to line the street leading from Munich. They were carrying flowers and hastily improvised banners and signs. The camp itself blossomed out with decorations of all sorts. Never had we seen such energy displayed in the camp. I don't think a visit from President Truman could cause as much excitement."[59] To the people in the camp, Heymont observed, Ben-Gurion "is God."

The most famous speech Ben-Gurion gave on this trip to Germany was at a hospital for camp survivors in the old Benedictine monastery of St. Ottilien near Munich, not far from Dachau. For once, at the sight of the Jewish orphans, his eyes welled up with emotion. But he swiftly pulled himself together: "I will not try to express the feelings within me . . . such a thing is impossible." Instead he put it to his audience, some of them still in striped prisoners' garb:

> I can tell you that a vibrant Jewish Palestine exists and that even if its gates are locked the *Yishuv* will break them open with its strong hands . . . Today we are the decisive power in Palestine . . . We have our own shops, our own factories, our own culture, and our own rifles . . . Hitler was not far from Palestine. There could have been terrible destruction there, but what happened in Poland could not happen in Palestine. They would not have slaughtered us in our synagogues. Every boy and every girl would have shot at every German soldier.[60]

Strong . . . power . . . our own rifles . . . These heroic words offered by the Zionist leader were precisely what the British didn't want to hear, even though in 1917 the British foreign secretary Arthur James Balfour had promised to make Palestine into "a national home for the Jewish people." The British were in a bind, for in the Balfour Declaration of 1917 the government had promised the Arab population of Palestine that "nothing shall be done which may prejudice the civil and religious rights of existing

non-Jewish communities in Palestine." Since the Arabs made up 91 percent of the roughly seven hundred thousand people in Palestine, this was
going to be a problem. Hence the White Paper, issued by the British government in 1939, limiting Jewish emigration to Palestine to ten thousand
persons a year between 1940 and 1944, to which twenty-five thousand
might be added in case of an emergency. The emergency came; just
enough Jews made it to Palestine to fill the utterly inadequate quota. Ben-
Gurion now insisted on moving at least a million Jewish survivors there by
all possible means, legal or not. President Truman, shocked by a report on
the condition of Jewish DPs in Germany,[61] argued in a letter to British
prime minister Clement Attlee that at least one hundred thousand Jews
should be permitted to emigrate. He added: "As I said to you in Potsdam,
the American people, as a whole, firmly believe that immigration into
Palestine should not be closed and that a reasonable number of Europe's
persecuted Jews should, in accordance with their wishes, be permitted to
resettle there."[62]

What Truman did not say in his letter was that he did not wish those
hundred thousand Jews to settle in the United States. The reason why the
British actively tried to stop Jews from moving to Palestine, sometimes
with the use of force against people who had barely survived Nazi death
camps, was practical. Palestine was still a British mandate. Britain, even
under a Labour government, wished to keep its influence in the Middle
East as the gateway to India. The Arabs, towards whom British Foreign
Office sympathies tilted anyway, would be up in arms if too many Jews
were allowed to settle in a majority Arab land. From the British point of
view this would be inopportune. And so Jews who tried to land illegally
were liable to be clubbed by British soldiers, shoved back onto their ram-
shackle boats, or even shot.

But British arguments were not always practical, and frequently disingenuous. If Zionism was formulated as a battle for Jewish identity, the
British put forward an alternative idea of identity. In response to the special U.S. report on DPs in Germany by Earl G. Harrison, American envoy
to the Inter-Governmental Committee on Refugees, the British Foreign

Office argued that it was wrong not only to segregate Jews from other DPs, as the report recommended, but also to conclude that there was no future in Europe for Jews. After all, "it would go far by implication to admit that [the] Nazis were right in holding that there was no place for the Jews in Europe." It was up to the Allies "to create conditions in which [the Jews] will themselves feel it natural and right to go home rather than to admit at this stage that such conditions are impossible to create."[63]

Quite how the British Foreign Office proposed to create those conditions in such countries as Poland, Lithuania, or Ukraine was not spelled out. Not that Jews were all agreed on the proper route to Zion. There was an intense rivalry between the Jewish Agency, incorporating all Zionist groups in Palestine, and the American Jewish Joint Distribution Committee, JDC, or "Joint" for short. Joint officials, trying to help Jewish refugees and DPs as best they could with money, food, and other necessities, disliked the Zionist indoctrination, which they found authoritarian and counterproductive. There were even cases of children being obstructed by the Jewish Agency from finding homes in Europe or the United States, since this might discourage "ascent" to the Jewish homeland.

It would take a few more years, but in the end, the Zionists got their way. The state of Israel was founded (1948) and millions of Jews found refuge there. Most countries in Europe, as well as the Soviet Union and the United States, were sympathetic, out of guilt perhaps, or because of the lingering nineteenth-century notion that every race needs its nation, or from recognition that for many Jews a state of Israel was the only plausible option. What Eden said about the Cossacks applied just as much to the European Jews: "We don't want them here."[64]

CHAPTER 5

DRAINING
THE POISON

N ations are not only physically damaged by war, occupation, or dictatorship but are morally corrupted too. Political legitimacy is lost. Civic sense is corroded by cynicism. Those who do well in tyrannies are often the least savory and most easily corrupted people. Those who carry most legitimacy, when the transition comes, are very often the most marginal while dictatorship lasts. In World War II this came down to the small number of men and women who joined the active resistance, perilously in countries under occupation, more safely in London, where the various "free" governments continued their pro forma existence in exile.

Resistance, quite deliberately romanticized after the war, played a tiny role in the military defeat of Nazi Germany or Imperial Japan. Violent acts of rebellion, followed by vicious reprisals against innocent citizens, frequently caused more trouble than they were worth, hence the common resentment among more cautious people towards the heroic figures whose actions led to even more savage repression. Of course, resistance has a symbolic value, as a demonstration that all is not lost, that the tyranny can be dented. But the real importance of resistance becomes clear only once the fighting is over. That some people stood firm against all the odds provides a heroic story to societies poisoned by collaboration or simple acquiescence in murderous regimes. Restoration of democracy rests on such stories, for they help to rebuild a sense not just of civic morale but also of political legitimacy for postwar governments. They are the foundation myths of national revival in postwar Europe.

In parts of central and eastern Europe the role of the resistance was more complicated, because there were two tyrannies to resist. Those who saw Stalin as the main enemy sometimes collaborated with the Germans. The most famous resistance hero in Ukraine was Stepan Bandera, leader of the Organization of Ukrainian Nationalists. When Ukraine finally became independent (1991) after the collapse of the Soviet Union, he was built up as the father of the fatherland, a kind of Ukrainian George Washington. Bandera statues were erected all over the place, along with Bandera monuments, Bandera shrines, and Bandera museums. But Bandera is hardly a unifying hero, for he came from western Ukraine, once part of the Austro-Hungarian Empire. In Russian Orthodox eastern Ukraine, Bandera is still regarded as a fascist for siding with the Nazis in 1941. Bandera's nationalists were also responsible for murdering roughly forty thousand Poles in 1944. The hero himself, after having declared independence from the Germans as well as the Soviets, was in a Nazi concentration camp when this happened. In 1959, living in exile in Munich, he was murdered by an agent of the Soviet KGB.

Things were less complicated in western Europe. The heroic myth was especially important in a country like France, whose bureaucracy, police forces, judiciary, industrial elites, and even many artists and writers were all deeply compromised by the collaborationist regime in Vichy. When General de Gaulle made his defiant radio broadcast from London on June 18, 1940, he was unknown to most people in France. The great father figure of the French *patrie* was still Marshal Pétain. Few people even heard de Gaulle on the radio declaiming in his halting, but strangely moving delivery: "Whatever happens, the flame of the French resistance must not be extinguished and will not be extinguished."

There was, in fact, little resistance in France during the first few years of the war. But de Gaulle came back to France in 1944 as the undisputed symbol of national rectitude, walking tall, in his uniform, at the head of French troops "liberating" Paris after the Allies had overwhelmed the Germans in Normandy. He was actually shot at by pro-Nazi snipers, but he marched on as though nothing was amiss. And so this seemingly untouchable figure was able to form a provisional government until the first postwar elections in October 1945, a government still manned by many Vichyistes and at odds with resistance groups, often led by communists, who distrusted de Gaulle's aims with some reason, just as he, with equal reason, distrusted theirs. But General de Gaulle bore the proud face of resistance, and so his leadership was regarded as legitimate. He was the man to lift his nation from moral bankruptcy.

Germany and Japan had no heroic symbols or leaders to build on (although something like a heroic myth of "anti-fascism" was cooked up in the communist zone of eastern Germany). The officers who had tried to assassinate Hitler in July 1944, and paid with their lives, were not yet regarded as heroes by most Germans. And since many of them came from the Prussian military aristocracy, they would have been associated by non-Germans, and many Germans too, with a militarist tradition ("Prussianism") that was widely blamed for the war. There were some Japanese who had resisted the wartime regime, but they were mostly communists or radical leftists who had spent the war in prison. Opponents of Hitler's Reich and Japan's Imperial government had by and large kept their thoughts to themselves, or, in the case of Germany, fled abroad.

But there were some active resisters in Germany, tiny groups of people who risked their lives in almost total isolation. One of them was Ruth Andreas-Friedrich, a journalist who joined the "Uncle Emil" resistance group in Berlin. She and her courageous friends had hidden Jews and others from Nazi persecution and secretly distributed anti-Nazi leaflets. Few people who did this kind of thing managed to stay alive. There were certainly not enough people like Andreas-Friedrich to create a national myth of resistance. Yet, once the fighting was over and danger was gone, people still felt a need for some kind of moral redemption. On May 15, 1945, barely surviving in the Russian-occupied ruins of Berlin, Andreas-Friedrich wrote the following words in her diary:

> Everywhere feverish political activity. As if there were a rush to make up for twelve years' lost time. "Antifascist" groups are shooting up like mushrooms. Banners and posters. Notices and signs. At every streetcorner some political group has been formed . . . Not all of these anti-Hitler groups can look back at a long struggle. With some of them resistance began only as Hitler's ended.[1]

Although not quite so blatant, similar hypocrisy could be observed in countries liberated from German occupation. But heroic narratives, even in those countries, let alone in Germany or Japan, were not enough to cope with moral collapse. For a postwar order to gain legitimacy, there had to be a purge in the ranks of Nazis, Japanese militarists, and their collaborators. The people responsible for the war, the dictatorships, persecution, slave labor, and mass murder, had to go. But where to start? How to go about it? How to define guilt? Was complicity enough reason to be purged? How to find the guilty? And what were the limits? If every German official who had been a Nazi, or worked with the Nazis, were to be purged, German society, already in tatters, might easily have disintegrated. There had been too many. In Japan, a complete purge of the wartime bureaucracy and political establishment would have left very few Japanese with either the knowledge or the skill to keep a country on the verge of starvation going. Yet something had to happen to make people feel that justice was done.

The oldest and simplest solution to a society gone wrong—apart from just killing the wrongdoers—is banishment. This was suggested by a conservative Christian senator in Belgium when wondering what to do with former collaborators: "If there really is no place in our country to re-integrate these people, wouldn't it be possible to let them go somewhere else? . . . There are countries, in Latin America, for example, where they could start new lives."[2] This option was indeed taken, albeit secretly, by a number of Nazi mass murderers, but it was hardly a viable government policy. And the idea of expelling all the collaborators of Europe, let alone all the Nazis in Germany, to Latin America was fanciful.

Nevertheless, at the July 1945 conference in Potsdam, the Soviet, British, and American leaders agreed that something radical had to be done to cleanse the defeated nations of their poisonous legacies and rebuild them as democracies that would never go to war again. Both Germany and Japan would be "demilitarized," and "democratized." Nazi organizations and police forces would be banned, naturally, but also "all military organizations and all clubs and associations which serve to keep alive the military tradition in Germany." And, as part of German democratization, "all members of the Nazi party who have been more than nominal participants in its activities and all other persons hostile to Allied purposes shall be removed from public and semipublic office and from positions of responsibility in important private undertakings."

Where the Soviets and their Western allies differed, of course, was on their idea of what constituted democracy. The other thing left unclear was the distinction, if there was any, between having been a Nazi or a "militarist," and being "hostile to Allied purposes." One can, after all, imagine a former Nazi who was quite prepared to work for Allied purposes, or a former anti-Nazi who fiercely disagreed with Allied policies—a communist, say, in the Western zones, or a liberal democrat in the Soviet zone. How to go about the purges also depended on how one viewed the German catastrophe. On this there was more agreement among the great powers. Prussian militarism, or Prussianism, was seen as the main problem; that is what needed to be uprooted. That this was somewhat off the mark became common knowledge only later.

The wording on Japan in Potsdam was a little different: "There must be eliminated for all time the authority and influence of those who have deceived and misled the people of Japan into embarking on world conquest, for we insist that a new order of peace, security and justice will be impossible until irresponsible militarism is driven from the world."

This, too, was a bit vague and indeed misleading. Is there such a thing as *"responsible* militarism"? And who exactly had misled whom? General Douglas MacArthur, the Supreme Commander for Allied Powers (SCAP), who was for the time being the highest authority in Japan, did not accept Emperor Hirohito's offer to take responsibility for the war. SCAP, the acronym by which MacArthur was generally known, was convinced that the emperor was needed to avoid chaos, so he was exempted from any guilt.

As the most powerful man in Japan, as well as a consciously contrived great white father figure, MacArthur received many letters from Japanese citizens, some addressing him with a bizarre reverence. The Supreme Commander's intention was to play the all-powerful shogun to the symbolic Japanese emperor. In a way, however, it was as if he had become a sacred figure himself. "Dear Sir," went one letter, "when I think of the generous measures Your Excellency has taken instead of exacting vengeance, I am struck with reverent awe as if I were in the presence of God."[3]

To many Japanese during the war, the emperor had been a sacred figure. But not to Japanese of a liberal or leftist bent. One letter writer to SCAP, possibly a Christian, wondered why the emperor had not been arrested as a war criminal: "To achieve true legal justice and human righteousness without shame before the world and before God, we ask you to strictly punish the present emperor as a war criminal. If you leave the emperor untouched simply to manipulate the people, then I believe that all the well-meaning policies of the Allied forces will come to naught after you leave."[4]

But there were other letters too, which warned of dire consequences should the emperor be touched: "This would obviously bring about the world's greatest tragedy. It would succeed only after the complete annihilation of the eighty-million Yamato [Japanese] people."[5] The phrase "Yamato" suggests an unreconstructed nationalist. MacArthur decided that this was the type of voice he should heed. As a result, the emperor, in whose name every wartime act, including the most atrocious, was committed, was supposedly "misled" himself. To depart from this narrative in public could lead to serious trouble, and on occasion still can.*

Since Japan had had no equivalent of the Nazi Party, let alone a Hitler, or a coup d'état comparable to what happened in Germany in 1933, instead "militarism," "ultranationalism," even "feudalism" were the poisonous weeds that needed to be eradicated. And so, in the words of a U.S. military directive: "Persons who have been active exponents of militarism and militant nationalism will be removed and excluded from public office and from any other positions of public and private responsibility."[6] When it came to propagandists, war criminals, and military leaders, this would be a fairly straightforward enterprise, but it would prove far more challenging to purge the bureaucrats, whose careers went back long before the Pacific War, or businessmen and industrialists who had certainly cooperated with and benefited from Japan's wartime governments, but in many cases could not be described as militarists or ultranationalists.

The idea that one can cut out "militarism," "feudalism," or "Prussianism," as though they were cancer cells in a human organism, had a wider appeal among Allied officials on the left than among conservatives. This was true also of Germans, Japanese, and citizens in former occupied countries. Since the left, including the communists, had played a dominant role in the resistance in many countries, leftist members of the resistance insisted that postwar societies should be shaped according to their wishes. To them, 1945 was the perfect opportunity for a final reckoning with the military, financial, and political establishments which had collaborated with fascism.

General MacArthur, although a conservative Republican himself, was surrounded in the early years of the Japanese occupation by idealistic lawyers and New Deal reformers who strongly pushed for purges as part of their efforts to democratize Japan. They were not experts with prewar

---

* In 1988, the mayor of Nagasaki, a Christian named Motoshima Hitoshi, stated that Emperor Hirohito should have borne some responsibility for the war. He became a target of the far right. Two years later, a hit man shot him in the back.

ties to the Japanese elites. There was, in their view, no special need for cultural expertise. Any country could be remade into a democracy, provided it was equipped with the right constitution and helped along by setting up independent trade unions and other progressive measures. The early purges in Japan were supervised by such figures as Lieutenant Colonel Charles Kades, a New Dealer working in SCAP's Government Section. His boss was Brigadier General Courtney Whitney, a former lawyer in Manila who had the same taste for bombastic rhetoric as his beloved boss: "MacArthur's philosophy, without precedent in the annals of military occupations of the past, will live as a standard and a challenge to military occupations of the future."[7] Their enemy in SCAP's byzantine Tokyo court was Major General Charles Willoughby, MacArthur's intelligence chief.

MacArthur liked to refer to Willoughby, born in Germany as Karl von Tscheppe und Weidenbach, as "my pet fascist." With good reason. A hunting man with a soft voice, silky manners, and a nasty temper, Willoughby had a tendency to see Jewish and communist conspiracies everywhere, including inside the U.S. military administration itself. The French ambassador, too, fell under his suspicion because he happened to have a Russian name. Willoughby enjoyed warmer relations with the conservative courtiers around Emperor Hirohito than with SCAP's New Dealers. After his retirement in the 1950s, Willoughby moved to Madrid to advise General Francisco Franco, a man he much admired. However, since he was formally in charge of the occupation police, it was Willoughby's duty to see to the dismissal of public figures he privately approved of. After listening to one of Willoughby's interminable rants against the purges, Whitney remarked: "I submit that anyone who is so opposed to a program is the wrong man to implement it."[8] And that, it turned out, was that, at least for the time being.

In Germany, the main thinker behind the purges of former Nazis was Franz Neumann, a Marxist who ended up working for the Office of Strategic Services (OSS), the forerunner of the CIA. Neumann was a Jewish refugee from Germany, where he had made a name before the war as a political theorist and labor lawyer. During his exile in the U.S., he prepared a denazification guide for the U.S. government together with Herbert Marcuse, one of several refugee Marxist scholars associated with the Frankfurt School. The Third Reich, according to their thesis, was a typical case of "totalitarian monopolistic capitalism."[9] Behind the Nazi movement stood the industrialists. Persecution of the Jews had been a maneuver to deflect popular discontent about monopoly capitalism.

Neumann, backed by the top military boss in the American zone, General Lucius Clay, helped to devise the notorious *Fragebogen* (questionnaire), the 131-point survey every German adult was required to fill out. On the basis of these detailed questions on past affiliations and sympathies, it was hoped, the U.S. military would be able to establish the guilt or innocence of at least twenty-three million people. A typical question would be: "Have you or any members of your family taken possession of property or assets stolen from others on the grounds of faith or race?" Another question concerned membership of university fraternities, as though these had been part of the Nazi apparatus instead of being banned after 1935. In truth, of course, answers were rarely honest. Submissions of the documents were postponed, sometimes forever. Endless appeals were launched. The Allies lacked sufficient staff, or knowledge, to assess the documents. Few Americans even spoke German, let alone read it. An already overwhelmed military administration, formally in charge of rebuilding democracy in Germany, was even further stretched by a new "Law No. 8," which became effective on December 1.

Ruth Andreas-Friedrich, the former resister in Berlin, made a note of this law in her diary, with approval:

> Three weeks ago the first measures were taken against Party members. Elimination of all Nazis from prominent positions in industry and commerce. Exclusion of Party members from cultural occupations. Former NSDAP members may only be employed as workers.[10]

Andreas-Friedrich was sympathetic to the idea of putting old Nazis to work at clearing rubble and other unpleasant menial tasks. But hers was an uncommon perspective, it seems. She recorded what she heard people saying around her: "Unbelievable, this terror! Outrageous, this latest injustice. They can't put twenty percent of the population under special law." To which she responded in the privacy of her diary: "But they can! Have they [the Germans] forgotten how easily it can be done? Has it escaped them that these special laws are almost identical to those of eight years ago against the Jews?"[11]

There was no sympathy for the protesting Germans from her. But the parallel she drew was part of the problem. Excluding people from society under a Nazi regime is one thing, but to do so in order to rebuild a democracy is an altogether trickier proposition. Besides, a simple admission of Party membership did not mean very much. Some 140,000 people lost their jobs, but many were petty officials and opportunists who had joined the Nazis out of fear or ambition, while bigger and more culpable figures remained untouched: the businessmen who didn't bother to join the Party, but made millions from plundered Jewish assets; the bankers who hoarded gold from the teeth of murdered Jews; the professors who promoted noxious racial theories; the lawyers and judges who meticulously followed the decrees of Hitler's Reich, prosecuting men and women for subverting the Nazi state or committing "racial shame" by falling in love with someone of an "inferior race."

Theodor Heuss had been a liberal journalist and politician before the war, and though not an active resister, he had loathed the Nazis. Heuss was the kind of German the Allies felt they could trust. In 1945, the Americans appointed him as Culture Minister of Baden-Württemberg. One of Heuss's problems was the lack of capable schoolteachers to wean the young from twelve years of Nazi propaganda. His task was made more difficult by the purges. In a desperate letter to the Military Administration, he wrote that in his view only between 10 to 15 percent of the people dismissed in the purges had been convinced Nazis. But so many teachers had been fired that children were being deprived of an education. It would not be difficult, he argued, "to scrape away the brown veneer" from older teachers, educated before the Third Reich, and "reawaken their powers of

My father, S. L. Buruma (far left),
with his fellow students in Utrecht

Soviet soldiers dancing in Berlin

Dutch girls celebrating with a Canadian soldier

British sailors and their girlfriends on VE Day in London

*A GI fraternizing
with a Japanese girl
in a Tokyo park*
(Associated Press/
Charles Gorry)

Dutch citizens cheering the bombers dropping food in May 1945

A "horizontal collaborator" is jeered by a mob in Holland.

Greeks receiving Allied aid

A woman being tarred
for collaboration in Amsterdam

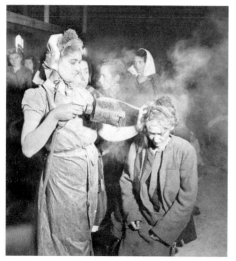

Delousing an inmate at Bergen-Belsen

Starved POWs at a Japanese camp in Malaya

The British Army setting fire to the last hut at Bergen-Belsen

Taking a break from clearing rubble in Berlin

Refugee children in Berlin

A Japanese man in the ruins of his home in Yokohama

Greek women mourning the dead (Associated Press)

*A German army general is tied
to the stake before his execution in Italy.*

(Associated Press)

*German POWs tend to American graves
near Omaha Beach in Normandy.*

(Associated Press/Peter J. Carroll)

German children walking into school in Aachen

*General Yamashita is sworn in
at his trial in Manila.*

*General de Gaulle in Lorient, a former U-boat base in France that
was badly damaged by Allied bombs* (AFP/Getty Images)

*Laval testifying in Paris at the trial of Marshal Pétain
(seated, right, behind Laval)*

*The Dutch National Socialist leader Anton Mussert is arrested
by the Dutch resistance in The Hague.*

The Japanese surrender to the Royal Air Force in Saigon.

Indonesian freedom fighters

Winston Churchill campaigning for reelection

Clement Attlee after his election victory
(Associated Press)

good." He begged the authorities for their confidence: "We promise to deliver the teachers from Nazism and to make them agents of new and better ideas, enabling them to educate youth in the right spirit."[12] He was turned down.

Carl Zuckmayer, who returned to Germany from his American exile to write a report for the U.S. War Department, argued that the American purges were so clumsy, and so often missed the real targets, that there was a danger of denazification leading to renazification. German conservatives saw denazification as a socialist plot. They believed that the Allied authorities deliberately favored German radicals, who were keen to purge every city and town of anyone who could be tarred with the fascist brush. Zuckmayer tells a joke he heard in Austria about a man who went to the local police station to have his name registered. Why would he want to do that? asked the policeman. Because I'm a Nazi, replied the man. Then you should have registered with us a year ago, said the officer. To which the man replied: A year ago I was not yet a Nazi.[13]

By the time this joke went the rounds, much of the task of sifting ex-Nazis from the supposedly innocent had been handed over, out of sheer necessity, to German committees. This move was formalized in the "Law for Liberation from National-Socialism and Militarism." It turned into a farce. German politicians had little enthusiasm for further purges. Purging committees, supposedly peopled by radical revolutionaries, were in fact often filled with former Nazis. Catholic priests warned that it was sinful for Germans to offer damaging evidence against their compatriots. Local bigwigs who had made fortunes during the Third Reich paid their way out of trouble, often by producing some pathetic survivor of Nazi persecution as a favorable witness. The key word of this period, starting in 1946, was *Persilschein*, Persil being a "whitewashing" laundry detergent. Countless ex-Nazis received their Persil document washing out every speck of brown dirt from their recent past. Certificates showing that one had been a former prisoner in a Nazi concentration camp could be bought on the black market; not cheap at twenty-five thousand deutsche marks, but affordable to many a former SS officer.

Things were little better in the eastern half of Germany, despite communist claims that the purges in the "democratic zone" had been a great
success. In the late spring of 1945, the kind of German "antifascist" committees described by Ruth Andreas-Friedrich were put in charge of the
purges. They were disbanded in the early summer when the German
Communist Party (KPD) took over. In theory, purges were indeed more
rigorous than in the Western zones. The foundation myth of the German
Democratic Republic, after all, would be its proud history of "antifascism";
this was the "better Germany," the Germany of resistance. Yet this myth
was muddled by the assumption of German collective guilt, of a deep-
seated Teutonic disease, which obsessed the communists. Some of their
own rhetoric seems to have been infected by this German virus. The KPD
demanded the total "liquidation" of the remnants of the Hitler regime.[14]
In one Brandenburg town, ex-Nazis were forced to pin swastikas onto their
clothes. There was much talk of severe punishment. The district magistrate of another locality warned: "The Nazis will be handled the same way
they handled us, that is: hard. We will force the slackers to work and if
need be stick them in a camp . . . By next year we want a Germany purged
of Nazis [Nazirein]."[15]

Still, despite all these hard measures, the purges were almost as inadequate in eastern Germany as they were in the "capitalist zones." Distinctions between "active" and "nominal" Nazis were supposed to be enforced,
but often proved to be elusive. The Soviets soon grew tired of this distinction and ordered *all* former Nazi Party members to be dismissed from
government posts, a task to be concluded in a few months—an impossibil-
ity, of course. They didn't trust the Germans to handle the purges anyway,
and never gave them proper guidelines. There was indeed reason for distrust in this matter. Many Germans refused to cooperate because it soon
turned out that too much purging would lead to a collapse in education,
social services, or any semblance of economic recovery. And so, Germans
in Leipzig and Dresden, as much as in Munich or Cologne, found ex-
cuses to reinstate ex-Nazis in their old jobs, or shield ex-Nazis from prosecution. Even the Soviet authorities connived in this, when purges

threatened to upset production quotas in factories under their control. Most "small" Nazis were comfortably absorbed into the Communist Party, whose authoritarian ways they would not have found unfamiliar. Files were kept on the more important former Nazis in case they should turn out to be troublesome.

The dilemma was the same in all zones. You couldn't really gut the German elites, however distasteful they may have been, and hope to re-build the country at the same time, no matter whether that country was to be a communist or a capitalist one. Very quickly the Allies saw economic recovery as a more important aim than restoring a sense of justice, albeit for opposite reasons. The Soviets wanted to rebuild their "antifascist" Ger-many as a buffer against capitalist imperialism; the United States, Britain, and their allies needed "their" Germany as a democratic bastion against communism.

General Patton's views in 1945 on denazification and former Nazis—that "this Nazi thing is just like a Democratic and Republican election fight" and that "we will need these people"—were historically crude and, so far as his own career was concerned, expressed too soon. Eisenhower had to fire him as military governor of Bavaria. But he was indiscreet rather than eccentric in his opinions. A year after Germany's defeat and the initial purges, most American officials took Patton's view. The British, in particular, had found the American keenness to punish the Germans ridiculous and counterproductive from the beginning. Con O'Neill, a Foreign Office official with total contempt for what he called "low-level zealots," had this to say about Law No. 8's stipulation excluding all Nazi Party members from anything but menial work: "As an example of system-atic and meticulous imbecility, it would be hard to beat."[16]

The story of Hermann Josef Abs is instructive. Compared to other businessmen and industrialists, his crimes as a banker during the Third Reich might appear to be minor. Unlike Alfried Krupp, say, he did not employ women and children to be worked to death as slaves. Nor was he a personal friend of Himmler's, like Friedrich Flick, whose coal and steel empire was a particularly brutal exploiter of concentration camp labor.

Abs wasn't even a Nazi Party member and SS officer, as were Wilhelm Zangen, chairman of Mannesmann in Düsseldorff, or Otto Ohlendorff, economic bureaucrat and leader of a murder squad in Ukraine.

Abs never got his own hands dirty. As a native Rhinelander he felt nothing but disdain for the Prussian military spirit. A suave Catholic Anglophile with fluent English who had worked for Jewish banks before the war and been a good friend of Sigmund Warburg, Abs would most probably never have had anything to do with the Nazis if he hadn't happened to be a highly ambitious German technocrat in the 1930s. But Abs was a director of the Deutsche Bank, and had enriched his concern by "Aryanizing" Jewish firms. Apart from handling Hitler's private account, Abs was also the banker for companies such as Siemens, Krupp, and I.G. Farben, which built vast slave camps around Auschwitz. Abs may not have acted out of vulgar ideological zeal. In fact, he almost certainly didn't. But without men like Abs, Hitler's criminal enterprise would have been a great deal less efficient.

When Abs was bundled into a British jeep after being found at the house of an aristocratic friend in June 1945, he feared the worst. Instead of finding himself in jail, however, he was ushered into one of the few hotels in Hamburg left standing, where his old friend from the City of London, a banker named Charles Dunston, greeted him with great warmth. Dunston had done business in Germany before the war, and rather admired the uniformed strutting of the Nazi movement. "It was like old times," Dunston recalled about their friendly reunion. "I didn't ask him about the war. It didn't matter." Abs excused his appearance, explaining the lack of proper shaving gear. But he looked just the same to Dunston: "Not a hair out of place. I immediately asked him whether he would help us rebuild the German banking system. Happily he agreed."[17]

Things did not go entirely as planned. The Americans, despite British protestations, still insisted that Abs should be arrested as a suspected war criminal. But once he was locked up in jail, Abs refused to give the British further financial advice unless he were released. It took the British three months to convince the U.S. authorities to let him go.

Alfried Krupp, who met his American captors in the hall of his country estate in Essen with the words "This is my house, what are you doing here?" was put on trial in Nuremberg. As was the industrialist Friedrich Flick. When the British came to arrest Baron Georg von Schnitzler, director of I.G. Farben, responsible for slave labor in Auschwitz, among other things, he greeted them suavely, dressed in a golfing outfit cut from the finest Scottish tweed. It was such a pleasure, he declared, to be free once more to resume his old friendships with Lord X and Lord Y, as well as the Du Ponts of Wilmington, Delaware. They were such wonderful friends and it had been most painful to be cut off from them in the last few years.[18] He was sentenced to five years for "plunder and spoliation." Schnitzler returned to business and society after one year. Krupp was sentenced to twelve years for slave labor, and served three. Flick, too, was released from the comfort of Landsberg Prison after serving three years of his seven-year sentence. During his time in captivity, Flick had sought and received financial advice from Hermann Abs, who went on to take a leading role in the reconstruction of West Germany, sitting on the boards of the Deutsche Bank, Daimler-Benz, and Lufthansa, among many other companies. When control of the Krupp company was transferred to a foundation in the 1960s, one of the main supervisors of this transaction was Hermann Abs.

. . .

AT LEAST SOME OF HITLER'S industrial elite had spent some time in prison, albeit with access to good food and very acceptable wines. Their Japanese colleagues were spared even that fate. The purges in Japan, apart from arrests of suspected war criminals, were meant to be "preventative," not "punitive." What they were meant to prevent was the resurgence of "militarism." The problem was that the Americans were unsure whom to purge, and too much inclined to view Japan as an Oriental version of the Third Reich.

Who exactly had "misled the people of Japan"? Not the emperor, since SCAP had already decided he was innocent. The military organization that most closely resembled a Nazi-type outfit was the military police, the *Kempeitai*, much feared by Japanese and non-Japanese alike for its expert use of torture and murder. About forty thousand *Kempeitai* officers lost their jobs; few Japanese tears were shed over them. Other patriotic organizations, having to do with the Shinto religion, emperor worship, martial arts, or wartime economic planning, may have looked like Nazi organizations, but were not really the same at all. Nor was the Imperial Rule Assistance Association, founded in 1940 as a reformist political umbrella group to mobilize politicians, bureaucrats, and intellectuals for the war effort. It lacked a coherent ideology, and some of its founders were actually socialists. The War Planning Board included a few left-wing economists too. Even the policy on what to do with officers in the armed forces was unclear. First it was decided that all officers down to the rank of major had to be purged. Surely no one lower than that could have been in a position to mislead anyone. When Major General Richard Marshall, deputy chief of staff, got wind of this, he erupted in a fury. In his experience, Japanese captains and lieutenants had been the worst fanatics. If they were not added to the list, he said, they would mislead the Japanese people again. So they were added to the list as well.[19] In short, SCAP's Americans didn't have much of a clue.

If any institution had played a major role in the Japanese war effort, it was the bureaucracy: the Home Ministry, in charge of policing dissent, but also the Ministry of Commerce and Industry (absorbed during the war into the Munitions Ministry), in control of wartime industrial planning. And even the Ministry of Finance, which had a big hand in exploiting the resources of conquered Asian countries. Industrial bureaucrats had been responsible for massive slave labor operations, in the puppet state of Manchukuo, in other parts of China, and in Japan itself, where large numbers of people were put to work in factories and mines, mostly in atrocious conditions. But the U.S. Occupation guidelines for dealing with these cases were vague. Senior figures in the top ranks were to be removed from office. Lower-ranking figures could remain in their jobs. The purged officials were not supposed to exert any more influence. It was never exactly clear how they could be prevented from meeting their former subordinates for informal consultations. And so they usually did.

It was on the question of what to do with the business and industrial elites that the U.S. administration was most divided. The Supreme Commander, in his typical pompous manner, intoned: "It was these very persons, born and bred as feudalistic overlords, who held the lives of the majority of Japan's people in virtual slavery, and who . . . geared the country with both the tools and the will to wage aggressive war." They, he insisted, had to be "removed from influencing the course of Japan's future economy."[20]

MacArthur actually said this in 1947, a year after the Tokyo War Crimes Tribunal (formally the International Military Tribunal for the Far East) had been convened, modeled on the Nuremburg trials. Other Americans took a very different view. The chief prosecutor of the Tokyo tribunal, Joseph B. Keenan, a former director in the U.S. Justice Department, said in that same year: "We have neither been offered nor have we found evidence of instances where prominent business and industrial leaders conspired with anyone to plan or initiate the war."[21]

How the Japanese themselves felt about purges depended on their politics. One letter writer to SCAP wanted him to understand that "99 percent of the Japanese people, at least until now, were absolute fanatics and militarists."[22] Another, more temperate correspondent claimed that the "bureaucrats are unprincipled, to the extent that they even allowed a fascist and a war criminal like . . . the former home minister, to keep his office. Even if there were a liberal among them, he would be timid and passive."[23]

What made things a little simpler in Japan is that only one of the Allied powers, the United States, was responsible for "demilitarization" and "democratization." There was no equivalent of SCAP in Germany, not even General Lucius Clay, who certainly would not have received letters such as the one that said, "We look to MacArthur as the second Jesus Christ."[24] But internally divided, in terms of bureaucratic turf and political persuasion, the Americans never really came up with a consistent purging strategy. The actual governing of Japan was left up to a Japanese cabinet, which instructed the bureaucracy to institute its own reforms. While these were perfunctory at best, there was another target which, despite the views of chief prosecutor Joseph Keenan, the American New Dealers took far more seriously. Individuals who "do not direct future Japanese economic efforts for solely peaceful ends" had to be removed, and "industrial and banking combines which have exercised control over a great part of Japan's trade and industry" must be dissolved.[25] These combines, or *zaibatsu*, were designated as the main economic warmongers.

This came as a shock to the industrialists, who, like the banker Hermann Abs and his colleagues in Germany, cherished their prewar contacts in the boardrooms of London and New York. Before the war was even over, the president of a large steel company, a Harvard graduate, exclaimed (in English) in a secret meeting of industrialists, "Our friend is coming."[26] Japanese business leaders with international experience, many of whom had studied in Europe or the United States, expected to be put in charge of the reconstruction of the Japanese economy by like-minded Americans. Instead, they were ousted and their business conglomerates pulled apart.

To the New Dealers in MacArthur's military government, this was their proudest achievement—this and the land reforms which broke the back of "feudalism" in rural Japan. Many Japanese leftists felt enormously encouraged by U.S. policies. In the first few years of occupation, Washington was seen as the left's best friend. Women's suffrage, the right to strike, collective bargaining, these were all great innovations pushed by the Americans and gratefully acted upon by the Japanese. Communists as well as socialists began to wield considerable power in trade unions and higher education.

But even some Japanese with leftist views who had no warm feelings for the industrialists were a little bemused by the special blame attached to the *zaibatsu*. In a letter to his friend Donald Keene, Theodore de Bary, then a naval officer, mentions a conversation with a businessman in

Tokyo named Miyauchi, who called himself a socialist and a democrat. De Bary asked him about the wartime role of the *zaibatsu*. Miyauchi replied that they had counted for little with the military establishment. Yes, some of the new *zaibatsu*, such as Nissan, had done well out of the war, but the "Big Four" old *zaibatsu* families, Mitsubishi, Mitsui, Sumitomo, and Yasuda, had been co-opted like everyone else: "They were weak, the zaibatsu were weak."[27]

De Bary is only half convinced. He had heard this line so often from Japanese that he suspected the influence of military propaganda. He writes: "The army, during the thirties, must have propagated the idea first and then have proved its truth by buying out or intimidating the *zaibatsu*."

One thing is certain: by going after the *zaibatsu* and leaving the bureaucracy more or less alone, the Americans showed that they had not really understood how the Japanese wartime system worked. But this was not just a matter of ignorance or misunderstanding; there was a confluence of views between idealistic American planners, who wanted to help build a new Japan, and the Japanese "reform bureaucrats" who were expecting to continue their wartime grip on the economy, albeit to more peaceful ends.

Not that nothing was done. By 1948, the careers of more than nine hundred thousand people had been screened, and more than one and a half million questionnaires examined. The Home Ministry was dissolved, the armed forces disbanded, and 1,800 bureaucrats were purged. But most of these (70 percent) were former policemen and other officials from the Home Ministry. Economic bureaucrats were hardly touched at all. From the former Ministry of Munitions only forty-two men were dismissed, and from the Ministry of Finance just nine.[28] The man who ran the Ministry of Munitions, after being in charge of slave labor in Manchuria, and who then helped to plan the Japanese imperialist enterprise known as the Greater East Asia Co-Prosperity Sphere, was arrested but never formally charged with war crimes. His name was Kishi Nobusuke, and his career flourished after his release from prison; he would go on to become prime minister of Japan.

. . .

IN THE HISTORY of the Greater East Asia Co-Prosperity Sphere, the Philippines occupies a curious place. The country was invaded and occupied by the Japanese on December 8, 1941, ten hours after the attack on Pearl Harbor. Douglas MacArthur, then officially Field Marshal of the Philippine Army, retreated to Australia in March of the following year, where he asserted, "I shall return." The Filipino president, Manuel Quezon, also left for Australia and thence to Washington, D.C., where he established a government in exile. This in itself was unusual; there was no Indonesian government in exile, or Burmese government in exile. There was a Thai government in exile, but Thailand was never a colony. By the time the Japanese invaded, the Philippines was somewhere in between a colony and a state. It already had commonwealth status and was supposed to become fully independent in 1946. The Japanese, in spite of promising, as General Homma Masaharu put it, to emancipate the Filipinos from the oppressive domination of the United States, in fact recolonized the country in a more brutal form. Even though the Philippines was formally declared an independent republic in 1943, under president José P. Laurel, the Japanese were fully in charge. Behind every Filipino government official was a Japanese "consultant," and behind every consultant stood the Japanese army and the dreaded *Kempeitai* military police. The republic, in short, was a sham.

There was, however, a tough Filipino resistance movement against the Japanese. The most effective anti-Japanese guerrillas, operating in the rural areas of the main island of Luzon, shared the politics neither of Quezon nor of Laurel. The Hukbalahap, meaning People's Anti-Japanese Army, were barefooted peasant revolutionaries whose enemies were not only the Japanese but also the big Filipino landowning families. Enriched by their vast sugar and coconut plantations, the landlords, masquerading as democrats, ran the country as a feudal oligarchy. The most famous Huk leader, named Luis Taruc, was a son of sharecroppers. Another colorful Huk was a huge and ferocious female warrior named Felipa Culala. Her nom de guerre was Dayang Dayang. Even the Japanese were afraid of Dayang Dayang.

Since many of the landlords had fled their plantations for Manila during the Japanese occupation, the Huks did what communists had done in
other countries: they took over the land and set up a kind of state within a
state. Their disciplined fighting "squadrons" were ruthless killers of Japanese, but also of any Filipinos suspected of collaboration or indiscipline.
Even the formidable Dayang Dayang was punished when she broke the
rules. Abiding by her own motto that "those who don't get rich in this war
have liquid brains," she went on a spree of looting anything from water
buffalo to jewelry. She was caught, tried, and shot.[29]

José Laurel and most of his cohorts in the puppet government, such as
Manuel Roxas and Benigno Aquino, were from the elite landowning families, whose power the Huks would have wished to overturn, even without
a Japanese occupation. In the sense of serving under the Japanese and
promoting an anti-American, pan-Asianist cause, these men were certainly collaborators. But like the collaboration of other Asian nationalists
in former Western colonies, their motives were complex. Laurel was an
impressive man, a graduate of Yale Law School, a senator, and an associate justice on the supreme court in Manila. Although a member of the
colonial elite, he may genuinely have believed that the Japanese brand of
militant "Asianism" was needed to wean Filipinos from their dependence
on the United States. Similar claims have been made by European quislings, who thought that a new order run by Nazi Germany would restore
some vim to their decadent societies. But they were betraying independent nations; Laurel, Sukarno, and others were operating under foreign
rule or domination, before and after the Japanese landed.

Laurel remained a prime target for Filipino guerrillas. While playing a
round of golf with Benigno Aquino at the Wack Wack Golf and Country
Club in June 1943, he was shot in the back by two assailants, one of whom
bore the name of "Little Joe." Later that year, after he had recovered from
his wounds, Laurel attended the Greater East Asian Conference in Tokyo,
where Asian brotherhood and cooperation were pledged. The following
year he agreed to declare war on the United States as the Japanese
demanded.

Meanwhile, in October 1944, General MacArthur made good on his promise to the Filipinos that he would return. To heighten the drama of this event, he waded through the surf of Leyte, a scowling figure in aviator glasses. Indeed, he waded through the surf more than once to get the image just right for the newsreels. And he reenacted the same scene in Luzon. In his usual biblical manner, sure to appeal to the Catholic as well as the mystical side of Filipinos, he intoned: "People of the Philippines, I have returned. By the grace of the Almighty God our forces stand again on Philippine soil—soil consecrated in the blood of our two peoples . . . Rally to me . . . The guidance of divine God points the way."

On their long and often bloody slog to Manila, American troops were actively helped by the Huks. The Filipino guerrillas drove out the Japanese from various parts of central Luzon, hoisted the Stars and Stripes along with the Philippine flag, and set up their own administration, expecting U.S. support for the independent Philippine socialist republic. This is not how it turned out, however. Despite some words of admiration for the fighting spirit of the Huks, MacArthur was persuaded to bring back the people he knew best, that is to say, the old landowning elite. Despite his vow to "run to earth every disloyal Filipino," MacArthur made Manuel Roxas, a loyal member of Laurel's puppet government, a brigadier general in the U.S. Army.[30]

The Huks were ordered to give up their arms. When they refused, they were arrested. Some were jailed without formal charges. One of them was Luis Taruc, who shared his prison cell with several former collaborators of the Japanese. When fifty thousand peasants marched in protest to the Malacañang Palace in Manila, Taruc was released, but many of his troops remained in prison. What followed is murky. Arms were twisted, money changed hands. The Manila press came out with stories about Laurel and his colleagues having acted as impeccable patriots during the war, shielding the Filipinos as best they could from the horrors inflicted by Japanese. MacArthur called Roxas "one of the prime factors in the guerilla movement." Filipinos were admonished to be above "petty jealousy" and "unnecessary misunderstanding," for such things would only "impede progress."[31]

As the first president of the Philippines after World War II, Manuel Roxas declared an amnesty for wartime collaborators. Thousands were released from jail. Luis Taruc took to the hills and the Huks became the Army to Liberate the People, forerunners of the Maoist New People's Army. And the old landowning families, firmly in charge of their possessions once more, continued to rule Philippine politics. This was still true in 1986, after "people power" had toppled Ferdinand Marcos, inspiring the world with the promise of Asian democracy. The People Power star was Corazon "Cory" Aquino, Benigno Aquino's daughter-in-law. Her vice president was "Doy" Laurel, José Laurel's son. As I write, the president is Benigno Aquino III, Cory's eldest son.

. . .

TO RESTORE LEGITIMACY to a ravaged country, it helps to have a symbolic figure to rally around. This can be a respected monarch, a resistance hero, even a foreign general who can plausibly pose as a savior. General Douglas MacArthur's style may have been a little too histrionic, even egomaniacal, for some tastes, but he played this role to perfection in both Japan and the Philippines. His use of the Japanese emperor as the symbol of continuity was calculated to complement his own performance as the temporary shogun. Heroism, including MacArthur's, is often a matter of theater, and in some cases a complete fiction. In North Korea, for example, "the Great Leader" Kim Il-sung was imposed by the Soviet Red Army as a great partisan hero who had single-handedly chased the Japanese from the Korean peninsula. In fact, he had spent most of the war in a Soviet army training camp near Khabarovsk.

When the figureheads of prewar regimes have lost credibility, and legitimacy is contested, you have the basis for civil war. This broke out in full force in Greece, and after a year of shadowboxing and skirmishes, it would soon cut loose in China too.

The Generalissimo Chiang Kai-shek, known to Americans as the Gimo, and to the U.S. commander in wartime China, General Joseph "Vinegar Joe" Stilwell, as "Peanut Head," was nominally in control of

China. But many parts of the country were clearly beyond his grasp. The Gimo presented himself, and was depicted in American wartime propaganda, as a great national leader, heroically battling the Japanese. But Mao Zedong, holed up with his guerrilla army in the northwest, promoted the idea—not entirely spurious—that Chiang had been passive at best, and a Japanese collaborator against the Communists at worst. The Communists claimed that *they* were the true resisters, and Mao the national hero. In fact, both sides often regarded the Japanese as a tedious sideshow which the U.S. would eventually take care of. The real enemies were at home. As two hostile Chinese armies squared up for the final battle, one heroic narrative was pitted against another.

The two leaders actually met, just after the war, at an extended meeting in the Nationalist wartime capital of Chungking (now spelled Chongqing). They couldn't really bear one another, but had a mutual respect for the other's toughness, like bosses of rival gangs. Mao toasted Chiang at the official banquet and wished him ten thousand years of prosperity. In an attempt to stave off an all-out civil war, polite talks were held about power-sharing, who would occupy which parts of the country, what kind of government might be shared, and so forth. No firm agreement was reached. Mao told his comrades that the statement of peaceful intentions ("democracy," "one army," Chiang's "leadership") was "a mere scrap of paper."[32] But the U.S. ambassador to China, the mentally unstable Patrick J. Hurley, who disconcerted his Chinese hosts by treating them to whooping Choctaw Indian war cries, still had hopes that he, a man who knew next to nothing about China, would bring the two parties together. Any American who harbored doubts on this issue, including diplomats with far greater expertise, was, in Hurley's fevered imagination, a traitor and probably a communist.

The *New York Times* reporter had it right. In a report on October 6, he wrote, "To Westerners who wonder why there is so much haggling, it should be pointed out that troops are the decisive factor in Chinese politics." Not only that, but arms were decisive too. Which is why Chiang insisted on his sole right to disarm the Japanese, and why Mao chose to ignore this.

In the summer of 1945, Chiang's Nationalists had an army of about four million men spread all over southern and central China. But they were badly trained, ill disciplined, and often led by corrupt and incompetent officers. "Puppet armies," set up by the Japanese in Manchukuo, northern China, and Nanking (Nanjing), the old Nationalist capital, numbered more than a million men. They were better equipped than the Nationalists and often superior fighters, and, rather than disarm them, Chiang preferred to absorb them into his own ranks. Then there was an assortment of provincial warlords whose loyalties were self-seeking and always fluid.

Chinese civilians dreaded the arrival of Nationalists in their villages and towns, for the troops tended to behave more like brigands than soldiers, looting property, robbing food, raping women, and shanghaiing peasants into the army. Puppet troops and warlord armies were not much better. The Communists, who had about a million soldiers and two million militiamen, could be ruthless masters too, but they at least understood the value of discipline. Their public relations were better; they realized that a war is partly won by propaganda. Being seen as a heroic people's army was one of their greatest assets.

Much of China was not just horribly damaged, but also corrupted by foreign occupation, warlord misrule, and many years of purges and counter-purges in a civil conflict that was often as brutal as the war with Japan. Donald Keene, the Japan scholar, was a young U.S. Navy officer stationed in Tsingtao (Qingdao), a port city on the Yellow Sea, known for its naval base, European architecture, and German-style beer breweries. The Japanese Imperial Navy was still in town when the U.S. Marines arrived, and Keene soon sensed "something fishy in the atmosphere," a stink of skullduggery and corruption; "the charge of collaborationist is no less pervasive than the generally suspicious character of the city itself."[33]

He found that Tsingtao was still run by Chinese who had been appointed by the Japanese, generally louche characters who had done well out of foreign occupation. He found Japanese naval officers bragging of their wartime exploits, and Chinese being purged for collaboration by other Chinese whose records were just as blemished; they simply wanted to loot the suspects' properties. Tsingtao was a place of seedy carpet-baggers, gangsters, spies with shifting loyalties, and Japanese who still behaved like a master race. None of this was unique to Tsingtao. Keene heard reports from other parts of China about heavily armed Japanese troops being asked by Nationalists to help contain the Communists. These reports were entirely accurate. Some right-wing factions in Chiang's government actually wanted to start a war with the Communists immediately with active Japanese assistance. The cautious Gimo did not wish to go that far, but large numbers of Japanese troops were used to guard Chinese railroads and many other installations against possible Communist attacks.

There were reprisals against the Japanese here and there, but on the whole, both Nationalists and Communists concentrated on their domestic enemies, and the Nationalists needed Japanese help. Besides, the relationship between Chinese and Japanese was often too tangled for simple solutions.

One of the most grotesque scenes of the immediate postwar period took place in Nanking, where tens of thousands, possibly hundreds of thousands, of Chinese had been massacred and raped by Japanese troops on an extended rampage in 1937. The Rape of Nanking still stands as one of the worst atrocities of World War II. General Okamura Yasuji was not directly involved in the massacre, but he was responsible for equally horrendous war crimes. In 1938, troops under his command murdered countless civilians with chemical weapons. His scorched-earth policy in 1942, known by Chinese as the "Three Alls" ("kill all, burn all, loot all"), caused the deaths of more than two million people. All men between fifteen and sixty were targeted for killing on suspicion of being anti-Japanese. And the systematic kidnapping of young women, mostly from Korea, to serve as sex slaves in Japanese army brothels, also happened on Okamura's watch.

But when this same Okamura surrendered to General Ho Yin-chin in Nanking on September 9, 1945, General Ho bowed to the Japanese general and apologized for the indignity of this humiliating ceremony. Ho, who had been trained at the military academy in Tokyo under Okamura, called him "sensei," teacher.[34] And so, Okamura continued to occupy the Foreign Ministry building in Nanking as though nothing had changed. After he was finally indicted for war crimes by a court in Nanking three years later, the Generalissimo himself shielded him from further indignities and kept him on as a military adviser to the Nationalists. Okamura Yasuji died peacefully in his bed in 1966.

The key to the Chinese civil war really lay in Manchuria. The first to take this heartland of heavy industries and mines, set up and run by the Japanese, would be in an almost unassailable position. As we have seen, the Soviets got there first and stripped all the industrial and financial assets that could be transported to the Soviet Union. Their first encounters with the Chinese Communists were not always cordial. The ill-kempt Chinese soldiers were often treated with disdain by Soviet Red Army officers, and the lack of interpreters made communication almost impossible. Besides, Stalin, for the sake of Big Power stability, had decided for the time being to recognize the Generalissimo as the legitimate Chinese leader.

Still, more and more Chinese Communists from the Eighth Route Army were trickling into Manchuria, and in some areas, with the help of sympathetic Soviet commanders, took over the local administration. Since most Communist cadres had neither knowledge nor roots in a region that most Chinese regarded as the Wild North, home of nomads and savages, this was not an easy task. Apart from tense relations with the Soviets, and the sinister presence of roaming gangs of puppet troops, the Eighth Route Army also had to deal with an assortment of local underground guerrilla bands, some attached to the Soviets, some belonging to provincial warlords, and some affiliated with the Nationalist camp. Just as the Nationalists wanted Japanese and American help to fight the Communists, the Communists asked for Soviet assistance to suppress "anti-Soviet bandits."[35]

Meanwhile, unnerved by the Communist advance into Manchuria, Chiang implored the Americans to transport Nationalist troops to the north. The U.S. complied, but halfheartedly, as the official policy was not to get involved in "fratricidal conflict." Nationalists often arrived in the northeast too late, not in enough numbers, and sometimes in the wrong places.

The curious nature of the snake pit that was Manchuria—things would get much worse; up to three hundred thousand civilians died of starvation and disease in the siege of Changchun by the Communists in 1948—might best be illustrated by the story of a famous brothel in Andong, on the North Korean border.

Andong, in the fall of 1945, was quite a cosmopolitan place, a kind of Casablanca of northeast Asia, filled not only with Manchurian Chinese, but also with Koreans, Russians, and about seventy thousand Japanese, not just resident soldiers and civilians, but refugees from other parts of the former puppet state. Terrified of what the advancing Soviet troops would do to them, particularly to the women, Japanese civic leaders decided to set up a "cabaret," in fact a brothel, to distract unwelcome Russian attentions from Japanese womenfolk. The task of running this establishment, named the Annei Hanten (Annei Inn), was a woman in her early forties named O-Machi. A former geisha in Japanese hot spring resorts, she recruited Japanese women, many of whom had no experience in this line of business, by appealing to their patriotism. They were asked to sacrifice themselves for the sake of Japan; they were the female kamikazes of Andong.[36]

There is still a stone memorial to O-Machi in her native town in Japan, erected by grateful Japanese whose lives she helped to save. O-Machi prided herself on being "apolitical" and treated all men, high and low, Russian, Japanese, or Chinese, equally. Although it was initially meant for the entertainment of the Russians, O-Machi's "cabaret" attracted other types of customers too, including Japanese ex-officers and community leaders, as well as Chinese collaborators with the Japanese who were now on the Nationalist side, and even Chinese and Japanese communists.

With the patrons fueled by sake, vodka, and Chinese wines, all kinds of information was exchanged at the Annei Inn.

O-Machi passed on to the Japanese what she heard from the Soviets about troop movements and planned arrests. Many Japanese, alerted in this way, managed to disappear at opportune times. There were spies and double-spies, "red radishes" (anticommunists pretending to be "reds"), and "blue radishes," or communist infiltrators in the guise of anticommunists. Plots were hatched, and counterplots. A marriage was arranged at the Annei Inn between a Japanese employee and a Chinese Communist spy (who may have been a red radish), so the Japanese might find out what the Communists were up to. A military coup from the right, planned by Chinese Nationalists and Japanese ex-officers who had hidden artillery in the hills above Andong, was organized at the Annei Inn, but fell apart when the expected Nationalist troops failed to arrive.

Instead, not much later, the Communist Eighth Army marched into town, replacing the Soviet Red Army. Nothing seemed to change at first. The Communists were treated to a Chinese banquet at the Annei Inn, albeit without female dalliance, which the cadres disapproved of. Perhaps the Japanese could be of assistance to the Eight Route Army? Former employees of the Japanese Manchukuo electric company set up a "red theater" troupe, hoping to stage socialist "people's plays."

But the honeymoon didn't last. The Communists decided that an international brothel was not what the new order called for. And, suspecting Japanese involvement in the failed Nationalist coup, the Communists arrested O-Machi and several Japanese community leaders as Nationalist spies. Not a great deal is known about what happened to them next. O-Machi was in prison for about a year, and then, in September 1946, she was executed on the bank of the Yalu River. Whether or not she was a spy, and for whom, remains a mystery.

. . .

FRANCE DESPERATELY NEEDED a sense of continuity and legitimacy. The embers of civil war had never stopped burning since the Revolution in 1789. Royalists and Catholic reactionaries had fought the Republic from its inception. German occupation and the Vichy regime had given them a temporary victory. General de Gaulle was hardly a man of the left, nor did he hold much truck with the messy business of multiparty democracy. But for the sake of continuity he set himself up as the natural heir of the Republic which he despised. Even though the National Assembly had voted constituent power to him in 1940, Marshal Pétain's Vichy government was declared illegitimate as soon as the war was over. De Gaulle's task in 1944 and 1945 was to stitch France back together again.

The fear of civil war was real enough. The communists, who had played such a major role in the resistance, had as far back as 1941 already prepared lists of enemies to purge. They wanted to go after the industrialists as much as the petty thugs in the pro-Nazi *milice*. The important thing for all former resisters was to punish the elite, the leaders, and not only the *"lampistes,"* the subordinates hanging from the lampposts while the bosses went free.[37] Aware that justice had to be seen to be done, and that France couldn't afford purges on a scale that would put intolerable strains on an already battered society, de Gaulle wanted to get the process over with as quickly as possible, preferably within a few months. The deadline was February 1945, which was of course impossible.

By then, however, much of the rough justice had already been done. Prisoners had been lynched, more than four thousand people summarily executed, some hanged by frenzied mobs. Especially in the south of France, some regions were almost in a state of anarchy. De Gaulle disapproved of this kind of thing; only the state should have the right to punish. A number of former resisters were, in fact, arrested for showing excessive zeal in executing suspected collaborators. But could de Gaulle really blame them? Pascal Copeau, a journalist and resistance leader in the south, wrote in January 1945:

> During four terrible years the best of the French learned to kill, to assassinate, to sabotage, to derail trains, sometimes to pillage and always to disobey what they were told was the law . . . Who taught

these Frenchmen, who gave them the order to assassinate? Who if
not you, *mon général?*[38]

For the state to regain the monopoly of force, the first thing de Gaulle
had to do was disarm the resistance. Since the *maquisards,* the underground fighters in the French resistance, had gained their weapons at
great risk during the war, while de Gaulle had lived in the safety of the
British capital, this was a delicate task. Communist resisters still had hopes
of a second French Revolution for which they would need their guns. But
this possibility was cut short, not only because the communists lacked
enough support for such a radical venture in France, but also because
Stalin made it clear that he would not back a revolution in the American
sphere of influence. Stalin had other fish to fry. So he told the French
communists to back off. And de Gaulle made a deal with the French communists. If they wanted permission for their leader Maurice Thorez, who
had deserted the French army in 1939 and fled to Moscow, to come home
without being tried for his treachery, they had to agree to disband their
armed fighters. Many weapons were still carefully hidden in remote
farms, under floorboards, or in warehouses. But the communists gave in,
and little by little the state regained control.

Some token figures, who had been particularly egregious or conspicuous during the occupation years, were put on trial. Pétain himself was
tried, but was deemed to be too old and too grand to be executed after
being convicted for treason, so he was banished instead to a small island
off the Atlantic coast. He died there, and was buried there, a demented
old man stripped of his military honors, an ignominious fate which enraged some of his loyal followers. An attempt was made by loyalists in 1973
to rectify Pétain's humiliation by disinterring his bones and transporting
them to the mainland for a more glorious burial in the cemetery for the
war dead. When the Maréchal's bones were discovered in the garage of
his lawyer, Maître Jacques Isorni, they were swiftly shipped back to the
island where, as far as is known, they remain.

Pétain's most powerful minister during the war, the unprepossessing and much loathed Pierre Laval, was less lucky, and his death sentence was carried out. He was shot in October 1945 after his attempt to take cyanide failed because the poison was too old to be effective.

There were other war crime trials too. But before they could be seen to be at all persuasive, the judiciary had to be purged. Since only one judge in wartime France had refused to sign an oath of loyalty to Marshal Pétain, this was a problem. A purge commission of judges and former resisters had to decide whether magistrates had behaved as loyal Frenchmen. According to this very loose definition, 266 were judged to have been deficient. The same criteria were applied to civil servants. Sanctions ranged from temporary suspension on half pay to losing one's job, as well as one's civic rights, entirely. Out of roughly a million civil servants, 11,343 received some kind of sanction and 5,000 lost their positions. As was true in other countries, the business and industrial elite was left largely unscathed. Notorious sympathizers with the Nazis, such as the founder of L'Oréal, the perfume manufacturer, were not touched at all.

Louis Renault, founder of the Renault motor car factory, was not a known Nazi. In his own account, he was given an awful choice by the Germans: either let his concern be taken over by Daimler Benz and see his workers shipped to Germany, or make vehicles for the German armed forces. He chose the latter. In communist resistance circles Renault was seen as the worst kind of industrial traitor, a class enemy of the first order. The communist newspaper L'Humanité wrote in August 1944: "The directors of the Renault factories must be made to pay for the lives of Allied soldiers killed as a result of their enthusiasm to equip the enemy."[39] Since so few other industrialists were purged, it is possible that Renault was a scapegoat, a bone thrown by the Gaullists to the left. Renault died of head wounds in prison before he could defend himself in a trial.

In many cases of purged magistrates and civil servants, they quickly returned to their former positions, or to respectable careers in the private sector. The case of Maurice Papon, the last Frenchman to be tried for war crimes, was typical in every way except for its final denouement. Responsible as a senior police official in Bordeaux for sending more than a thousand Jews to the camps, he was never tried in 1945. On the contrary, he went on to become an important bureaucrat in various governments: secretary of state under de Gaulle, prefect of Corsica, prefect in Algeria where he helped to crush the anticolonial rebellion, and Paris police chief, again under de Gaulle, who presented him with the Legion of Honour for services to the French state, and finally budget minister under President Valéry Giscard d'Estaing. What was unusual about Papon's illustrious career is that he lived long enough for his unsavory past to catch up with him. His trial began in 1995. He was jailed in 1999, released in 2002, and fined the equivalent of about three thousand dollars for illegally wearing his Legion of Honour decoration, of which he had been stripped.

De Gaulle mended France in the same way Japan was "mended," or Italy, or Belgium, or even Germany: by keeping damage to the prewar elites to a minimum. He could not afford to polarize his nation further. The expertise of businessmen, financiers, lawyers, professors, doctors, and bureaucrats was needed. They had the right contacts.

Men and women of the resistance had played their roles as brave mavericks risking their lives while others kept their heads down. They had done this for all manner of reasons: religious faith, political ideology, boredom, rage, a thirst for adventure, or just a sense of decency. But in the choices they made they were less representative of most people than were the opportunists and sycophants.

Punishment for wrongdoing, in France no more or less than anywhere else, was frequently symbolic anyway, and the distribution was hardly fair. While the establishment remained relatively untouched, a former prostitute and possible spy named Marthe Richard lobbied in December 1945 to close the brothels in Paris. A year later the *Loi Marthe Richard* closed all the brothels in France. The reason given for this most un-French zeal was that brothels during the German occupation had been the principal centers of "collaboration."

CHAPTER 6

THE RULE
OF LAW

Once the Communist Eighth Route Army had reached Manchuria in the late fall of 1945 and began to take city after city from the Chinese Nationalists who had replaced the Japanese in some places, and the Soviet Red Army in others, so-called people's trials quickly followed. Justice was swift, the rituals of law rudimentary, if not primitive.

In some instances, Chinese newspapers would advertise for witnesses, asking anyone with a complaint against former officials of Manchukuo, the Japanese puppet state, to come forward. In Andong, on the northern border with Korea, a primary school was set up as a "people's court." Many of the charges were trivial, sometimes driven by the sour residue of long repressed resentments. A rickshaw puller accused a Japanese businessman of smashing his lantern without offering compensation. A young man remembered how his father was worked so hard as a coolie for a Japanese

firm that he died from exhaustion. The accused, who usually had no rec-
ollection of their misdeeds, were lucky if they got off with very stiff fines.

There were far more serious accusations too. People's justice proved to
be just as quick in those cases. In December three hundred Japanese and
Chinese functionaries in Andong Province were executed on the banks of
the Yalu River. These were all men who had worked in the Manchukuo
administration. There is an eyewitness account of what happened to two
of them, the ex-governor of Andong, a Chinese named Cao, and his Japanese vice-governor, Watanabe.

Black hoods were placed over their heads, and Manchukuo decorations pinned to their chests—badges of honor transformed into badges of
shame. They were then paraded through the main street of Andong in
horse-drawn carts, with their heads bowed down in a show of contrition,
holding up wooden signs daubed with crimson characters for all to see.
One said "reactionary," the other "puppet." The people's court was held in
the open air, with large crowds trying to get a glimpse of the culprits. The
people's judge shouted out: "What shall we do with them?" "Kill! Kill!"
the mob screamed back. And so it was decided. The men were led to the
banks of the river, made to kneel, and shot from behind. (It is said that
Watanabe's ears were cut off first, but this is disputed.)[1]

What is interesting about this account is not the almost farcical nature
of such summary trials, but the need for them. Why should the Chinese
Communists have insisted on trials at all? Why not simply shoot the ras-
cals? Clearly they wanted the executions to appear lawful. Establishing a
form of legality is a necessary condition of legitimacy, even in a dictatorship, or perhaps especially in a dictatorship. But the concept of the law in
show trials is entirely political. The trial is a ritual to demonstrate the authority of the Communist Party. The accused in Andong were charged
not only with being instruments of the Japanese puppet state, but also,
after liberation, of collaborating with the "reactionary" Chinese Nationalists, something they could hardly have avoided as the Nationalists took
over Andong before the Communists arrived. Since the Communist Party
supposedly represented the power of the people, the role of the people in

this ceremonial affair was to shout out the verdict that was expected of them.

China was neither exotic nor unusual in this respect. Similar people's courts sprung up wherever communists took control. The Hungarian writer Sándor Márai was in Budapest when the Hungarian "antifascists" appointed by the Soviet Red Army came to power in 1945. This was not yet a communist regime. Stalin decided that a gradual takeover would be better; he didn't wish to startle the Western Allies too soon. Elections were held in November in which the communists did not do well. But the Soviets decided who would serve in the government anyway, and the communists, in the words of their leader Mátyás Rákosi, cut off their rivals "like slices of salami" until 1949, when the People's Republic of Hungary finally came into being.

Budapest in 1945 had been badly damaged in the siege by Soviet and Romanian troops which had lasted for several months. The Royal Palace was a wreck, electricity was down, telephones didn't work, bridges had collapsed into the Danube like wounded steel monsters. Food was scarce. Strangers would walk into people's houses, expecting to be fed, or just to make trouble (to express their "hatred," wrote Márai). Rich bourgeois homes were popular targets for popular anger. A new set of authorities had taken over the old torture chambers of the fascist Arrow Cross, and gangsters raced through the potholed streets in imported American cars. Márai noted a strangely feverish activity in town, which only later changed into a sullen listlessness. He wrote in his memoir that "dishonesty spread like the bubonic plague." Law and justice, he said, "did not exist anywhere, but People's Tribunals were already operating, and political executions afforded daily entertainment to the unemployed rabble, as in the time of Caligula in Rome."[2]

Since 1920, in the absence of the king, Hungary had been under the reign of Admiral Miklós Horthy, officially His Serene Highness the Regent of the Kingdom of Hungary. This peculiar arrangement followed one year of Communist Party rule in 1919, under Béla Kun. White Terror followed Red Terror. Horthy, a very reactionary figure, though not exactly a fascist, had a lifelong horror of communism, which he, like many others, tended to associate with Jews, whom he disliked but not to the extent of wishing them all dead. He foolishly formed an alliance with Nazi Germany in the late 1930s, but balked when Hitler asked for his assistance in the Holocaust. Hungarian Jews were harassed but were shielded from mass murder until 1944, when the Germans decided to take things in hand and invaded the country. German armies were being decimated in the Soviet Union, with supply lines overstretched, materiel in short supply, and transportation routes cut off by enemy forces. But in a show of where true Nazi priorities lay, more than four hundred thousand Hungarian Jews were deported with ruthless efficiency. Most were killed in Auschwitz-Birkenau. Horthy was forced to step down and the fiercely anti-Semitic Arrow Cross leader Ferenc Szálasi ruled for 163 days with great brutality, offering Adolf Eichmann, officially in charge of the Final Solution in Budapest, all the help he needed.

The antifascist regime in 1945 made it clear that the entire Arrow Cross government would have to be tried, and execution was a foregone conclusion. A common factor in people's justice was that the outcome of the trials was rarely in doubt. This was not just a matter for the people's tribunal itself. The press too had to play its part. Béla Imrédy, a former banker turned Jew-baiter and prime minister in 1938, was described during his trial by a well-known journalist as "a spindly gnome, fumbling about in terror," "a pitifully despicable figure," "wriggling like a grey lizard under the weight of evidence."[3] It should be said that the Western press was often no less lurid when it came to prosecuting Nazis.

A Hungarian legal expert made it clear what the real purpose of the people's trials was. It was not to try and punish the war criminals for "simple breaches of the law," but "to retaliate against them for the political mistakes they made . . ."[4] The courts consisted of Party people and trade unionists, led by professional judges. Sometimes the professionals, especially in the court of appeal, called the National Council of People's Courts, were criticized for being too lenient. The communist paper *Szabad Nép* cried out that "the professional judges sitting in the Council have completely forgotten that they are the people's judges. The people do not play around with documents; they do not look for mitigating circumstances in the case of war criminals but demand merciless retaliation against those who are responsible for their misery, suffering, and humiliation."[5]

The past, too, was placed firmly under control of the new order, which, to repeat, was Soviet-controlled but not yet a communist regime. Judges held some of the defendants, such as László Bárdossy, prime minister in 1941, responsible for crushing "democracy" in 1919. What had been crushed was, in fact, Béla Kun's communist dictatorship of the proletariat, which had its own forms of thuggishness and summary justice. It wasn't just men, however, who were on trial, but the system they represented. László Budinszky, the minister of justice in the Arrow Cross government, was sentenced to death because, according to the National Council, "twenty-five years of an oppressive ruling system" had "brought the country to the brink of destruction."[6]

In terms of numbers, Hungary was actually not among the harshest nations. More than 57,000 people were prosecuted for collaboration in Belgium.[7] In the Netherlands 50,000 collaborators were sentenced.[8] In Hungary it was closer to 27,000. In Greece, 48,956 people were held in prison by the end of 1945. But they were all leftists.

Greece is the best example of a country where both communists and anticommunists abused trials for political ends, occasionally even at the same time. People's Courts were set up already in 1943, in areas liberated by the left-wing National People's Liberation Army, the military arm of the National Liberation Front, controlled by communists. The courts were part of the effort to set up a socialist state in occupied Greece. People's Courts, consisting of ELAS fighters and other "comrades"—farmers, truck drivers, and the like—dealt with criminals, war criminals, and collaborators.[9] Sentences tended to be severe. Many people were executed, after a quick trial, or sometimes without any trial, by the guerrillas.

The most common crime in rural Greece appears to have been cattle thieving. In the village of Deskati, in central Greece, the guerrillas were too busy to deal with cattle thieves, however. Villagers were simply told that cattle thieving had to stop, since "we have no prisons or exiles to detain thieves. If one of you is caught stealing, he will just tell us what he prefers that we cut, his head or his feet. The decision is yours."[10] Apparently this was effective. The thieving, in Deskati at any rate, stopped. The People's Court did deal with the curious case of a young man, who declared his love to one girl, but then proposed to marry another. The court gave him a stark choice, marry the first girl or be executed. He hesitated until the very last minute before deciding that he would rather live.

People's Courts were merciless to collaborators. This meant policemen and gendarmes who worked for the Germans, promoters of fascism, Slavic-speakers in Macedonia who cooperated with the Bulgarian efforts to slice off a chunk of Greek territory, or class enemies who stood in the way of the revolution. When Greece was liberated from the Germans in the spring of 1944, there was a short period when it was run by a Government of National Unity, but even after that government established official courts to prosecute collaborators, People's Courts continued to function in certain areas well into 1945. That Greece had two distinct legal systems, one official one with only limited authority, the other unofficial but with more territory under its control, shows how little consensus there was about political legitimacy. There was no Greek General de Gaulle to patch things over between communists and conservatives, between royalists and liberals. The scars of war were too raw, the rifts ran too deep.

Some efforts were made by the official government courts to try top wartime collaborators, such as the Greek prime ministers under the Germans, but the trials were slow, and frequently awkward. The quisling prime ministers claimed patriotism, as quislings always do, as their reason for staying in office. Indeed, they said, with some evidence, they had been told to stay in their posts to make the best of an appalling situation by the Greek government in exile. The head of the exiled government was none other than the first post-Liberation prime minister, Georgios Papandreou, whose son and grandson would later serve as prime ministers too.

More violent collaborators, such as the vicious Security Battalions, were hardly prosecuted at all. In fact, after the so-called Varkiza

Agreement was signed in February 1945, compelling the left to lay down its arms in anticipation of a national referendum about the future government, the Greek world turned topsy-turvy. Former right-wing collaborators, who refused to hand in their weapons, terrorized everyone they suspected of left-wing sympathies. People were arrested, and sometimes shot, just for having been part of a People's Court. This time the state within the state was run by rightist militias beyond the government's control. Since the police were mostly on the side of the right, courts could not rely on them to arrest former collaborators. Instead, old partisans and their supporters were beaten up, tortured, and jailed by armed men who had worked for the Germans. For every former collaborator in prison in 1945, there were ten supporters of ELAS.

An ex-partisan named Panayiotis gave up his gun in February 1945. A few weeks later he was picked up by former members of a Security Battalion, taken to a nearby school, suspended upside down, beaten with rifle butts. They then whipped his bare feet to a pulp so that he had to crawl all the way to his house. Still, he mused from his later home in Australia, he had been lucky "to be the victim only of the first flood of Fascist revenge," for he "missed the second flood when the Fascists sentenced thousands to death in their courts."[11] Liberation in Greece, then, was not the end of civil strife and the seemingly endless cycles of vengeance, but the beginning of much worse to come.

. . .

ALMOST TWO AND A HALF thousand years before, Athens was the setting for Aeschylus's great tragedy the *Eumenides*. It is all about a murder case. Orestes had killed his mother to avenge her slaying of his father. These foul deeds set off the furies of vengeance, the agents of an eye for an eye to see that justice was done. Pallas Athena, goddess of wisdom and the city's patroness, convinced Orestes to submit to a trial. Only through rational argument in a court of law, she told him, could the furies of vengeance be pacified. But even rational argument in court does not always lead to a clear conclusion; the jury was tied, and so it was up to Athena's divine judgment to let Orestes go. But the furies were indeed calmed by her decision:

> And never more these walls within
> Shall echo fierce sedition's din,
> Unslaked with blood and crime;
> The thirsty dust shall never more
> Suck up the darkly streaming gore
> Of civic broils, shed out in wrath
> And vengeance, crying death for death![12]

Not much has changed since Athena watched over her great city. Ending the cycle of vengeance is still the best reason for conducting trials. But one problem with trials after a war, or the fall of a dictatorship, is that there are too many potential defendants. Stalin was perhaps indulging in one of his dark little jokes when he told Churchill at the Teheran Conference in 1943 that fifty thousand German officers should be shot out of hand. Churchill, apparently, was not amused and stomped out of the room in a fury. But Stalin had a point. Even if there is no such thing as collective guilt, there are far more guilty people than can possibly be tried. Yet justice must be seen to be done. This does not mean that individuals put on trial for crimes committed by thousands, and abetted by millions, are scapegoats. But there are cases where people are tried symbolically, as it were, because others cannot be put on trial, because they are too numerous, or out of reach, or protected for political reasons.

One of the worst Japanese war criminals was a medical doctor named Ishii Shiro, an arrogant loner who first made a name for himself as the inventor of a water filtering system. He once startled the Japanese emperor at a demonstration of his device by urinating into his filtered water and inviting His Majesty to take a sip. The emperor politely declined. Ishii was also an early and rather obsessive promoter of bacteriological and chemical warfare. In 1936 the Imperial Army gave him permission to build a vast secret facility near Harbin in Manchukuo, where he could experiment to his heart's content. Not only did Ishii, and his able staff of Unit 731, including a microbiologist named Kitano Masaji, experiment with bubonic plague, cholera, and other diseases, but thousands of prisoners were used for anything that took the doctors' fancy. The human guinea pigs, mostly Chinese, but also Russians and even a few American POWs, were known as "logs," or "monkeys." Some were exposed to freezing experiments, some were hung upside down to see how long it would take before they choked, some were cut open without anesthesia and had organs removed, and some were injected with lethal germs. Another specialty of Unit 731 was to infect large numbers of rats with deadly bacteria and drop them over Chinese cities together with thousands of fleas in porcelain bombs suspended from little parachutes.

The "water filtering facility" near Harbin was destroyed by the retreating Japanese, along with the remaining prisoners in the summer of 1945, just before the Soviet Red Army arrived. The ruins now contain a "patriotic museum" with waxworks of Ishii and his colleagues conducting live vivisections. Ishii, Kitano, and some others actually made it back to Japan. More junior doctors were captured by the Soviets, who put them on trial for war crimes. Even as General MacArthur promised to try Japanese war criminals (always excepting the emperor himself), Ishii quickly disappeared from sight. He managed to convince his interrogators, led by Major General Charles Willoughby, MacArthur's "pet fascist," that the data culled from his experiments in China would be of great interest to the U.S. Army. Willoughby was convinced that the human experiments, not as readily available to U.S. doctors, had produced vital information. There was considerable worry that the Soviet Union was ahead of the U.S. in this type of research, and, as a U.S. Army medical specialist later wrote in a memo to State Department officials, human experiments were better than animal experiments, and since "any war crimes trial would completely reveal such data to all nations, it is felt that such publicity must be avoided in the interest of defense and national security of the US."[13]

Lieutenant General Ishii Shiro died peacefully in Tokyo in 1959. The commissioner of his funeral was his deputy and later successor at

Unit 731, Lieutenant General Kitano Masaji. Kitano, an expert in blood experiments, went on to head Green Cross Corporation, the first commercial blood bank in Japan. There are few traces left by these men, except for the ruins of the prison labs near Harbin, and one curious monument found in a disused rat cellar in China, erected by Kitano in honor of the rodents he dissected for research purposes.

• • •

THE FIRST WAR CRIME TRIAL in the Pacific War theater was that of General Yamashita Tomoyuki, also known (respectfully in Japan, fearfully elsewhere) as "the Tiger of Malaya." General Yamashita actually spent very little time in Malaya, but he had earned his sobriquet by taking Singapore in February 1942 against a much superior force; thirty thousand Japanese against more than one hundred thousand British and Commonwealth troops. The humiliating scene of Yamashita facing Lieutenant General Arthur Percival, with the Japanese general demanding an immediate answer to his question whether Percival would surrender, "yes or no!", can still be seen as a waxwork tableau in the amusement park on Singapore's Sentosa Island.

The wartime prime minister, General Tojo, who disliked and distrusted Yamashita, perhaps because of the latter's superior military skills, or perhaps because of Yamashita's skepticism about Japan's war with the Western powers, whisked him away from Southeast Asia and sidelined him in Manchukuo, where he had no chance to shine on any battlefield. Yamashita was dispatched back to the region only after Tojo lost power in 1944. He was handed the thankless task of defending the Philippines after it had become indefensible.

At his trial during the fall of 1945, Yamashita was accused of permitting one of the worst atrocities committed during World War II: the Massacre of Manila.

There was no dispute about the events. Trapped in Manila by advancing U.S. forces in February 1945, more than twenty thousand Japanese, mostly from the Imperial Japanese Navy, were ordered to fight to the death and to lay as much of the Philippine capital to waste as they could while they were at it. After plunging into the ample supplies of beer and rice wine put at their disposal, the troops went on an orgy of violence. Women of all ages were raped and murdered. Babies and children were smashed against walls or ripped apart with bayonets. Men were mutilated for sport and massacred. Hospitals were raided and patients burned alive. Houses and buildings were torched. And all the while, the city was being bombarded and shelled by U.S. tanks and howitzers while Japanese fought off American attacks using flamethrowers and bazookas. After one month of mayhem, Manila was a flaming ruin. The devastation was on a par with that of Warsaw, and up to one hundred thousand Filipinos were murdered in this extended bloody spree.

Manila had been General Douglas MacArthur's stamping grounds before the war. His rooms at the Manila Hotel had been badly damaged in the carnage. He recorded his state of shock as he watched the attack on the hotel from a distance: "Suddenly the penthouse blazed into flame. They had fired it. I watched, with indescribable feelings, the destruction of my fine military library, my souvenirs, my personal belongings of a lifetime . . . I was tasting to the last acid dregs the bitterness of a devastated and beloved home."[14]

For MacArthur, what happened in Manila in 1945, and what had happened there three years earlier when he had been driven out by the Japanese Imperial Army under General Homma Masaharu, was a personal affront. So the trials held against both Homma and Yamashita in Manila were rather personal too. Orders came from Washington to arrange for speedy trials, following decisions made by the Allies in June 1945 to prosecute war criminals. But they were to be held by military commissions under MacArthur's command. The judges were appointed by MacArthur, and the procedures were managed by MacArthur. This left many people who were there with the distinct impression that these were not trials to still the fires of vengeance; they *were* a form of vengeance.

Someone had to pay for the heinous crimes in Manila, as well as other brutalities perpetrated under Japanese occupation: the Bataan Death

March in April 1942, the starving of POWs, the destruction of Filipino villages and towns, the torture prisons under the *Kempeitai*. Since the collaborators in the Filipino elite were largely shielded from prosecution, and the most active Filipino resisters were being crushed in the name of anti-communism, a villain was badly needed to show Filipinos, who had suffered so much, that justice was still being done; a brutal face had to be matched to the nameless mass of killers. Someone had to hang.

Yamashita Tomoyuki certainly looked the part: a squat, bullnecked figure with narrow, myopic eyes, his was the cartoon image of the Japanese war criminal. Filipinos were encouraged to come and watch him being tried in the old High Commissioner's residence. One old woman was so embittered by her wartime experiences that she carried rocks in her purse to throw at the monstrous Japanese general. And some American reporters did their best to condemn him before he was convicted. As the trial reporter for *Yank* put it nicely: "From the very beginning of the proceedings, you couldn't find a sucker to bet two *pesos* to 200 on Yamashita's acquittal."[15]

Yank continued: "In the bullet-scarred High Commissioner's office, where he once ruled as a conqueror, general Yamashita stood before a tribunal of five as a war criminal. He was receiving a fair trial, according to law—something the general hadn't bothered to give his victims."

This is almost entirely wrong. Yamashita had never been in the High Commissioner's office before and certainly not as a conqueror. He arrived in the Philippines for the first time just before MacArthur waded ashore in the Leyte Gulf. Defending the country was by then a hopeless cause. Yamashita didn't know the terrain. The chain of command was in tatters. His troops were scattered all over the Philippine islands. Communications had been largely cut. Food was no longer getting to most soldiers roaming in the mountains. Gasoline was barely available. Troops were badly trained and demoralized by hunger, exhaustion, and the tropical climate. Harassed by Filipino guerrillas and overwhelmed by superior U.S. forces, Yamashita had no chance to even see his troops, let alone lead them as a conqueror.

The Manila Massacre was at least partly the result of Japanese disarray. Yamashita's headquarters were in the mountains almost two hundred miles from Manila. Knowing that he could not defend the capital, he ordered all Japanese troops to withdraw, including the marines who were nominally under his command. Manila would be an open city, with only sixteen hundred soldiers left behind to guard military supplies. But naval commanders dithered. Some wanted to fight to the last man. Others talked about a retreat but not before wrecking the harbor facilities. It wasn't clear who commanded whom. Orders went unanswered. As so often happened in the Japanese armed forces, middle-ranking officers took things into their own hands and the most zealous prevailed. By the time a furious Yamashita insisted once again on their retreat, the soldiers and sailors were stuck in Manila with no way out but death.

Yamashita certainly didn't face a fair trial. The judges were military desk officers whose knowledge of the law was as scanty as their understanding of battlefield conditions. One of them was so bored that he spent much of the time in deep slumber. MacArthur put all necessary resources at the disposal of the prosecution, whereas the defense lawyers were picked at the last possible minute. There was no time to investigate the more than sixty criminal charges, and even more were added just before the trial began. Rules of evidence and other procedures seemed to be arbitrary, if not rigged. In a "special proclamation" from MacArthur, the rules established by the Allies in June were restated: "The Tribunal shall not be bound by technical rules of evidence. It shall adopt and apply to the greatest possible extent expeditious and non-technical procedure, and shall admit any evidence which it deems to have probative value. All purported admissions or statements of the accused are admissible."[16]

Alas for Yamashita, this included dubious affidavits as well as statements by a shady couple of former collaborators who tried to cleanse their reputations by subjecting the court to wild allegations of the Japanese general's alleged plans to exterminate the entire Filipino people. There was also a succession of traumatized witnesses who told their stories about horrific violence during the sacking of Manila. In the words of the *Yank* report: "Sobbing girl witnesses told of repeated attacks by Jap soldiers. Many of the girls said they were forced to submit at bayonet point . . . An extract of the testimony: '. . . A 12-year old was lying on a mat on the floor. She was covered with blood and the mat where she was lying was saturated with blood.'"

Again, few doubted the truth of such stories. The question was whether Yamashita could have known about them, and even then, could have done anything to stop the violence. At the Nuremberg trials, which were taking place at that same time, German generals were prosecuted only for war crimes which they ordered, abetted, or personally participated in. There was no proof of Yamashita's having done any of these things. Indeed, his orders pointed in the opposite direction. And so he was charged with a crime that had not existed before, namely, of not being able to stop atrocities committed by troops over whom he had no control and who deliberately went against his orders. *Yank* stated with confidence that Yamashita had been treated fairly "according to law." If so, it was no law that Yamashita, or any other military commander, had been even remotely aware of. On December 7, 1945, the anniversary of the Japanese attack on Pearl Harbor, Yamashita Tomoyuki was sentenced to death by hanging. He bowed to his judges and thanked the United States for giving him the benefit of "upright American officers and gentlemen as defense counsel." Major Robert Kerr told a newspaper reporter that he had come to the Pacific expecting to shoot Japs on the beaches, not to hang them, but that it was all the same to him.[17]

An appeal for mercy was turned down by MacArthur. Yamashita's lawyers tried, without much hope, to get the U.S. Supreme Court to declare the trial invalid. Their claim was that military commissions had no right to try former enemies in peacetime, and that the trial had not been conducted fairly. The Supreme Court decided not to contest the legitimacy of the military court, but two justices were highly critical of the trial. In the dissenting words of one of them, Justice Wiley B. Rutledge Jr.: "It is not in our tradition for anyone to be charged with crime which is defined after his conduct . . . Mass guilt we do not impute to individuals, perhaps in any case but certainly in none where the person is not charged or shown actively to have participated in or knowingly to have failed in taking action to prevent the wrongs done by others, having both the duty and the power to do so."[18]

Yamashita declared that his conscience was clear. The evidence of the Manila Massacre, of which he claimed to have been ignorant when it occurred, had shocked him profoundly. He told his lawyers that it would have been hard for him to return to Japan anyway after leaving so many dead men behind. After hearing his sentence, he wrote a short poem:

The world I knew is now a shameful place
There will never come a better time
For me to die.[19]

Yamashita was hanged on February 23, 1946, at Los Baños, a picturesque hot spring resort south of Manila.

· · ·

GENERAL MACARTHUR HAD a peculiar and interesting justification for his implacability in the case of his Japanese adversary. Yamashita, in his view, had brought dishonor to the military profession.

The traditions of the fighting men are long and honorable. They are based on the noblest of human traits—sacrifice. This officer . . . has failed this irrevocable standard; has failed his duty to his troops, to his country, to his enemy, to mankind; has failed utterly his soldierly faith. The transgressions resulting therefrom as revealed by the trial are a blot upon the military profession, a stain upon civilization and constitute a memory of shame and dishonor that can never be forgotten.[20]

In his grandiose way, MacArthur was voicing a common sentiment of his time: the trials against the German and Japanese war criminals, as well as their accomplices, were not just about restoring the rule of law, but about restoring "civilization." This was the language of prosecutors in the Nuremberg and Tokyo trials as well. It was typical of MacArthur to equate civilization with "soldierly faith." The idea of conducting trials to blot out the "memory of shame and dishonor," on the other hand, was most important in countries humiliated by foreign occupation. Perhaps MacArthur was thinking of the Philippines. But that memory was like a shadow everywhere hanging over trials of national leaders who had collaborated with the occupiers, even when they had done so for what were in their own minds honorable reasons.

One thing Pierre Laval, the highest-ranking minister in two Vichy governments, and Anton Mussert, "the Leader" of the Dutch National Socialist Movement (NSB), had in common was that they saw themselves as honorable men, patriots who had done everything in their power to serve the interests of their countries. They faced their executioners, after being swiftly tried for treason in the fall and winter of 1945, convinced that they were dying as martyrs and would one day be not only vindicated but recognized as saviors. The other thing they had in common was that they died as the most hated men in their respective nations. There were worse, more brutal people. Neither Laval nor Mussert had a taste for violence. On the contrary, Laval had been a left-wing pacifist during World War I and never lost his personal loathing for military action, even, some would argue, in defense of his nation. He was a born appeaser, confident that he could outwit even the devil in negotiations. As he told his lawyer: "To collaborate to me meant to negotiate."[21] Both men, in fact, had stood up to the Germans on occasion to defend the interests of some of their compatriots, usually without much success. And yet they were almost universally loathed. Which is why the outcome of their trials had to be a foregone conclusion.

Laval and Mussert, like Yamashita Tomoyuki, were physically unprepossessing, which can't have helped. Mussert was a pudgy, round-faced little man so utterly unsuited to the black uniforms and leather coats of his fascist party that he always managed to look ridiculous. Laval, never a booted and uniformed rabble-rouser, but a professional politician in striped trousers and a habitual white necktie, had the air of a disreputable merchant of questionable goods: short, dark, greasy-haired, with hooded eyes and a perpetual cigarette staining his crooked teeth and bushy moustache. Mussert started his professional life as an engineer (he designed autobahns, among other things), and Laval as a lawyer. Laval was by far the more successful politician. He led the French government twice before the war and in 1931 was *Time* magazine's Man of the Year—"calm, magisterial and popular"—for shepherding France through the Great Depression.[22] Mussert was already somewhat of a figure of fun to most Dutch people at the end of the 1930s; strutting around in black shirts was not the Dutch style.

Neither man wished for a German invasion of his country; they *were* nationalists, after all. In Laval's Man of the Year profile, *Time* magazine actually praised him for being tough on Germany. He made a short-lived pact, in 1935, with Britain and Italy, to stop German rearmament. Anything to avoid another war. Yet, when it happened, both Mussert and Laval saw German occupation as an opportunity, as though their finest hour had finally come. Mussert had visions of a new Europe, dominated by "Germanic peoples," led by Hitler, to be sure, but with an autonomous National Socialist Netherlands under the leadership of Mussert himself. Fascist idealism held no attraction for Laval. But after having spent the last years of the 1930s in the political wilderness, he saw a role for himself as France's savior in difficult times. With the old Marshal Pétain as the patriarchal figurehead, Laval would negotiate the best terms he could for France. More than that: he, too, saw possibilities in the new Europe, with France as Germany's chief ally in purging the continent of that twin modern scourge: Anglo-Jewish capital and Russian bolshevism. As he said in a radio speech in 1942, in words that would come back to haunt him three years later: "I desire the victory of Germany, for without it, bolshevism would tomorrow install itself everywhere."[23]

Before the war, neither Mussert nor Laval had shown any evidence of a personal animosity towards Jews. Mussert had few close friends, but one of the few happened to be Jewish, and in the 1930s he encouraged Jews to become members of his movement. There were "good Jews," in his thinking, and "bad Jews." The bad ones were Jews who refused to join him, or criticized the Dutch National Socialist Movement (NSB), and were thus "un-Dutch." Unfortunately, Mussert's German comrades had more rigorous views on the matter, which was one of several issues of contention between him and the German SS. In 1940, he was obliged to expel the few remaining Jewish members from the NSB. For this, Mussert claimed deep regret. How deep is not clear, since he did develop a detailed plan in 1938 to move European Jews to Dutch, French, and British Guiana, a scheme that failed to interest either Himmler or Hitler. (What the British and French thought is unrecorded.) And Mussert had no scruples about enriching himself, as well as his friends and relatives, from robbed Jewish properties.[24]

Laval never shared the strong anti-Semitism of the French far right. He, too, had Jewish friends and worked closely with Jewish colleagues. Yet he was minister of state in 1940 when, unprompted by the Germans, the Vichy French *statut des juifs* (statute on Jews) deprived Jews of their civil rights. He later tried to save French-born Jews from deportation, but only at the price of delivering tens of thousands of foreign-born Jews into the maw of the Third Reich. This included naturalized French citizens who were deprived of their citizenship during the war.

By setting themselves up as saviors through collaboration, vainglorious figures like Mussert and Laval walked straight into a trap the Germans had laid for them, Mussert from a mixture of ideological delusion and vanity, and Laval from being morally obtuse and putting too much stock in his own cleverness. Neither of them realized that his nationalist illusions—France and the Netherlands as significant partners in the new Europe—hardly fit German plans for total domination. These patriotic quislings were useful to the Germans, as long as they took the heat for unpopular, indeed criminal, German enterprises. Bit by bit, they gave in, sometimes grudgingly, sometimes carelessly. Mussert incorporated his storm troopers into the German SS and swore an oath of loyalty to Hitler, who was, in Mussert's cloudy imagination, the Führer not just of Germany but of all the "Germanic peoples." Laval collaborated not only by handing over French workers to German industry in exchange for some French POWs, but also by establishing a militia against French partisans and sending large numbers of Jews to their deaths. It was Laval, not the Germans, who insisted that Jewish children should be deported to Poland with the adults in July 1942, ostensibly to keep families together.

As a result of their behavior, both men were despised and distrusted by the Germans as "bourgeois nationalists" and detested by their own countrymen as the embodiments of everything that was sordid and shameful about the occupation. They were hated even by the most ardently pro-German Nazis in their own countries, the kind of people who enthusiastically worked for Hitler's Reich. Since Mussert and Laval had so few people on their side, after Liberation they were the perfect candidates for trials and punishment. Making examples of the two most conspicuous faces of collaboration made millions who had not shown conspicuous courage themselves feel better.

Pétain was tried and sentenced to death as well, but age and distinction saved him. His trial was never part of de Gaulle's plans. The general would have much preferred for the old man to have stayed in Swiss exile. Pétain had requested the trial himself. If this proved to be an embarrassment, the French certainly could not bring themselves to shoot the hero of Verdun. So he was banished instead. Laval, in a sense, took his place as an object of blame. In the words of a popular French ditty of the time: "Pétain, to sleep / Laval to the stake / de Gaulle to work." *Time* magazine, the very same journal that had praised Laval so effusively more than a decade before, wrote:

Last week Pierre Laval came to judgment. With him came none of the dreadful pity, the sense of terrible duty that had been in every Frenchman's heart during the trial, sentence and commutation to life imprisonment of old Marshal Pétain. The elimination of Pierre Laval, a necessary chore, might have been a satisfying vengeance. He made it a shameful farce.[25]

This was a trifle unfair. The trial was a farce, to be sure, but Laval was not the main culprit. De Gaulle did not like the business of purges and trials, but had to get to work, as the ditty demanded, and wanted this one to be over with as quickly as possible. A referendum on the postwar constitution was scheduled for October 21, so Laval's verdict had to be in by then. Laval sat in his prison cell, smoking five packets of American cigarettes a day, fuming because he was denied access to the documents he had carefully accumulated for his defense. A note retrieved from his suitcase when he was flown back to France from his temporary refuge in Germany revealed his bitter state of mind: "It is a strange paradox. Here I am, obliged to justify myself before a court for policies and conduct which should have earned me the recognition of my country. Both before the war, and during those unhappy years of occupation, I know I fulfilled my duty."[26]

Mussert, always prone to delusions, had found a new fantasy in his prison cell on the Dutch North Sea coast: he had designed a giant submarine vessel. Since, in his view, the Americans would surely wish to make full use of his invention, he was expecting to be sent to the United States. The last weeks of his life were spent learning English, another venture that ended in failure.

One of the blemishes on Laval's trial, which Laval himself was not slow to point out, was the fact that his judges and prosecutor had served the same Vichy regime that he did, and pledged their allegiance to Pétain as well. The attorney general, André Mornet, had even sat on a committee to denaturalize Jews. The jury was made up of members of parliament and of the resistance.

Jacques Charpentier, head of the Paris bar, sensing the ritual air of a fight to the death in a Spanish corrida, recalled: "Like Andalusian urchins who leap into the arena, members of the jury insulted the accused and intervened in the proceedings. The court judged [Laval] without giving him a hearing . . . Just as they revitalized Robespierre to drag him to the scaffold, Laval's corpse was revived so they could throw a still living traitor to the lions of the people."[27]

The dramatic high point of the trial was Laval's protest against the bias of the judges: "You can condemn me!" he shouted, banging the table with his briefcase engraved with his presidential title: "You can do away with me; but you do not have the right to vilify me!" Whereupon one of the jurors shouted: "Shut up, traitor!" Laval screamed in fury that he was a Frenchman who loved his country. And the jurors shouted back that he was a "bastard" (*salaud*) who "deserved twelve bullets" from the firing squad.[28] Laval concluded that he would prefer to remain silent rather than be an "accomplice" in a "judicial crime." When a juror shouted, "He'll never change!" Laval replied with as much truth and conviction: "No, and I never will."[29]

The trial in the Royal Palace in The Hague against Mussert was more dignified, but the result there too was never in doubt. The prosecutor, J. Zaaijer, observed in his opening statement that "even without a trial, we already know what sentence Mussert deserves," which was a rather odd way to begin a legal proceeding. Mussert's able defender, Wijckerheld Bisdom, later recalled that in those early postwar days there was a consensus of opinion that the "worst National Socialists—and first of all Mussert, who was seen as the essence of the Dutch National Socialism—could not get away with anything less than a death sentence."[30] The trials were driven by public sentiment; the law was responding to the street.

Mussert defended himself in a rousing speech against the charge of treason. Waving his arms, as though still addressing a party rally, he claimed that his aim had never been to deliver his country to alien rule. On the contrary, his ideal had always been to form a Dutch government to secure Dutch interests when a victorious Germany would change the order in Europe. Aiding the German cause, he explained, had been essential "to keep Asia from Europe's door." Overcome with the fire of his own rhetoric, Mussert forgot himself and addressed the court as "my loyal followers," a phrase that provoked a ripple of laughter in what were otherwise pretty grim proceedings.[31]

The former Dutch leader's execution, too, was a more sober occasion than the end of Laval. He was taken into the dunes outside The Hague, where the Germans had shot many Dutch partisans before, and tied to a simple stake. When a Protestant minister bade him farewell, Mussert apologized for the fact that he was no longer able to shake his hand. Twelve men aimed their rifles and Mussert was dead.

Laval fretted for a long time that he would be disfigured by a shot in the face. His lawyers reassured him that executions were done quite neatly these days. He then botched a suicide attempt by swallowing an old cyanide capsule that was no longer strong enough to kill him quickly. Nursed back to life, but still limping, Laval was taken to a site near the prison walls, dressed in a dark suit with his customary white tie and a scarf in the French red, white, and blue. He insisted that his lawyers remain in eyesight, as he "would like to see you while I die." His last words were "*Vive la France!*" The shots rang out and he slumped to the right. A sergeant then did what Laval had most dreaded and shot him again, just to make sure, making a mess of his face. A young journalist who was there described the scene: "People ran towards the stake and picked up fragments of the wood. The most valued splinters were soaked in blood."[32]

To call Mussert or Laval scapegoats would not be quite right. There is no doubt that they were guilty of giving aid to the enemy. They had chosen to cooperate with the Nazi occupation. And their trials served the purpose for which they were mainly intended, in Mussert's case to avoid the type of "wild" vengeance that had claimed so many lives in France. His swift—all too swift—trial also served as a justification for the Dutch authorities to let go of many lesser figures who were flooding already overcrowded jails and prison camps. The violent deaths of Mussert and Laval were shows of justice; they demonstrated that the postwar governments were doing their work. Laval's fatal end, like Mussert's, was a way to wind down retribution and start rebuilding his country.

But if these trials fulfilled one of Athena's aims in the *Eumenides*, by slaking the thirst for revenge, the speed of the trials, their foregone conclusions, and especially in Laval's case, the highly flawed procedures made the cause of due legal process rather dubious. In the perhaps overdramatic conclusion of one observer, "Laval's trial is unpardonable because it made the French doubt the reality of French justice . . . Now the harm is done. French justice is discredited. Laval had won the last round and completed the demoralization of the country."[33]

· · ·

SOME ARGUED IN 1945 that the cause of law would have been better served by dispensing with legal niceties altogether and simply shooting the main culprits out of hand. George F. Kennan, who was actively involved in European policy as a U.S. diplomat, noted his distaste for war crime trials in his memoirs. In the case of the Nazi leaders, he said, their crimes had been so awful that there was nothing to be gained in keeping them alive. He wrote: "I personally considered that it would have been best if the Allied commanders had had standing instructions that if any of these men fell into the hands of Allied forces they should, once their identity had been established beyond doubt, be executed forthwith."[34]

These views were shared by others. U.S. Secretary of State Cordell Hull, for example, told his British and Soviet colleagues that he would ideally "take Hitler and Mussolini and Tojo and their arch accomplices and bring them before a drumhead court-martial. And at sunrise the following day there would occur a historic incident."[35] Hull, incidentally, was the winner of the Nobel Peace Prize in 1945. The British Foreign Office circulated a memorandum during the war voicing its opposition to postwar trials against such figures as Heinrich Himmler, leader of the SS, because their "guilt was so black" that it was "beyond the scope of any judicial process."[36] Churchill, too, took the view that it would be best "to line them up and shoot them." This sounds a little harsh, but trying men, especially in the company of Soviet judges whose own hands were far from clean, knowing that there could be only one outcome, might do

more harm than good to the rule of law. The Soviets, who insisted on trials even as Churchill was still resisting the idea, startled the Allied judges
by proposing a toast to the execution of the German leaders before the
trials in Nuremberg had even begun.

In a curious way, Germans in 1945 might have been more impressed
by executions too. Visiting Hamburg, the English poet Stephen Spender
was told that most Germans regarded the trial against the men and women
responsible for the atrocities at Bergen-Belsen as mere propaganda: "These
Germans said that if the accused were really guilty, and if we knew they
were, why didn't we dispose of the whole matter quickly and condemn
them?"[37]

By speaking of the extreme nature of Himmler's guilt, the Foreign Office memo was on to one serious problem: were the laws as they stood at
the time really equipped to deal with crimes which went a long way beyond conventional war crimes? People may not yet have been aware of the
full scale and nature of the Nazi attempt to exterminate an entire people
on ideological grounds. The word "Holocaust" was not yet in use. But the
Allies had seen enough to know that they were dealing with something
previously unheard of. The legal implications were already clear before
Nuremberg.

Only Soviet troops had actually seen what remained of the Nazi death
camps in Poland. But Western Allies were profoundly shaken by what they
found in concentration camps, such as Dachau, Buchenwald, and Bergen-
Belsen. General Eisenhower visited a subsidiary camp to Buchenwald
called Ohrdruf on April 12, 1945. The SS had only just vacated this camp
near Weimar. They had not had enough time to burn all the corpses
which lay around like smashed dolls amidst the prisoners who were too
weak to get up. The reporter for *Yank* wrote: "The cold had preserved their
bodies and deadened the stench so that you could walk around them and
inspect them at fairly close range." The same reporter, Sergeant Saul Lev-
itt, noted that "Blood had caked the ground around the bodies into pancakes of red mud."[38]

Eisenhower wrote to his wife, Mamie: "I never dreamed that such cruelty, bestiality, and savagery could really exist in this world." He wanted American soldiers to see it, so they would be in no doubt why they were fighting this war. He wanted reporters to visit the camps so that no one could ever pretend that these horrendous crimes were figments of propaganda. American senators and congressmen, as well as British members of Parliament, were asked to tour the camps. The reason why Eisenhower wanted everything to be recorded—the piles of rotting corpses, the crematoria and torture rooms—is that this was something "beyond the American mind to comprehend."[39] Churchill received a message from Eisenhower saying that "the discoveries, particularly at Weimar, far surpassed anything previously exposed."[40]

Not only were local German citizens forced to walk through the camps, pinching their noses behind handkerchiefs, averting their gaze, vomiting around the pits filled with blackened corpses, but people in Allied cities too were meant to see what the Germans had done. This was not always welcome. In London, moviegoers "unable to stomach atrocity newsreels" tried to walk out of the Leicester Square Theatre, only to be blocked at the door by British soldiers. The *Daily Mirror* reported that "people walked out of cinemas all over the country, and in many places there were soldiers to tell them to go back and face it." One soldier was quoted as saying: "Many people don't believe such things could be. These films are proof. It is everybody's duty to know."[41]

Or, as the *Times* of London put it: "That the civilized world should part with the last pretext for persisting in a skeptical and therefore indifferent response to such atrocities is of paramount importance for civilization itself."[42] This idea, very much espoused by Eisenhower, that knowledge of the human capacity for evil would make the rest of us behave better, that to learn about the worst would be a civilizing process, was one of the chief motives for the ensuing war crime trials.

That the horrors of Ohrdruf still paled in comparison to the death factories in Poland was not yet fully acknowledged, which is why some contemporary reports referred to the German concentration camps as "death camps." That most of the victims in many of these camps were

Jews was also a point that was rarely stressed in news reports of the time. But Eisenhower wanted the world to know, for the sake of civilization, and one of the ways to record what had happened, and to give the people of Germany, as well as everywhere else, a moral education, was to broaden the scope of war crime trials. On June 2, Eisenhower asked the Combined Chiefs of Staff to prosecute the people who had been responsible for these atrocities.

The first concentration camp trial actually took place in Bergen-Belsen under British, not American, jurisdiction. This dress rehearsal, as it were, of the Nuremberg Trials of 1945–46, showed how difficult it would be to apply existing laws and legal procedures to the Nazi crimes. Several of the defendants, including the vile Belsen commandant Josef Kramer and the camp doctor Fritz Klein, had worked at Auschwitz-Birkenau as well. It was decided that they should also be tried for what they had done there, so their active roles in mass extermination were yoked to their criminal neglect in an insanely overcrowded concentration camp where thousands of starving people were left to die of typhus and other diseases. Newspaper headlines, even in the august pages of the *Times*, shouted daily about "Scenes Worthy of Dante"; "Witness from Gas Chamber"; "Millions Done to Death"; "Girls Hanged"; "Story of Girl Beaten to Death." Kramer ("the Monster of Belsen") and the twenty-two-year-old blond female guard, Irma Grese ("the beautiful beast" or "the hyena from Auschwitz"), became household names from a Nazi chamber of horrors. Whether this really helped people understand the Nazi crimes is doubtful. Being shocked by the depravity of individual "beasts" and "monsters" was, in a way, to miss the point of the criminal system that made their deeds seem almost normal. The much criticized report by Hannah Arendt on the Eichmann trial in Jerusalem in 1961 was clearer on this matter. When mass murder on ideological grounds becomes government policy, everyone, all the way down from the Reichsführer SS to the petty bureaucrat in charge of railway schedules, is complicit. The beasts just got their hands dirtier than most.

The Belsen trial, like so many others, had to be completed as quickly as possible; the outraged public demanded no less. But the British took pride in staging a proper and fair trial, with none of the antics that discredited the proceedings against Laval. The problem was with the law itself. A British Military Court, such as the one operating in the showy nineteenth-century school building in Lüneburg, could prosecute only war crimes, defined as "violations of the law and usages of war."[43]

After lengthy legalistic wrangling between the lawyers about the right of the court to try the defendants in the first place, several witnesses gave shocking accounts of what they had seen. Sophia Litwinska, from Lublin, had survived Auschwitz as well as Belsen. She described how on Christmas Eve, 1941, women were stripped of their rags, chased from their barracks, and made to stand naked in the freezing cold until 5 A.M. on Christmas Day, when they were dumped in front of the gas chamber from a tip-up truck.

Dr. Hadassah Bimko, from Sosnowiec, who later married Josef Rosensaft, the Zionist organizer, took the stand on September 21, under a bank of 3,000-watt lamps. She had lost her parents, brother, husband, and six-year-old son in Auschwitz. As a medical orderly she had had a close view of what went on there: the selections, in which both Kramer and Dr. Klein had taken part; the medical experiments; and the gas chambers, where Jewish prisoners in the *Sonderkommando* (the death camp work unit) were made to do the most terrible work: cutting the hair, removing the dead bodies, operating the crematorium. Those selected for the gas chambers, she told the court in words reported by the *Times*, "were taken away naked and waited several days without food or drink till trucks arrived to take them to the crematorium." After choking to death in the gas chamber, she continued, "the dead were removed on trolleys which ran on rails out of a room at the opposite side from the changing room. Every so often members of the *Sonderkommando* were killed and their places taken by others. However, it was generally possible to preserve some sort of record." From this, she related, friends of hers in the camp calculated that four million Jews had been destroyed.[44]

Dr. Bimko's friends overestimated the numbers, but the bare facts of the Jewish genocide had been laid before the British Military Court. Counsel for the defense tried to probe the witnesses for inconsistencies and memory lapses. Kramer's lawyer, Major Winwood, perhaps pandering to prejudices which were still far from rare, described the inmates of Belsen as "the dregs of the ghettoes of central Europe," a remark for which he later apologized by claiming that he had "acted only as the mouthpiece of the accused."[45] But few people could have been left in any doubt that the atrocities described had taken place. This was, however, a military court, and some of the lawyers could think only in military terms. Major Winwood compared his client to a "Battalion Commander in whose area is a prison, the orders for which come from Battalion Headquarters." SS Hauptsturmführer Kramer was a simple soldier who had followed orders. There was no evidence of any "deliberate attempt" to "ill-treat the internees."[46]

Colonel Herbert A. Smith, professor of international law at London University, was brought in by the defense to argue that no war crimes had been committed. What happened in the camps had had "nothing to do with the war," and were not considered to be crimes at all at the place and time they were committed. After all, he said, Himmler had been chief of police and was entitled to give orders which "as such had the force of law."[47]

None of these arguments saved Kramer or Grese or Dr. Klein from the gallows. But two things, at least, could be concluded from the Belsen trial. People may not yet have fully grasped the difference between death camps and concentration camps, or known how much killing had already been done in eastern Europe before the gas chambers even got going. But that the Nazi murder machine was systematic should have been known to anyone who read a newspaper in 1945. This is what made remarks about deliberate "ill-treatment" so obtuse. In his pedantic way, Professor Smith had made another thing clear: existing laws and conventions on war crimes were no longer adequate to deal with the nature and scale of what the Nazis had done. This set the stage for the biggest war crimes trial of all, which began in Nuremberg on November 20, four days after the "beasts" of Belsen received their death sentences.

. . .

ONE THING TO BE SAID about the twenty-one defendants at Nuremberg is that they did not look like beasts. Observers remarked how utterly ordinary they appeared, these pale, tired figures in their ragged suits: Joachim von Ribbentrop, chin raised and eyes shut in a show of wounded dignity; Hermann Goering slumped in his chair, using his handkerchief to wipe spittle from his smirking lips; Hans Frank hiding his eyes behind dark glasses; Fritz Sauckel, the slave labor chief, looking like a timid concierge; Hjalmar Schacht turning away from the others as though in fear of contamination; and Julius Streicher twitching and fidgeting. Rudolf Hess, rocking back and forth, his eyes staring madly under his thick eyebrows, did look rather strange, but he was quite possibly demented.

There was only one man in the Nuremberg Palace of Justice, apart from some of the witnesses, who had felt the full force of what these men had engineered. Few would have known his name, or even noticed his presence among the hundreds of lawyers, translators, court clerks, judges, military policemen, and journalists. Ernst Michel was a junior reporter for a German press agency. Next to his byline it said 104995, his number as a prisoner at Auschwitz. Michel was still a schoolboy when he was arrested in his hometown of Mannheim, Germany, in 1939 simply for being a Jew.

Just before the Soviet troops arrived at the Auschwitz camp, Michel was forced to go on a deadly march across the icy borderlands of Poland and Germany to Buchenwald. When the U.S. Army approached Buchenwald, he was marched off again, weighing eighty pounds. Somehow, he found the strength to make a dash for the woods, and survived for some time in the Soviet zone, covering his concentration camp garb for fear that people might find out that he was a Jew. Back in Mannheim at long last, he discovered that his parents had been murdered. All his relatives had disappeared as well. Since he had some high school English, he was given a job by American war crime investigators as an interpreter. He told me in New York City, "Germans always said they had helped the Jews. The hell they had! I even knew one of the people who said this, and he was a real Nazi."

Michel's next job was as a reporter at the Nuremberg trial. Anxious about his lack of professional qualifications, he was told just to write down what he saw. So there he was, six months after escaping a death march from Buchenwald, Auschwitz prisoner no. 104995, in the same room as Goering. He recalled in New York, more than six decades later: "I knew all their faces. And I was a free man, the only survivor to attend the trial. They were talking about *me*."

This is what Ernst Michel wrote in his first dispatch for the German news agency, the *Deutsche Allgemeine Nachrichtenagentur*:

> Often in those difficult hours in the camp I had been sustained by the faith that there would be a day when those responsible for this regime would be called before the bar. This faith gave me strength to keep going. Today this day is here. Today, only a few feet away from me, are the men who for all prisoners in the camps were symbols of destruction and who are now being tried for their deeds.[48]

No matter how flawed the Allied war crimes tribunals may have been—and flawed they certainly were, in Tokyo even more than in Nuremberg—Michel's statement could serve as an argument why they were just nonetheless. The other thing to be said in Nuremberg's favor is that the trial was, for the most part, extraordinarily boring. Rebecca West, who was there for the last few weeks before the verdicts, described the Palace of Justice as "a citadel of boredom." Everybody, she wrote, "within its walk was in the grip of extreme tedium . . . this was boredom on a huge historic scale. A machine was running down, a great machine, by which mankind, in spite of its infirmity of purpose and its frequent desire for death, has defended its life."[49]

At least, in Nuremberg, the law was taken seriously. This was not a quick trial driven by popular rage. Everything had to take its course, and so it went on, and on, and on, turning boredom into a sign of probity. Later trials, at the International Criminal Court in The Hague, would be molded in Nuremberg's image, in this respect above all. Tedium spiked the guns of vengeance. That was the whole point. Already in 1942, the Inter-Allied Commission on the Punishment of War Crimes was established by nine governments-in-exile in London. The Declaration of St. James's, named after the palace where they met, was written with the danger in mind of "acts of vengeance on the part of the general public." Which was why "the sense of justice of the civilized world" demanded that the free governments "place among their principal war aims the punishment, through the channel of organized justice, of those guilty of or responsible for these crimes."[50]

Awareness of the Nazi genocide of the Jews may still have been low at the time of the Nuremberg trials. But it was certainly not absent. In December 1942, just months after the gas chambers in the death camps began their operations, the German government was accused by the U.S. and European Allies of "a bestial policy of extermination of the Jewish people in Europe." That this didn't yet resonate fully with the public had the following reasons: what was happening was still unimaginable, and neither the U.S. nor British governments saw fit to give it much publicity; they did not want people to think that the war was fought to save the Jews.[51]

Although the Soviet Union had not joined the Western Allies in their condemnation of the Jewish genocide in 1942, and long after the war still chose to speak of victims of fascism without specific reference to the Jews, the Soviet prosecutors did mention it during the Nuremberg trials. General Roman A. Rudenko, one of five chief prosecutors at Nuremberg, had carried out bloody show trials himself, and was not above spreading mendacious propaganda at Nuremberg, such as blaming the Germans for murdering more than twenty thousand Polish officers in the woods of Katyn in 1940, knowing full well that the massacre had, in fact, been perpetrated by the Soviet secret police. But about the nature of the Jewish genocide, he left no doubt. Ernst Michel quoted Rudenko's speech in one of his dispatches: "The fascist conspirators planned the extermination to the last man of the Jewish population of the world and carried out the extermination throughout the whole of their activity from 1933 onwards.

The bestial destruction of the Jewish people took place in Ukraine, Belarus and the Baltic states."[52]

This was in fact a slight exaggeration; the extermination began in 1941, not 1933. Rudenko probably used the earlier date to stress the notion of a Nazi conspiracy, not just to kill the Jews, but to wage an aggressive war against the Soviet Union.

Since existing war crime laws, as already noted in the Belsen trial, applied only to acts of war, new ones had to be devised to cover the Third Reich before 1939, and for the systematic extermination of a people. That laws against killing Jews, or other innocent civilians, had not existed in Nazi Germany could not be allowed as an excuse. Nor were superior orders accepted as a valid reason for taking part in mass murder. The new legal category, "crimes against humanity," laid down in the London Charter of the International Military Tribunal of August 1945, broadened the concept of war crimes. Another legal novelty was "crimes against peace," meaning the planning and execution of an aggressive war. The planning preceded the actual warfare. This is where the idea of conspiracy came in. In Anglo-American law, people can be found guilty of conspiring to commit crimes. This law was applied to the Nazis (and later, on far more dubious grounds, to the Japanese military and government as well).

Sentencing people for breaking laws that were made after the crimes were actually committed is legally questionable. Submitting defendants from a defeated nation to the judgment of the victors is also vulnerable to criticism. Conducting the Tokyo Trials in 1946, as though wartime Japan had been the Asian mirror image of Nazi Germany, led to great distortions as well. Ernst Jünger, the right-wing nationalist writer, saw a great moral danger in making scoundrels into the victims of injustice. He described the Nuremberg court as one "consisting of murderers and puritans, their butcher's knives held by moral handles."[53]

But then Jünger, as an unreconstructed German nationalist whose contempt for the Americans more than matched his hatred of Soviet bolshevism, would say that. On balance, it was better to have held the trials, even if presided over by bloodstained or puritanical judges, than to have done what Churchill, Hull, and Kennan had suggested. Summary executions would have put the Allied victors on the same moral plane as the vanquished Nazis. Even though most Germans recognized the merits of the Nuremberg trials only later, when the bitterness of defeat had subsided and life was more secure, the trials provided a model for Germans to try Nazi war criminals themselves. That the Japanese didn't follow suit had many reasons: victors' justice was more blatant in Tokyo, more mistakes were made, the war itself was not perceived in the same manner, and there was no Nazi regime, no Holocaust, no Hitler.

So was justice done? Were the purges and trials enough to ensure that justice was seen to be done? The answer has to be no; too many criminals walked free, some to have flourishing careers, while others with far less guilt were punished as scapegoats. But total justice, even in the most favorable circumstances, is a utopian ideal. It would have been impossible to carry out, for both practical and political reasons. You cannot try millions of people. Punishment of the guilty had to be balanced by other interests. Too much zeal would have made the rebuilding of societies impossible. Too little effort to call the worst criminals to account would undermine any sense of decency. It was a delicate calibration that would inevitably be flawed. To grow up in Germany after the war, with ex-Nazis as teachers, doctors, university professors, diplomats, industrialists, and politicians, must have been galling. And not just in Germany or Japan. In many countries that had suffered German occupation, the old elites who came to terms with the Third Reich rarely fell very far from their high perches after the Nazis had left.

But perhaps the opportunism of man is sometimes his most useful quality. In June 1945, the former resistance fighter in Berlin, Ruth Andreas-Friedrich, discussed this very matter with a close friend, another brave resister. Her friend, Frank, said:

The Führer is dead. If you want to live you must eat. If you want to eat, and eat well, you'd better not be a Nazi. So they aren't Nazis. Therefore they weren't Nazis and they swear by all that's holy that they've never been . . . Denouncing and condemning don't help in the perfection of men. Help them get up when they've fallen. Give them a chance to atone for their sins. And then no more reprisals. Once and for all.[54]

That these words came from a man who had risked his life to resist the Nazis gives them moral weight. The same opportunism that made the banker accommodate himself to a murderous regime, financing companies that exploited slaves and set up factories near the death camps, could make him a loyal citizen of the postwar German democracy and an agent of its reconstruction. This may be unjust, even morally repellent. And Germany, as well as Japan, and even Italy, eventually paid a price. All three nations were plagued in the 1970s by revolutionary extremists whose acts of violence were inspired by a zealous conviction that their countries had never changed, that fascism was still alive in a different guise, carried on by some of the same people who had waged war in the 1940s. They believed it was their duty to resist, precisely because their parents had once failed to do so.

Robert H. Jackson, another of the chief prosecutors at Nuremberg (and a justice of the Supreme Court of the United States), was far from a revolutionary extremist. But he was convinced that the trial was more than an exercise in establishing guilt and punishing the guilty. He believed that he was speaking for civilization. The world would be a better place after Nuremberg. In his opening statement, he proudly claimed: "That four great nations, flushed with victory and stung with injury, stay the hand of vengeance and voluntarily submit their captive enemies to the judgment of the law is one of the most significant tributes that Power has ever paid to reason." But it was of the future that he was thinking when he added: "We must never forget that the record on which we judge these defendants is the record on which history will judge us tomorrow. To pass these defendants a poisoned chalice is to put it to our lips as well."[55]

Jackson was an idealist. The trials were part of an effort to build a better world, where the horrors of the past would never be repeated. After the trial was finally over, Jackson, accompanied by the British barrister Peter Calvocoressi, took a trip to Salzburg to attend the first music festival held there since 1939. They heard *Der Rosenkavalier*, and were particularly impressed by a young German singer named Elisabeth Schwarzkopf, who sang beautifully.

The great soprano actually had a small cloud hovering over her head; she had been a member of the Nazi Party since 1940, had performed recitals for SS officers on the eastern front, and had been romantically linked to an SS general and Nazi governor of Lower Austria. Perhaps she had done all these things out of conviction. Perhaps she was an opportunist. But her reputation soon recovered after the war. The person who was most responsible for this revival was the man she married in 1953, the British music impresario Walter Legge, a Jew.

PART 3

NEVER AGAIN

CHAPTER 7

BRIGHT CONFIDENT MORNING

Ernst Michel, the Nuremberg trial reporter, was one of thousands of men forced to leave Buchenwald on a cold and very often deadly march on April 8, 1945. Others left behind with a reduced number of SS guards knew that, if the Americans didn't arrive soon, they would surely be forced to follow the same hideous route, or be killed on the spot. Buchenwald, built on the crest of the lovely Ettersberg, was among the worst German concentration camps. One of the many tortures devised by the SS was to suspend men from trees with their elbows tied behind their backs. The screams of pain gave the name "singing forest" to this gruesome place where Goethe once contemplated the beauty of nature and conversed with a young poet friend who made notes of the great writer's observations.

There was a small underground organization in the camp, led by communists, who had hidden some guns in the barracks, as well as a

shortwave radio transmitter built by a Polish engineer. A desperate message went out on April 8: "To the Allies. To the army of General Patton.
This is the Buchenwald concentration camp. SOS. We request help. They
want to evacuate us. The SS wants to destroy us." Three minutes later
the answer came back: "KZ Bu. Hold out. Rushing to your aid. Staff of
Third Army."[1]

Few of the inmates had enough strength left to attack the SS guards,
or even to celebrate when the Americans finally came. But the fitter members of the camp resistance had decided not to wait for the Third Army's
arrival. The knowledge that deliverance was at hand was encouragement
enough. So they stormed the watchtowers and used the guns they had
hidden for just such an occasion to kill the remaining guards.

While the U.S. soldiers tried to get water and food to the desperately
ill and dying, the communist resistance leaders were already turning their
minds to the future. Almost immediately the gate of Buchenwald, with its
cast iron words *Jedem das Seine* ("To each his own"), was plastered with
signs that read: "Never Again!"

Never Again was a sentiment that all people who had suffered in history's worst human conflict would have shared. But it was, for many, more
than a sentiment; it was an ideal, perhaps a utopian ideal, a belief that a
new and better world could be created from the ashes. Even as many
people, including my father, pined for normal life to resume, others knew
that this could never be. The world would not simply revert to what it had
been before. The destruction of much of Europe and many parts of Asia,
the moral bankruptcy of old regimes, not least the colonial ones, the collapse of Nazism and fascism, all these things encouraged the belief that
there would be a completely new start. The year 1945 would be a blank
slate; history would be happily discarded; anything was possible. Hence
such phrases as "Germany, Year Zero" (*Deutschland, Stunde Null*), adopted by Roberto Rossellini as the title of his film about life in the ruins
of Berlin, or the *Gruppe Neubeginnen* (Group Starting Afresh), formed by
German social democrats exiled in London.

Of course, anything was not possible. There is no such thing as a blank slate in human affairs. History cannot be wished away. Besides, even though almost everyone agreed that past horrors should never recur, there was less agreement on just how to make sure of this. Utopian ideals, or even the more modest ambitions for political change, come in many different shapes.

We know what kind of revolutions the Soviet and Chinese communists had in mind. It is also clear what Asian nationalists in European colonies were hoping for. The goals of communist parties in western Europe, held in check by Stalin for his own geopolitical reasons, were more complicated. In any case, significant power—all the bravery of French or Italian partisans notwithstanding—would remain beyond their grasp. And yet a remarkable change did take place in western Europe, instigated by social democrats who had been planning for peace long before the war was over. The most radical change came not in formerly occupied countries, but in that conservative island country, that fortress of tradition whose heroic defiance had kept European hopes alive in the bleakest days of the war, when the Nazis appeared to be invincible: Great Britain.

· · ·

MY BRITISH GRANDMOTHER, rising to the patriotic fervor of a typical immigrants' daughter, was outraged when, in July 1945, her compatriots had the gall to vote against Winston Churchill's Conservatives: Winston out, Clement "Little Clemmie" Attlee, leader of the Labour Party, in, with a landslide. In a letter to my grandfather, still waiting to be released from army duty in India, she lamented the "black ingratitude" shown by the British towards "that great man to whom we owe everything." My grandfather, who was also born in a family of Jewish immigrants, was less vehement, but then he was in the army, and had been exposed to other views.

Even the victors in the July election were so surprised by the sheer scale of their triumph that there was a kind of hush before the celebration.

Trade union delegates, gathered in drafty northern hotels, watched in silence as figures displayed on giant screens went up and up. The final results: 393 seats to Labour, 213 to the Conservatives. A report in the *Manchester Guardian:* "The thunder on the Left changed to lightning as the election results flashed out Labour's victory. The only slow-motion today was in the rather stunned way people at first took it all . . . Through it all Mr. Attlee remained calm and discreet. He looked a little tired."[2]

A genuinely radical program came with an outward show of modesty. The most famous note of triumphalism only came a year later, when Hartley Shawcross, one of the chief prosecutors at Nuremberg and a far more glamorous figure than his party leader, told Parliament: "We are the masters at the moment and shall be for some considerable time."[3] That this instance of crowing was held against him for the rest of his life shows how careful the new guard was about not looking too proud.

After the election, the *Guardian* carried a comment from the United States: "Queer that England should go Socialist when America is getting rid of the New Dealers and going right back to the Centre."[4]

There were other interesting reactions from abroad. In Palestine, Jews rejoiced because Labour was thought to be more pro-Zionist than the Tories. The Greek royalists were shaken, but the embattled left was jubilant, hoping in vain for a change in its own fortunes. The Soviet news announced the Labour victory without comment. General Franco's fascist government in Spain expected a break in diplomatic relations. And in India, the ex-premier of Bengal, a Muslim grandee named Sir Khwaja Nazimuddin, observed: "It appears the British electorate has thrown overboard the one person who saved them from annihilation, and this has taken place even before the war is over."[5]

Perhaps it is true what a French politician said at the time, that ingratitude is the characteristic of a strong people. Actually, Churchill was still revered. The impossible ideal for many voters might have been a Labour government with Churchill as prime minister. But as the political correspondent of the *Guardian* said: "The country has preferred to do without Mr Churchill rather than to have him at the price of having the Tories too." The Tory party "is not merely condemned for its past: it is rejected because it has no message for the times. Great Britain, like the Continent, is clearly straining after a new order."

Churchill himself was a little dazed by it all, but took his defeat in relatively good humor. His wife, Clementine, perhaps hoping to see more of her husband at home, had told him it may well turn out to be a blessing in disguise. To which Churchill responded: "At the moment it seems quite effectively disguised." He had wanted the national coalition government of the war years to continue, at least until the defeat of Japan. In fact, since he was never very keen on party politics (he changed parties twice), he probably felt more comfortable presiding over a national government than one consisting of a single party. But, according to Harold Nicolson, the diarist and diplomat who lost his seat in the election, Churchill didn't complain. He showed a "calm, stoical resignation—coupled with a shaft of amusement that fate could play so dramatic a trick, and a faint admiration for the electorate's show of independence."[6]

Some of Churchill's colleagues in the Conservative Party were more understanding of their opponents than my grandmother was. Harold Macmillan, who must have sensed the mood in the British Army, wrote in his memoir that given the tremendous difficulties of rebuilding the nation, "it may well be that by a sound instinct the British people felt that it would be wiser for a government of the Left to be in control."[7] He added, however, that many people had been persuaded during the war that "immediately the struggle was over there would follow a kind of automatic utopia." The socialist state, under British leadership, they thought, in Macmillan's reading, "would bring about unexampled prosperity in a world of universal peace."[8] Such naïve idealism may have been in the air. But the notion that Churchill's Britain had passed, and the time had come for a more equitable society, could not be dismissed simply as a pipe dream. What Macmillan was perhaps reluctant to acknowledge was the resentment felt by people who had done most of the heavy work towards men of his own class.

This didn't escape the notice of Harold Nicolson. In the unmistakable tones of a different kind of class peevishness, Nicolson noted in his diary on May 27 that people felt "in a vague and muddled way, that all the sacrifices to which they have been exposed . . . are all the fault of 'them' . . . By a totally illogical process of reasoning, they believe 'they' mean the upper classes, or the Conservatives. Class feeling and class resentment are very strong."[9]

But was it so illogical to feel that things could not go back to what they had once been, to the "normal" state of class deference, the natural acceptance of privileges or the lack thereof, of being excluded by birth from enjoying the benefits of a decent education, a solid house, or proper medical care? Much has been written after the war about the solidarity of people linked at a time of national peril, of the good-natured "London-can-take-it" British bulldog spirit, when everyone mucked in together. But those same leveling experiences had also created a new sense of entitlement, where the old inequalities would no longer do. That was the British version of Never Again.

The American critic Edmund Wilson attended a Labour Party meeting in an industrial town of narrow coal-dark row houses. He watched Harold Laski, the party chairman and Marxist academic, make a speech on a gray afternoon to grimly attentive men and women dressed in worn-out army surplus clothes and ill-fitting "demob" suits. Laski reminded his audience that Winston Churchill was "in favor of the traditional Britain, with a few measures of practical construction." But in the "traditional Britain," he would have them know, only 1 percent of the population had owned 50 percent of the wealth, and only 1 percent of army officers came from working-class families.

As Wilson listened to Laski talking about the blessings of socialist government, he noticed an elderly woman (who may have looked older than she actually was), staring at the speaker with a hungry intensity that reminded him of other pale and gaunt Europeans who seemed different from the poor in times of peace, as though they belonged to a peculiar "breed with ravenous eyes like an animal's" that saw "only with appetites that were simple and stringent." And there, "erect before this woman and all her silent companions," stood Laski, "slight, bespectacled, high-browed, making them promises which could perhaps not always be real-ized," and "talking to some degree the mere cant of politics." And yet "he held to his post by some tension that magnetized and turned him toward that craning grey-faced chicken-eyed woman."[10]

In Greece, Wilson had the chance to mingle with British army men. Somewhat to his surprise, he found a peculiar animus among the common soldiers, not just against their officers, but against Churchill himself. One man "expressed himself very strongly on the subject of Churchill's cigar." Whenever British soldiers met their American counterparts, they couldn't but notice how much better the GIs were being treated by their officers. In Delphi, of all places, Wilson detected "the almost complete class line-up, on the issue of the Churchill government, between the English officers and the English troops." He "found no English soldier who had not voted for Labour and only one officer who had."[11]

This observation is impossible to disprove, but there may have been a slight element of projection here; Edmund Wilson was himself rather sensitive to the subtle and unsubtle ways by which the English express superior status, towards Americans as much as to the lower ranks. In fact, the shifts in British society cannot be entirely explained by class warfare. Wilson got only part of the story. Noel Annan, a senior military intelligence officer in 1945 and later provost of King's College, Cambridge, among other grand positions, was typical in almost every respect of the English *haute bourgeoisie*, except perhaps for his strong intellectual interests. He voted Labour in 1945, as did quite a few other young officers. Annan relates why in his memoir. It wasn't that he didn't admire Churchill; he simply "doubted whether [Churchill] understood what the country needed after the war."[12]

Another reason, aside from class feeling, why the war changed social and political attitudes was that people were becoming better educated. The British wartime government had put much effort into cultural improvement. The Council for the Encouragement of Music and the Arts (CEMA) organized classical music concerts and theater performances in factories, church halls, and air-raid shelters. Debates and education pro-grams were set up for the intellectual elevation of the troops abroad. In Cairo, where many soldiers were stationed, a mock parliament was formed by leftist servicemen in 1943 to discuss politics, in the words of one air-man, "as though we were living in the yearned-for peace . . ."[13]

Some Conservatives found this development profoundly disturbing. The MP for Penryn and Falmouth wrote a letter to Churchill's parliamen-tary secretary: "I am more and more suspicious of the way this lecturing to and education of the forces racket is run . . . for the love of Mike do something about it, unless you want to have the creatures coming back all pansy-pink."[14]

Cyril Connolly, an old Etonian esthete with Francophile tastes, started his literary journal *Horizon* in 1940, determined to keep the flames of art and culture going even as—in his phrase—the lights were dimming over Europe. Soldiers and sailors were encouraged to subscribe at heavily reduced rates. Connolly too believed it was time to climb down from his high-minded perch and bring culture to the people. *Horizon* found its way into a surprising number of khaki backpacks. In June 1945 Connolly wrote an article explaining why he voted Labour. It was not because Labour politicians supported the arts more readily than Tories. The contrary was more often true. But he voted Labour because every human being should be entitled to a civilized life: "To make England a happy country, there must be a leveling up which socialism alone will provide."[15]

One of the most curious films made in wartime Britain, or at any time really, was *A Canterbury Tale*, directed by Michael Powell and Emeric Pressburger, one a conservative English genius, the other a Jewish Anglo-phile born in Hungary. Too odd to be well received when the movie first came out in 1944, *A Canterbury Tale* tells us a great deal about the yearn-ings of that time, which were spiritual as much as political. An English soldier and an American GI find themselves thrown together by chance with a young English woman in rural Kent. The woman, a shopgirl from

London, is accosted at night by a mysterious stranger known as the "glue man," who is in the habit of secretly tipping pots of glue over women's hair. It doesn't take them long to unmask the glue man as a highly cultivated local gentleman farmer and magistrate. His aim, it turns out, was to stop young women from wasting their time going out with soldiers instead of immersing themselves in the glories of English history and the English countryside. All four characters end up in Canterbury, as modern-day pilgrims, each receiving a kind of personal blessing.

The glue man might easily be seen as a crazy pervert. Yet, though undoubtedly eccentric, he is also an idealistic, almost saintly figure, trying in his peculiar way to articulate why England is worth fighting for. The film shows an idea of England, particularly of rural England, that is intensely patriotic, and romantic, a Tory version of Blood and Soil, perhaps, except that it dissolves the traditional barriers of class. When the young woman tells the glue man that she was never accepted by her fiancé's parents because they were of good family and she was just a shopgirl, he answers that such categories mean nothing any more in "the new England," which in the movie is a metaphysical place, its landscape a source of spiritual feeling. That would be like an earthquake, says the young woman. We *are* in an earthquake, the glue man replies. This earthquake, to the glue man, was more than just social or political; it was a religious epiphany in the green fields of England.

The socialism of Clement Attlee would seem to be far removed from Powell and Pressburger's Tory romanticism. Attlee, a quiet pipe-smoking solicitor's son, was not a romantic in any sense. Yet his politics weren't as far removed from A *Canterbury Tale* as all that. British socialism had strong Christian antecedents, steeped in the improving traditions of the Victorian age, with aesthetic links through arts and crafts to the idea of a pristine rural England. "Jerusalem," William Blake's hymn to "England's green and pleasant land" among the "dark satanic mills," is an expression of patriotic religiosity, of Christ turning England into a version of heaven. Blake was a dissenter. His hymn was often sung on working-class marches against their oppressors. Socialist Britain was sometimes referred to as the New Jerusalem. The spirit of the Powell-Pressburger movie, set in the sun-dappled fields of Kent and ending in Canterbury Cathedral, is strikingly similar to Blake's vision.

In the month leading up to the July election, Churchill and Attlee laid out their very different patriotic visions of England. Churchill tried to land the first blows by accusing the Labour Party of being in thrall to foreign notions "abhorrent to the British ideas of freedom." He growled that this "Continental conception of human society called Socialism, or, in its more violent form, Communism" would inevitably lead to a police state; that a socialist government would "have to fall back on some form of Gestapo." This would never work "here, in old England, in Great Britain, in this glorious island . . . the cradle and citadel of free democracy." For the British, said Churchill in the rousing tones of his finest wartime speeches, "do not like to be regimented and ordered about . . ."[16]

Regimentation was all very well in times of national peril, Churchill went on: "We all submit to being ordered about to save our country." But once the war is over, proud Britons would cast off those self-imposed shackles and burdens and "quit the gloomy caverns of war and march out into the breezy fields, where the sun is shining and where all may walk joyfully in its warm and golden rays."

This was Churchill's laissez-faire notion of the green and pleasant land. It misfired badly. For once, now that peace was at hand, Churchill was tone-deaf to the sentiments of his people. There was "a good deal of bewilderment" among British soldiers abroad, according to the *Guardian*: "The transformation of Mr Churchill, the national leader, into the Churchill of the 'Labour Party Gestapo' speech has puzzled men everywhere."[17]

In response, Attlee, too, accused his opponent of taking his ideas from dubious foreign sources, in Churchill's case a Viennese economist named Friedrich Hayek who had left his native country in the 1930s and blamed Continental totalitarianism on the follies of central planning. Churchill had been reading Hayek's seminal book, *The Road to Serfdom*. "I shall not waste my time," said Attlee in his radio broadcast, "on this theoretical stuff which is merely a second-hand version of the academic views of an Austrian professor . . ."

Where Churchill saw the abolition of wartime planning and controls as the quickest route to those sunny English fields, Attlee believed that wartime controls should be extended to build the New Jerusalem. The common good should not be left in the hands of private individuals, out to swell their personal profits. Indeed, he argued, "the war has been won by the efforts of all our people, who, with very few exceptions, put the nation first and their private and sectional interests a long way second . . . Why should we suppose that we can attain our aims in peace—food, clothing, homes, education, leisure, social security and full employment for all—by putting private interests first?"[18]

Attlee, like so many Europeans of his time, put his faith in government planning. This was more than an opportunistic exploitation of conditions made necessary by war. Distrust of liberal economics, blamed for the booms and busts and high unemployment rates that caused so much political turbulence in the 1930s, had existed for many decades, on the right as well as the left. Hjalmar Schacht, Hitler's first minister of economics, was a planner who believed in a state-directed economy as much as Attlee. In East Asia, so did the Japanese "reform bureaucrats," more national socialists than social democrats, who cooperated with the Imperial Army to wipe out Western-style capitalism. Planning the perfect society was one of the twentieth century's great faiths.

Plans for a makeover of Britain had already been devised in the early years of the war. The Beveridge Report on Social Insurance and Allied Services calling for a National Health Service and full employment was published in 1942. A system of secondary education for all was outlined in a paper published in 1943. Social insurance followed in 1944, and a document on housing policy in 1945. But the overwhelming popular mandate to carry these plans out came in July 1945, when not only Britain but much of Europe was exhausted, virtually bankrupt, and in ruins, the perfect landscape for dreams of doing everything over.

· · ·

THE WORD FOR NEW JERUSALEM in France was *"progressisme."* Left-wing ideals, infused with a great deal of patriotism, inspired former members of the resistance just as they had British socialists. Communists, social democrats, even many Gaullists, did not fight Vichy and the Germans only for the love of the traditional *douce France.* They had political ideals for which so many of them gave their lives, and wanted them to be implemented after the war, preferably by the ex-resisters themselves. The National Council of the Resistance, dominated by the left, was designed to be a kind of government-in-waiting.

This is how Stéphane Hessel, a young Jewish *résistant* who had survived the Gestapo's torture and Buchenwald, remembered it sixty-six years later: "In 1945, after a horrendous drama, the members of the National Council of the Resistance dedicated themselves to an ambitious resurrection." The Council, in words that echoed Attlee's program exactly, proposed "a rational organization of the economy that makes sure private interests are subordinated to the common good." New plans would have to be made to ensure universal social insurance. Coal, gas, the big banks, electricity would be nationalized. All this, Hessel recalled, to "emancipate the common good from the dictatorship created in the image of fascist states."[19]

Hessel was not a communist. He had joined de Gaulle's forces in London and was parachuted into occupied France in March 1944, an act of extraordinary bravery, especially for a Jew, even with false papers. (He was betrayed and arrested in July.) But Hessel's political ideals were certainly well to the left of de Gaulle's idea of France. De Gaulle was viewed by the French left much as Churchill was by many people in Britain, a great man of his time, no doubt, but a reactionary obstacle to progress. Marguerite Duras, who had been part of a left-wing resistance group, described de Gaulle as "by definition a leader of the Right." De Gaulle, she wrote, "would like to bleed the people of their vital strength. He'd like them to be weak and devout, he'd like them to be Gaullist, like the bourgeoisie, he'd like them to *be* bourgeois."[20]

She wrote this in April 1945. The feeling would persist, and grow even stronger, as colonial wars in North Africa and Indochina became ever grimmer. But de Gaulle, although undoubtedly a conservative, and quick to block the former resistance from taking political power, knew that compromises with *progressisme* had to be made. It was under de Gaulle that the Renault motor factories and five big banks were nationalized in 1945, as well as coal, gas, and public transport. And it was to de Gaulle, in December of that same year, that Jean Monnet, a technocrat from Cognac who had spent much of the war in Washington, D.C., presented his plans for modernizing the French economy. His schemes to put the state in charge of industry, mining, and banking were typical of the faith in planning. Planning, and yet more planning, was the way to a better future, not just because it promised greater fairness, but because it would prevent Europeans from embarking on a catastrophic war again.

And so it went all over Europe. Arthur Koestler, that consummate European survivor, a Jewish ex-communist who had escaped from a fascist jail in Spain, wrote with considerable misgivings that "if we are in for an era of managerial super-states, the intelligentsia is bound to become a special sector in the Civil Service."[21] Even though the resistance organizations failed to become the political force they had hoped to be, many of their left-wing ideals were indeed carried out. Social democratic governments were elected in the Netherlands and Belgium. Land reforms in Sicily, Romania, Czechoslovakia, Hungary, and Poland made smallholders out of millions of peasants, often at the expense of unpopular minorities such as the Germans in East Prussia and the Sudetenland. In the Soviet zone of Germany, the social democrats were trying, in vain as it turned out, to make common cause with the communists.

There was, in fact, a strong pan-European element in all of this; New Jerusalem as a European rather than just a national idea. Major Denis Healey, later to become an important cabinet minister in several Labour governments, landed with the British Army in Sicily and Anzio. His explanation for the left-wing leanings of his fellow soldiers was "contact with the resistance movements and a feeling that a revolution was sweeping

Europe."[22] Healey had been a communist, but broke with the party in 1939 over the Nazi-Soviet Non-Aggression Pact, also known as the Molotov-Ribbentrop Pact. But a cold splinter of his old communist heart was still in evidence in 1945 when he told the Labour Party conference to help socialist revolutions in Europe. Labour, he insisted, should not be "too pious and self-righteous when occasionally facts are brought to one's notice that our comrades on the Continent are being extremist."[23]

In the case of Cyril Connolly, his Francophilia and love of European culture, as much as his political views, led him to conclude that only a united Europe would serve as a barrier to another suicidal conflict. "Every European war is a war lost by Europe," he wrote in *Horizon* in December 1944, and "a war lost by Europe is a war lost by England; a war lost by England leaves the world poorer." Never again, to him, meant "a European Federation—not a nominal federation, but a Europe without passports—a cultural entity where everyone is free to go where they like . . . If Europe cannot exchange economic nationalism for international regionalism it will perish as the Greek City States perished, in a fizzle of mutual hate and distrust under the heel of an invader."

That Connolly was not just a Europhile eccentric is proved by the fact that many others shared his views, including Churchill himself, even though it was never quite clear whether the former prime minister wanted Britain to be part of the new European construction. Probably not. In a speech he gave in Zurich a year after the war, Churchill expressed his enthusiasm for a "United States of Europe." But it would be a united Europe with "Britain and the British Commonwealth of Nations" among its "friends and sponsors."[24] However, the role of the left remained highly contentious. Connolly believed that a European Federation could only be brought about by the left, that is "a European Front Populaire which is determined to be strong and also to avoid a Third World War." Similar ideas were being promoted by the Soviet Union, especially in Germany, whose unity, as Moscow saw it, was supposed to be achieved under communism. After having lunch at the French embassy in London, Harold Nicolson wrote in his diary about the dangers of communist propaganda:

"To combat this we must provide an alternative ideal; the only possible ideal is a federal Germany in a federal Europe."[25]

The other argument for Europe was a patriotic one, the idea that national grandeur could be regained only in a united Europe. This notion was most pronounced in France, held by technocrats in the Vichy regime no less than by some of their opponents. The key figure was again Jean Monnet, whose dreams of unity transcended French borders. His life, recorded in his memoirs, was a constant attempt to seize "exceptional moments" to overcome diversity and forge unity. May 1940, when the Germans were rampaging across France, was such a moment. One year before, Monnet had tried to interest Neville Chamberlain in a union between France and Britain. In 1940, Churchill was prepared to go along with idea, which then foundered on mostly French suspicions.

State planning was Monnet's patriotic contribution to France. This, he told de Gaulle, was the only way back to French *grandeur*. To achieve this, it was essential to capitalize on the unity of all French citizens. This time, 1945, was the perfect moment for such "collective efforts, because the patriotic spirit of Liberation was still present and had not yet found a way to express itself in a grand project."[26] The first grand project was the modernization of France by nationalizing the economy and directing German coal to French factories. The next project was European, the Coal and Steel Community, then the European Economic Community, and finally, in Monnet's dream, the full *grandeur* of a United Europe.

De Gaulle liked to call this European dreamer, not without affection, "*L'Americain.*" Monnet was that rare Frenchman who felt as much at home in Washington and London as he did in Paris. Yet there was something Continental, something faintly Roman Catholic, something not entirely in tune with liberal democracy, about Monnet's unifying obsessions. There was a whiff of Holy Roman incense wafting over his European dreams. And his unease with party politics, naturally competitive as they were, and free market economics, uncontrolled by state bureaucrats, suggested a technocratic faith which had antecedents on the right as much as the left. Or, rather, right and left were less than meaningful categories in the technocratic utopia. It was more a belief that social justice would be delivered most efficiently by a benign authoritarian government. Churchill was not entirely wrong that this might not suit the British as much as the left-wing planners of 1945 might have hoped.

. . .

GERMAN TECHNOCRATS WORKING for the Third Reich were great planners too. One of the more shadowy tales of World War II is the cooperation between German planners and their European counterparts under Nazi occupation. Architects, urban planners, builders of dams and motorways, found one another, not as fellow Nazis, but as kindred spirits and fellow engineers of a new European order. For them, too, destruction was often the "exceptional moment" of opportunity.

Rotterdam was the first city in western Europe to have its heart ripped out by bombs. The damage was not as vast as in Warsaw, bombed eight months before Rotterdam in September 1939, but the center of the city was pretty much obliterated. Plans to rebuild Rotterdam were made almost immediately. Unhindered by democratic procedures or private interests, a committee of Dutch urban planners and engineers set out to have the rubble cleared, private property expropriated, and the city rebuilt according to rational blueprints. They were not Nazis; in fact, most were not in the least sympathetic to the German occupiers, but these highly practical men had long been impatient with the indecision, the bickering, and the general messiness of liberal democracy. Much like Jean Monnet, they believed in unified action under strong leadership. In this sense, the Nazi government gave them an opportunity to do what they had wanted all along.

For the Germans, though not necessarily for the Dutch technocrats, there was an important pan-European dimension as well. Rotterdam would be one of the major hubs in a greater region of Germanic peoples. In the racist jargon of the German occupiers, "The Netherlands form a part of the European *Lebensraum*. As a member of the Germanic tribe, the Dutch people will follow the destiny of this natural bond."[27] There would be no room in the new order for the "plutocratic" prewar liberal market economy. All economies, including the Dutch, would be made to conform to a Continental planned economy (*Kontinentalwirtschaft*). Collective interests would trump any private interests, unless, of course, those interests happened to be those of Nazi leaders.

The talk about Germanic tribes held no appeal for a man like Dr. J. A. Ringers, the engineer put in charge of rebuilding Rotterdam in 1940. In fact, he was later arrested for helping the Dutch resistance. But he was convinced that planned cities were the right way forward. And in the first few years of the war, the Germans were happy to share their considerable expertise with Ringers and other Dutch technocrats. This didn't mean they always agreed. German plans to rebuild Rotterdam in the monumental fascist style were not at all what the Dutch had in mind. And, besides, the modernization of Rotterdam was not allowed to come at the expense of German port cities, such as Hamburg or Bremen. So in 1943, by which time Ringers had already been arrested, plans to rebuild came to a halt. But Ringers survived, despite a grueling time in a German concentration camp. As soon as the war was over, he was appointed minister of public works in charge of rebuilding the Netherlands. Ringers would be one of the chief engineers of the Dutch New Jerusalem, whose blueprints owed something to Karl Marx, something to prewar socialist planning, and perhaps a little more to the Nazi occupation than people care to remember.

· · ·

THE BIGGEST PLANNERS of all were the Japanese. During the 1930s and early 1940s, Manchukuo, Japan's Manchurian puppet state, was the most perfectly planned colony in the world, a kind of dream palace of Japanese pan-Asianism. It could not officially be called a colony, of course, as Japan was ostensibly the liberator of Asia from Western imperialism. And since the Japanese empire was also set against "selfish" Western-style free market capitalism, Manchukuo would be not just a pseudo-independent Asian state, but a showcase of collective social justice and egalitarianism. In fact, it was nothing of the sort; Japanese-built mines and factories relied on Chinese slave labor, and life for Chinese and Koreans under the

Japanese Kwantung Army was brutal. But the economy, like everything else in the puppet state, was strictly controlled by the military government, and ably assisted in this enterprise by government-favored Japanese industrial companies and banks.

The capital city of Manchukuo, known in Japanese as Shinkyo or New Capital, was little more than a small railway junction called Changchun when the Japanese set up the puppet state in 1932. Almost at once teams of Japanese planners, engineers, architects, and bureaucrats of the South Manchurian Railway and the Kwantung Army set out to design the most modern, most efficient, cleanest, most orderly city in Asia, to be built in the "New Asian" style. Shinkyo's blueprint bore the marks of Western influence—Haussmann's Paris, nineteenth-century British ideas on the Garden City, German Bauhaus—but the huge, modernist government buildings would be adorned with gabled Oriental roofs copied from various Japanese temples and Chinese palaces.

On the flat northern Chinese landscape, covered in snow all winter, a brand-new city arose in five years of high-speed construction under the auspices of the State Council of Manchukuo. If Albert Speer had been Japanese, this would have been his monument to totalitarian planning: grandiose bureaucratic fortresses in the New Asian style flanking wide and perfectly straight boulevards leading to massive round plazas like the spokes of a giant wheel.* Everything had been worked out with mathematical precision. And everything worked, from the sleek South Manchurian high-speed railway trains, the "Asia Express" which always ran on time, to the flushing toilets in public housing, an innovation that was unheard of in most homes back in Japan.

The public face of Manchukuo was Chinese, all the way up to Henry Pu'yi, the effete "last emperor" of the Qing Dynasty. Behind his throne and every Chinese official stood a Japanese puppeteer, or "deputy." To call the Japanese rulers fascists would be inexact. Many of them were

---

* These buildings are still there. Their bombastic style appealed to the Chinese Communists. The transition seemed entirely natural: the former Kwantung Army building is now the Communist Party headquarters, and so on.

militarists, all were Japanese nationalists, and quite a few believed in the pan-Asian ideal of their official propaganda, a new Asia, led by Japan, free from Western-style capitalism and imperialism.

All the military and government bureaucrats were dedicated to planning, unhindered by democratic procedures or the individual interests or desires of Manchukuo's mostly Chinese subjects. Behind the sinister force of the Kwantung Army, the murderous *Kempeitai* police, and an assortment of Japanese gangsters and carpetbaggers was an army of highly sophisticated bureaucrats, managers, and engineers who saw the puppet state as a kind of drawing board for running a perfectly planned economy. Their plans were coated in a cultlike imperialism, revolving around the divine Japanese emperor and his royal vassal in the old "Salt Palace" in Shinkyo, the bemused, hapless, and utterly humiliated puppet emperor Pu'yi.

Some Japanese planners were distinctly right-wing in their dedication to conservative military order; some were socialists who shared with the militarists an aversion to free market capitalism. But even the right-wing bureaucrats believed in Soviet-style five-year plans. The typical Manchukuo "reform bureaucrat" might best be described as a right-wing radical who had more in common with communists than with liberals. Kishi Nobusuke was of this type. A suave rabbit-faced bureaucratic operator, Kishi hardly looked like a strongman who ruled over huge numbers of industrial slaves. However, barely forty years old, he was one of the most powerful men in the Japanese empire. His brief was to turn Manchukuo into a state-controlled powerhouse of mining, chemicals, and heavy industries.

Industrial policy was set, not for the profit of businesses and corporations, or not in the first place, and certainly not to satisfy Japanese consumers, who were increasingly squeezed by wartime rationing, but to expand the power of the state. Some companies did very nicely out of this. Nissan, for example, moved its headquarters to Manchukuo in 1937, where, in partnership with the government, it established a new industrial and banking conglomerate, or *zaibatsu*, making five-year plans and producing everything from military vehicles to torpedo boats. The Mitsubishi *zaibatsu* manufactured fighter planes, and Mitsui enriched itself and the Manchukuo government by monopolizing the opium trade in China. Two major figures in this sordid business were Ayukawa Gisuke, founder of the Nissan corporation, and Kishi Nobusuke, the industrial bureaucrat whose contacts with the criminal underworld would always be carefully maintained. But the interests of big business and the military did not always coincide. Even Ayukawa disapproved of Japan's alliance with Nazi Germany. War with Britain and the U.S. was not necessarily good for business, and corporations, even when they benefited from special tax breaks and subsidies, did not always take kindly to bureaucratic interference.

What Kishi and others pioneered in Manchukuo was later put into practice in Japan itself. From the beginning of the war in China, in 1937, till the end of the Pacific War, the Japanese economy was effectively controlled by such government organs as the Cabinet Planning Board, the Finance Ministry, and the Ministry of Commerce and Industry. The men who ran the war economy were recruited from the same network of reform bureaucrats, strategic planners, and antiliberal ideologues from left and right who had industrialized Manchukuo with callous efficiency. The minister of Commerce and Industry was none other than Kishi Nobusuke himself. In 1943, the Ministry of Commerce and Industry was renamed Ministry of Munitions, more in keeping with the true nature of the Japanese war economy. Kishi, officially as vice munitions minister, continued to run the war economy for another year. In August 26, just days after the Japanese defeat, by imperial ordinance, the Ministry of Munitions disappeared and became the Ministry of Commerce and Industry once more.

One of the mysteries of the U.S. occupation of Japan is how the Americans allowed the Japanese to get away with such conjuring tricks. After all, Never Again was what the victors had in mind for Japan as well. There, too, 1945 would be Year Zero, the perfect moment to create a new society on the ruins. Clearly some people had to be purged. Kishi Nobusuke was arrested as a Class A war criminal, as was Ayukawa Gisuke. But the institutions they built in Japan were left pretty much intact, even as the industrial stock of Manchukuo was being systematically looted by the Soviet Red Army.

Quite how Japan would rebuild itself was a matter of much dispute. There was a strong current of opinion in Washington that Japan should no longer be involved in heavy industry at all, but should instead specialize in products more in keeping with a quaint Oriental nation: toys, ceramic figurines, silk, paper goods, porcelain bowls, and the like. Cocktail napkins for export to the United States was one helpful suggestion.[28] Japanese had different ideas. Just before the U.S. troops arrived, the head of the Mitsubishi *zaibatsu* wrote a letter to one of his executives talking about a "great hundred-year plan."[29] Even though this phrase, borrowed from the Chinese classics, was not meant to be taken literally, planning was still very much on Japanese minds. A year later, a report drafted by the Japanese Foreign Ministry explained that the age of laissez-faire was over, and the world had "at last entered an era of State capitalism or an age of controlled, organized capitalism."[30]

This was close to what some influential American New Dealers, sent out to help General MacArthur remake Japan into a peaceful democracy, thought as well. Some of the early drafts of their plans could have been written by Leninists. Owen Lattimore, a leftist British scholar of China at Johns Hopkins, was influential for a time. He believed that Asians were more interested in "actual democratic practices, such as the ones they can see in action across the Russian border," than they were in Western democratic theories, which come "coupled with ruthless imperialism." The only true democracy in China, he claimed to know, was to be found "in Communist areas."[31] Other "China hands" in the State Department looked carefully at the ideas for postwar Japan of Nozaka Sanzo, the leader of the Japanese Communist Party who had spent the war in China indoctrinating Japanese POWs. Factory committees and workers' groups were supposed to take over from "fascist" bureaucrats to run food distribution and other vital services. Even though this particular idea fell by the wayside, New Deal administrators were serious about land reforms and independent trade unions, and were convinced that the U.S. occupation authorities should "favor a wider distribution of ownership, management and control of the economic system."[32]

The New Deal for Japan was rather like Attlee's plans for Britain. Of course, neither Attlee nor the New Dealers were communists. On the contrary, they were, like most social democrats, very much opposed to communism. A serious concern among the U.S. administrators, including the New Dealers, was that Japanese, driven to extremes by economic destitution, would become susceptible to communist temptations. The solution was to make sure Japan could feed itself as quickly as possible by rebuilding its industrial capacity, undistracted by military interests or big business greed. And the best way to do this was to hand economic policy over to the Japanese with the most experience, to civil servants who knew how to plan for the future, who would put the public good over private interests, whose ideals were patriotic and egalitarian; that is to say, to the largely unpurged bureaucrats in the Ministry of Finance and the Ministry of Commerce and Industry.

In 1948, Kishi Nobusuke was released from Sugamo Prison without his case ever coming to trial. During his time in jail he had kept up with old friends from the worlds of right-wing politics and organized crime, some of whom shared his cell. In 1949, the Ministry of Commerce and Industry ceased to exist. In its place came the Ministry of International Trade and Industry, or MITI, the most powerful government force behind the Japanese economic miracle of the 1960s and '70s. In 1957, Kishi was elected prime minister.

. . .

WHEN KOREANS HEARD on the radio that Japan had surrendered on August 15, 1945, the first thing many of them did was throw away their Japanese wartime uniforms—the unsightly peasant trousers for women and the woolen khaki breeches for men. Dressed in traditional white Korean clothes, thousands of people swarmed into the streets waving Korean flags, singing patriotic songs and shouting "Korean independence for ever!" The streets of Seoul were gutted, the electricity had been cut off, there wasn't enough food, but people were crying with happiness. For the first time in many years, they could openly behave like Koreans again, without being punished for not bowing to images of the Japanese emperor or refusing to go by a Japanese name.

There were some misunderstandings at first. People thought the Soviets were coming, so welcoming parties were sent off to Seoul's railway station to greet the Russian liberators who never arrived. Similar parties waited in vain at railway stations in other cities across southern Korea, in Taegu, Kwangju, and Pusan, waving Soviet and Korean flags and banners expressing thanks for Soviet help in restoring Korean independence.

Others made for the nearest Japanese Shinto shrines, the main symbols of colonial oppression, and tried to bring them down with hammers, clubs, and even their bare hands, before setting them on fire. First in the northern city of Pyongyang, and then all over Korea, the hated shrines burned brightly through the night to the horror of Japanese who held them sacred.

And yet the Japanese themselves, by and large, escaped from molestation, except in the north where women and girls of all ages were treated by Soviet soldiers as war booty. On the morning of August 16, in Seoul, a Korean resistance hero named Yo Un-hyong, a devout Christian with leftist views and a taste for smart English tweed suits, formed the Committee for the Preparation of Korean Independence with other patriots, including communists just released from Japanese jails. His speech, to thousands of people gathered in a high school playground, was remarkable for two reasons. One was its spirit of generosity: "Now that the Japanese people are about to part from the Korean people, we should let bygones be bygones and part on good terms." And then there was a strong note of utopianism: "Let us forget what we suffered in the past. We must build on this land of ours an ideal society, a rational paradise. Let us set aside individual heroism and progress together in an unbreakable union."[33]

The crowd sang the patriotic Korean anthem, expressing undying love to the nation, set to the tune of "Auld Lang Syne," which apparently gave some Japanese the illusion that Koreans were bidding a fond farewell to their Japanese masters.

North of Seoul, above what would become known as the "38th parallel," about a week before the Soviet troops arrived in Pyongyang, an equally venerable left-leaning Christian patriot named Cho Man-sik, known because of his gentle ways and his native Korean garb as the "Korean Gandhi," also prepared for national independence. Like Yo in the south, Cho had many former political prisoners from the Communist Party in his entourage, but was not yet dominated by them. In both north and south, Korean People's Committees quickly took over from Japanese administrators. Most members were either communists or moderately left-wing, often Christian, nationalists.

As was true in Europe, east and west, leftists, including communists, had the best patriotic credentials. While the conservative elites in government, business, and higher education had usually collaborated with the Japanese, sometimes grudgingly, sometimes keenly, in the name of modernization or progress, or out of self-interest, resistance since annexation to the Japanese empire in 1910 had a strong left-wing slant. Korean rebellions against their own elites, as well as the Japanese, often had a messianic streak, a mixture of Korean shamanism and Christian influences. Marxist-based resistance against Japanese rule was in many ways a modern incarnation of old peasant revolts against the Korean landowning gentry.

Unity, however, Yo Un-hyong's fine words notwithstanding, was brittle. It was indeed a rarity in Korean history. The country was torn by regional differences, especially between north and south, as well as by explosive political rivalries. The year 1945 was no different. Even though Cho Man-sik and Yo Un-hyong had a common ideal of Korean unity, the left was riven by factions, and communists were ready to grab power where and when they could. When Yo established the Korean People's Republic in Seoul, he faced a challenge from the right as well, in the shape of the Korean Democratic Party, led by landowners and other members of the old elite, many of whom had collaborated with the Japanese. There were also various Korean politicians in exile, in China and the United States, who were far from united.

But almost all Koreans, whatever their political views, agreed about one thing. Never Again, to them, meant never to be dominated by foreign powers. These were the fighting words of the declaration of the Korean People's Republic on September 14:

> We are determined to demolish Japanese imperialism, its residuary influences, antidemocratic factions, reactionary elements, and any undesirable foreign influence in our state, and to establish our complete autonomy and independence, thereby anticipating the realization of an authentically democratic state.[34]

There is a word in Korean, *sadae*, literally "serving the great," a term used to describe the traditional tribute paid to the Chinese imperial throne by peripheral kingdoms, such as Korea. In modern times, *sadae* came to mean groveling to any foreign power, usually to gain advantage over Korean rivals. Collaborators with the Japanese were guilty of *sadae*. In the "rational paradise," envisaged by Yo, the shame of *sadae* would be wiped out forever.

The Koreans never had a chance.

When the U.S. troops finally landed in the southern port city of Inchon several weeks after the Japanese surrender, they had no clue about the country or the aspirations of its people. Lieutenant General John R. Hodge had been chosen to be the man in charge just because he happened to be in the neighborhood—on the Japanese island of Okinawa. His political advisers hardly knew any more about Korea than he did. None spoke a word of Korean. But there was immense goodwill, certainly on the Korean side. *Yank* magazine reported that "native Koreans" greeted U.S. jeeps, trucks, and reconnaissance cars with "shouts, grins, lifted arms, bows and cries of 'Hubbah, hubbah!'"[35]

Despite strict nonfraternization orders, a Japanese-American military intelligence officer named Warren Tsuneishi fell into a conversation with a Mr. Kim, a hotel manager in Seoul. Mr. Kim said: "And we have you to thank for our liberation. Deeply, deeply, I thank you. You have suffered so much to liberate us and make us independent." Tears welled up in Mr. Kim's eyes, which made Tsuneishi suddenly feel "ill at ease."[36]

By then, the first U.S. blunder had already been made. Before he had even disembarked from his ship, General Hodge received a request to see Yo Un-hyong's brother, Yo Un-hong, a moderate figure representing the provisional Korean government. The general, suspecting Japanese or perhaps communist skullduggery, refused to talk to him. The next day in Seoul, Hodge announced that the Japanese governor and his entire administration would stay in place until further orders. Koreans were furious and flooded the streets to protest against this slap in the face. Embarrassed by the reaction, the U.S. State Department quickly announced that the Japanese would no longer be in control after all. The Americans would take charge. But since the Americans still lacked sufficient troops, Japanese were ordered to stick to their posts anyway.

This is how *Yank* described the Japanese surrender ceremony: "Outside the Japanese Governor's palace in Seoul, a brief retreat ceremony was held around the flag pole. The 184th formed a hollow square of fatigue-clad men, and the 7th division played *Americans We*. The Jap flag was hauled down, displayed briefly for the inevitable photographers and replaced by the U.S. flag as the band played the U.S. national anthem." Then, the American troops "marched out the gates of the palace. *The Bringers of Justice* whom Koreans had welcomed to their ancient Land of the Three Kingdoms had begun their occupation duty."[37]

Although the Soviet Red Army occupied Korea above the 38th parallel, Soviet authority was not quite so crudely imposed. A Soviet official remarked to an American reporter that Russians liked the English and Americans, because "they look like us." But, he continued, "we don't like the Koreans. We will stay until a suitable stable government has been set up, then we'll go."[38] General Hodge, incidentally, didn't like Koreans any better. He regarded most of them as "poorly-educated Orientals strongly affected by forty years of Jap control . . . with whom it is almost impossible to reason."[39]

The Soviets stuck to their word, but their idea of a suitable stable government was not what patriots, such as Yo Un-hyong or Cho Man-sik, would have wished. Northern Korea was first run by Korean People's Committees. People's Courts were set up to purge collaborators and "reactionary elements." Officials of the colonial government were ousted, sometimes with considerable violence. Korean landlords, and others who had nothing to gain from revolutionary politics backed by Soviet officials, began to move to the south very swiftly. Cho Man-sik was still in charge of the People's Political Committee, but this central organ had only limited control over the regional committees. Nor could it stop the Soviets from dismantling and looting Japanese-built factories.

In the south, the American military authorities, who, unlike the Soviets, did assert direct government control, embarked on a policy which would be repeated on many occasions when the U.S. decided it knew best how to bless the natives with good government. Partly out of ignorance, partly out of a not always unreasonable distrust of communist intentions, the U.S. military government relied on conservative members of the Korean elite who spoke English, or, better still, were educated at American institutions. To lead the future Korean government, they brought in a man from the United States who was indisputably a nationalist, but also a figure with staunch anticommunist views: Syngman Rhee, a Christian, educated at Harvard and Princeton. Rhee was not a total unknown in Korea, but he had no popular base there, either. Although he had been regarded by U.S. officials as a nuisance while in exile, a lady from the passport division of the State Department thought Rhee was "a nice patriotic old gentleman." Her opinion, combined with Rhee's anticommunist credentials, was thought to be good enough. On October 11, Rhee was welcomed back to his native country by General Hodge, who called him "a great man who has given his entire life to the freedom of Korea."[40]

A similar scene took place in Pyongyang three days later, when a relatively obscure Korean guerrilla fighter, a pudgy man in his thirties with a pudding-bowl haircut, who had spent most of the war in a Soviet army training camp near Khabarovsk, was welcomed by the top Soviet commanders as "a national hero" and "an outstanding guerilla leader." Seventy thousand people had been mobilized to pay tribute to "General Kim Il-sung," who, in his capacity "as a representative of the grateful Korean people," delivered a speech written by his Soviet handlers honoring the Soviet army.[41]

Precisely one week after that the first glimmer of a Kim Il-sung cult appeared in a Pyongyang newspaper, describing heroic exploits that would soon become part of a quasi-religious liturgy celebrating all manner of divine interventions on the Korean peninsula, echoing the messianism of so many political movements in the Korean past. In December Kim took over the leadership of the North Korean Communist Party. But the center of Korean politics was still in the south. There was no question, quite yet, of two independent Korean nations.

Koreans, always conscious of their nation's history of *sadae*, had ample reasons to worry at this point. In November 1945, Donald Keene, still based in the Chinese city of Tsingtao, had dinner one night with some resident Koreans. For once, he reported in a letter, there was no contentious argument over Korean independence. "The only subject discussed which led to any controversy was that of Russo-American relations." Keene found it "very difficult" to persuade his Korean friends that "America and Russia have no quarrel and can get along in a world of peace." These Koreans, he explained, had "braved severe punishment [from the Japanese] by listening to American shortwave broadcasts during the war," and so they thought the U.S. should help their country against the Russians. Keene observed, with a hint of impatience: "A solution based on cooperation is viewed as out of the question. All they can see are two different factions in Korea, each striving to win all; cooperation in such a case they would consider betrayal."[42]

They were right: the fate of the Koreans would indeed be decided by foreign powers. But there were many more than two factions. At first, at a December conference of foreign ministers in Moscow, it looked as though

Keene's optimism was justified and the United States and the Soviet Union could come to an agreement. A "trusteeship" would be established in Korea under a joint commission drawn from U.S. and Soviet military commands. United States and Soviet authorities would help the Koreans form a provisional government and guide the country towards full independence with the help of Britain and China. This undertaking could take up to five years.

The Soviets had little trouble persuading their Korean allies in the north to back this arrangement. Dissenters were quickly dealt with. When Cho Man-sik, to whom a trusteeship smacked of yet more colonialist meddling in Korean affairs, protested, he was put under house arrest. House arrest later turned into imprisonment, and around the time of the Korean War, he disappeared entirely, never to be seen again.

The situation in the south was more fraught. Almost all south Koreans opposed a trusteeship, either for nationalistic reasons or political ones; conservatives wanted nothing to do with Soviet interference. They could not see how a national government could possibly include the Korean Communist Party. The conservatives, however, lacked popular support. The leftist Korean People's Republic, despite American efforts to crush it, still had more patriotic credibility. But the issue of trusteeship proved to be its undoing.

When an attempt by leftists and conservatives to form a coalition collapsed, the left became more sympathetic to the idea of a trusteeship. This was followed by chaos: a coup attempt, led by another former exiled nationalist known as "the assassin," was thwarted; workers went on strike in protest against the U.S. military government. And Syngman Rhee's conservatives rose as the true patriots, accusing the Korean left of being Soviet stooges—*sadae,* in other words. The Americans backed Rhee, naturally, and now claimed that trusteeship had been a Soviet plot from the beginning, and that South Korea should set up its own conservative government under the benevolent stewardship of the U.S.—something that might be described, and *would* be described by what remained of the left in future years, as another form of *sadae.*

And so the Korean People's Republic was doomed. What followed was a tragedy. The country would effectively be split into two, with Kim Il-sung in charge of the provisional Communist Party government in North Korea, and Rhee controlling the South. Keene's Korean friends in Tsing-tao soon proved to be more correct than even they could possibly have anticipated. The ghastly Korean War, started by an invasion from the North in 1950, ended in a stalemate after more than two million civilian deaths. Seoul, having survived World War II more or less intact, lay in ruins, as did Pyongyang in the North. The North continued to be ruled by a tyrannical quasi-imperial dynasty, and the South endured decades of military rule.

At the height of the Cold War, in 1961, a staunch anticommunist took power in South Korea by coup d'état. Following the Japanese wartime model of a planned economy under military rule, boosted by Korean *zaibatsu* operating in tandem with the government, the South Korean economy grew apace. The strongman in question had graduated in 1942 at the top of his class from the Manchukuo Military Academy in Shinkyo, and had been a lieutenant in the Japanese Kwantung Army. In 1948, he was expelled from the South Korean Army for taking part in a plot against Syngman Rhee. His Japanese name during the war was Takagi Masao. His real name was Park Chong-hee. One of his greatest Japanese supporters was Kishi Nobusuke, a fellow veteran of the Manchukuo puppet state.

. . .

UTOPIAN DREAMS ARE DESTINED to end in a junkyard of shattered illusions. But they don't all end in the same way. And they tend to leave traces. New Jerusalem in Britain foundered on what John Maynard Keynes, the greatest economist of his time, called a "financial Dunkirk." Keynes had hoped that Britain might have the benefit of U.S. aid—a constant supply of material goods on highly generous terms—under the Lend-Lease Act at least until the end of 1945. That would have given the government some time to stave off bankruptcy. Failing that, it was hard to see where the money would come from to plug the near-catastrophic balance of payments deficit, let alone to pay for Britain's socialist dreams. Keynes prayed that "the Japanese would not let us down by surrendering too soon."[43]

His hopes were dashed by the atomic devastation of Hiroshima and Nagasaki, events that prompted the following entry in Harold Nicolson's diary, describing the reaction of his wife, Vita Sackville-West: "Viti is thrilled by the atomic bomb. She thinks, and rightly, that it means a whole new era."[44]

Japan's war was over in August.

The misery of economic austerity, the rationing of goods that went on longer in Britain than in other countries, the endless queuing for meager services, the sheer dreariness of life, and the postwar fatigue coupled with the realization that Britain not only had depleted its treasury but was also rapidly losing its standing as a major power in the world, all this helped to deflate the spirit of optimism. Even though planning for public housing, education, culture, health, and full employment still went ahead, the nation's finances were dire, and the enthusiasm of 1945 was quickly dissipated. Two years after the victories over Germany and Japan, the Labour chancellor Hugh Dalton wrote in his diary: "Never bright confident morning again."[45]

In 1951 Winston Churchill was back as prime minister. The Labour Party had to wait another thirteen years for a second chance at governing, this time under Harold Wilson, who had been president of the Board of Trade in Attlee's cabinet.

Similar things happened in other western European countries, where stability and continuity—normality of a kind—promised by Catholic and Christian Democratic parties eclipsed the revolutionary élan of the left. The Dutch social democrats lost power in 1956. General de Gaulle established the French Fifth Republic in 1958. The near hegemony of the Italian Christian Democratic Party began in 1948, much helped by American anticommunist propaganda and financial support. The first social democratic government in West Germany was elected only in 1969. In East Germany, the Social Democrats saw their dreams of working with the communists to build a better antifascist Germany collapse even before the German Democratic Republic was founded in 1949. Germans living in the Soviet zone stubbornly refused to support the Communist Party and much preferred the Social Democrats in 1945. As a result, in the following year, the Soviet authorities forced the east German Social Democrats to merge with the Communist Party, which quickly gobbled them up.

One way of looking at the demise of the noncommunist left in Korea, or indeed Japan, where socialist government lasted for exactly one year, from 1947 till 1948, is to blame it on the Cold War. The U.S. occupation authorities in East Asia may have been fumbling, and often conservative, but the Soviet Union was just as responsible for the debacle of the moderate left. Where the Soviets were in control, in North Korea as much as in eastern and central Europe, socialists were crushed.

Stalin did agree not to stir up revolutions in the American spheres of interest; French and Italian communists were told to forget their dreams of taking power. Indeed, the Italian communist leader, Palmiro Togliatti, was rather a middle-of-the-road figure who avoided violent confrontations with conservatives, even though the right was still tainted by Mussolini's legacy. But the United States and its conservative allies, in East and West, were so suspicious of communist intentions that they did everything they could to keep anything left-wing away from power. This was especially true in states on the front lines of the Cold War, which happened to be Germany, Italy, and Japan. From the late 1940s, Japan, like West Germany, had to be reconfigured as a bastion against communism. The New Deal enthusiasms of 1945 quickly vanished as military rearmament, industrial development, crackdowns on trade unions, "red purges" in the civil service and education, as well as active support of conservative politicians, some of whom only recently had been awaiting trials as war criminals, became the new policy. This so-called reverse course by the U.S. authorities, who had been so encouraging to the Japanese left at the start of the occupation, never ceased to be seen as a betrayal of the idealism of 1945.

And yet Hugh Dalton had been a little too pessimistic when he lamented the end of Britain's "bright confident morning." The ecstasy of liberation may have faded, but many of the institutions erected in that bright new start were not dismantled so quickly; some, for better or worse, have lasted to this day. Neither the Conservative governments in Britain, nor the Christian Democratic parties on the Continent, seriously attempted to tear down the foundations of European welfare states, conceived by prewar planners and idealistic members of the wartime resistance. In fact, Churchill's Tories built more public housing than Attlee's Labour Party. Many Christian Democrats were almost as suspicious of laissez-faire economics as were the socialists. The western European welfare systems began to corrode around the edges only in the 1970s, and, especially in Margaret Thatcher's Britain, to get seriously dented a decade later. The economies of Japan and South Korea, even compared to continental Europe, are still quite tightly controlled by government planners.

But the main monument of postwar planning is Europe itself, or rather the European Union, rotting and battered, yet still standing. In 1945, most people believed in European unity as a noble ideal. It had always appealed to Catholics, inspired by echoes of the Holy Roman Empire. Frenchmen and Francophiles liked the idea of Europe as a center of Western civilization, centered in Paris, that could stand up to the crass materialism of the United States. Socialists and other economic planners were drawn to Brussels, where essential institutions of the European Union are based, as the capital of a new technocracy. Above all, however, a united Europe would ensure that Europeans would never go to war with one another again. In this sense, at least, so far, the idealism of 1945 has paid off.

CHAPTER 8

CIVILIZING THE BRUTES

In 1943, Noël Coward wrote a song called "Don't Let's Be Beastly to the Germans," which gave rise to misunderstandings. The song was briefly banned by the BBC for appearing to be too sympathetic to the enemy:

Don't let's be beastly to the Germans
When our victory is ultimately won,
It was just those nasty Nazis
Who persuaded them to fight,
And their Beethoven and Bach
Are really far worse than their bite!

In fact, as Coward carefully pointed out before singing his song on-stage, the sting was aimed at "a small minority of humanitarians who in my view took rather too tolerant a view of our enemies."

To say that the Allied occupations of Germany and Japan were carried out entirely in the spirit of such humanitarians would be an exaggeration, but not too much of one. For the occupations, at least in the first couple of years, were unique in their earnest endeavors not to exact revenge, but to reeducate, civilize, change hearts and minds, and turn dictatorships into peaceful democracies so that they would never wreak destruction on the world again.

In the beginning, it is true, there were plans, made in Washington mostly, to punish the former enemies and render them harmless by destroying any means of becoming modern industrial nations. As was already mentioned, the Morgenthau Plan, named after Henry Morgenthau, secretary of the Treasury under President Roosevelt, was to dismantle German industries, break up the nation into smaller bits, and reduce the Germans to being a pastoral people with barely a stick to defend themselves with. Similar ideas did the rounds about Japan.

These schemes came to nothing, and were replaced by the three Ds: Demilitarization, Denazification, Democratization. It was the third D that involved reeducation, not just to change patterns of behavior promoted and enforced by militaristic and dictatorial governments, but to change ways of thinking, the "national character," by reaching into the minds of the conquered peoples. An instructional film, entitled *Our Job in Japan,* made by the U.S. War Department, located the problem quite precisely. "Our problem," the narrator explains, as the image of a Japanese skull appears on the screen, "is in the brain inside the Japanese head." At the end of the film, he sums up the mission: "We're here to make it clear to the Japanese brain that we've had enough of this bloody barbaric business to last us from here on in."[1]

Reforming the natives is a strategy that might be traced back as far as the civilizing efforts of the ancient Romans. Some argue that it came from the Enlightenment conviction that human nature is rational and can be reshaped by the right education. Some recall colonial strategies, such as the French *mission civilisatrice.* Or the missionary zeal of Christianity. Or the molding through education of immigrants into good American citizens. British accounts have even brought up the faith in character building developed in Victorian boarding schools: the production of sportsmanlike gentlemen with a working knowledge of the classics. Re-education was also seen as an extension of psychological warfare, the military use of propaganda.

Punch magazine published a poem in 1939 by A. P. Herbert that intimated the need for a reeducation program:

We have no quarrel with the German nation
One would not quarrel with the trustful sheep
But generation after generation
They cough up rulers who disturb our sleep . . .

We have no quarrel with the German nation
In their affairs of course we have no say
But it would seem some major operation
(On head and heart) may be the only way.

Even as the crowds were celebrating victory in Europe on May 8, the following letter appeared in the *Times* of London, written by a man who was to have a significant influence on education policies in occupied Germany, Robert Birley, headmaster of Charterhouse, the famous private boarding school. "Sir," he wrote, "it is becoming clear that the reeducation of Germany by the allies is not just a pious aspiration, but an unavoidable duty." The problem with the Germans, as A. P. Herbert also indicated in his poem, and most people believed at the time, was that for more than a century they had been "fatally ready to accept any government which would save them from having to make decisions for themselves." They had become, in Birley's view, sheeplike, always following leaders, devoid of individuality, like militarized robots.

Birley then went on to make another, more interesting point, which in the end failed to impress British military occupation authorities, namely that reeducation, to be successful, had to be based on a national tradition. Germany should not be treated as a tabula rasa; Germans had to be persuaded "that they themselves have such a tradition, however completely forgotten now, on which a decent society can be based. There was once a Germany of Goethe, a country which the young Meredith visited because it was a land of liberal thinkers, one with universities which inspired Americans like George Bancroft." *

Birley's ideas were certainly popular among Germans who were longing to slough off the brown coat of Hitlerism and cloak themselves in the glories of Goethe, Kant, and Beethoven. As the educational adviser to the British Military Government in Germany in 1945, Birley helped to establish libraries, amply stocked with suitable English and German literature, as well as adult education centers, called *Die Brücke* (The Bridges), promoting intellectual and cultural exchanges between Britain and Germany. Alas, this promising start ran into opposition from British officials, some of whom had very odd ideas. Only the "extensive mixing of blood with other nationals" would cure the German disease, was one such opinion.[2] Another middle-ranking zealot suggested that all ex-Nazis and their families be confined to an island in the North Sea. Birley replied with proper sarcasm that their children, going to school on the mainland, might then infect innocent classmates with their Nazi ideas. Like the Morgenthau Plan, this, too, was quickly scrapped.

A more serious criticism of Birley's project to revive the best of German culture was that it didn't do enough the promote the best of British culture. General Brian Robertson, Birley's immediate superior, and incidentally a former pupil of Charterhouse, ruled that the Military Government needed more protection against criticism of its policies in Germany. In the words of another general, there needed to be more "projection" of "British civilization," and promotion of British policies.[3] Birley resigned and went back to England.

---

* George Bancroft (1800–1891), American historian and statesman.

Authorities in the American Zone were initially more inclined to punish than to educate. More effort was spent on purges of teachers suspected of Nazi taints than on remolding the German mind. Some Germans exiled in the U.S. advised the American authorities that reeducation would be futile. The novelist Alfred Döblin said, "Educating the Germans is almost hopeless because the majority of the professional classes are Nazis." His friend Lion Feuchtwanger, an equally famous German novelist, was convinced that "Three million Nazis must be arrested, killed, or exiled to forced labor."[4] Others talked as though teaching Germans to become better people was as misguided as trying to impart civilization to baboons.

Still, the Potsdam Declaration made the official Allied position clear: "German education shall be so controlled as completely to eliminate Nazi and militarist doctrines and to make possible the successful development of democratic ideas."[5] As far as Japan was concerned, the aims of Postdam sounded less harsh, or at least less controlling: "The Japanese Government shall remove all obstacles to the revival and strengthening of democratic tendencies among the Japanese people. Freedom of speech, of religion, and of thought, as well as respect for the fundamental human rights shall be established." It is hard to explain this difference in tone, especially in light of what actually happened during the occupation, which was a great deal more radical in Japan than in Germany.

And yet the task of reeducating (a term, by the way, detested by Birley, who preferred the simple "educating") the Germans was seen as a less complicated affair than doing the same for the Japanese. Germany, after all, was part of Western civilization, largely Christian, the land of Goethe and Kant. The foundations were believed to be sound. What needed to be done was to destroy Nazi ideology and "Prussianism." Denazification and demilitarization would go a long way towards solving the German problem. To this end, German guilt in recent crimes had to be emphasized through the distribution of such films as *Nazi Concentration Camps*, commissioned by the U.S. Army, or *Death Mills*, which contained the following lines in the narration:

Here is a typical German barn at Gardelegen. Eleven hundred human beings were herded into it and burned alive. Those who in
their anguish broke out were shot as they emerged. What sub-
humans did these things?[6]

These films were not popular in Germany. People refused to see them
or dismissed them as propaganda. Günter Grass was seventeen in 1945, a
prisoner in an American POW camp after having served briefly in an SS
Panzer division. He was instructed, with his fellow prisoners, by an American education officer in a "crisply ironed shirt." They were shown the
photographs of Bergen-Belsen, Buchenwald, the piles of corpses, the living skeletons. And they didn't believe any of it: "We kept repeating the
same sentences: 'Germans did that?' 'Never.' 'Germans would never do
such things.' And among ourselves we said: 'Propaganda. All this is just
propaganda.'"[7]

Discussion groups, organized by well-meaning American officials,
were often just as fruitless. Earnest talks about "how we do [democracy] in
the States" did not always attract enough people, since they were held in
English, and such topics as "the Nazi state" foundered on defensiveness:
we didn't know, Hitler did many good things, and so on.[8] Whenever the
education officer in Günter Grass's camp lectured the Germans on the
horrors of racism, the POWs embarrassed him with questions about
the treatment of "niggers" in the U.S.

Hungry people also had other things to worry about, as the freezing
winter approached. Hans Habe, a Hungarian-American journalist put in
charge of establishing newspapers in postwar Germany, remarked: "The
idea that the nation should look back, questioning and repenting, was the
concept of a conqueror . . . the people only worried about how to fill their
stomachs and their stoves . . ."[9] Habe, who was Jewish and spent time in a
concentration camp, had no reason to feel particularly warmly toward the
Germans.

Teaching the blessings of democracy was not necessarily easier. In an

article for *Yank* magazine, entitled "Re-education of Germany," there is a
wonderful interview with a ten-year-old German schoolboy in Aachen
named Ernst. Asked whether he knew that the German armies had
all been defeated, he replied: "The Americans had many guns and many
Jews." Next question: "Has anyone told you anything about democracy?"
Answer: "The teachers are telling about it." So was he interested in what
he heard about democracy? Answer: "It does not sound like so much fun
as singing."[10]

Aachen, Charlemagne's old capital in the heart of Europe, was where
the reeducation of Germany began, not for sentimental historical reasons,
but because it was the first town under Allied occupation. Few schools
were left standing after the bombings. Out of a prewar population of
160,000 only 14,000 remained. Eighty-five percent of the town lay in ruins. The beautiful early medieval cathedral, where Charlemagne is buried, somehow survived the damage. But now, in the words of *Yank*: "The
war of bombs . . . has given way to a new war of ideas. The effort to
de-hoodlumize young Germans is an experiment that all the world will
watch."

A Major John P. Bradford, representing the U.S. military government,
told the German city officials who had not been purged that they had a
great opportunity: "You are to be allowed to teach the German youth, to
re-educate it, to turn it away from the baseness of Nazism."[11]

The first problem was the lack of suitable teachers; conscripted men
were either dead or still stuck on various battlefronts, as POWs, or they
had been dismissed as Nazis. The poet Stephen Spender asked a group of
schoolchildren in Hamburg what they were learning at school. Latin
and biology, they said. Nothing else? No, they replied, "You see, the History, Geography, English and Mathematics teachers have all been
purged."[12]

The next problem was textbooks. Much had been destroyed in the
bombings. What was left were usually highly unsuitable: books in praise
of the Führer and his master race, or the biological need to rid Germany

of the Jews. Even pre-Nazi textbooks contained stories honoring the German martial spirit, or the heroic deeds of such figures as Frederick the Great. But, since there was not much else, these would have to do. Plates were made in London of one of these Weimar-era books, shipped back to Germany, and printed at an old newspaper plant in Aachen.

The director of schools in Aachen, Dr. Karl Beckers, was confident that the smaller children could be convinced fairly easily that their future lay with "all the people everywhere and not with that of a 'greater Germany.'" With the older children, however, Dr. Becker thought it might be necessary to be "very firm." But, he stated, even "in dealing out punishment in the classroom, we shall try to use democracy. Sometimes when a boy or girl causes trouble in the classroom, we will let the class decide how best to punish the culprit." Dr. Becker was "opposed to whipping," he said, "except in the most extreme cases."[13]

Dr. Becker was a Catholic conservative. Concerned to "replace the trappings of Nazis with something concrete and good," he saw a revival of Christian spiritual values as the answer. Many Germans believed this, which explains the dominance in future West German elections of the Christian Democratic Union. The future leader of the Christian Democrats, and the first postwar chancellor, was another Catholic Rhinelander, Konrad Adenauer. Stephen Spender went to see him at the town hall of Cologne, where Adenauer was mayor before Hitler came to power, and again in 1945.

Through the windows of Adenauer's office Spender gazed at what little was left of the streets of Cologne. There were still walls standing, but these were "a thin mask in front of the damp, hollow, stinking emptiness of gutted interiors." But Adenauer, in his interview, stressed a different kind of ruined landscape. "You can't have failed to notice," he told Spender, "that the Nazis have laid German culture just as flat as the ruins of the Rhineland and the Ruhr. Fifteen years of Nazi rule have left Germany a spiritual desert."[14] What was needed, then, as much as food and fuel, were more schools, books, films, music, theater: "The imagination must be provided for."[15]

Hunger for culture was certainly real, but the motives could be quite odd. One reason many Germans had stopped reading books was that Nazi literature was, on the whole, deadly boring. Now some people spoke about the need for high culture as though it were a kind of penance. Spender met a lady in Bonn, "the most unctuous type of respectable pious *hausfrau*," who was outraged by the frivolous taste for popular entertainments. There should be no place for cabarets, let alone jazz music, in the moral ruins of the Third Reich, she thought. German culture should be serious, for that was the "least one would expect, after all that the Germans have done." Germans should "be compelled" to have only "good" culture: "Mozart, Beethoven, Goethe. Nothing else should be allowed."[16] It is doubtful that Adenauer would have been quite so severe.

The hunger for culture was illustrated better, perhaps, by the first postwar revival in Berlin of Brecht's *Threepenny Opera*, a play that had been banned under the Nazis, of course. People walked for hours to get to the Hebbel Theater in the American zone, one of the few theaters that survived the war more or less unscathed. The performance started at four o'clock in the afternoon so that people could walk home safely before criminals stalked the streets at night. The premiere was on August 15 (the day after the Japanese surrender, but that was surely a coincidence). Rehearsals had taken place under very difficult circumstances: rain had come pouring through the roof, the actors were hungry, the costumes were stolen, the props destroyed.

Ruth Andreas-Friedrich, the former resistance fighter, was in the audience. "I feel choked with emotion," she wrote in her diary. Songs "of our illegal days," which had provided so much "solace and comfort during many desperate hours," could now be heard in freedom. But even in these heart-warming moments, her sensitivity to the false note, the hint of bad faith, did not desert her. There was "a storm of applause" at Brecht's famous words: "First give us something to eat, then we can talk about morals . . ." She was instantly roused "out of my self-absorption." The burst of self-pity was offensive to her. "Must we begin our first attempt at free expression by criticizing others?"[17]

. . .

IT WOULD HAVE MADE more sense, in a way, if Brecht's highly political opera, so full of left-wing moralism, had been revived in the Soviet zone rather than in the U.S.-occupied Kreuzberg area of Berlin. After 1949, it was indeed in the "democratic" (communist) German state that Brecht would build his own theater, even though he prudently held on to his newly acquired Austrian passport. The Soviet Union, too, made a strenuous effort to reeducate the Germans. The Soviets actually took culture more seriously than the Anglo-American allies. A British occupation official complained in a dispatch that the "free and personal culture" promoted in the West couldn't compete with the "politicized culture" of the Soviets. In the Soviet sector, he said, "Theatrical, book-publishing, art, and musical activities are conducted with a hustle which conveys the impression that something new and lively is going on."[18]

Something was indeed going on. The "democratic" elements of the German intelligentsia were actively courted by the Soviet authorities with special clubs, extra food rations, and general assistance with artistic endeavors. "Democratic" culture was often marked by a mixture of German nationalism and communist ideology. One of the prime German cultural movers was Johannes Becher, the Marxist poet and chairman of the Soviet-initiated *Kulturbund*, or, to give it the full name, Cultural Association for the Democratic Renewal of Germany. Rather like the British educator Robert Birley, Becher saw the "German spirit" as the proper foundation for renewal, as long as this spirit was "progressive." He wasn't thinking of Goethe so much as of the communist martyrs who died in Nazi prisons. "Antifascist art" was the "real" German art.

In fact, this formula proved to be too flexible for the Soviet military commissars, who had a narrower and more provincial concept of progressive culture. They were happy to promote Russian classics in the German theater, such as works by Chekhov or Gogol, as well as modern Soviet plays and even some progressive German playwrights, such as Friedrich Wolf, father of Markus Wolf, the future East German spy chief, as long as they were produced in the Soviet fashion. To this end, they liked to tell German writers and theater producers precisely what to include, what to delete, and how to stage the plays.

The popular appeal of musical, cinematic, and theatrical performances in the Soviet zone was probably not enhanced by the official insistence that they be accompanied by pamphlets and long introductions on stage by political figures explaining the correct political line. Communist authorities did not stint on advertising such films as *Lenin in October*, or *Lenin in 1918*, but the audience, even though starved of entertainment, remained largely unconvinced. Even members of the Socialist Unity Party of Germany (SED) could not muster much enthusiasm for much official Soviet culture. Johannes Becher, whose communist credentials were impeccable, was never really trusted by the Soviets. As well as being German, he was perhaps too "cosmopolitan." And there was a dangerous whiff of Trotskyism in his past. In November 1945, a Soviet cultural official in Potsdam accused the *Kulturbund* of tolerating "bourgeois tendencies in art and literature; futurism, impressionism, etc."[19]

There was another aspect to life and culture in the Eastern zone, which was to remain a feature until the Berlin Wall came down in 1989: the hectoring, hyperbolic tone of official Nazi rhetoric was carried over seamlessly into the communist style—as well as goose-stepping, mass calisthenics, and a penchant for military marches, often accompanied by slogans roared by vast crowds punching their fists in the air, extolling friendship and peace. Besides attending the postwar premiere of *The Threepenny Opera*, Ruth Andreas-Friedrich was also at the inauguration of the *Kulturbund*. Her boredom with the endless speeches soon turned to disgust. She noted in her diary on July 3:

> Hardly anyone of the eight notables, who are talking here about coming to terms with the past and renewing our cultural life, seems to notice how little they've so far managed to renovate their own way of talking. It is still about the greatest, the ultimate, the largest, and most magnificent . . . 'With firm steps we're marching

into the battle for pacifism,' a politician proclaimed the other day, probably not realizing how paradoxical his well-meant zeal sounded being phrased that way. Learning to cut out the exaggeration might not be so easy.[20]

. . .

EVEN THOUGH AMERICAN CULTURE WAS, on the whole, more entertaining than the culture promoted by Soviet authorities, you would not necessarily get that impression from the earliest magazines put out in the Western zones. Rather than leaving this task to the Germans themselves, U.S. occupation officials began by publishing their own magazines for German readers. The first issue of a monthly journal, entitled *The American Observer*, aimed at German intellectuals, contained articles on humanism and faith, the political philosophy of Thomas Jefferson, and a piece entitled "Rebirth of the Tennessee Valley." A magazine called *Heute* (*Today*) featured stories on the Nazi occupation of the Netherlands, "Men in the Hell of Concentration Camps," and "Community Work in the Tennessee Valley Authority."[21]

Reception of these journals among the German readers was, in the words of one American observer, "spotty."[22]

The Soviets, on the other hand, allowed dependably "democratic" Germans to produce their own magazines from the start, an altogether more fruitful strategy. The first one, *Aufbau*, published articles by Thomas Mann, Paul Valéry, and Ernest Renan, as well as pieces about German war guilt. It sold out almost instantly.

Since Germans had been deprived of Hollywood movies for more than a decade, the thirty-two feature films specially selected to promote the American way of life were popular, regardless of the intended message. The selectors made sure to avoid the darker sides of American society, so no gangster pictures. *Gone With the Wind* (1939) and *The Grapes of Wrath* (1940) were also considered too negative. But the Germans got to see pretty much the same slightly dated Hollywood films as many other western Europeans at the time: Charlie Chaplin's *The Gold Rush* (1942),

Deanna Durbin in *One Hundred Men and a Girl* (1937), the biopic *Abe Lincoln in Illinois* (1940), and the 1944 musical *Going My Way*, starring Bing Crosby as a golf-loving priest.

Some choices backfired, however, and had to be withdrawn. *Action in the North Atlantic* (1943), a war picture starring Humphrey Bogart as a merchant seaman being attacked by German U-boats, caused violent scenes in a cinema in Bremen. Having to watch documentary films about Nazi atrocities was one thing; to be subjected to entertainments featuring helpless Americans being machine-gunned at sea by vicious German U-boat crews was intolerable. Outraged veterans of the German navy tried to force other people the leave the cinema with them.

The main problem with American, and to a lesser extent British, re-education was a perhaps irresolvable and certainly unresolved dilemma; the aim was to teach Germans, and later the Japanese, the virtues of free-dom, equality, and democracy. Yet the lessons in freedom of speech came from military authorities, whose power was almost absolute, whose propa-ganda was often an extension of psychological warfare, and who used cen-sorship whenever it suited their purposes. To be sure, culture and education were nowhere near as oppressive as under the Nazis or the Japa-nese wartime regime, and it was certainly a bit rich for Hitler's ex-soldiers such as Günter Grass to mock the Americans for their racism, but the Allies were vulnerable to accusations of hypocrisy. Praise of democracy could sound a little hollow coming from occupiers who refused even to show *Gone With the Wind*, or countenance any views, or indeed factual information, that put their own policies in a negative light.

On August 31, the occupation of Germany was given a new, official status. Although still divided into different zones, the country was to be officially governed by the Allied Control Council, consisting of the United States, the Soviet Union, Great Britain, and France. Once more Ruth Andreas-Friedrich's ear for the false note was acute. She wrote in her diary:

Now at least we know who governs us. Why is there so much talk in the papers about democracy? Democracy means the people rule. We are ruled by the Control Council. We should beware of abusing that beautiful word [democracy].[23]

Bookstores and libraries all over the American zone were combed through by American Book Control teams. Not all the books they removed were written by Nazis. Popular travel accounts describing Americans or non-German Europeans as uncouth or degenerate were banned too, as were such authors as Oswald Spengler (*Decline of the West*), and the historian Heinrich von Treitschke, who was indeed a fierce Prussian nationalist but died in 1896, long before Hitler was ever heard of. Spengler, though initially sympathetic to the Nazis, had fallen out with them before his death in 1936. He had the peculiar distinction of having some of his books banned by the Nazis as well as the Americans.

Banning Nazi propaganda, in books, films, or other entertainments, was the least of it. Officers from the Information Control Division also engaged in censorship of the news. The American journalist Julian Bach spent much of 1945 observing such officers in various places in Germany. He described their attitudes with a sharp sense of the absurd. Germans, they surmised, had been systematically starved of free thinking during the Nazi years. Just as starving people in liberated concentration camps cannot be fed with too much food, because of their shrunken stomachs, shrunken minds cannot take too rich a diet of information either. In Bach's words: "According to the American 'mental surgeons' in charge of healing the German mind, the Germans' hunger for news and fresh ideas must be satisfied only gradually."[24] That most of these surgeons had very little idea of German history, culture, or society cannot have been helpful in assessing the required doses.

At first, the only newspapers available to Germans were written and edited by occupation officers. Even so, a little bit went a long way. Copies of these newssheets sold on the black market for twenty times their original price. When the first issue of a paper in Cologne appeared in the street, there was such a mob scene that a nervous American colonel in the vicinity felt the need to reach for his gun. In contrast to the Nazi press, even these occupation papers must have smelled of freedom. And access to American and British books and periodicals in the so-called America Houses and British Centers, opened in cities all over the Anglo-American zones, was a blessing to many people, and remained so for a long time.

The Western Allies couldn't have it all ways, however. By preaching the virtues of democracy and free speech, and encouraging the rebuilding of German political parties, they provoked criticism that ham-handed military censors had tried so hard to avoid, specifically, criticism of the military occupation and its policies. American policies favoring free enterprise over a planned, socialist economy annoyed social democrats. In the British zone, run by representatives of Attlee's socialist government, it was often the reverse; German conservatives protested against the "Bolshevik" economy planned by the occupiers. Criticism from Christian Democrats sometimes had more sinister overtones. In the state of Hessen, in the American zone, a speaker at a youth rally warned that denazification would lead to the "Bolshevizing" of Germany. "Emigrants in Allied uniforms" (Jews, in other words) were blamed for this unfortunate tendency.

. . .

IF AMERICA WAS THE MODEL to follow, and its culture, from Bing Crosby musicals to Lucky Strikes, from swing music to chewing gum, the dominant postwar influence, this was viewed by many Germans with a degree of ambivalence. It went against the widely held view among Christian conservatives that religion and classical German *Kultur* were the only routes to spiritual renewal and redemption. Suspicion of American culture had a conservative pedigree that went back much further than Hitler's rise. Its popular appeal had long made American culture seem like a threat to traditional values, defined and promoted by the intellectuals. This disturbed some left-wing intellectuals too. Theodor Adorno, the Frankfurt School philosopher who had spent the war years in exile in the U.S., was scathing about jazz music and other popular American art forms, albeit from a Marxist perspective. To him, jazz was part of what he called the "culture industry," a capitalist ploy to exploit the masses by daz-zling them with commercial entertainments.

Such opinions were not confined to the Germans. After becoming the first chairman of the Arts Council of Great Britain in the summer of 1945, John Maynard Keynes succinctly explained his aims in a radio program by exclaiming: "Death to Hollywood!" This, when the British, like Ger-mans, Dutch, and other Europeans, were flocking to the cinema to watch American movies. When the United Artists Corporation protested, Keynes wrote a letter to the *Times*, asking UA to forgive him for his "ec-centricity." What he had meant to say was that countries should "develop something . . . characteristic of themselves." What he had *really* meant was: "Hollywood for Hollywood."[25]

Keynes was being a little disingenuous. His disdain for "Hollywood" was all too typical of many European intellectuals, even if they couldn't quite repress their excitement about New World culture, either. In an ar-ticle published in *Horizon* in the spring of 1945, Cyril Connolly wondered where the European cultural revival might come from. What the world needed most, he argued, was "a positive and adult humanism." Could America supply it? On balance, he thought not. For America was "too money-bound and machine-dry." No, it had to come from his beloved France. Only France would be "capable of a bloodless 1789, of a new proclamation to the world of the old truth that life is meant to be lived and liberty is its natural temperature . . ."

Paris was to many people the symbolic antidote to "Hollywood." The Paris of Jean-Paul Sartre philosophizing at the Café de Flore, of literary journals with roots in the *Résistance*, of young men and women living lives of sexual and political liberation. This hopeful view of France stretched all the way to Japan, which was subjected to an even greater and more concentrated dose of American culture than Germany. The top ten publications in 1946 in Japan included three foreign books in translation: Sartre's *Nausée*, André Gide's *Intervues Imaginaires*, and Erich Maria Re-marque's *Arc de Triomphe*.[26] And in Berlin, Ruth Andreas-Friedrich noted the fashion among the young for sporting French berets after the war:

"Anyone who felt they had something to say wears a black beret." In Japan, this Francophile fashion adopted by intellectuals lasted at least until the end of the twentieth century.

Francophilia never had mass appeal, however. Besides, many people in France were as infatuated by America as people in other countries, north, south, east, and west. Even Sartre himself. In November 1944, a dozen French reporters were invited to visit the United States to learn more about the American war effort. Simone de Beauvoir recalled that she "had never seen Sartre so elated" as the day when he was asked to join the party. De Beauvoir described the allure of America in her memoir. She could have been speaking for millions all over the world:

> It meant so many things, America! To begin with, everything inaccessible; its jazz, cinema and literature had nourished our youth, but it had always been a great myth to us as well . . . America was also the country which had sent our deliverance; it was the future on the march; it was abundance, and infinite horizons; it was a crazy magic lantern of legendary images; the mere thought that they could be seen with one's own eyes set one's head whirling. I rejoiced, not only for Sartre's sake, but also for my own, because I knew that one day I was sure to follow him down this new road.[27]

Then there was Boris Vian and his band of *zazous*, who had rebelled against the frowzy Pétainism of the war years by affecting an Anglo-American style, throwing wild parties, and reading clandestine copies of Hemingway and Faulkner. They were the French counterparts of the German *Swingjugend*, who, at far greater risk, showed their defiance of the Nazis by dancing to forbidden jazz music in private apartments. After the Spring of '44, Vian and the *zazous* dressed in American surplus blue jeans and checked shirts, and played and listened to nothing but jazz, jazz, jazz.

Disillusion often follows exposure to the real thing. Sartre returned from the U.S., in Beauvoir's account, "a little stunned by all he had seen."

He had liked the people all right, and was impressed by Roosevelt, but, in Beauvoir's words, "apart from the economic system, segregation and racism, there were many things in the civilization of the Western Hemisphere that shocked him—the Americans' conformism, their scale of values, their myths, their optimism, their avoidance of anything tragic . . ."[28]

It stands to reason that France was seen by many, especially in France itself, as the obvious cultural counterweight to America. Like the United States, the French Republic was born from a revolution with universalist aspirations; France as an enlightened civilization whose fruits could, and indeed should, grow with profit everywhere. Americans have a similar view of their own republic and its mission in the world. This was certainly true in 1945, when the U.S. was in a somewhat better position to preach, and sometimes impose its values, than France. It was different in the early nineteenth century, when Napoleon spread French universalism with brutal force, especially in the German lands. The German reaction then was the growth of a romantic nationalism, a defensive consciousness of blood and soil whose hideous perversion would lead to the Third Reich.

Reeducation American-style in 1945 was a gentler enterprise, despite an initial thirst to mete out punishment. Perhaps this was one reason why Germans, not without ambivalence and even resentment, took to the American century more readily than the French. Knowing what they themselves had done to the Slavic countries, let alone to the Jews, most Germans can only have been deeply relieved by the way they were treated by the Americans. Life in the Anglo-American zones was certainly to be preferred to the Soviet zone, or even, certainly in the beginning, to the much smaller French zone in the Rhineland along the French border. The main city under French occupation was the elegant spa town of Baden-Baden, now bereft of guests to take the waters. That France should have a zone at all was far from obvious. The United States had been against it, since France, despite General de Gaulle (whom Roosevelt had always distrusted) and his Free French forces, had hardly played a vital role in defeating Nazi Germany. Still, de Gaulle's will, as usual, prevailed. The other problem with France was the desire among many of its citizens to wreak vengeance, and to extract as much loot from Germany as they could get away with.

This was especially true in the first year of occupation, during which the French, more even than the Americans or the British, behaved like conquerors. Troops were sometimes undisciplined. Natural resources, such as coal, were shipped to France. There were French plans, which came to nothing in the end, to annex parts of Germany, specifically the industrial Rhineland and Westphalia and the coal-rich Saarland. These schemes were abandoned because none of the other Allies supported them. There was opposition from some French generals too, who feared that such moves would provoke just the kind of German revanchism that had led to the war that had just ended.

But the French, as always inspired by their *mission civilisatrice*, were serious about culture, especially the export of French culture to civilize the Germans. And not just the Germans. Exhibitions of French art, concerts featuring French composers, and French cinema and literature were promoted in other Allied zones as well, to show, in the words of René Thimonnier, head of French cultural affairs, that "in the order of cultural values, France is still a great nation, indeed perhaps the greatest of all."[29]

In terms of denazification, the French did pretty much what the Americans did: purge teachers and others with a Nazi past, ban books from libraries, and check the content in German papers and radio programs produced by reliable German journalists under French control. One of the people combing through contemporary German writing in Baden-Baden was the novelist Alfred Döblin, who had become a French citizen in the 1930s. He was struck by the wooliness of German prose produced immediately after the war, the tendency towards mysticism, the air of intellectual confusion. Germans, he surmised, "hadn't read or learned very much." The German soil, at first, "only sprouted grass and weeds."[30]

Like the American officials of the Information Control Division, French officials did not think the Germans were quite ready in 1945 to be exposed to political ideas. Their view was that the press ought to concentrate instead on the problems of daily life and cultural affairs, on subjects such as "contemporary French ceramics" or "French painting." The idea was to bring the Germans, who had been deprived of modern artistic developments outside the Third Reich, back into the civilized world. The center of the civilized world was, of course, Europe, and the cultural capital was, of course, Paris.

There was a political point to this, apart from restoring French amour propre. Even though France was unable to annex the borderlands along the Rhine, something more important would soon happen there. Its rich supplies of coal and steel would be put under the control of a pan-European institution to the benefit of Germany, France, and the other members of the European Coal and Steel Community, founded in Paris in 1951. The French zone was the birthplace of what would later become the European Union. The initiative to share sovereignty had come from France. The man who officially proposed it was the French statesman Robert Schuman, born in Luxembourg of a French father and German mother. The chancellor of West Germany, who agreed to share sovereignty over one of Germany's wealthiest areas, was the former mayor of Cologne, Konrad Adenauer.

To say that Germany was lucky to be divided into Allied zones in 1945 would be cruel to those who had to endure communist dictatorship for four decades. But perhaps these divisions best suited the federal nature of Germany. The Allied occupiers were never able to centralize German education, or flatten regional differences in culture and politics. Whether Germans were really reeducated is doubtful. The greatest Allied achievement may have been to leave western Germany without animosity. Wishing to reeducate a former foe may be patronizing, but it is a more benign and much less dangerous policy than vengeance. Helping the old enemy to its feet may have been more than some Germans deserved, but it was better than squeezing the country dry. This time there would be no "stab in the back" legend, or armed bands of desperadoes wanting to avenge their nation's defeat. What really shaped Germany's future, however, had less to do with culture or education, justice, or even common decency, than with political circumstances, the Cold War, the need to build strong democracies in Europe, the opportunism of the German elites, American interests, and the utopian project designed, in the words of Robert Schuman, to "make war [in Europe] impossible" and "encourage world peace."

In terms of military and political clout, the French occupation of the Rhineland may not have amounted to much, but it helped to knit one of the bloodiest fissures in Europe together again. A united Europe was not only a Franco-German, but also a Christian Democratic, dream. De Gaulle, with a great degree of skepticism, likened it to "resuming Charlemagne's enterprise."[31] The social democrats in Germany had opposed it, as had the French communists. De Gaulle was against it, too, because he thought France was not strong enough yet to dominate the union. Perhaps the general was irritated because he wasn't in power at the time. For in 1945, inspired by Jean Monnet, de Gaulle had actually spoken in favor of integrating the Ruhr and the Saarland into a European federation. (He was a little vague about whether Britain should be part of this.) Whatever the future of the currently troubled Union may bring, this dream of unity did more to bring Germany back into the fold of European nations than all the reeducation programs put together.

. . .

ON DECEMBER 15, 1945, the *Saturday Evening Post* featured an article about the occupation of Japan with an extraordinary headline—extraordinary now, not then. It read: "The G.I. Is Civilizing the Jap." Written by William L. Worden. Dateline: Tokyo, By Bomber Mail.

Above the dateline is a summary of Worden's article: "While the Nipponese wait to be told what to think, and their slippery countrymen duck the job, the living example of the American soldier is proving effective."

Later on in the piece, the reader is informed that "The average Japanese is a simple person not far removed from the savage—as evidenced in the war."

But there is some hope, for, "The man who, at the moment, seems to be most effective in democratizing and civilizing the Japanese is the G.I., even as he was so effective in pacifying him."

This image of the "Jap" as a savage was widespread during the war. After the A-bombs had killed around two hundred thousand people in Hiroshima and Nagasaki, President Truman wrote to a friend that "when you have to deal with a beast, you have to treat him as a beast."[32]

What is remarkable about the occupation is how quickly such views disappeared. Which is not to say that the idea of reeducating the Japanese to become peaceful democrats was not viewed in some quarters with the greatest skepticism. Experts on Japanese culture and society in the State Department, collectively known as "the Japan hands," were quick to point out the top-down collectivist nature of traditional Japanese life. The Japanese, they claimed, would never behave like individuals. They were used to obeying orders from people of superior rank. The emperor was revered as a sacred figure. His subjects, in the words of one Japan hand, were "inert and tradition bound." The Japanese, according to the British representative in occupied Tokyo, were "as little fitted for self-government in a modern world as any African tribe, though much more dangerous."[33]*

Pitted against the Japan hands, whose theories on the Japanese character were often based on what they heard from their elitist Japanese contacts, were the China hands, frequently people with left-wing sympathies, and New Dealers from the old Roosevelt administration. These were the officials whose opinions prevailed, at least in the first years of the occupation. The pivotal date was August 11, when Joseph Grew, doyen of the Japan hands and former ambassador to Tokyo, was replaced as undersecretary of state by Dean Acheson. Acheson stated in September that "the present social and economic system in Japan which makes for a will to war will be changed so that the will to war will not continue."[34]

General MacArthur, a deeply religious man, whose wartime theories about the "Oriental mind" as childlike and brutal were often remarkably crude, was convinced that he had been destined to reeducate the Japanese. His guides in this mission, he liked to say, were Washington, Lincoln, and

* His chief aide was Brigadier John Profumo, the politician who was eventually brought down by his liaison with the call girl Christine Keeler.

Jesus Christ. Ideally, Japanese should be converted to the Christian faith. But in any case—and here MacArthur's ideas concurred with those of Konrad Adenauer—renewal had to be spiritual as well as political, social, and economic. MacArthur, however, went further than anything conceived by the German Christian Democrat. His occupation of Japan, he said, would result in "a spiritual revolution . . . an unparalleled convulsion in the social history of the world."[35] Herbert Hoover, on a visit to Tokyo, rather oddly called MacArthur "the reincarnation of St. Paul."[36] Yet the American viceroy had no interest in exploring Japanese culture, or learning much about the place. He spent most of his evenings at home watching cowboy movies. His translator, Faubion Bowers, later recalled that during MacArthur's five years in Japan, "only sixteen Japanese ever spoke with him more than twice, and none of these was under the rank, say, of Premier, Chief Justice, or president of the largest university."[37]

Unlike Germany, Japan was not divided into Allied zones (the Soviets had wanted to claim the northern island of Hokkaido, but made no fuss when the U.S. said no). The Japanese occupation was an American show, and MacArthur, the Supreme Commander of the Allied Powers, had almost absolute authority, even though he reigned over an elected Japanese government, which did most of the actual governing. There are several possible reasons why the reeducational zeal in Japan was greater than in Germany. It may be that experiences in Germany set the stage for what followed in Japan. Efforts that were frustrated in Germany by the other Allies, or by German recalcitrance or regional differences, had more chance of success in Japan where the U.S. was almighty. But the main reason might be contained in SCAP's idea of the Japanese as childlike savages, as simple souls ripe for conversion. They were not Christians, nor was their culture rooted in Western civilization. As far as the Japanese mind was concerned, this truly seemed like Year Zero.

Considering how vicious the fighting in the Pacific War and how brutal the wartime propaganda on both sides had been, the Japanese were surprisingly willing pupils. The way the Japanese paid tribute to MacArthur when he left Japan in 1951, after he had been dismissed by President

Truman from his post for insubordination in the Korean War, would have been unthinkable in Germany. A law was enacted to make him an honorary Japanese citizen. Plans were drawn up to build a memorial to the Supreme Commander in Tokyo Bay. And hundreds of thousands of Japanese lined his route to the airport, many of them in tears, shouting their thanks at his limousine. One of the main Japanese newspapers exclaimed in an editorial: "Oh, General MacArthur—General, General, who saved Japan from confusion and starvation."[38]

Here is a letter to SCAP from a Japanese lawyer with strong communist leanings: "For the future of the Japanese people, [the leaders of the Occupation] have brought the peaceful dawn of liberty, equality, and benevolence. They have ably assisted and conscientiously directed the Japanese in the building of a democratic nation . . . to show our gratitude for their accomplishments, we will hold a mass rally to welcome the occupation forces."[39] And this was written in November, just three months after Hiroshima and Nagasaki.

One way of reading Japanese behavior is to see it as an example of Oriental flattery, insincere, self-serving, and fitting a long tradition of appeasing powerful rulers. There may have been an element of this, but it is far from the whole story. I am convinced that much of the gratitude was genuine. Compared to most German (non-Jewish) civilians, whose living conditions, fattened by the loot from conquered countries, were not so bad until the last stages of the war, Japanese had suffered more. Not only did most of their cities go up in flames, as was true in Germany too, but the Japanese had been living on hunger rations for several years. And the bullying by Japanese military authorities and security police forces was probably even more intrusive than in Germany. Unlike many Germans in 1945, who still thought fondly of the Führer, few Japanese had anything good to say about their military regime, which had brought them nothing but misery.

So when the Americans—so wealthy, and crisply turned out, so tall, and in the main so free and easy—settled in, they really were regarded as liberators, and many Japanese were ready to be taught how they might become more free and easy themselves. It wasn't the first time in Japanese history that people decided to learn from a great outside power. China had been the model for many centuries, and Europe and the U.S. had been the examples to emulate since the latter half of the nineteenth century. Militant Japanese nationalism in the twentieth century was in some ways a reaction to an extraordinary run of Westernization, meaning economic liberalism, mass media, Hollywood movies, political parties, Marxism, individualism, baseball, jazz, and so forth. After the disaster of World War II, most Japanese were more than happy to return to modernity, which they associated with the Western world, and, after 1945, with America in particular.

Whether this could really be called reeducation is a moot point. But the new masters, and many of their pupils, clearly thought in those terms. Quite how to "remake" Japan was the question. Japan hands found the whole idea absurd, and the officials most eager to take Japan's reeducation in hand knew very little about the country and its history. To them, there could be no equivalent of denazification, of stripping off a recent layer of toxic ideology from a mature civilization, since Japan was not deemed to have such a thing. Japanese culture itself was thought by reformers to be rotten to the core.

Nevertheless, the need for a total makeover was no more apparent to the old Japanese elites in the imperial court and the bureaucracy than it was to the Japan hands. They would have been perfectly content to stay with small reforms, undertaken slowly. But for Colonel Charles Kades and other New Dealers around SCAP, these reforms wouldn't go nearly far enough. In his words: "[The Japanese leaders] wanted to take a tree that was diseased and prune the branches . . . We felt it was necessary to, in order to get rid of the disease, take the root and branches off."[40]

To purge Japan of its "feudal" culture, it was not enough to tear down Japanese rising sun flags (known as "meatballs" to the GIs), or ban the musical or visual celebrations of Japanese military prowess, or even abolish the Japanese armed forces, or indeed write a new constitution banning Japan's sovereign right to wage war.

All these things were thought to be necessary, to be sure; preparations were already made in 1945 to write the pacifist constitution. (Quite who thought of this novelty first is unclear; some say it was Shidehara Kijiro, the Japanese prime minister in 1945, a longtime pacifist, who suggested it to MacArthur.) "Feudal" family laws were abolished and women's rights guaranteed. This was upsetting to members of Japan's governing elites, even men who were relatively liberal, such as the ex-foreign minister Shigemitsu Mamoru ("Shiggy" in the U.S. press), who wrote in his diary: "The occupation army is thinking along lines that are radically different from any mere compliance with the Potsdam Declaration . . . They propose a remodeling of Japan from top to bottom."[41]

He was right; that is what the reformers set out to do. All Japanese customs and habits, thought to be "feudal," had to be rooted out. American soldiers or civilians who spotted Japanese women breastfeeding in public tried to stop this practice at once. Wooden swords in traditional theater productions were confiscated. Kabuki plays featuring samurai heroes were banned. Earl Ernst, who later became a distinguished scholar of the Kabuki theater, walked into the Imperial Theater in Tokyo one night to halt a performance of *Terakoya*, a scene in a famous eighteenth-century play about a former samurai lord who is ordered to sacrifice his son. Out of loyalty to his lord, a former retainer kills his own son instead. This type of theatrical "barbarism" could not be tolerated. Instead, to edify the Japanese public, the theater company was required to stage a performance of Gilbert and Sullivan's *Mikado*. Rather than being edified, however, the Japanese public was apparently rather nonplussed.

Nothing that could be remotely associated with "feudalism" was allowed. Even the depiction of Mount Fuji, a sacred spot in the ancient nature religion that is Shinto, was banned, in movies, artworks, and on the tiled walls of public bathhouses, where the Fuji was a popular adornment. Since the nineteenth century Shinto had indeed been transformed into a kind of state cult to promote emperor worship and the notion of the Japanese as a unique race, blessed with divine bloodlines, destined to rule the lesser breeds in Asia. Prohibiting the use of Shinto as a state religion was actually not a bad idea. The SCAP directive of 15 December stated:

> The purpose of this directive is to separate religion from the state, to prevent misuse of religion for political ends, and to put all religions, faiths, and creeds upon exactly the same legal basis, entitled to exactly the same opportunities and protection.[42]

Ordering Emperor Hirohito to announce on the radio that he was a human being like everyone else did not seem like such a bad idea, either. What the emperor actually said was that his ties with the Japanese people were not "predicated on the false conception that the emperor is divine." This satisfied the Americans. Most Japanese were hardly surprised by the statement, since they never doubted his humanity. But they saw him as a ruler descended from the Sun Goddess, something he never repudiated. In any case, few Japanese seem to have cared much one way or another. Only ultranationalists were upset, and have remained so ever since, arguing that Shinto should not be treated as any other religion, but as the essence of Japanese culture.

Some of the cultural reeducation was merely irritating, and usually not long-lived, such as the banning of Kabuki plays or swordfight movies. Some of it was so eccentric as to be amusing, like the American soldier in charge of a rural district who thought that teaching the Japanese square dancing would enhance their democratic spirit. But in some things the Americans could go too far, even for the relatively pliant Japanese. For example, the possibility of abolishing Chinese characters and romanizing the Japanese writing system was extensively studied, and then recommended by a U.S. education mission. Nothing came of it. The education system, on the other hand, unlike in Germany, was radically revised. Single-sex elite schools made way for a system of coeducational comprehensive schools, with three years of elementary school, three years of lower secondary, and three years of upper secondary school.

The town of Omi, in the middle of the country, not too far from Kyoto, could serve as the Japanese equivalent of Aachen. In the fall of 1945, a U.S. Army patrol decided to check on a primary school there. The sight of the American soldiers terrified the pupils so much that they started screaming. When asked whether they "liked Americans," there was a vigorous shaking of heads. Schoolrooms were still decorated with wartime posters showing Japanese soldiers striking heroic poses. One of the teachers was a former army officer. A bloodstained sailor's cap was found in a desk drawer. All this would not do at all, so the school principal was ordered to fire the ex-army officer and make sure all references to the war were removed.

Six months later, some of the same Americans returned to the scene in a jeep. This time, the children appeared to be less afraid. One of the officers began to whistle "Swanee River," and to the American party's intense satisfaction, the children sang the song with him in Japanese, followed by renderings of "Auld Lang Syne" and the "Maine Stein Song." The party was equally pleased to note that the textbooks had been properly doctored; all "feudal" passages, referring to the war, to Japan's warrior past, to the emperor, and so on, had been blacked out with India ink. The principal, full of goodwill, spoke in English. He promised that all the wartime posters would be put on a bonfire and several more teachers, three of whom had served in the army, dismissed.[43]

However relieved many Japanese may have been by the relatively benign behavior of the American victors, and however grateful for the democratic reforms forced on their political elites, there were also more complicated feelings about American-style reeducation. A fascinating letter to the *Asahi* newspaper from a junior high school student perfectly expressed a common reaction among young Japanese to the volte-face by their elders; one day they were taught to worship the emperor and support the holy war in Asia, and the next, by the very same teachers, to denounce Japanese feudalism and support *demokurashii*.

The student begins his letter by observing that many adults are worried how hard it will be to change young minds raised with militarism. In fact, he says, recent experience has made teenagers much more politically conscious. All they had ever known was that Japan was permanently at war. Peace was like "emerging from the dark into dazzling sunlight." Everything they had been taught before was shown to be utterly wrong: "How could they ever trust their leaders, or indeed any adults again?" In fact, it was the adults, still often confused and ambivalent about the recent past, who should give cause for worry, for they clearly had more difficulty in freeing themselves from the spirit of militarism.[44]

His was the voice of one of the most politically active generations in Japan's modern history. Most were on the left, and all were filled with distrust of the old Japanese establishment and felt deeply betrayed when the Cold War prompted the same Americans who had come to Japan as teachers of freedom, pacifism, and democracy to embrace that old establishment, many of whose members had the blood of the last war on their hands. Japanese much like the young letter writer to the *Asahi* would pour into the streets of Tokyo in 1960 when Prime Minister Kishi Nobusuke, the Albert Speer of wartime Japan, ratified a security treaty with the U.S. that would turn Japan into a perpetual base for U.S. military operations in Asia. They protested against Japan's indirect—and highly lucrative—involvement in the Vietnam War, which seemed to echo earlier wars in Asia. The Japanese left, enraged by Japan's role in U.S. "imperialism," and the right, just as enraged by having to abide by an "American" pacifist constitution, had one thing in common. To either side, the U.S. occupation seemed never to have ended.

To some people postwar *demokurashii* had come a little too easily, as a kind of gift from the foreign conquerors. A well-known cartoon by Kato Etsuro showed an ecstatic Japanese crowd, some still in military caps, raising their hands to the skies, from which parachuted canisters drop like manna from heaven bearing the words "democratic revolution."[45] To receive something one ought to have fought for oneself was a little humiliating.

Some of the humiliation was intended, but it was not directly aimed at the common Japanese people. The most emblematic photograph of the

Occupation, published in September 1945, was taken on the occasion of Emperor Hirohito's official visit (more an audience, really) to General MacArthur at SCAP's official residence. The emperor, forty-four years old, a mere stripling compared to the Supreme Commander, who was sixty-five, stands stiffly to attention in full morning dress. Next to him stands MacArthur, his superior authority made visible not just by his great height, but a studied casualness: the open-necked khaki shirt, hands comfortably lodged behind his hips.

The photo was printed in all the major newspapers, and the Japanese government, shocked by an image reeking of lèse-majesté, promptly forbade further publication. The following day, MacArthur revoked the ban and ordered new measures to guarantee press freedom. This did not mean that the Americans didn't censor the news as actively as they did in Germany. They did. Mention of Hiroshima was prohibited, for example, as were negative reports about the United States, or any criticism of SCAP's administration. (In 1946, a Japanese film titled *The Japanese Tragedy* was even banned for being too critical of the emperor's wartime role, since MacArthur, after all, had absolved him from all blame.)

Still, democracy was not just an empty word. Some of the revolutionary change dropped in those parachuted canisters was real enough. But there was still that lingering sense of shame, poignantly articulated by Takami Jun, one of the most thoughtful and honest Japanese writers of his time. He wrote in his diary on September 30:

> When I think back to the fact that freedom, which naturally should have been given by the people's own government, could not be given, and instead has been bestowed for the first time by the military forces of a foreign country . . . I cannot escape feelings of shame. I am ashamed as someone who loves Japan, ashamed for Japan's sake.[46]

The feeling is understandable, but such utterances are a bit misleading. One of the conceits of the Occupation, still often heard, is that the

Americans built modern Japanese institutions from scratch, that "Westernization" began in 1945, and that the Japanese, thanks to benevolent U.S. guidance, jumped from "feudalism" to democracy in a year or two after their wartime defeat. In fact, democratic institutions, flawed and fragile as they may have been, were already in place by the 1920s. In Japan, as in the Western zones of Germany, after the war Western Allies created the conditions for those institutions to be restored on a firmer basis. This was not always automatic. Japanese politicians and bureaucrats often had to be forced to carry out democratic reforms which most people welcomed. What neither the Americans nor the Japanese could have anticipated, however, was that the one thing the Americans did concoct entirely by themselves would become both the cornerstone, and the burden, of the postwar Japanese identity.

Article 9 of the Japanese constitution, although it was written only in 1946, and thus outside the scope of this book, is still worth quoting, since it, more than anything else, expresses the idealism of 1945:

> (1) Aspiring sincerely to an international peace based on justice and order, the Japanese people forever renounce war as a sovereign right of the nation and the threat or use of force as means of settling international disputes. (2) To accomplish the aim of the preceding paragraph, land, sea, and air forces, as well as other war potential, will never be maintained. The right of belligerency of the state will not be recognized.

In 1953, on a visit to Japan as Eisenhower's vice president, Richard Nixon shocked the Japanese by declaring that Article 9 had been a mistake. There was no reason why the Japanese shouldn't revise it. The United States wouldn't object. Indeed, the United States wanted Japan to be a strong ally against communism. But most Japanese disagreed. They refused to change their constitution because they were proud of it. Pacifism had given a nation which had slaughtered millions of people in several terrible wars a new sense of moral purpose, even superiority. Japan would lead the world into a new era of peace. In Japanese eyes, it was the Americans, in Korea, Vietnam, and later in Iraq or Afghanistan, who ought to be condemned for refusing to relinquish the habit of war.

This, more or less, was the tone of public discourse in Japan for at least fifty years after the war. But pacifism came with a price. Idealism and reality soon diverged, and the Japanese, contrary to the words of their constitution, did rebuild their armed forces, disguised at first as police forces, and later as the Japan Self-Defense Forces (JSDF). Not only was this hypocritical, but it failed to address another problem, resented almost equally by Japanese on both the right and the left. Japan was still dependent on the U.S. for its security; pacifism was professed under the nuclear umbrella of its former conquerors. There never was the equivalent in East Asia of NATO, or a European Union, allowing Japan to build trust and find a new place among its neighbors.

Article 9, still clung to by most people, but fiercely resented by the nationalistic right, has also muddled Japanese attitudes towards their own history. So long as liberals and leftists defend the pacifist clause as an essential penance for wartime guilt, the right maintains that Japan was no more guilty than any other country at war. If the Rape of Nanking or the Manila Massacre are reasons to deprive the nation of a sovereign right, then there is every reason to minimize the importance of those "incidents." This hopelessly polarized political dispute, masquerading as a historical debate, has poisoned Japan's relations with the rest of Asia for decades. Apart from the one-sided dependence on the United States, this too has been part of the legacy of 1945, a year of many catastrophes that ended with such high hopes.

CHAPTER 9

ONE WORLD

rian Urquhart, the young British army intelligence officer mentioned earlier in this book, the man who had been told to go on sick leave after he alerted his superior officers to the colossal risks of dropping Allied forces near the Dutch town of Arnhem in September 1944, could easily have ended up as a cynic. Operation Market-Garden, costing thousands of young lives, went ahead anyway. "Monty" wanted to outshine his American rival, General George Patton, no matter what. A little more than six months later, already disillusioned by the arrogant stupidity of his own side, Urquhart was among the first Allied soldiers to enter Bergen-Belsen. First, the idiocy, then the horror. When the war was finally over, he could not summon up much joy.

And yet, somehow, he avoided the trap of cynicism. He recalled in his memoir: "I did not meditate that things would never be the same. I hadn't had too much experience of the old order and did not feel I would miss it. I *did* think that the greatest task at hand would be to help prevent such disasters from ever happening again."[1]

Before the war, Urquhart had been excited by the League of Nations. His internationalist enthusiasm had been inspired, he recalls, by his childhood connection to a private girls' boarding school, Badminton, run by an eccentric headmistress named Miss Beatrice M. Baker, known to all as BMB. Urquhart's mother taught at Badminton School. His aunt Lucy was the formidable BMB's partner, in the school and in life. At the age of six, Urquhart was the only little boy among more than two hundred girls. BMB's sympathies were very much on the left. Like many people at the time, she took a benign view of "Uncle Joe" Stalin. BMB also took in Jewish refugees from the Continent during the 1930s, not something most private boarding school headmistresses would have done at the time. She even made her girls, including my mother, who was a pupil during the war, march through the streets of Bristol under banners that read "Workers of the World Unite!"

After the war was over, Urquhart was briefly taken on by the historian Arnold Toynbee in a special department at the Foreign Office set up to gather intelligence from Nazi-occupied Holland. Since Holland was no longer under Nazi occupation, there was nothing much to do—a small example of the many bureaucratic oddities left over from the war. This assignment didn't last long, however. Urquhart's next employer was Gladwyn Jebb, the British diplomat in charge of organizing the recently established United Nations, whose charter he helped draft. For the rest of his professional life, Urquhart remained a loyal servant of that world institution whose ideals continued to move him, even as he viewed its flaws in practice with due skepticism.

Four decades later he wrote of that heady time in the fall of 1945:

> . . . it is hard to recapture the freshness and enthusiasm of those pioneering days. The war was still vivid in everyone's mind and experience. Many of us had been in the armed forces, and others had only emerged from underground resistance movements a few months before. To work for peace was a dream fulfilled, and the

fact that everything had to be organized from scratch was an additional incentive.[2]

One of Urquhart's closest friends in the UN secretariat was another man mentioned before, the French resistance fighter Stéphane Hessel, who was arrested and tortured by the Gestapo before being sent to Buchenwald and Dora. He was born in 1919, the same year as Urquhart. Hessel, too, had an unusual background. His father, Franz Hessel, a distinguished German writer and translator of Proust, was the model for Jules in *Jules et Jim*, the story of a fatal Franco-German love triangle, later made into the famous film by François Truffaut. Like Urquhart, Stéphane Hessel wanted to build a better world on a global stage. His ambition was spurred by something more remarkable than the usual loathing of war and longing for peace. He wrote in his memoir that it was "the cosmopolitanism of the concentration camps," where men from many nations and classes were thrown together, that "pushed me towards diplomacy."[3] Three years after the end of the war, he helped to draft the first Universal Declaration of Human Rights (adopted in 1948). Hessel died in 2013, at the age of ninety-five.

No doubt, Urquhart and Hessel were extraordinary men. But their idealism, born from the experience of devastation, was not out of the ordinary. The idea that a new world order had to be built, governed by a global organization, more robust and effective than the League of Nations, was widely believed. Some took this notion very far. Even before the atomic bombs were dropped on Hiroshima and Nagasaki, proponents of world government often spoke in apocalyptic terms. Arnold Toynbee's pronouncements during the war that a Third World War could be prevented only by a world government, with a worldwide police force, would seem to be on the zany side, but he was taken seriously enough by senior figures in the U.S. State Department. A Gallup poll taken in April 1945 revealed that 81 percent of Americans wanted the U.S. to enter "a world organization with police power to maintain world peace."[4]

Since the concept of world government or world federation was quite vague, thinkers along these lines tended to project their personal ideals on the future. Mahatma Gandhi, not surprisingly, held that a world federation should be based on his principles of nonviolence. Toynbee argued that the worldwide police force, at least for some time to come, should be an Anglo-American operation. The idea was to create a "democratic Anglo-American World Commonwealth."[5] He was not alone. Lord Lothian, the ambassador to Washington in 1939, saw the British Empire as the model for a federal world government. This, too, might strike one as not only self-serving but utterly fanciful. Yet the idea of a kind of liberal Anglo-Saxon hegemony was not unusual in Britain or the U.S. Churchill believed in it for a while. Indeed, the notion still pops up on occasion to feed the self-esteem of English-speaking dreamers, including one or two occupants of the White House.

The *New Yorker* writer E. B. White commented in that magazine that San Francisco was just the right place for a conference to draft the first United Nations Charter in the spring of 1945. After all, he said, the "United States is regarded by people everywhere as a dream come true, a sort of world state in miniature."[6] If this kind of smugness feels rather stale today, it, too, has not totally vanished. Even so, E. B. White was quite aware of certain blemishes on the American dreamscape. He noted on May 5, a week after the San Francisco Conference had begun, that somewhere in California "a group of preservationists (we saw by the papers) were attempting to restrict residence in a certain area to 'people of the Caucasian race.'"[7]

Then there were the Europeans, often in the anti-Nazi, antifascist resistance, who saw European unity as the first step towards a united world. Already in 1942, the French resistance group Combat (also known as the Mouvement de Libération Nationale [MLN]) published a manifesto declaring that "The United States of Europe—a stage on the road to world union—will soon be a living reality for which we are fighting."[8] One of the main figures in Combat was Albert Camus, not a man usually given to hyperbole. He was later in close touch with another group of antifascist resisters who issued a manifesto for European unity even earlier, in 1941, from the tiny volcanic island of Ventotene, off the coast of Naples, where Altiero Spinelli and other Italian leftists were incarcerated by Mussolini in a bleak eighteenth-century prison built by the Bourbons. The so-called Ventotene Manifesto, written by one of the prisoners, the political thinker Ernesto Rossi, declared that national politics was for reactionaries, and all progressives should struggle for "a solid international state." First a federal Europe, then a federal world.

The ideal of a united Europe is much older, of course, going at least as far back as the Holy Roman Empire in the ninth century. Since then the European ideal went through many changes, but there were two constant themes. One was the ideal of a unified Christendom, with Europe as the spiritual and political core. This goal would remain popular among Catholics—Erasmus for one—and especially French Catholics. Maximilien de Béthune, the duke de Sully (1560–1641), for example, conceived of a Christian European republic which the Turks could join only if they converted to the Christian faith.

The related ideal was eternal peace. In 1713, another Catholic Frenchman, the Abbé de Saint-Pierre, published his "Project for the Creation of Eternal Peace in Europe." There would be a European senate, a European army, and the larger member-states would have equal voting rights.

Eternal peace and Christian unity were often identical in the minds of early pan-Europeanists. Peaceful unification was a religious notion, a Christian utopia. Not necessarily meant to be confined to the European continent, it was, like Christianity itself, a universalist aspiration. National borders, ideally, should be abolished in the earthly kingdom of God.

After the Enlightenment, a new version of this religious universalism was adopted by rationalists with only minor rhetorical changes. The French nineteenth-century poet and statesman Alphonse de Lamartine wrote a rationalist ode to European unity titled the "Marseillaise of Peace" (1841): "In the course of enlightenment, the world rises to unity / I am the fellow citizen of every thinking person / Truth is my country." As foreign minister of France in the revolutionary year of 1848, Lamartine published a Manifesto for Europe, promoting the French Republic as a model not just for Europe, but for all mankind.

A similar switch from religious to rationalist idealism took place at the end of World War II. In 1940, before the U.S. had even joined the war, an outfit called the Federal Council of the Churches of Christ in America set up a commission to work on a "Just and Durable Peace"—a bit premature, perhaps, but always a subject worth pursuing. Protestant ministers and lay-men were sometimes joined by Jews and Catholics in this endeavor. "Na-tional missions on world order" were established in major U.S. cities. The need for a world organization was set out in a statement by the commission called the "Six Pillars of Peace." Lest anyone suspect the statement was the work of idle dreamers, the chairman of the commission was John Foster Dulles, an admirer of Hitler in the early 1930s and a fierce cold warrior in the 1950s when he served as Eisenhower's secretary of state.

Dulles played a major role in some very shabby, not to say morally dubious, policies: he supported the French colonial war against the Viet-minh nationalists, and he also helped to bring down the democratically elected Iranian government of premier Mohammad Mosaddeq in 1953. Mosaddeq was regarded as soft on communism and a threat to Anglo-American oil interests. A coup, engineered by British agents and the CIA, led by Dulles's brother Allen, was the result. But Dulles's anticommunism was not only dictated by corporate business. He was a Christian moralist who believed that the war against godless communism was above all a moral enterprise. He also claimed to believe in what he called the "moral power" of the United Nations, and acted as an adviser to the U.S. delega-tion in San Francisco.[9] His response to the use of atomic bombs against Japan might seem unusual, not just for the time, but for a man associated with American conservatism, but it was not untypical of him: "If we, as a professedly Christian nation, feel morally free to use atomic energy in that way, men elsewhere will accept that verdict."[10]

It was indeed the devastation of Hiroshima that changed "one world" rhetoric from something that was often inspired by religious morality to something more secular, and immediate. Scientists were among the first to warn about the implications of a weapon some of them had helped to create. The fearsome explosion of the first atomic bomb in the desert of New Mexico, on July 16, 1945, even prompted a quasi-religious response from Robert Oppenheimer, a leading figure in developing the bomb. He quoted words from the Hindu scripture Bhagavad Gita:

If the radiance of a thousand suns
Were to burst at once into the sky,
That would be like the splendor of the Mighty One . . .
Now, I am become Death, the shatterer of worlds.

Einstein's first words on hearing about the bombing of Hiroshima were more prosaic: "Oh, weh!"[11]

Two months later, Einstein cosigned a letter to the *New York Times*, along with such prominent figures as Senator J. W. Fulbright and Owen J. Roberts, associate justice of the Supreme Court. They wrote, "The first atomic bomb destroyed more than the city of Hiroshima. It also exploded our inherited, outdated political ideas."[12] These ideas included national sovereignty. The United Nations Charter agreed upon in San Francisco was just a beginning, they proclaimed: "We must aim at a Federal Constitution of the world, a working world-wide legal order, if we hope to prevent another atomic war."

John Foster Dulles had argued for UN control of nuclear energy, before he changed his mind fast once the Soviet Union exploded its own bomb. Einstein, in an interview published in the *Atlantic Monthly* in November 1945, thought that the "secret of the bomb should be committed to a World Government, and the United States should immediately announce its readiness to give it to a World Government."

The case for moral reason was perhaps made most succinctly by that old Christian socialist, the British prime minister, Clement Attlee, in a speech to the Canadian houses of parliament in the same month that Einstein's interview appeared in the *Atlantic Monthly*. Speaking partly in French, and very much with Hiroshima in mind, Attlee proposed that science and morality had to be brought into harmony. He believed, as the *Times* of London reported, "that without a moral enthusiasm equal to that which savants bring to their researches, the civilization built over the centuries would be destroyed."[13]

. . .

THE WAY THE ACTUAL WORLD was beginning to be remade in 1945 might have owed something to the high-minded idealism of former resistance fighters and soldiers for peace, shocked scientists and Christian one-worlders, but not nearly as much as they might have wished. What shaped international institutions after the war (and, in fact, already during the war) was not so much religion or moral ideals, as politics. Since political solutions are never ideal, the new order was bound to be imperfect.

The origin of the UN Charter that would be worked out in San Francisco was a meeting of Churchill and Roosevelt in Placentia Bay, off the coast of Newfoundland, in August 1941. Britain had survived in the Battle of Britain, if only just. Germany had just invaded the Soviet Union, on June 22, and Pearl Harbor was soon to come (December 7, 1941). Roosevelt was keen to nudge American voters gently towards accepting a more active U.S. role in the European conflict. And so the two leaders arrived on their respective battleships, Roosevelt on the USS *Augusta*, Churchill on HMS *Prince of Wales*, to draft an "Atlantic Charter."

Curiously, it was Churchill who was keen to include mention of a future world organization in the Charter. Roosevelt, disillusioned by the failure of the League of Nations and nervously aware of domestic resistance to international entanglements, struck out Churchill's suggestion. Nor was Roosevelt keen on British imperialism, although he did believe, in line with Toynbee, that Britain and the U.S. should jointly police the world for some years. Roosevelt invoked his "Four Essential Human Freedoms," first announced to the world in January of that same year, as the reasons for fighting fascism. They were immortalized in the sentimental illustrations of Norman Rockwell: Freedom of Speech, Freedom of Worship, Freedom from Want, and Freedom from Fear.

The Atlantic Charter, in fact, turned out to be little more than an elaboration of these fine principles. But one clause did have a significant and long-lasting impact. It was very much the work of the Americans. Not only did the Charter express "the hope that self-government may be restored to those from whom it has been forcibly removed." It went further: "the right of all people to choose the form of government under which they will live" would be respected as well.[14]

News of this aspiration immediately got through to those who were fighting to be free from colonial empires. Nationalist leaders such as Ho Chi Minh in Vietnam and Sukarno in Indonesia would quote the words of the Atlantic Charter over and over in their demands for political independence—and for U.S. support. The Algerian protesters in Sétif, who were gunned down on May 8 by French settlers for demanding equality, carried banners that read: "Long Live the Atlantic Charter!"

Jawaharlal Nehru, in prison for "civil disobedience" when the Atlantic Charter was drawn up, sensed hypocrisy in the Anglo-American pronouncements; he dismissed the Charter as a set of pious platitudes. But in his "Quit India" campaign of the following year, Nehru echoed the Charter's call for national self-determination. He also called for a "world federation" that would guarantee such rights.

Churchill had to move fast to reassure Parliament that the right to "self-government" referred only to nations under Nazi occupation. The colonies were an entirely different matter. After all, as he famously remarked in 1942, he had "not become the King's First Minister in order to preside over the liquidation of the British Empire." Roosevelt had no time for this kind of bluster, and was sympathetic to Nehru, but did not want to push Churchill too hard while there was still a war on. Churchill, for his part, resented being "school-marmed" by the U.S. on imperial affairs, since the U.S. itself had anything but clean hands, notably in the Philippines. This was true enough, but Churchill forgot to mention that the U.S. had already promised independence to the Philippines before the war, a process that was interrupted by the Japanese invasion.

From the Atlantic Charter, it was but a short step to the United

Nations, albeit not yet as a world organization for global security, but as an alliance against the Axis Powers. Twenty-six nations, including China and the Soviet Union, signed up for it in January 1942. Despite his earlier reservations about international organizations, it was Roosevelt who gave the alliance its name, just weeks after the attack on Pearl Harbor, when Churchill, in a very fine mood, was visiting the White House for a conference code-named "Arcadia." Roosevelt had been thinking about what to call the new worldwide alliance. Then, before breakfast one day, inspiration hit. Barging into Churchill's bathroom, he shouted at the prime minister, who was still dripping from his bath: "The United Nations!" And Churchill said it was good.

The main question, worked on all through the war by bureaucrats, planners, diplomats, and the Allied leaders, was how to transform the wartime alliance into a stable postwar international order for peace. How to avoid another worldwide economic slump. How to stop future Hitlers from starting another world war. And how to do this without stirring up American conservatives, who were quick to brand such international enterprises as the dark doings of "communists." Whatever the new world organization would look like (Churchill still thought in terms of the "English-speaking peoples," Stalin of "peace-loving" peoples, and Roosevelt of a harmonious Big Power coalition), it had to have real clout. For that was precisely what the old League of Nations had lacked. The new UN would need the capacity to impose peace, by force if necessary. To assert such authority effectively, the major powers had to get along, hence the conferences in Moscow, Teheran, and Yalta, where the postwar order was thrashed out, sometimes on the back of envelopes, by Churchill, Roosevelt, and Stalin, making their moves as though the world were a giant chessboard, with Poles, Greeks, and other peoples, pushed around like pawns.

In the U.S., meanwhile, new international bodies were created to deal with humanitarian aid and food shortages in the countries ruined by war. The United Nations Relief and Rehabilitation Administration (UNRRA) was formed in 1943, an organization Churchill, at first, found hard to take seriously. Once again in his bathroom, he was heard to sing "UNRRA!,

UNRRA!, UNRRA!" as though it were a music hall turn. After the war, UNRRA was inevitably accused by Republicans in the United States of being soft on communism. There was some reason for this: since western European governments were deemed to be able to take care of their own problems, much of the relief went to eastern European countries and Soviet republics, where the spoils tended to go to political favorites. UNRRA was often a shambolic enterprise, especially in the early stages, and yet without it many more people would have perished in dreadful conditions.

By the time Stalin's Red Army was driving back the exhausted Germans across the icy plains of the Ukraine and the Western Allies had secured their beachheads at Normandy, the Big Powers had a rough idea what the future UN organization would look like. It would have a General Assembly, and a Security Council controlled by the Big Powers themselves. Economic cooperation to defeat Germany—Lend-Lease, and so on—provided the basis for an international monetary system, with international rules to contain the excesses of economic nationalism and noxious forms of speculation. And there would be an International Court of Justice.

The monetary system was set up in 1944 at a resort hotel in New Hampshire named Bretton Woods. The meeting, formally titled the United Nations Monetary and Financial Conference, was held at Bretton Woods for two reasons: the New Hampshire senator on the congressional banking and currency committee was a Republican opponent of currency regulation who needed to be brought around, and the hotel accepted Jewish guests, which was not always the case in rural establishments of this sort. It would hardly have done for Treasury secretary Henry Morgenthau, among others, to be turned away at the door.

In November 1944, Roosevelt won his fourth term as president of the United States. That he was by then fully committed to a postwar UN was obvious from his campaign statements. The world needed a global New Deal, in his view, and the UN needed to be empowered to secure global peace. As he said at the time: "To my simple mind it is clear that, if the world organization is to have any reality at all, our American representatives must be endowed in advance by the people themselves, by constitutional means through their representatives in Congress, with authority to act."[15] Even though the voices that associated Roosevelt and his ideals with "communism" had not been stilled, most American citizens now appeared to agree with him.

Just before Roosevelt's fourth election, there had been one more conference on the UN, held discreetly at Dumbarton Oaks, a plush estate in Georgetown, Washington, D.C. The United States, Britain, and the Soviet Union, the so-called Big Three, had decided Allied policies during the war. This time, a Big Fourth, China, was invited to take part as well. These Big Four, it was hoped, would jointly police the postwar world, even though there was limited confidence that China would be able to play its part. Neither Churchill nor Stalin had much respect for Chiang Kai-shek's regime, but the Americans were very keen to give the Generalissimo face. (Later, in San Francisco, the Big Four became the Big Five, with France in urgent need of face-saving as well.)

There were still disagreements at Dumbarton Oaks, however, about the exact shape of the United Nations. Which countries would be eligible for membership? Should the UN mission confine itself to security (the Soviet position) or also include economic and social affairs, which is what the U.S. wanted (and got)? Should there be an international air force? Who would supply UN troops? Should every member have the right to veto UN actions, as was the case in the League of Nations, or just the Big Powers? Exactly what should be subject to veto—just the actions, or investigations and topics for discussion too? Compromises were struck, and hard questions (the veto) left unresolved. Membership, in principle, would be open to all "peace-loving states," a phrase that appealed to the sentimental side of the Americans, but meant something more specific to Stalin, who habitually denounced critics of the Soviet Union as enemies of peace. Finland, for example, which had defied the Soviet Red Army in 1940, was an enemy of peace.

And so the stage was set for San Francisco, where, on April 27, 1945, the peace-loving world would unite and the UN be transformed from a wartime alliance to a "democratic organization of the world," as Roosevelt liked to say.[16]

Sadly, the president, already gravely ill and fatally exhausted by the conference at Yalta, where, despite the grandeur of the tsar's old summer palace, conditions were not comfortable (bedbugs were a particular torment), died on April 12. But the new president, Harry S. Truman, actually cranked up expectations for a democratic world order even higher than his predecessor had done. Upon receiving an honorary degree in June from the University of Kansas City, not long before putting his signature to the UN Charter, Truman declared in a burst of Yankee optimism: "It will be just as easy for nations to get along in a republic of the world as it is for us to get along in the republic of the United States."[17]

. . .

THE FLAGS OF FIFTY NATIONS snapped in the Pacific breeze, as five thousand delegates arrived, and hundreds of thousands of spectators flooded the streets for the opening ceremony at the San Francisco Opera House. All the world—except Germans, Japanese, and their allies, of course—was there. Or actually, not all the world; there were exceptions. And perhaps not everyone that was there, should have been. Argentina, whose military junta, until the very end of the war, had been distinctly sympathetic to the fascist camp, was invited because of some gamesmanship between the U.S. and the Soviet Union. The latter wanted the Soviet republics of Ukraine and Belarus to be full members, so the U.S., needing Latin American support, insisted on the inclusion of Argentina.

Poland, on the other hand, the country where World War II began, was not invited, because there was no agreement over a legitimate government. The Soviet Union had sponsored a provisional Polish government, known as the Lublin Committee, while the Polish government-in-exile continued to make its claims from London. As long as this was so, there was no question of inviting the Lublin Committee to San Francisco, as the Soviets wanted. Stalin had assured Churchill and Roosevelt at Yalta that Poland would have free elections, and sixteen leaders of the Polish wartime underground had even been invited for a friendly chat with the Russians. That nothing more was heard from these Polish leaders since was ominous. In the words of E. B. White in the *New Yorker*, "Over the city the Polish question hovered like a foul bird."[18]

Still, there was enough optimism to get on with. Arab delegates had a particularly exotic appeal for the local gawpers. According to *Yank* magazine, "American celebrity hounds jostled one another to look at the Aye-rabs from close up and said, to a man, 'Sheeks, huh? How about that?'"

And the Arabs responded with similar bafflement. A Mr. Farid Zeineddine of Syria described his impressions to *Yank*: "The Americans seem to me like a nation of people in spectacles, all chewing gum. Maybe they have to wear spectacles because the buildings are so high and they strain their eyes to see up and down them."[19]

Others surveyed the scene with a more acid eye. Michael Foot, the future leader of the British Labour Party, was there as a columnist for the *Daily Herald*. A good European socialist, he was worried about the "dangers of America's present status." The U.S. was simply too rich, too unscathed by war, too powerful. "America's economic prospects," he observed, "seem to dwarf the conference itself." What was more, newsreels shown at local cinemas of the Nazi concentration camps did not, as he put it, "incite to mafficking" (rejoicing, as British crowds did during the Boer War when the siege of Mafeking was lifted).[20]

Other films in the American cinemas that spring, no doubt aimed at lifting the flagging war spirit in the last months of the Pacific War, were John Wayne's *Back to Bataan*, and *Objective, Burma!* with Errol Flynn. But there was more cheerful entertainment on hand as well, including MGM's *Son of Lassie*, Dorothy Lamour in *Medal for Benny*, and *Here Come the Co-Eds* with Abbott and Costello.

Accommodations, for which delegates were supposed to pay themselves, were certainly more plush than at Yalta. Gladwyn Jebb, who had attended most wartime conferences, including Yalta, as Churchill's diplomatic adviser, described the San Francisco experience as "an appalling outbreak of hospitality."[21] The Big Four Powers (soon to be Five), presided over by U.S. Secretary of State Edward R. Stettinius Jr., met in the circular library of a penthouse apartment at the top of the Fairmont Hotel—"with a blue ceiling and two love seats upholstered in green," in the words of *Time* magazine.[22] The lesser delegations worked on the floors below.

Agreement on general principles came swiftly between the Big Powers. But there were tensions between them and the rest, between the aim of Big Power dominance and a democratic world organization. The smaller countries, represented by the grandiloquent Australian foreign minister, Dr. Herbert Evatt, resented the veto rights of the Big Powers in the Security Council, but they had to give way. The Soviet foreign minister, Vyacheslav Molotov, took the most extreme Big Power position. He continued to insist on the right to veto any subject the Soviet Union did not wish to be discussed in the UN. This attitude almost sank the conference, until a U.S. diplomatic mission was sent to Moscow, and Stalin instructed Molotov to back down.

All appeared to be fine, among the Big Three at least, when Molotov organized a lavish banquet for his British and U.S. counterparts, the suave Anthony Eden, and Edward Stettinius, described by Brian Urquhart as "a man with theatrical good looks and unnaturally white teeth."[23] As usual at these Russian affairs, huge amounts of food and drink were consumed. Photographs were taken of the three men toasting one another, in which even the colorless Molotov, known in Soviet Party circles as "Steely Ass" for the long hours spent at his desk, managed to contrive an air of bonhomie. It was getting late. The gentlemen were beginning to feel distinctly woozy.

Then something extraordinary happened. Still in an expansive mood of chummy goodwill, Molotov announced to his esteemed colleagues that he could finally divulge what had happened to the sixteen leaders from the Polish underground. They had been arrested for "diversionist activity" against the Soviet Red Army, a crime that carried the death penalty. Eden, first shocked, then furious, demanded a full explanation. Molotov, ruffled by Eden's sharp tone, became sullen and defensive. The festive mood instantly evaporated. Once more, the conference was in danger.

This storm, too, blew over, however. Wishful thinking kept reality at bay. American liberals were told by the *Nation* magazine that once "truly free elections" were held in Poland, "Russia's moral position" would be "greatly strengthened" and "distrust reduced to a minimum."[24] The vague promise of free elections was the fig leaf, eagerly grasped at by the Western Allies at Yalta, which no one yet wished to throw away. Only the Soviets knew that the sixteen brave Poles who had risked everything by resisting the Germans in the most ghastly conditions had already been tortured by the Soviet secret police and tried as "Nazi collaborators." They were sentenced on June 21, while the San Francisco conference was still going on. All but two were later murdered in Soviet prisons.

Even as the sixteen Poles were being tortured in Moscow, the Big Powers discussed a declaration on human rights for inclusion in the preamble to the Charter (the Universal Declaration of Human Rights came later, in 1948). This noble fruit of Enlightenment thinking, as well as Christian universalism, the idea that human rights should benefit not just one community, defined by faith or culture or political borders, but mankind, was seen by Stéphane Hessel and many others as the greatest contribution of the postwar order. Universal human rights were linked to the law, adopted in Nuremberg, on "crimes against humanity," which in turn was linked to the concept of genocide, defined in 1944 by the Polish lawyer Raphael Lemkin as "the deliberate and systematic destruction, in whole or in part, of an ethnic, racial, religious, or national group."

Not that anyone suggested for a minute that human rights would or could be enforced. Quite to the contrary. In the words of a British foreign policy adviser at San Francisco, the historian C. K. Webster, "Our policy is to avoid '*guarantee* of human rights,' though we might not object to a declaration."[25] And a declaration duly arrived, based on a draft written by General Jan Smuts, the South African statesman and hero of the Boer War, who had assisted at the birth of the League of Nations, as well as of the UN. These were the words decided upon in San Francisco by the Big Powers in June: "We the peoples of the United Nations determined . . . to reaffirm faith in fundamental human rights, in the dignity and worth of the human person, in the equal rights of men and women and of nations large and small . . ."

Michael Foot, in his column for the *Daily Herald,* singled out the moral leadership of the Soviet Union for special praise. He pointed out that before the war the British government under Neville Chamberlain had suppressed the news of Nazi atrocities. But then, of course, "the victims were only Liberals, Socialists, Pacifists and Jews." Nowadays, he observed with a touch of superciliousness, "these types will have the advantage of their rights being included in the preamble of the Charter of Fundamental Freedoms drawn up by General Smuts. This Charter will even apply to black people in South Africa. Or will it?" Foot's doubts on this score were not unfounded, but he, too, was happy to overlook the foul stench of the Polish question. Indeed, he commended the Soviets for expressing "a far more logical and unequivocal view" on "the political rights of dependent peoples than any other nation."

There was one more crisis before the Conference reached its conclusion at the end of June. The action, this time, was in the Levant, where on May 29 French troops were fighting Syrians in the streets of Damascus, and dropping bombs, not just on the ancient capital, but on Aleppo, Hama, and Homs. The French had called for reinforcements after Syrian demands that they transfer special Syrian forces under French command to the Syrian national army.

The next day, Syrian president Shukri al-Quwatli, a deft diplomatic operator, wrote a letter to President Truman expressing the same sentiments as Ho Chi Minh and Sukarno, though with a much more successful outcome. Here were the French, he wrote in perfectly justified indignation, killing Syrians with weapons bought with money borrowed from the United States to fight the Germans. The United States had recognized Syria as an independent country in 1944. So: "Where now is the Atlantic Charter and the Four Freedoms? What can we think of San Francisco?"[26]

The Americans needed little encouragement to take the side of the Syrians. European imperialism was not popular in Washington, and

French imperialism least of all. Unlike Indochina, which was rather more alien territory to the Americans in those days, Syria and Lebanon had long been regarded with the kind of benevolent paternalism bestowed on the Chinese as well, a mixture of missionary zeal and commercial interest: the American University in Beirut, Christian missions in Jerusalem, an Open Door economic policy. The popular phrase among U.S. policymakers at the time was "moral leadership." No doubt, as appears to be true of John Foster Dulles, the moral sentiment was sincere, but so was the ambition to lead.

Since the Allies had already promised to recognize postwar Syrian independence when British troops occupied the Levant in 1941, they could hardly ignore Quwatli's plea now. So Churchill instructed his man on the spot, General Bernard Paget, to drive the French back into their barracks. This was not a difficult task, as the French were far too few in number to resist. The left-leaning *Manchester Guardian* reported the event with patriotic delight. Its reporter "marched into Damascus with the sailors . . . while crowds of surprised Damascenes clapped their hands . . . The people of Damascus hissed and booed the long line of lorries, tanks, and Bren-gun carriers taking French troops out of the city, escorted by British armored cars . . ."[27]

General de Gaulle responded with fury to what he saw as a heinous Anglo-Saxon conspiracy: "We are not in a position to open hostilities against you at the present time. But you have insulted France and betrayed the West. This cannot be forgotten."[28]

On the surface, the Syrian crisis was the perfect test for the new world order that was being shaped in San Francisco. If ever there was a legitimate case for living up to the words of the Atlantic Charter and the ethos of the UN, this was it. The French, despite promises made in 1941, were trying to restore their colonial authority. The British were quite right to put them in their place, hence the proud tone of the *Guardian's* report.

It wasn't, of course, quite as simple as that. As they had elsewhere in the Middle East, the British played a double game, making different promises to different people. With the end of the Ottoman Empire in sight in 1916, Britain and France in the Sykes-Picot Agreement had carved up the Levant into spheres of interest: France would have the run of Syria and Lebanon while Britain took charge of Transjordan and Iraq. In 1941, a year after France had been defeated by Germany, British forces moved into Damascus, promising to support Syrian independence while recognizing France's privileged position. These were obviously not compatible aims. In fact, what the British really wanted was to become the major players in the Levant themselves. So they were quite happy to see the Syrians provoke the French. Violent French retaliation was just the excuse needed to kick them out altogether. And this, in effect, is what was happening in the early summer of 1945.

There was something quaintly old-fashioned, indeed redolent of late-nineteenth-century imperial skirmishes, about the Syrian crisis. In any event, though this was not yet clear in San Francisco, Britain and France would both lose their preeminent positions in the Middle East. The United States and the Soviet Union would soon call the shots. One British wartime plan offered a glimpse of the not too distant future. It was hoped in London that Britain and the U.S. would jointly police the postwar world by establishing military bases under the auspices of the UN; the U.S. in Asia, and the British in the Middle East. The Americans had already made it clear that local sovereignty would not stretch to areas selected for U.S. military installations—the so-called strategic trust territories. Already in the first months after the war, the dim shape of a more informal empire was starting to be visible. What the British had not quite realized was how minor their role in this new world was destined to be.

The Syrians were not alone in demanding independence. Indeed this was one of the talking points of San Francisco. And Michael Foot was not wrong to say that the Soviet Union, for its own not strictly philosophical reasons, was more supportive of such aspirations than its western European allies. But, although the General Assembly would, in time, become a vital forum for anticolonial agitation, decolonization was not yet on the agenda in 1945. The most that colonial powers would concede was the promise, enshrined in the UN Charter, to look after "the well-being" of the inhabitants of the "non-self-governing territories." Self-government would be promoted "according to the particular circumstances of each territory and its peoples and their various stages of advancement." The former governor of the Punjab, Baron (William Malcolm) Hailey of Shahpur and Newport Pagnell, could reassure the readers of the London *Times* that there was "nothing here which is not already implicit in our own policy." And, more important, there was "clearly no intention that the United Nations Organization should intervene in the application of the principles of the charter by the colonial powers concerned."[29] All that Britain, France, and other imperial powers were obliged to do was to report regularly to the Secretary General of the UN on conditions in the "territories" they continued to possess.

. . .

GIVEN THE HIGH EXPECTATIONS in some quarters for a world government, the final outcome of the San Francisco conference was bound to disappoint. For a world government to work, national governments would have had to give up their sovereign rights. Of the Big Powers, only China, represented by T. V. Soong, business tycoon and politician, talked about "yielding if necessary a part of our sovereignty."[30] China had even been prepared to give up on Big Power veto rights. But since Chiang Kai-shek's sovereignty in China itself was already looking shaky, Chinese magnanimity in this matter did not cut much ice.

In his dispatches for the *New Yorker*, E. B. White had put his finger on the main paradox of the conference. He wrote that "the first stirrings of internationalism seem to tend toward, rather than away from, nationalism."[31] He saw in the national flags, the uniforms, the martial music, the secret meetings, the diplomatic moves, "a denial of the world community." Under all the fine internationalist rhetoric, he heard "the steady throbbing of the engines: sovereignty, sovereignty, sovereignty."

Another observer in San Francisco was John F. Kennedy, recently discharged from the U.S. Navy. He agreed with the "world federalists" that "world organization with common obedience to law would be the solution." But he realized that nothing would ever come of this unless the common feeling that war was the "ultimate evil" were strong enough to drive governments together. An unlikely event, in his view.[32]

Even the dropping of two atomic bombs failed to bring that sentiment about. A week after Nagasaki was devastated, Ernest Bevin, the British foreign secretary, made a speech at a luncheon welcoming Gladwyn Jebb and his UN Executive Committee to London. It was a very high-powered committee. Andrei Gromyko was there for the Soviet Union; Lester Pearson for Canada; Stettinius for the United States, assisted by the tall and dapper Alger Hiss, later to be prosecuted as a Soviet spy. Britain was represented by Philip Noel-Baker, a great believer in internationalism. And the historian C. K. Webster was there to assist him, wearing a tennis visor in protest against photographers' lights. This excellent committee, said Bevin, would soon complete the work begun in San Francisco. The terrible new weapons dropped on Japan made it all the more imperative that the world organization should work. However, Bevin continued, he recognized that "the idea of world government" would have to be "carefully nurtured." Nations had histories, collective memories, traditions. All this might be overcome in time, just as he, Ernest Bevin, had managed to overcome his working-class origins. The "basic principle" of San Francisco was right. But it would take time to create "the right atmosphere." Until then, "cooperation between nations, and notably large ones, who are the greatest influence for good and for ill, is the only practical method which we can adopt."[33]

Bevin was right. But without meaning to, he revealed the great defect in the ideal of world government. It depended for its working on an alliance of Big Powers. If the alliance kept together, a kind of global authoritarianism—a repeat of Metternich's Holy Alliance after Napoleon's defeat—threatened. If it didn't, the fledgling world organization would be powerless, and another, perhaps even more devastating war loomed.

In the event, the Big Powers failed to stick together. Exactly when the Cold War began is hard to say. Serious rifts were already apparent at Yalta, no matter how much Roosevelt tried to keep Stalin on his side—to the point of needlessly bullying Churchill. John Foster Dulles did not yet call it the Cold War, but he claimed to have witnessed its birth, in London, at the end of September 1945.

The foreign ministers of the Big Five powers—the United States, Britain, the USSR, France, and China—had gathered there to discuss various peace treaties, notably with Italy, Finland, and the Balkan countries. They did not disagree on anything substantial. Indeed, the U.S., for the sake of harmony in the Big Power alliance, had already agreed to recognize the Soviet-imposed provisional government in Poland without being too fussy about its nature, and was prepared to do the same in the case of Hungary. In his report on the conference, U.S. secretary of state James F. Byrnes stated that his government "shares the desire of the Soviet Union to have governments friendly to the Soviet Union in eastern and central Europe."[34]

But Molotov had another agenda. Communism was a major force in two of the Big Powers, apart from the Soviet Union: in France, where the Communist Party was still very powerful, and China, where simmering civil war would soon come to the boil. If Molotov could humiliate the Chinese Nationalists and the French, and implicate the U.S. in their humiliation, the communist cause would be greatly strengthened. His tactic was to demand that France and China withdraw from the treaty discussions, since they had not been signatories to the surrender terms of the relevant countries. The aim was to bully the French, insult the Chinese, and rattle the British. John Foster Dulles, in his memoir, couldn't help but admire Molotov's cold-blooded diplomatic skills: "Mr. Molotov at London in 1945 was at his best."[35]

The French foreign minister, Georges Bidault, a former leader of the resistance and future president, was constantly slighted, provoked, and humiliated. One of Molotov's tricks was to ask his British and American colleagues to postpone a meeting without informing Bidault, so the Frenchman would turn up to an empty room. The hope was that Bidault would stomp off to Paris in high dudgeon. The Chinese minister was simply ignored, as though he weren't in the room at all. And Bevin, who had a temper, was needled into explosions of fury, followed by sheepish apologies that might result in concessions to the Soviet view.

When these tactics failed to have the desired result, the Soviets tried blackmail. Bevin and Byrnes were told that the Soviet Union would no longer cooperate if France and China did not withdraw. Byrnes refused to lend himself to the further humiliation of his allies and the conference was abandoned. To Dulles, this was the moment of truth. It marked "the end of an epoch, the epoch of Teheran, Yalta, Potsdam. It marked the ending of any pretence by Soviet Communists that they were our 'friends.' It began the period when their hostility to us was openly proclaimed throughout the world."[36]

The old Cold Warrior was surely not wrong about this. And he wasn't the only one to see cracks appearing in the postwar world order. Hanson W. Baldwin was the military editor of the *New York Times*, a liberal, unlike Dulles. In a column written for his paper on October 26, he argued that the invention of atomic bombs meant that the world, and the two Big Powers in particular, were faced with a harrowing choice. One was to strengthen the United Nations. Inevitably, in that case, the Big Powers would have to give up a great deal of national sovereignty, and veto power in the Security Council would be abolished. Russians would have the right to inspect American atomic facilities, and vice versa.

This was Baldwin's own preferred solution, not on moral grounds, but for the sake of self-preservation. Dulles, as always, took a more moralistic view. The UN would always remain weak, he wrote, because there was no worldwide "consensus on moral judgment."[37] To him, the Cold War was a moral as well as a political conflict, a war of good against evil.

Hanson Baldwin was not naïve, however. He did not expect the Soviets, or the Americans for that matter, to agree to his proposed solution. And that would mean, in his words, "a world divided into two blocs, each suspicious of the other, a world that may be stable for many years, but eventually would trend toward major war."

So it came to pass. By the time autumn turned to winter, the high hopes of the spring of '45 were already fading. There would be no world

government, let alone a world democracy; there would not even be four or
five world policemen. What powers were still left to the two European
countries represented in the Security Council would soon be further depleted by the bloody demise of their empires. The Soviets and the United
States were drifting into open animosity. And China, a gravely wounded
country after Japanese occupation, was itself divided into two blocs, with
corrupt and demoralized Nationalists holding out in major cities south of
Manchuria, and the Communists dominating the countryside and much
of the north.

In the fall and winter of 1945, American newspapers were still reporting on positive developments in the Chinese wartime capital of Chungking, where negotiations between Communists and Nationalists continued as a kind of shadow play. There was talk of "compromise" and "truce"
and "democracy," and the reluctance on both sides to "start" a civil war.
In an article published in the *New York Times Magazine* on October 14,
full confidence was expressed in the leadership of the Generalissimo Chiang Kai-shek. It makes for very curious reading now:

> Notwithstanding his democratic ideology, Chiang now has more
> power than any world leader except Stalin, and he has more titles
> than Stalin. Besides being President of China, Commander of the
> Army and chief of the Kuomintang, he is the head of at least forty-
> three other organizations . . . the Generalissimo is China. His
> word is law and he has his word on many things that other national
> leaders would delegate to subordinates.

It would not do him any good. Exactly four years later, the Generalissimo would be reduced to wielding his authority over a small island off
the Fujian coast, formerly known as Formosa, and now as Taiwan.

. . .

AND SO YEAR ZERO FINALLY came to an end, on a mixed note of gratitude and anxiety. Grateful that a kind of peace had been achieved, in

most places, people had fewer illusions about a glorious future and growing fears about an increasingly divided world. Millions were still too cold
and hungry to celebrate the coming new year with any semblance of joy.
Besides, the news was often grim: food revolts were expected in occupied
Germany; acts of terrorism were creating chaos in Palestine; Koreans were
furiously protesting against their semicolonial status; fighting continued
in Indonesia, with British soldiers and Dutch marines, "fully supplied
with American equipment," trying to crush the native rebellion.[38]

But the sense one gets from newspapers around the world on the last
day of 1945 is that most people were too anxious to get on with their own
lives to care much about the global news anymore. During a worldwide
war, everywhere matters. In times of peace, people look to home.

So the British talked about the weather and sports. According to the
Manchester Guardian, "The war-time ban on weather reporting has left
us a little out of practice in assessing the sort of fog we had last night in the
North-west." But it was good to know that "the Derbyshire and Lancashire
Gliding Club hopes to be the first gliding and sailplane club in the coun-
try to resume activities which were suspended when war broke out."

The French talked about food. American GIs, who just one year ago
had been fighting in the bloody snow of the Ardennes, were now being
treated to a skiing holiday in the French Alps. "The cuisine," reported *Le
Monde* from Chamonix, "was prepared by French chefs to everyone's delight. One is surprised to see to what extent this aspect of French civilization is appreciated." The paper was also happy to announce that the
"fourth litre of wine in December" could be obtained with J3, M, C, and
V rations.

The *Frankische Presse* of Bayreuth struck a more somber note with
reminiscences of the terrible hardships suffered by the German population, "huddled in cellars and bunkers, a shattered, exhausted mass of
people with feverish eyes and shivering hearts, with only one hope, not
even of victory, but of an end to the war." There was other news: two German men had come forward as volunteers to execute the war criminals at
Nuremberg. Erich Richter, from the town of Marburg, said he would be

happy to chop their heads off for nothing. Josef Schmidt, from a DP camp in Leipzig, was prepared to hang or behead the convicts, but would exact "a price for each head." The solace of culture was not neglected. For the first time in years, the Bayreuth Symphony Orchestra would perform music by Claude Debussy, "the French composer who . . . worked systematically to free French music from the influence of German Romanticism and neo-Romanticism." And this in Bayreuth, the Mecca of Wagnerism!

In Tokyo, the main editorial of the *Japan Times* proclaimed: "Ring out the old! Ring in the new! Japan will ring out the old year which has just ended with no regrets. For it was a year of pain and suffering, disillusionment and confusion and humiliation and punishment. Such a year of bitter memories can be relegated to the limbo with hearty relief." The paper also revealed that "Japanese plans for using flour made of ground silkworms, locusts, mulberry leaves and a dozen other food substitutes to avert a food crisis when American forces invaded . . . [are] still being developed." And a reporter named Nishizawa Eiichi explained that although most heroes in Kabuki plays were regrettably feudal, there were some rare exceptions. The seventeenth-century village headman Sakura Sogoro, for example, crucified for impudently asking the shogun to reduce the tax burden on poor peasants, "was a martyr in the democratic cause."

The tone of the *New York Times* was a bit more upbeat: "New York's Bacchanalian barometers flew storm warnings yesterday, indicating the city was headed tonight for its most exuberant New Year's Eve since 1940." But more than the articles, it is the advertisements in the *Times* that showed the almost unimaginable gulf between the new and the old worlds: "It's different—the creamy smooth peanut butter that melts in your mouth—spread it thicker, Mom, it's Peter Pan!"

If there is anything to be gleaned from these glimpses of the global mood on New Year's Eve, it is that a certain sense of normality was beginning to seep back into the daily lives of people who were lucky enough to be able to lift their heads from the direst misery of the immediate postwar period. This was not a luxury available to those who were still displaced in

Germany, in Japanese POW camps, or in whatever sordid limbo they found themselves.

Set to the task of rebuilding their shattered countries, they had no more time for feasting, or even much mourning. There was work to be done. This made for a more sober perception of reality, grayer, more orderly, less exciting than the upheavals of war and liberation. In some places, of course, new wars, against colonial masters, or domestic enemies in civil conflicts, would continue, and new dictatorships were imposed. But for millions of others, there had been enough excitement to last a lifetime, years of drama that some preferred to forget, and others, who had perhaps been more fortunate, would look back on with a tinge of nostalgia—things would never be as interesting again.

Year Zero itself has been rather eclipsed in the world's collective memory by the years of destruction that preceded it, and new dramas that still lay in store, in Korea, Vietnam, India-Pakistan, Israel, Cambodia, Rwanda, Iraq, Afghanistan, and on and on. But for those who came of age after Year Zero, when so much was created amidst the ruins of war, it was perhaps the most important year of all. Those of us who grew up in western Europe, or indeed in Japan, could easily take for granted what our parents had built: the welfare states, economies that just seemed to grow, international law, a "free world" protected by the seemingly unassailable American hegemon.

It wouldn't last, of course. Nothing ever does. But that is no reason not to pay tribute to the men and women who were alive in 1945, to their hardships, and to their hopes and aspirations, even though many of these would turn to ash, as everything eventually does.

EPILOGUE

Did the war really end in 1945? Some have claimed 1989 as the year that hostilities finally came to a close, for it was only then that Poland, Hungary, Czechoslovakia, East Germany, and other parts of east and central Europe were released from communist rule. The division of Europe, inflicted by Stalin in 1945, was one of the rawest wounds of World War II. Bad faith had followed bad faith. Czechoslovakia, a parliamentary democracy, was first carved up by Hitler in 1938, with the connivance of France and Britain—as Neville Chamberlain said, it was "a quarrel in a far away country between people of whom we know nothing." In 1939, Britain had gone to war with Germany, supposedly to restore the integrity of Poland, a promise that was never fulfilled.

But in 1989, with the fall of the Soviet empire, there was hope that the gash running through the spine of Europe might heal at last. More than that: hope that the world would finally come together briefly flickered again in that miraculous year, despite what happened in China in June, when citizens asking for an end to their dictatorship were murdered by their own soldiers. Now there was only one Big Power left. There was talk of a new world order, even of the end of history. The Berlin Wall was finally breached.

My sisters and I decided to celebrate the eve of hope, December 31,

1989, at the Berlin Wall, with our father. He had been back to Berlin only once before since he saw its destruction in 1945. In the shadow of a family calamity, we had spent Christmas and New Year's in Berlin in 1972. It was a depressing occasion. The city was dark and freezing. Crossing the border between West and East was a long and tiresome process, with snarling border guards checking the bottom of our car with mirrors to make sure we weren't carrying contraband or human cargo.

In 1972, East Berlin was still much as my father remembered it. Despite the pumped-up grandeur of empty Stalinist avenues, it was a dark city with the ruins of war still visible. Drawing up in his brand-new Citroën to the gates of the old factory where he had been forced to work for the Nazi war effort gave him a certain grim satisfaction. It was a large, forbidding-looking building of red brick, a kind of Wilhelminian industrial fortress. Nearby was the camp where my father was housed in flimsy wooden barracks, open to ice, fleas, lice, snow, and Allied bombs. Everything was still there, as though the past was quite literally frozen: the watchtower, the crater which the inmates used as a public toilet, as well as a public bath.

In 1989, the camp was gone, transformed, I think, into a parking lot with a shabby stand hawking sausages in a vapor of greasy curry sauce.

The sun was shining as we walked through the Brandenburg Gate, something that had been unthinkable for almost four decades. Anyone who might have attempted it would have been shot. I remember the flush of excitement on my father's face as we joined Germans from East and West, as well as Poles, Americans, Japanese, French, and others from all corners of the globe, tasting the simple freedom of taking a short stroll through the very center of Berlin. There were still men in uniform, but they looked on, powerless to intervene, some of them with smiles, relieved that they didn't have to shoot a fellow citizen. For once, all seemed well with the world.

The night of December 31 was cold, but not freezing. We could hear the crowds cheering from a long way off as we approached the Brandenburg Gate, our father proceeding with a certain reluctance; he was not keen on crowds, particularly German crowds. Nor did he like loud bangs; they brought back too many memories. Tens of thousands of people, most of them young, had gathered near and on top of the wall, singing, shouting, popping corks off bottles of the sweet sparkling wine Germans call Sekt. There was a smell of Sekt everywhere. People were showering one another with the sticky foam.

Some were chanting: *"Wir sind das Volk!"* ("We are the people!"). Others sang: "We are one people!" But there was nothing nationalistic or menacing in the air of that night. It was an international crowd, a kind of political Woodstock without rock bands, celebrating freedom, togetherness, and hope for a better world, in which the bitter experiences of the past would not be repeated; no more barbed wire, or camps, or killing. It was good to be young. If ever Beethoven's anthem of "All Men Will Be Brothers" (*"Alle Menschen werden Brüder"*) had meaning, it was on that extraordinary New Year's Eve in Berlin.

Suddenly, at around a quarter past midnight, we realized we had lost our father in the crowd, which had grown so dense that it was difficult to move. We looked for him everywhere, as fireworks exploded and rockets lit up the sky. The noise was deafening. Laughing faces around us, illuminated by the fireworks, now looked slightly hysterical. There was no way we could find our father in this mass. Without him, our appetite for celebration waned. We were worried and returned to our hotel.

Hours later, after we had found some fitful sleep, the door opened, and there he was, his face plastered with a bandage. Just as the Berlin crowds saw the new year in with a bang, round about the stroke of midnight, pretty much on the same spot where my father once had to dodge British bombs, Stalin Organs, and German sniper fire, a firecracker had somehow found its way to him and hit him right between the eyes.

ACKNOWLEDGMENTS

I cannot imagine how I could have written this book without my stint as a fellow of the Cullman Center for Scholars & Writers at the New York Public Library. Thanks to its excellent director, Jean Strouse, her invaluable deputy director, Marie D'Origny, and the ever helpful Paul Delaverdac, the center is a writer's paradise.

While doing my research, I benefited greatly from the advise of Robert Paxton, Fritz Stern, Hata Ikuhiko, Avishai Margalit, Ben Bland, and Geert Mak. At the NIOD research institute in Amsterdam, I was given a great deal of help by David Barnouw and Joggli Meihuizen.

Mark Mazower and Geoffrey Wheatcroft were kind enough to read the manuscript at various stages and managed to save me from making errors I would never have caught. Any infelicities that might remain in the text are, of course, entirely my own responsibility.

Andrew Wylie, Jin Auh, and Jaqueline Ko, of the Wylie Agency, have offered me their constant support, for which I am deeply grateful. Scott Moyers was involved in the book first as my agent at the Wylie Agency, then as my editor at The Penguin Press, and was equally superb in both capacities. Thanks also to Mally Anderson, at The Penguin Press, who has seen the book through to its completion.

Finally, I owe a great debt to my father, Leo Buruma, and my friend, Brian Urquhart, who have taken the time to relate their personal experiences of 1945. As a small token of my gratitude and esteem, I dedicate my book to them.

I am grateful to my wife, Eri, for her patience and encouragement.

NOTES

CHAPTER 1: EXULTATION

1. Quoted in Ben Shephard, *The Long Road Home: The Aftermath of the Second World War* (New York: Alfred A. Knopf, 2010), 69.
2. Martin Gilbert, *The Day the War Ended: May 8, 1945: Victory in Europe* (New York: Henry Holt, 1994), 128.
3. Brian Urquhart, *A Life in Peace and War* (New York: Harper & Row, 1987), 82.
4. This story is well told in David Stafford, *Endgame, 1945: The Missing Final Chapter of World War II* (New York: Little, Brown, 2007).
5. From Zhukov's memoir, quoted in Gilbert, *The Day the War Ended*.
6. Simone de Beauvoir, *Force of Circumstance* (New York: G. P. Putnam's Sons, 1963), 30.
7. Gilbert, *The Day the War Ended*, 322.
8. Ibid., 319.
9. Urquhart, *A Life in Peace and War*, 85.
10. David Kaufman and Michiel Horn, *De Canadezen in Nederland, 1944–1945* (Laren, The Netherlands: Luitingh, 1981), 119.
11. Michael Horn, "More Than Cigarettes, Sex and Chocolate: The Canadian Army in the Netherlands, 1944–1945," in *Journal of Canadian Studies/Revue d'études canadiennes* 16 (Fall/Winter 1981), 156–73.
12. Quoted in Horn, "More Than Cigarettes, Sex and Chocolate," 166.
13. Ibid, 169.
14. Quoted in John Willoughby, "The Sexual Behavior of American GIs During the Early Years of the Occupation of Germany," *Journal of Military History* 62, no. 1 (January 1998), 166–67.
15. Benoîte Groult and Flora Groult, *Journal à quatre mains* (Paris: Editions Denoël, 1962).
16. See Patrick Buisson, *1940–1945: Années érotiques* (Paris: Albin Michel, 2009).
17. Rudi van Dantzig, *Voor een verloren soldaat* (Amsterdam: Arbeiderspers, 1986).
18. Buisson, *1940–1945*, 324.
19. Urquhart, *A Life in Peace and War*, 81.

NOTES

20. Ben Shephard, *After Daybreak: The Liberation of Bergen-Belsen, 1945* (New York: Schocken Books, 2005).
21. Ibid., 99.
22. Ibid., 133.
23. Richard Wollheim, "A Bed out of Leaves," *London Review of Books*, December 4, 2003, 3–7.
24. Shephard, *After Daybreak*, 138.
25. Atina Grossmann, *Jews, Germans, and Allies: Close Encounters in Occupied Germany* (Princeton, NJ: Princeton University Press, 2007), 188.
26. Shephard, *The Long Road Home*, 299.
27. Ibid., 70.
28. Norman Lewis, *Naples '44: An Intelligence Officer in the Italian Labyrinth* (New York: Eland, 2011), 52.
29. John Dower, *Embracing Defeat: Japan in the Wake of World War II* (New York: W. W. Norton, 1999), 126.
30. Ibid., 102.
31. Theodore Cohen, *Remaking Japan: The American Occupation as New Deal*, Herbert Passin, ed. (New York: Free Press, 1987), 123.
32. Letter to Donald Keene, in Otis Cary, ed., *From a Ruined Empire: Letters—Japan, China, Korea, 1945–46* (Tokyo and New York: Kodansha, 1984), 96.
33. William L. Worden, "The G.I. Is Civilizing the Jap," *Saturday Evening Post*, December 15, 1945, 18–22.
34. For more information on the *panpan* culture, John Dower's *Embracing Defeat* is an excellent source.
35. Dower, *Embracing Defeat*, 134.
36. John LaCerda, *The Conqueror Comes to Tea: Japan Under MacArthur* (New Brunswick, N.J.: Rutgers University Press, 1946), 51.
37. Ibid., 54.
38. Dower, *Embracing Defeat*, 579.
39. Giles MacDonogh, *After the Reich: The Brutal History of the Allied Occupation* (New York: Basic Books, 2007), 79.
40. Klaus-Dietmar Henke, *Die Amerikanische Besetzung Deutschlands* (Munich: R. Oldenbourg Verlag, 1995), 201.
41. Dagmar Herzog, *Sex After Fascism: Memory and Morality in Twentieth-Century Germany* (Princeton, NJ: Princeton University Press, 2005), 69.
42. Willoughby, "Sexual Behavior of American GIs," 167.
43. Groult, *Journal à quatre mains*, 397.
44. MacDonogh, *After the Reich*, 236.
45. Nosaka Akiyuki, *Amerika Hijiki* [*American Hijiki*] (Tokyo: Shinchōsha, 2003). First published 1972.
46. MacDonogh, *After the Reich*, 369.
47. *The Times* (London), July 9, 1945.
48. Willoughby, "Sexual Behavior of American GIs," 158.
49. *New York Times*, June 13, 1945.
50. Anonymous, *A Woman in Berlin: Eight Weeks in the Conquered City: A Diary* (New York: Metropolitan Books, 2005).
51. Nagai Kafu, *Danchotei Nichijo* II (Tokyo: Iwanami Pocket Books, 1987), 285.
52. Ibid, 278.
53. Quoted in Donald Keene, *So Lovely a Country Will Never Perish: Wartime Diaries of Japanese Writers* (New York: Columbia University Press, 2010), 149.
54. LaCerda, *The Conqueror Comes to Tea*, 23–24.
55. Henke, *Die Amerikanische Besetzung Deutschlands*, 199.

56. Ibid.
57. Richard Bessel, *Germany 1945: From War to Peace* (New York: HarperCollins, 2009), 204.
58. Elizabeth Heineman, *What Difference Does a Husband Make?* (Berkeley, CA: University of California Press, 2003), 100.
59. Quoted in Willoughby, "Sexual Behavior of American GIs," 169.
60. Keene, *So Lovely a Country*, 171.
61. Willoughby, "Sexual Behavior of American GIs," 160.
62. Curzio Malaparte, *The Skin*, David Moore, tr. (New York: *New York Review of Books*, 2013), 39. First published 1952.
63. Quoted in Herman de Liagre Böhl in *De Gids*, periodical, May 1985, 250.
64. Ibid., 251.
65. Buisson, *1940–1945: Années érotiques*, 411.

CHAPTER 2: HUNGER

1. J. L. van der Pauw, *Rotterdam in de tweede wereldoorlog* (Rotterdam: Boom, 2006), 679.
2. *New York Times*, May 12, 1945.
3. Shephard, *After Daybreak*, 109.
4. Edmund Wilson, *Europe Without Baedeker: Sketches Among the Ruins of Italy, Greece, and England* (London: Secker and Warburg, 1948), 125.
5. Ibid., 120.
6. Antony Beevor and Artemis Cooper, *Paris After the Liberation: 1944–1949*, revised edition (New York: Penguin Books, 2004), 103. First published 1994.
7. Stephen Spender, *European Witness* (New York: Reynal and Hitchcock, 1946), 107.
8. Ibid., 106.
9. Wilson, *Europe Without Baedeker*, 136.
10. Ibid., 146.
11. Ibid., 147.
12. Sándor Márai, *Memoir of Hungary 1944–1948* (Budapest: Corvina in association with Central European University Press, 1996), 193–94.
13. Carl Zuckmayer, *Deutschlandbericht für das Kriegsministerium der Vereinigten Staaten von Amerika* (Göttingen: Wallstein, 2004), 142.
14. Spender, *European Witness*, 15.
15. *New York Herald Tribune*, December 31, 1945.
16. Cary, ed., *From a Ruined Empire*, 54.
17. Dower, *Embracing Defeat*, 103.
18. Ibid., 63.
19. MacDonogh, *After the Reich*, 315.
20. Ronald Spector, *In the Ruins of Empire: The Japanese Surrender and the Battle for Postwar Asia* (New York: Random House, 2007), 56.
21. Quoted in Bessel, *Germany 1945*, 334.
22. *New York Times*, October 27, 1945.
23. Julian Sebastian Bach Jr., *America's Germany: An Account of the Occupation* (New York: Random House, 1946), 26.
24. *Daily Mirror*, October 5, 1945, quoted in Shephard, *The Long Road Home*, 129.
25. Quoted in Shephard, *The Long Road Home*, 156.
26. Joint Chiefs of Staff directive 1380/15, paragraph 296, quoted in Cohen, *Remaking Japan*, 143.
27. MacDonogh, *After the Reich*, 479.
28. Statement to Congress quoted in Cohen, *Remaking Japan*, 145.

29. Quoted in Norman M. Naimark, *The Russians in Germany: A History of the Soviet Zone of Occupation, 1945–1949* (Cambridge, MA: Harvard University Press, 1995), 181.
30. Cohen, *Remaking Japan*, 144.
31. Ibid., 142.
32. Herman de Liagre Böhl, *De Gids*, 246.
33. Willi A. Boelcke, *Der Schwarzmarkt, 1945–1948* (Braunschweig: Westermann, 1986), 76.
34. Sakaguchi Ango, *Darakuron*, new paperback version (Tokyo: Chikuma Shobo, 2008), 228. First published in 1946.
35. Dower, *Embracing Defeat*, 139.
36. Fujiwara Sakuya, *Manshu, Shokokumin no Senki* (Tokyo: Shinchōsha, 1984), 82.
37. Quoted in Bessel, *Germany 1945*, 337.
38. Zuckmayer, *Deutschlandbericht*, 111.
39. Irving Heymont, *Among the Survivors of the Holocaust: The Landsberg DP Camp Letters of Major Irving Heymont, United States Army* (Cincinnati: The American Jewish Archives, 1982), 63.
40. Carlo D'Este, *Patton: A Genius for War* (New York: HarperCollins, 1996), 755.
41. See Shephard, *The Long Way Home*, 235.
42. *Yank*, August 10, 1945, 6.
43. Quoted in Stafford, *Endgame, 1945*, 507.
44. Alfred Döblin, *Schicksalsreise: Bericht u. Bekenntnis: Flucht u. Exil 1940–1948* (Munich: Piper Verlag, 1986), 276.

CHAPTER 3: REVENGE

1. Norman M. Naimark, *Fires of Hatred: Ethnic Cleansing in Twentieth-Century Europe* (Cambridge, MA: Harvard University Press, 2001), 118.
2. Tadeusz Borowski, *This Way for the Gas, Ladies and Gentlemen* (New York: Viking, 1967).
3. Gilbert, *The Day the War Ended*, 38.
4. Shephard, *After Daybreak*, 113.
5. Ruth Andreas-Friedrich, *Battleground Berlin: Diaries, 1945–1948* (New York: Paragon House, 1990), 99.
6. Hans Graf von Lehndorff, *Ostpreussisches Tagebuch* [East Prussian Diary Records of a Physician from the Years 1945–1947] (Munich: DTV, 1967), 67.
7. Ibid., 74.
8. Naimark, *The Russians in Germany*, 72.
9. Bessel, *Germany 1945*, 155.
10. Okada Kazuhiro, *Manshu Annei Hanten* (Tokyo: Kojinsha, 2002), 103.
11. Ibid., 128.
12. Naimark, *The Russians in Germany*, 108.
13. Anonymous, *A Woman in Berlin: Eight Weeks in the Conquered City: A Diary* (New York: Metropolitan Books, 2005), 86.
14. Naimark, *The Russians in Germany*, 79.
15. Quoted in Buisson, *1940–1945: Années érotiques*, 387.
16. Ibid., 251–52.
17. Jan Gross, *Fear: Anti-Semitism in Poland after Auschwitz* (New York: Random House, 2006), 82.
18. Anna Bikont, *My z Jedawabnego* [We from Jedwabne] (Warsaw: Prószyński i S-ka, 2004). Translated excerpt by Lukasz Sommer.
19. Testimony of Halina Wind Preston, July 26, 1977: www.yadvashem.org/yv/en/righteous/stories/related/preston_testimony.asp.

20. Tony Judt, *Postwar: A History of Europe Since 1945* (New York: Penguin Press, 2005), 38.
21. Gross, *Fear*, 40.
22. Naimark, *Fires of Hatred*, 122.
23. Shephard, *The Long Road Home*, 122.
24. Christian von Krockow, *Hour of the Women* (New York: HarperCollins, 1991), 96.
25. Christian von Krockow, *Die Reise nach Pommern: Bericht aus einem verschwiegenen Land* (Munich: Deutscher Taschenbuch-Verlag, 1985), 215.
26. Herbert Hupka, ed., *Letzte Tage in Schlesien* (Munich: Langen Müller, 1985), 138.
27. Ibid., 81.
28. Ernst Jünger, *Jahre der Okkupation* (Stuttgart: Ernst Klett, 1958), 213–14.
29. Krockow, *Hour of the Women*, 110.
30. MacDonogh, *After the Reich*, 128.
31. Margarete Schell, *Ein Tagebuch aus Prag, 1945–46* (Bonn: Bundesministerium für Vertriebenen, 1957), 12.
32. Ibid., 48.
33. Ibid., 99.
34. Ibid., 41.
35. MacDonogh, *After the Reich*, 406.
36. Dina Porat, *The Fall of the Sparrow: The Life and Times of Abba Kovner* (Stanford, CA: Stanford University Press, 2009), 214.
37. Ibid., 212.
38. Ibid., 215.
39. Abba Kovner, *My Little Sister and Selected Poems, 1965–1985* (Oberlin, Ohio: Oberlin College Press, 1986).
40. Judt, *Postwar*, 33.
41. Harold Macmillan, *The Blast of War, 1939–1945* (New York: Harper & Row, 1967), 576.
42. Wilson, *Europe Without Baedeker*, 147.
43. Figures quoted in Roy P. Domenico, *Italian Fascists on Trial, 1943–1948* (Chapel Hill, NC: University of North Carolina Press, 1991), 149.
44. Wilson, *Europe Without Baedeker*, 157.
45. Macmillan, *The Blast of War*, 193.
46. Ibid., 501.
47. Allan Scarfe and Wendy Scarfe, eds., *All That Grief: Migrant Recollections of Greek Resistance to Fascism, 1941–1949* (Sydney, Australia: Hale and Iremonger, 1994), 95.
48. Macmillan, *The Blast of War*, 499.
49. Mark Mazower, ed., *After the War Was Over: Reconstructing the Family, Nation, and State in Greece, 1943–1960* (Princeton, NJ: Princeton University Press, 2000), 27.
50. Macmillan, *The Blast of War*, 547.
51. *The Times* (London), July 13, 1945.
52. Macmillan, *The Blast of War*, 515.
53. Wilson, *Europe Without Baedeker*, 197.
54. Spector, *In the Ruins of Empire*, 90.
55. Cheah Boon Kheng, "Sino-Malay Conflicts in Malaya, 1945–1946: Communist Vendetta and Islamic Resistance," *Journal for Southeast Asian Studies* 12 (March 1981), 108–117.
56. Gideon Francois Jacobs, *Prelude to the Monsoon* (Capetown, South Africa: Purnell & Sons, 1965), 124.
57. Spector, *In the Ruins of Empire*, 174.
58. Benedict Anderson, *Java in a Time of Revolution: Occupation and Resistance, 1944–1946* (Jakarta: Equinox Publishing, 2005).

59. L. de Jong, *Het koninkrijk der Nederlanden in de tweede wereldoorlog*, 11c, Staatsuit-geverij, 1986.

60. Theodore Friend, *Indonesian Destinies* (Cambridge, MA.: Harvard University Press, 2003), 27.

61. Jan A. Krancher, ed., *The Defining Years of the Dutch East Indies, 1942–1949: Survivors' Accounts of Japanese Invasion and Enslavement of Europeans and the Revolution That Created Free Indonesia* (Jefferson, NC: MacFarland, 1996), 193.

62. Spector, *In the Ruins of Empire*, 179.

63. De Jong, *Het koninkrijk der Nederlanden*, 582.

64. Anderson, *Java in a Time of Revolution*, 166.

65. Spector, *In the Ruins of Empire*, 108.

66. Jean-Louis Planche, *Sétif 1945: Histoire d'un massacre annoncé* (Paris: Perrin, 2006), 139.

67. Martin Evans, *Algeria: France's Undeclared War* (New York: Oxford University Press, 2012).

68. Françoise Martin, *Heures tragiques au Tonkin: 9 mars 1945–18 mars 1946* (Paris: Editions Berger-Levrault, 1947), 133.

69. David G. Marr, *Vietnam 1945: The Quest for Power* (Berkeley: University of California Press, 1995), 333.

70. Martin, *Heures tragiques au Tonkin*, 179.

71. Ibid., 129.

72. Spector, *In the Ruins of Empire*, 126.

CHAPTER 4: GOING HOME

1. For a detailed analysis, see Timothy Snyder's magisterial book *Bloodlands: Europe Between Hitler and Stalin* (New York: Basic Books, 2010).

2. Imre Kertész, *Fateless* (Evanston, IL: Northwestern University Press, 1992).

3. Quoted in Dienke Hondius, *Holocaust Survivors and Dutch Anti-Semitism* (Westport, CT: Praeger, 2003), 103.

4. Ibid., 101.

5. Roger Ikor, *Ô soldats de quarante! . . . en mémoire* (Paris: Albin Michel, 1986), 95.

6. Marguerite Duras, *The War* (New York: Pantheon Books, 1986), 15.

7. Ibid., 14.

8. Ibid., 53.

9. Ango, *Darakuron*, 227.

10. Dower, *Embracing Defeat*, 58.

11. *Koe*, vol. 1 (Tokyo: Asahi Shimbunsha, 1984), 103. No author, this is a collection of letters sent to the newspaper.

12. Ibid., 104.

13. Bill Mauldin, *Back Home* (New York: William Sloane, 1947), 18.

14. Ibid., 45.

15. Ibid., 54.

16. Nicholai Tolstoy, *The Minister and the Massacres* (London: Century Hutchinson, 1986), 31.

17. Quoted in Gregor Dallas, *1945: The War That Never Ended* (New Haven, Conn.: Yale, 2005), 519.

18. Tolstoy, *The Minister and the Massacres*, 13.

19. Ibid.

20. Nicholas Bethell, *The Last Secret: The Delivery to Stalin of over Two Million Russians by Britain and the United States* (New York: Basic Books, 1974), 86.

21. Ibid., 87.
22. Borivoje M. Karapandić, *The Bloodiest Yugoslav Spring: Tito's Katyns and Gulags* (New York: Carlton Press, 1980), 73.
23. Macmillan, *The Blast of War*, 436.
24. Shephard, *The Long Road Home*, 80.
25. Bethell, *The Last Secret*, 18, 19.
26. Ibid., 133.
27. Ibid., 138.
28. Ibid., 142.
29. Ibid., 140.
30. Dallas, *1945*, 560.
31. *Yank*, August 24, 1945.
32. Dallas, *1945*, 549.
33. Naimark, *Fires of Hatred*, 109.
34. Ibid., 110.
35. Lehndorff, *Ostpreussisches Tagebuch*, 169.
36. Hupka, *Letzte Tage in Schlesien*, 265.
37. Jünger, *Jahre der Okkupation*, 195.
38. Author's communication with Fritz Stern.
39. Quoted in Bessel, *Germany 1945*, 223.
40. Hupka, *Letzte Tage in Schlesien*, 64.
41. *Yank*, September 21, 1945, 16.
42. Naimark, *Fires of Hatred*, 112.
43. Ibid., 115.
44. Antony Polonsky and Boleslaw Drukier, *The Beginnings of Communist Rule in Poland* (London and Boston: Routledge and Kegan Paul, 1980), 425.
45. Grossmann, *Jews, Germans, and Allies*, 199.
46. Quoted by Grossmann, 148.
47. Ibid., 147.
48. *New York Herald Tribune*, December 31, 1945.
49. Heymont, *Among the Survivors*, 21.
50. Grossmann, *Jews, Germans, and Allies*, 181.
51. Quoted in Hagit Lavsky, *New Beginnings: Holocaust Survivors in Bergen-Belsen and the British Zone in Germany, 1945–1950* (Detroit: Wayne State University Press, 2002), 64.
52. Rosensaft himself never settled in Israel. He apparently told some Israelis, "You danced the hora while we were being burned in the crematoriums." (Quoted in Shephard, *The Long Road Home*, 367.)
53. Heymont, *Among the Survivors*, 47–48.
54. Quoted in Shabtai Teveth, *Ben-Gurion: The Burning Ground, 1886–1948* (Boston: Houghton Mifflin, 1987), 853.
55. Avishai Margalit, "The Uses of the Holocaust," *New York Review of Books*, February 14, 1994.
56. Tom Segev, *The Seventh Million*: The Israelis and the Holocaust (New York: Hill and Wang, 1993), 99–100.
57. Teveth, *Ben-Gurion*, 871.
58. Ibid., 870.
59. Heymont, *Among the Survivors*, 66.
60. Teveth, *Ben-Gurion*, 873.
61. The Harrison Report, so called after Earl G. Harrison, the U.S. representative on the Inter-Governmental Committee on Refugees.
62. Letter dated August 31, 1945.

63. PRO FO 1049/81/177, quoted in *Life Reborn*, conference proceedings, edited by Menachem Rosensaft (Washington, D.C., 2001), 110.
64. Bethell, *The Last Secret*, 8.

CHAPTER 5: DRAINING THE POISON

1. Andreas-Friedrich, *Battleground Berlin*, 27.
2. Luc Huyse and Steven Dhondt, *La répression des collaborations, 1942–1952: Un passé toujours présent* (Brussels: CRISP, 1991), 147.
3. Sodei Rinjiro, ed., *Dear General MacArthur: Letters from the Japanese During the American Occupation* (New York: Rowman & Littlefield, 2001), 70.
4. Ibid., 87.
5. Ibid., 78.
6. Directive from the State, War, Navy Coordinating Committee, quoted in Hans H. Baerwald, *The Purge of Japanese Leaders Under the Occupation* (Berkeley: University of California Press, 1959), 7.
7. Quoted by Faubion Bowers in "How Japan Won the War," *The New York Times Magazine*, August 30, 1970.
8. Cohen, *Remaking Japan*, 85.
9. See Franz Neumann, *Behemoth: The Structure and Practice of National Socialism, 1933–44*, with a new introduction by Peter Hayes (Chicago: Ivan R. Dee, 2009; published in association with the United States Holocaust Memorial Museum). First published 1942.
10. Andreas-Friedrich, *Battleground Berlin*, 100.
11. Ibid., 101.
12. James F. Tent, *Mission on the Rhine: Reeducation and Denazification in American-Occupied Germany* (Chicago: University of Chicago Press, 1982) 55.
13. Zuckmayer, *Deutschlandbericht*, 137.
14. Timothy R. Vogt, *Denazification in Soviet-Occupied Germany: Brandenburg, 1945–1948* (Cambridge, MA: Harvard University Press, 2000), 34.
15. Ibid., 38.
16. Tom Bower, *The Pledge Betrayed: America and Britain and the Denazification of Postwar Germany* (Garden City, NY: Doubleday, 1982), 148.
17. Ibid., 8.
18. Henke, *Die Amerikanische Besetzung Deutschlands*, 487.
19. Cohen, *Remaking Japan*, 161.
20. Jerome Bernard Cohen, *Japan's Economy in War and Reconstruction* (Minneapolis: University of Minnesota, 1949), 432.
21. Cohen, *Remaking Japan*, 154.
22. Rinjiro, *Dear General MacArthur*, 176.
23. Ibid., 177.
24. LaCerda, *The Conqueror Comes to Tea*, 25.
25. Cohen, *Remaking Japan*, 45.
26. Dower, *Embracing Defeat*, 530.
27. Cary, ed., *From a Ruined Empire*, 107.
28. Chalmers Johnson, *MITI and the Japanese Miracle: The Growth of Industrial Policy, 1925–1975* (Stanford, CA: Stanford University Press, 1982), 42.
29. Teodoro Agoncillo, *The Fateful Years: Japan's Adventure in the Philippines, 1941–1945* (Quezon City, The Philippines: R. P. Garcia, 1965), 672.
30. Stanley Karnow, *In Our Image: America's Empire in the Philippines* (New York: Random House, 1989), 327.
31. Ibid., 328.

32. Jay Taylor, *The Generalissimo: Chiang Kai-shek and the Struggle for Modern China* (Cambridge, MA: Harvard University Press, 2009), 323.
33. Keene's letter to T. de Bary in Cary, ed., *From a Ruined Empire*, 128.
34. Spector, *In the Ruins of Empire*, 41.
35. Odd Arne Westad, *Cold War and Revolution: Soviet-American Rivalry and the Origins of the Chinese Civil War, 1944–1946* (New York: Columbia University Press, 1993), 90.
36. Two books on the Annei Hanten are Okada Kazuhiko, *Manshu Annei Hanten* (Kojinsha, 2002), and Fujiwara Sakuya, *Manshu, Shokokumin no Senki*, cited in chapter 2 above.
37. Peter Novick, *The Resistance Versus Vichy: The Purge of Collaborators in Liberated France* (New York: Columbia University Press, 1968), 40.
38. Ibid., 77–78.
39. Quoted in Beevor and Cooper, *Paris After the Liberation*, 104.

CHAPTER 6: THE RULE OF LAW

1. Fujiwara, *Manshu, Shokokumin no Senki*, 175.
2. Márai, *Memoir of Hungary*, 188.
3. István Deák, Jan Tomasz Gross, Tony Judt, eds., *The Politics of Retribution in Europe: World War II and Its Aftermath* (Princeton, NJ: Princeton University Press, 2000), 235.
4. Ibid.
5. Ibid., 237.
6. Ibid., 235.
7. Ibid., 134.
8. Ibid., 135.
9. Mazower, ed., *After the War Was Over*, 31.
10. Lee Sarafis, "The Policing of Deskati, 1942–1946," in Mazower, ed., *After the War Was Over*, 215.
11. Scarfe and Scarfe, *All That Grief*, 165–66.
12. Translation by E. D. A. Morshead.
13. Quoted in John W. Powell, "Japan's Germ Warfare: The US Cover-up of a War Crime, "*Bulletin of Concerned Asian Scholars* 12 (October/December 1980), 9.
14. Lawrence Taylor, *A Trial of Generals: Homma, Yamashita, MacArthur* (South Bend, IN: Icarus Press, 1981), 125.
15. *Yank*, "Tiger's Trial," November 30, 1945.
16. Taylor, *A Trial of Generals*, 137.
17. A. Frank Reel, *The Case of General Yamashita* (Chicago: University of Chicago Press, 1949), 34.
18. Richard L. Lael, *The Yamashita Precedent: War Crimes and Command Responsibility* (Wilmington, DE: Scholarly Resources, 1982), 111.
19. Taylor, *A Trial of Generals*, 195.
20. Lael, *The Yamashita Precedent*, 118.
21. Quoted in J. Kenneth Brody, *The Trial of Pierre Laval: Defining Treason, Collaboration and Patriotism in World War II France* (New Brunswick, NJ: Transaction, 2010), 136.
22. *Time*, January 4, 1932.
23. Geoffrey Warner, *Pierre Laval and the Eclipse of France* (New York: Macmillan, 1969), 301.
24. For a detailed description of Mussert's criminal venality, see Tessel Pollmann, *Mussert en Co.: de NSB-leider en zijn vertrouwelingen* (Amsterdam: Boom, 2012).

25. *Time*, October 15, 1945.
26. Jean-Paul Cointet, *Pierre Laval* (Paris: Fayard, 1993), 517.
27. Jacques Charpentier, *Au service de la liberté* (Paris: Fayard, 1949), 268.
28. Hubert Cole, *Laval* (London: Heinemann, 1963), 284.
29. Cointet, *Pierre Laval*, 527.
30. Jan Meyers, *Mussert* (Amsterdam: De Arbeiderspers, 1984), 277.
31. Ibid., 275.
32. Cointet, *Pierre Laval*, 537.
33. Quoted in Novick, *The Resistance Versus Vichy*, 177.
34. George Kennan, *Memoirs 1925–1950* (Boston: Atlantic Monthly Press, 1967), 260.
35. Dower, *Embracing Defeat*, 445.
36. Telford Taylor, *The Anatomy of the Nuremberg Trials: A Personal Memoir* (New York: Alfred A. Knopf, 1992), 29.
37. Spender, *European Witness*, 221.
38. *Yank*, May 18, 1945.
39. Website of the Dwight D. Eisenhower Memorial Commission.
40. *The Times* (London), April 20, 1945.
41. *Daily Mirror* (London), April 20, 1945.
42. *The Times* (London), April 28, 1945.
43. Shephard, *After Daybreak*, 166.
44. *The Times* (London), September 24, 1945.
45. Ibid., November 9, 1945.
46. Shephard, *After Daybreak*, 171–72.
47. *The Times* (London), November 8, 1945.
48. Ernst Michel, DANA report, January 9, 1945.
49. Rebecca West, *The New Yorker*, October 26, 1946.
50. Telford Taylor, *Anatomy of the Nuremberg Trials*, 25.
51. Ibid., 26.
52. Ernst Michel, DANA, February 15, 1946.
53. Jünger, *Jahre der Okkupation*, 176.
54. Andreas-Friedrich, *Battleground Berlin*, 63–64.
55. Telford Taylor, *Anatomy of the Nuremberg Trials*, 167–68.

CHAPTER 7: BRIGHT CONFIDENT MORNING

1. See Hermann Langbein, *Against All Hope: Resistance in the Nazi Concentration Camps, 1938–1945* (New York: Paragon House, 1994), 502.
2. *Manchester Guardian*, July 27, 1945.
3. *Daily Telegraph* (London), July 11, 2003.
4. *Manchester Guardian*, July 27, 1945.
5. Ibid.
6. Harold Nicolson, *The Harold Nicolson Diaries, 1907–1964*, Nigel Nicolson, ed. (London: Weidenfeld & Nicolson, 2004), 321.
7. Harold Macmillan, *Tides of Fortune, 1945–1955* (New York: Harper & Row, 1969), 32.
8. Ibid., 33.
9. Nicolson, *Diaries*, 318.
10. Wilson, *Europe Without Baedeker*, 135.
11. Ibid., 186.
12. Noel Annan, *Changing Enemies: The Defeat and Regeneration of Germany* (New York: W. W. Norton, 1996), 183.
13. Paul Addison, *Now the War Is Over: A Social History of Britain, 1945–51* (London: Jonathan Cape and the British Broadcasting Corporation, 1985), 14.

14. Ibid., 13.
15. Cyril Connolly, *Horizon*, June 1945, reprinted in *Ideas and Places* (London: Weidenfeld & Nicolson, 1953), 27.
16. *Manchester Guardian*, June 5, 1945.
17. Ibid., June 26, 1945.
18. Roy Jenkins, *Mr. Attlee: An Interim Biography* (London: Heinemann, 1948), 255.
19. Stéphane Hessel, *Indignez vous!* (Montpellier, France: Indigène Editions), 10.
20. Duras, *The War*, 33.
21. Arthur Koestler, *The Yogi and the Commissar* (New York: Macmillan, 1945), 82.
22. Addison, *Now the War Is Over*, 18.
23. Annan, *Changing Enemies*, 183.
24. Winston Churchill, "Speech to the Academic Youth," Zurich, September 9, 1946.
25. Nicolson, *Diaries*, 333.
26. Jean Monnet, *Mémoires* (Paris: Fayard, 1976), 283.
27. See Tessel Pollmann, *Van Waterstaat tot Wederopbouw: het leven van dr.ir. J.A. Ringers (1885-1965)* (Amsterdam: Boom, 2006).
28. Dower, *Embracing Defeat*, 537.
29. Ibid.
30. Ibid., 538.
31. Owen Lattimore, *Solution in Asia* (Boston: Little, Brown, 1945), 189.
32. Cohen, *Remaking Japan*, 42.
33. Morita Yoshio, *Chosen Shusen no kiroku: beiso ryōgun no shinchū to Nihonjin no hikiage* (Tokyo: Gannando Shoten, 1964), 77.
34. Bruce Cumings, *The Origins of the Korean War: Liberation and the Emergence of Separate Regimes, 1945–1947* (Princeton, NJ: Princeton University Press, 1981), 88.
35. *Yank*, November 2, 1945.
36. Cary, ed., *From a Ruined Empire*, 32.
37. *Yank*, November 2, 1945.
38. Cumings, *Origins of the Korean War*, 392.
39. Spector, *In the Ruins of Empire*, 163.
40. Ibid., 160.
41. Ibid., 148.
42. Cary, ed., *From a Ruined Empire*, 197.
43. Robert Skidelsky, *John Maynard Keynes, 1883–1946: Economist, Philosopher, Statesman* (New York: Penguin Books, 2005), 779.
44. Nicolson, *Diaries*, 325.
45. Judt, *Postwar*, 88.

CHAPTER 8: CIVILIZING THE BRUTES

1. Dower, *Embracing Defeat*, 215–17.
2. Annan, *Changing Enemies*, 160.
3. Ibid., 162.
4. Döblin and Feuchtwanger quoted in Tent, *Mission on the Rhine*, 23.
5. Quoted in Tent, *Mission on the Rhine*, 39.
6. Nicholas Pronay and Keith Wilson, eds., *The Political Re-education of Germany and Her Allies after World War II* (London: Croom Helm, 1985), 198.
7. Günter Grass, *Beim Haüten der Zwiebel* (Göttingen: Steidl, 2006), 220–21.
8. John Gimbel, *A German Community Under American Occupation: Marburg, 1945–52* (Stanford, CA: Stanford University Press, 1961), 168.
9. Pronay and Wilson, eds., *The Political Re-education of Germany*, 173.
10. *Yank*, July, 20, 1945.
11. Ibid.

12. Spender, *European Witness*, 229.
13. *Yank*, July 20, 1945.
14. Spender, *European Witness*, 44.
15. Ibid., 46.
16. Ibid., 158.
17. Andreas-Friedrich, *Battleground Berlin*, 82.
18. Naimark, *The Russians in Germany*, 399.
19. Ibid., 402.
20. Andreas-Friedrich, *Battleground Berlin*, 66.
21. Bach, *America's Germany*, 228.
22. Ibid.
23. Andreas-Friedrich, *Battleground Berlin*, 92.
24. Bach, *America's Germany*, 218.
25. *The Times* (London), July 11, 1945.
26. Dower, *Embracing Defeat*, 190.
27. De Beauvoir, *Force of Circumstance*, 17.
28. Ibid., 33.
29. Corinne Defrance, *La politique culturelle de la France sur la rive gauche du Rhin, 1945-1955* (Strasbourg: Presses Universitaires de Strasbourg, 1994), 126.
30. Döblin, *Schicksalsreise*, 273.
31. Quoted in Monnet, *Mémoires*, 339.
32. Barton J. Bernstein, ed., *The Atomic Bomb: The Critical Issues* (Boston: Little, Brown, 1976), 113.
33. Dower, *Embracing Defeat*, 218.
34. Ibid., 77.
35. Edward T. Imparato, *General MacArthur: Speeches and Reports, 1908–1964* (Paducah, KY: Turner, 2000), 146.
36. Bowers, "How Japan Won the War."
37. Ibid.
38. *Mainichi Shimbun*, quoted in Dower, *Embracing Defeat*, 549.
39. Rinjiro, *Dear General MacArthur*, 33.
40. Dower, *Embracing Defeat*, 77.
41. Quoted by Bowers in "How Japan Won the War."
42. Quoted in "The Occupation of Japan," a seminar sponsored by the MacArthur Memorial Library and Archives, November 1975, 129.
43. LaCerda, *The Conqueror Comes to Tea*, 165–66.
44. *Koe*, 115.
45. Dower, *Embracing Defeat*, 67.
46. Keene, *So Lovely a Country*, 118.

CHAPTER 9: ONE WORLD

1. Urquhart, *A Life in Peace and War*, 85.
2. Ibid., 93.
3. Stéphane Hessel, *Danse avec le siècle* (Paris: Editions du Seuil, 1997), 99.
4. Mark Mazower, *Governing the World: The History of an Idea* (New York: Penguin Press, 2012), 208.
5. Ibid., 194.
6. E. B. White, *The Wild Flag: Editorials from* The New Yorker *on Federal World Government and Other Matters* (Boston: Houghton Mifflin, 1946), 72.
7. Ibid., 82.
8. Menno Spiering and Michael Wintle, eds., *European Identity and the Second World War* (New York: Palgrave Macmillan, 2011), 126.

9. John Foster Dulles, *War or Peace*, with a special preface for this edition (New York: Macmillan, 1957), 38. First published 1950.
10. Neal Rosendorf, "John Foster Dulles' Nuclear Schizophrenia," in John Lewis Gaddis et al., eds., *Cold War Statesmen Confront the Bomb: Nuclear Diplomacy Since 1945* (New York: Oxford University Press, 1999), 64–69.
11. Joseph Preston Baratta, *The Politics of World Federation: United Nations, UN Reform, Atomic Control* (Westport, CT: Praeger, 2004), 127.
12. *New York Times*, October 10, 1945.
13. *The Times* (London), November 20, 1945.
14. Townsend Hoopes and Douglas Brinkley, *FDR and the Creation of the U.N.* (New Haven, CT: Yale University Press, 2000), 41.
15. Dan Plesch, *America, Hitler, and the UN: How the Allies Won World War II and Forged a Peace* (London: I. B. Tauris, 2011), 170.
16. Roosevelt's words are quoted in Mazower, *Governing the World*, 209.
17. "Remarks Upon Receiving an Honorary Degree from the University of Kansas City," June 28, 1945, trumanlibrary.org/publicpapers/viewpapers.php?pid=75.
18. White, *The Wild Flag*, 82.
19. *Yank*, June 15, 1945.
20. *Daily Herald*, May 1945.
21. Author's conversation with Gladwyn Jebb's grandson, Inigo Thomas.
22. *Time*, May 14, 1945.
23. Urquhart, *A Life in Peace and War*, 94.
24. *The Nation*, June 30, 1945.
25. Mark Mazower, "The Strange Triumph of Human Rights, 1933–1950," *The Historical Journal* 47, no. 2 (June 2004), 392.
26. William Roger Louis, *The British Empire in the Middle East, 1945–1951: Arab Nationalism, the United States, and Postwar Imperialism* (New York: Oxford University Press, 1984), 163.
27. *Manchester Guardian*, June 4, 1945.
28. Louis, *British Empire in the Middle East*, 148.
29. *The Times* (London), October 6, 1945.
30. White, *The Wild Flag*, 80.
31. Ibid., 81.
32. Arthur M. Schlesinger Jr., *A Thousand Days: John F. Kennedy in the White House* (Boston: Houghton Mifflin, 1965), 88–89.
33. *The Times* (London), August 17, 1945.
34. Report by Secretary Byrnes, http://avalon.law.yale.edu/20th_century/decade18.asp.
35. Dulles, *War or Peace*, 27.
36. Ibid., 30.
37. Ibid., 40.
38. *New York Times*, December 31, 1945.

INDEX

Urquhart, Brian, 15, 16, 21, 29, 31, 307–9,
    321
Ustaša, 102, 145, 149
Utrecht, 48
Utrecht University, 2–3, 6–7

Valéry, Paul, 286
van Berkum, Carla, 118–19
van Berkum, Peter, 117–18
Varkiza Agreement, 208–9
V-E Day, 17–22, 48
Velouchiotis, Aris, 108
vengeance, *see* revenge
Venizelos, Eleftherios, 107
Ventotene Manifesto, 311
veterans:
    return home, 139–45; *see also*
        homecomings
    violent acts committed by, 144
Vian, Boris, 291
Vietminh, 120–21, 124, 312
Vietnam, 102, 106, 120–22, 124–27
Vietnam War, 142, 303

War, The (Duras), 138–39
Warburg, Sigmund, 182
war crimes trials, 210–37
    at Bergen-Belsen, 228–30, 234
    of Homma, 213
    in Hungary, 206–7
    of Ishii, 210–12
    of Japanese war criminals, 212–18
    of Laval, 200, 218–25, 229
    of Mussert, 218–21, 222–24
    new legal categories devised for, 234, 322
    Nuremberg, 183, 185, 216–18, 226, 228,
        230–37, 244, 322, 331
    Tokyo War Crimes Tribunal, 185, 234
    of Yamashita, 212–17, 218
Warsaw, 60–61, 75–76, 256
Warsaw Ghetto Uprising, 161
Webster, C. K., 322, 327
Westerling, Raymond "Turk," 119–20
West, Rebecca, 232
West Germany, 183, 271, 272, 282, 336
White, E. B., 310, 320, 326

White Paper, 167
Whitney, Courtney, 176
Willoughby, Charles, 176, 211
Wilson, Edmund, 57, 59, 104, 106, 107, 110,
    246–47
Wilson, Harold, 271
Winwood, Major, 230
Wolf, Friedrich, 284
Wolf, Markus, 284
Wollheim, Richard, 31
Woman in Berlin, A, 42, 83
women:
    independence of, 8, 23
    voting rights for, 51, 85, 186
    see also sexuality
Worden, William L., 295
world government, 309–11, 327, 329–30
    Atlantic Charter and, 314–15, 323, 324
    atomic bomb and, 313
    British Empire as model for, 310
    League of Nations and, 9, 308, 309, 314,
        316, 318, 322
    United Nations and, *see* United Nations

Yalta Conference, 92, 151, 155, 316, 319–20,
    322, 327–29
Yamashita Tomoyuki, 40, 212–17, 218
Yank, 61, 72, 154, 159, 214, 215–16, 226, 265,
    266, 281, 320
Yasuda, 187
Yediot Ahronot, 161
Young Hearts (*Hatachi no Seishun*), 38
Yo Un-hong, 266
Yo Un-hyong, 263–64, 266, 267
Yugoslavia, 102, 103, 146–50
    Tito and Partisans in, 103, 145, 146,
        148–51

Zaaijer, J., 223
zaibatsu, 186–87, 260, 261
Zangen, Wilhelm, 182
zazous, 291
Zeineddine, Farid, 320
Zhukov, Georgy, 17–18, 21, 79
Zionism, 99, 100, 161–68, 244
Zuckmayer, Carl, 40, 60, 71, 179

IMAGE CREDITS